DECOMPOSITION

A Music Manifesto

ANDREW DURKIN

Pantheon Books New York

Pantheon Books and colophon are registered trademarks
of Random House LLC.

Grateful acknowledgment is made to the following for permission to reprint
previously published material: Alfred Music: Excerpt from "So You Want To Be
a Rock 'n' Roll Star," words and music by Roger McGuinn and Chris Hillman,
copyright © 1966, copyright renewed, by Reservoir Media Management, Inc. and
Sixteen Stars Music. All rights for Reservoir Media Music (ASCAP) administered
by Reservoir Media Management, Inc. Reservoir Media Music (ASCAP)
administered by Alfred Music. All rights reserved. Reprinted by permission of
Alfred Music. · Hal Leonard Corporation: Excerpt from "The Entertainer," words
and music by Billy Joel, copyright © 1974, copyright renewed, by Joelsongs.
All rights administered by Almo Music Corp. All rights reserved. Reprinted by
permission of Hal Leonard Corporation.

Getty Images: Photo of Saxophone and Big Jay McNeely and Crowds and
Audience by Bob Willoughby/Redferns, United States, circa 1951. Reprinted
by permission of Getty Images. · akg-images Ltd: "Ludwig van Beethoven
and intimates, listening to him playing," painting by Albert Graefle, image
AKGORD5193. Reprinted by permission of akg-images.

Library of Congress Cataloging-in-Publication Data
Durkin, Andrew.
Decomposition : a music manifesto / Andrew Durkin.
pages cm
Includes bibliographical references and index.
ISBN 978-0-307-91175-9 (hardcover : alk. paper).
ISBN 978-0-307-91176-6 (eBook).
1. Music—Philosophy and aesthetics. 2. Music appreciation—Psychological
aspects. 3. Music appreciation—Social aspects. 4. Sound recordings—Social
aspects. 5. Music and technology. I. Title.
ML3800.D93 2014 781.1—dc23 2014017686

www.pantheonbooks.com

Jacket design by Peter Mendelsund

Printed in the United States of America
First Edition
2 4 6 8 9 7 5 3 1

For John Paul Ryan, who loved both art and ideas

CONTENTS

DECOMPOSITION

INTRODUCTION

There are so many approaches to listening to music, and music has been designed in so many ways to meet these approaches, that some ethnomusicologists have declared that there is no universal phenomenon of music.

—Robert Jourdain

The eighteenth century musician was taught to see the whole of musical history as a hill rising gently and undulatingly out of darkness, with the music of his own time standing on the sunlit summit; the modern musician is encouraged to view it as a rather alarming slope, studded like Easter Island with titanic heads, far larger than life. And he may even have an uneasy suspicion that the slope is a downward one, and that the noisy and polemical modernists who lead the way are, like the maiden in one of Ernest Bramah's incomparable stories, uttering loud and continuous cries to conceal the direction of their flight.

—Thurston Dart

The title of this book comes from the old joke about what Beethoven is doing these days. It's a cheap laugh, to be sure, but the punch line ("decomposing!") is a nice metaphor for my purpose: to demythologize music without demeaning it. A composer myself, I contend that the exalted view of musical composition associated, in the Western tradition, with Beethoven—though it is by no means limited to him—has a way of interfering with the fullness of our musical life. By constraining musical understanding within the limits of traditional notions of authorship, and a blind faith in authenticity, that exalted view distracts us from the processes that produce music—not the conscious creative processes of the individual composer (many composers are only too happy to talk about how they work) but the much less obvious contributions of a broad array of collaborative and mediating activity. We have become accustomed to focusing on the end result of musical production as if that's all there is to it. And when this distraction occurs, when the final stage of a creative arc is presented as the entire thing itself, something valuable in our experience of music is lost.

Perhaps that seems too dramatic a way of putting it. Perhaps our experience of music is doing just fine, thank you very much. And yet today even many emphatic fans articulate ennui and despair about the art form. The last few years have seen the emergence of a kind of death cult for music, greatly expanding on the infighting angst that has always marked particular genres in the modern era (as evidenced, for instance, by the "jazz is dead" meme). What we see now is something more thorough, a simultaneously economic, aesthetic, and philosophical cri de coeur, the impact of which is discernible, for instance, in the presumptuous eschatology of *Frontline*'s episode "The Way the Music Died" (2004), Andrew Shapter's documentary *Before the Music Dies* (2006), and Andrew Keen's book *The Cult of the Amateur* (2007), which divided its discussion of music into two chapters, "The Day the Music Died [side a]" and "The Day the Music Died [side b]."

Keen claims that in the wake of postmodernity "it's quite conceivable that we will see the end of a cultural economy"—by which he means the end of a marketplace in which art is bought and sold. Others have suggested that the problem is more strictly aesthetic. "For more than half a century we've seen incredible advances in sound technology but very little if any advance in the quality of music," composer Glenn Branca wrote in the *New York Times* in 2009, in an article whose title—"The End of Music"—echoed *Frontline,* Shapter, and Keen (and like them seemed a brazen attempt to get a rise out of audiences). Many responded with variations of the same rebuttal: if you don't know any good modern music, you're not looking in the right place. "Curmudgeons are eternal," wrote one commenter. "This could have been written any time in the last 30 (100?) years."

But whether or not the curmudgeons are right, this is a time of great concern about the future of music, even for those of us who never stopped loving it. Working musicians worry publicly about how to adapt to the changed landscape of the twenty-first century—notwithstanding the fact that many of them, like singer-songwriter Jonathan Coulton, or folk songstress Amber Rubarth, or geek rocker Adam Rabin, or guitarist and producer Chris Schlarb, or singer and improviser Fay Victor, or clarinetist and vocalist Beth Fleenor, or solo bassist and blogger Steve Lawson, have come up with creative new definitions of what it means to have a music career. Fans today enjoy greatly expanded access to a universe of musical offerings unthinkable even fifteen years ago—whether or not they choose to partake of it legally or fairly. And the industry's institutions wobble topheavily between mandating an increasingly outdated conception of what a musical community should look like, on the one hand, and tapping into new dynamics for that community, on the other. All the while, there has been a great deal of anxiety about how we value music—but also about what music means, what it is for, and even what it is.

In *Decomposition* I wish to explore a suspicion that something important has been ignored or forgotten in the wake of this tumult, obscured by our myths about music. In biology, decomposition involves the breakdown of once-living matter, so it can be recycled for future life. As a metaphor for this book, I mean the word as an alternative to the mainstream story of authorship and authenticity—a counternarrative focusing on the less ostentatious, more organic aspects of musical creativity. Decomposition in this sense is also a way of giving the lie to music's death cult; it points to the inevitability of regeneration in art. But it requires, as Cornel West suggests, that we talk about corpses. One has to acknowledge that artists, works, audiences, discourses, and traditions do not last forever as they are experienced and appreciated at any particular moment. "Absolutely, read the poetry of John Donne, he'll tell you about corpses that decompose," West tells Astra Taylor in her film *Examined Life.* "See, that's history. The raw, funky, stinky stuff of life. That's what bluesmen do. That's what jazzmen do."

My concern with decomposition comes from my own experience as a "jazzman"—more specifically, as a composer, musician, bandleader, writer, educator, blogger, and occasional critic. The mythology I have observed in practice, weighing us down like the proverbial albatross, is two-pronged. First, there is the persistent assumption that music is always created by solitary individuals. An easy example here is the film (and earlier, the play) *Amadeus,* and the way it draws its dramatic power from the legend of Mozart. Here is our most flattering stereotype of authorship: that works spring full-blown and ex nihilo from the minds of isolated geniuses. Second, there is the obsession with authenticity: the quest for a singularly true, ideal experience of music (whether a recording, live performance, score, or transcription) that trumps all others, disregarding the variability of audience perception, and accessible only to those with "correct" knowledge and "proper" understanding.

My interest in critiquing these myths will most likely be familiar—perhaps even a bit too familiar—to anyone who has spent any time in a university or college humanities department over the last few decades. It might very well be overdetermined by the stereotypical postmodern take on art. But with this book I want to demonstrate the benefit of thinking about authorship and authenticity from a broader, more vernacular perspective—without, I hope, the distraction of academic posturing. That task is more challenging than it seems. While authorship and authenticity simplify our understanding and perception of music, neither notion is simple in itself or easy to discuss. Each is informed by degrees of truth. Each can be defined extremely or moderately. Each has a long history and a wide variety of contexts not necessarily coherent or consistent, and sometimes downright contradictory. For instance, the same Romantic era that gave rise to the modern notion of the solitary godlike genius also glorified folk culture, with its emphasis on communal and anonymous creativity. Similarly, "authenticity" is often deployed with maddening slipperiness: one writer might refer to it for historical verification; another might invoke it as a barometer of emotional honesty in a performance; still another might use it to determine the supposed success or failure of a cultural appropriation. "Authenticity" has become a classic weasel word—or, more frustratingly, a classic weasel concept, as sometimes it is invoked in practice without being invoked by name.

Yet despite, or perhaps because of, haziness of definition, we deal with musical authorship and authenticity on a daily basis, so persistent are these ideas in our culture. And while their influence is by no means universal, neither is it limited to a geographical region or genre, as it once narrowly characterized Western classical music. Rather, "authorship" and "authenticity" have been imperfectly yet widely disseminated as governing concepts by the global music ecosystem, thanks to that ecosystem's dramatic expansion in recent years. Thanks also to population growth, the development of music education, greater access to the technological means through which music is recorded and distributed, more nebulous boundaries between the "professional" and the "amateur," and a self-help industry devoted to emerging artists, there has been in our time an explosion of preprofessional and semiprofessional music making. Emphasis on authorship and authenticity is the conceptual glue holding this unwieldy network together—connecting superstars like Lady Gaga, Yo-Yo Ma, and U2 with the local rockabilly-reggae-polka ensemble selling its music independently on Bandcamp.com.

The fact that it is possible to speak of a "global music ecosystem" at all is of course a testament to the ruthless success of market capitalism, which undoubtedly influences the way we think about music too, and provides a fertile ground for the flourishing of authorship and authenticity. But the relationship is symbiotic. In modern times, authorship and authenticity have, by simplifying our understanding, helped transform the perception of music from an amorphous, multifaceted, irrational, unmarketable process into a tangible, manageable commodity—what in the business is called "product" (or what pianist Ethan Iverson recently called, with unintended foreboding, an "interesting property").

In the context of human history, this commodification of music is a relatively new development, certainly less than a few centuries old as a cultural trend, and probably less than a century old as a widespread phenomenon. Mentioning its prevalence now is not to suggest its total absence in past societies. Some indigenous cultures used songs as gifts, which could be individually owned, shared, or passed on to others. In certain Pacific Northwest Native American tribes, for instance, singing a song that you did not own would "invite the severe punishments due to thieves." And in the tradition of Somali sung poetry, some compositions are treated as private property and cannot be recited by other poets without attribution.

Yet there is a difference worth noting: the foregoing cultures lacked technology to "store" their music. In the global music ecosystem, in contrast, the order of the day can best be described as "reification"—

succinctly defined by pianist Charles Rosen as "the reduction in capitalist society of, for example, a human being, a work of art, or even an idea to a material object." The difference is that reified music has been reduced while being objectified. Carolyn Abbate similarly suggests that for many, music has become a "souvenir"—"one of the things taken away from the experience of playing or listening"—kept like a knickknack in a drawer, and once in a while "contemplated as a way of domesticating that experience." Lydia Goehr and Richard Taruskin have both used the metaphor of the museum—a collection of things—to make the same point. Christopher Small, in *Music of the Common Tongue,* writes, with apparent regret, that Westerners—particularly those ensconced in the classical music tradition, though I think his observation has farther-reaching implications—tend to perceive "music primarily in terms of entities, which are composed by one person and performed to listeners by another." Daniel Cavicchi similarly argues that "seeing music as an open 'process' and not a closed 'object' remains a radical idea" because "people still buy music in pre-packaged plastic cases and then play 'it' on their stereos and react to 'it,' something that effectively masks their own part in constituting that music and that constitution's place in broader social processes." Although we enjoy, idealize, and even fetishize live performance, our fundamental understanding of music is now deeply dependent on a certain concreteness: the "track," the "album," the "score"—allegories of cultural experiences involving the record, the cassette, the CD, and other media hard-copy forms.

Reification is complicated by the immateriality of digital music, to be sure. By the second decade of the twenty-first century, fewer and fewer consumers were buying their music in traditional brick-and-mortar stores, opting instead for purchases in cyberspace, where recorded music consists primarily of bits—MP3s, WAVs, AIFFs, and other digital files. Strictly speaking, these are not "things," not objects in the sense of LPs, cassettes, or CDs. Streaming and cloud technologies have further contributed to an impression that music is no longer (or will soon no longer be) an item to be owned, but rather an experience to be accessed.

And yet as trumpeter and composer Kris Tiner has pointed out, perhaps one object has been replaced with another, while an under-lying mind-set has endured. For those who have been liberated from the hard-copy recording itself, there is now playback technology to fetishize. Such technology—handheld MP3 players, music-dispensing smartphones, and so on—readily invites its own objectification, through attractive packaging, hip marketing campaigns, extensive accessoriz-ing, and user-friendliness. So while many of us no longer collect CDs or LPs, we continue to rely on a tactile relationship with the devices that play our music. Modern playback technology is designed to be handled, even caressed—think of the touch screen—and is as portable as previ-ous generations of sound media. The typical smartphone is about the size of an audiocassette, a fact capitalized upon by a recent iPhone case design. All of this facilitates objectification. More than a decade into the "digital revolution," old habits of musical understanding endure: most musicians continue to refer to their work as "records" or "albums," stressing the physicality of something that, as the industry lingo goes, "drops" on a given release date. Composers still speak of "unveiling" new pieces. Fans still refer to a favorite song as "the bomb."

In short, the impulse toward reification lingers. And it may not be going anywhere soon. After all, it took some effort to get to where we are now. As recently as the late 1800s, Small points out, Europe-ans were still visiting "pleasure gardens" where they could experience music, often at negligible cost, as process—not as background sound, but woven into the fabric of an outing—instead of consuming it as a detached, objectified work of art. And Evan Eisenberg, in his *The Recording Angel*—the second chapter of which is provocatively called "Music Becomes a Thing"—notes how listeners resisted the commodi-fication of music in the early years of the new industry. While Eisenberg places responsibility for the conceptual shift to reified music squarely with the invention of recording, and Small attributes it to the growth of industrial capitalism, with its underpinnings of scientific rational-ism, a crucial role was also played by the concepts of authorship and authenticity. In a sense, these concepts—which predated both record-ing technology and modern commerce—provided the theoretical and intellectual justification for the mind-set that drives the global music ecosystem, long before that ecosystem actually existed. And so today we live in a world where, for most listeners, these concepts are deemed axiomatic.

THE PROFUSION PROBLEM

If there was anything the human race had a sufficiency of, a sufficiency and a surfeit, it was books . . . the cataracts of books, the Niagaras of books, the rushing rivers of books, the oceans of books, the tons and truckloads and trainloads of books that were pouring off the presses of the world at that moment.

—Joseph Mitchell

One of Bach's students once asked him, "Papa, how do you ever think of so many tunes?" The composer's response, according to Stephen Nachmanovitch, was telling: "My dear boy, my greatest difficulty is to avoid stepping on them when I get up in the morning." One could do worse than this as a description of the twenty-first-century musical landscape. (My own CD collection is so out of control that my greatest difficulty when entering my office is to avoid stepping on it too.) The global music ecosystem now extends far beyond the short list of artists who appear on the charts that track album sales, and as the known corpus of musical works continues to grow, it becomes increasingly difficult for an individual listener to grasp the lineaments of a genre—or, for that matter, the total output of an artist. Several decades ago, Anthony Storr suggested that even a Mozart scholar would be hard pressed, despite a lifetime of study, to "claim familiarity with everything which Mozart composed." Today, the task of claiming familiarity (let alone expertise) has become many times more difficult.

The emergence of an era of musical profusion presents the listener with an interesting critical-aesthetic predicament—how to choose what to listen to? If you are a serious music fan in the early twenty-first century you are confronted with a seemingly infinite number of options akin to Borges's Library of Babel ("for every sensible line or accurate fact there would be millions of meaningless cacophonies, verbal farragoes, and babblings"). In an exchange on the "Music Thoughts" e-mail list, Los Angeles–based singer-songwriter Jimi Yamagishi gave voice to this dilemma:

> I have EXACTLY one hour a day @ the gym at 5 am to listen critically during my workout. That's a CD a day, no repeats. With listening to referrals online from people on these lists, hearing & seeing artists live, I don't have TIME to search XM or Sirius for good stuff. . . . Most of my friends also multitask in real life, & have little time to hear new stuff. Sometimes, if I put a CD in their hands or give 'em a referral, they'll listen 'cuz they want to see what I'm talkin' about. Usually, it takes a trip to the store or a gig with 'em in the car to get 'em to listen. They mostly prefer the comfort of what they already know, & actually get upset when a favorite artist goes off rotation on their favorite radio station, & that's when they might do a Kazaa or MP3 or even seek out the CD to buy it.

While the CD is an arbitrary unit of musical consumption, keeping track of CD listening is nevertheless one way to measure how much music people listen to. If we take Yamagishi's comments at face value (is it, for instance, really possible to listen "critically" while one is working out?), they can be seen as a response to what the futurist Alvin Toffler called "overchoice": too many possibilities, without the means to consume them all. Even if we were to double Yamagishi's listening rate of one CD per day, there is still inevitably a vastness that will prove elusive. "I listen to some 700 CDs a year," says critic David Adler, "and it's hard for me to swallow the notion that I'm not checking out enough music. And yet it's true. At this point it's a given that whatever offbeat and excellent music I'm taking in, there are probably scores of other deserving titles I overlook."

Others give this abundance a positive spin; the term "celestial juke-box," coined in the early days of the Internet, perfectly evokes the cosmic *jouissance* that an endless selection of music is supposed to provide. The online service eMusic recently sought my renewed membership with an optimistic plea for me to "start downloading today. There are 13+ million tracks waiting for you." (I couldn't help wondering how much free time they thought I had.) To help navigate the surfeit, most listeners look for guideposts, which savvy retailers are only too happy to provide. Arriving at the homepage of Amazon.com, or iTunes, or most other online music stores, surfers are immediately greeted with a list of recommendations, exhortations to try X if you liked Y, or pop-ups touting the latest best sellers. Some consumers resist such classification schemes, believing that they interfere with the pleasures of accidental discovery. But imposed organizational systems—whether consumer portals, genre, academic canons, year-end lists, branding, or, as is my concern in this book, the privileging of authorship and authenticity— facilitate our interaction with hyperabundance. Their raison d'être is to be reductive, to lead audiences through the seemingly impenetrable thicket of artistic productions, eliminating many and organizing what is left. As a result, talking about music becomes easier, more efficient and elegant.

If imposed organizational systems make talking about music easier, how can we at once talk about music while critiquing such systems? For that matter, how do we posit a reliable definition of "music" from such a position? The answer to the latter question is that perhaps we can't. Explicitly articulating a general notion of music—one that works consistently across geographies, histories, cultural contexts, biological differences, and so on—may satisfy the taxonomical impulses of social science, but for everyday listeners it is an act fraught with problems. This does not mean it is pointless to ask the question—"What is music?"—but we must start from the premise that there is no easy answer, and maybe no answer at all.

Here I focus less on what music "is," and more on how we idiosyncratically engage with it. In my view, music is an extensive network of individuated aural perceptions, which are always the result of deeply complex collaborative and mediating processes. Naturally, I have my own listening biases. In this book I will repeatedly turn to the music that gets called "jazz," "rock," "pop," and "classical"—not for philosophically absolutist reasons but because these are the kinds of music I know best. At the same time, I am fully aware that my choices are arbitrary and problematic. The very existence of genre categories contributes to the reification I have described, and one of the points of this book is to "decompose" that reification.

Ultimately, rather than defining music, I am interested in how we discuss whatever it is we think music is, as well as what that discussion obscures. Every time we treat authorship and authenticity as reifications—as synecdoches, to borrow a term from literary terminology—consequences for understanding ensue. The word "composer," which assumes an individual, comes to stand for and eventually replace a complex network of creativity that involves performers, audiences, recording engineers, music copyists, instrument manufacturers, record label executives, DJs, and many others who are typically thought of as being outside the creative act. Similarly, calling music "authentic" distracts us from the artistry of listening, its participation in the making of the music itself—for listening is much more than a transparent apprehension of data as it moves from point A (the artist) to point B (the listener).

In *The Practice of Everyday Life,* Michel de Certeau homes in on this discursive habit by which simplicity trumps complexity. Certeau evokes the immeasurability of experience by describing people walking in a city, whose footsteps "are myriad" and "cannot be counted because each unit has a qualitative character." Taken as a whole, the "swarming mass is an innumerable collection of singularities." Maps are important for getting around in this space, as they provide the shorthand necessary to plan a physical journey. But from an experiential point of view, they are woefully incomplete. A map permits users "to grasp only a relic set in the nowhen [Certeau's temporal analogy for 'nowhere'] of a surface of projection. Itself visible, it has the effect of making invisible the operation that made it possible. These fixations constitute procedures for forgetting. The trace left behind is substituted for the practice."

In a similar way, authorship and authenticity encourage us to focus on the "trace left behind," on what is merely immediately perceivable about music. We acknowledge the author's name, the work itself, the copyright information, the work's authentic or inauthentic status. But we forget or ignore the collaborative trajectories that led to it, the mediation that makes it perceivable, and the fact that the end result is itself the starting point for a new flow of creativity that may or may not already be manifest.

HEARING BEYOND BOUNDARIES

The problem of musical authorship and authenticity is perpetuated by the insularity of much musical discourse. Consider the underappreciated relationship between jazz and technology, for instance. For many writers on jazz, technology seems irrelevant to expressive authenticity (a notion that we will look at in more detail in chapter 3). In his biography of John Coltrane, Ben Ratliff notes that after Coltrane damaged his saxophone mouthpiece in the early 1960s, "some of his comments about his 1962 recordings suggest that he never found real satisfaction with new mouthpieces, but finally decided that mind-over-matter was the way to move on." Ravi Coltrane (John's son) dismisses the idea that his father would have been hindered by technical considerations. "Some people have said that he fucked up his mouthpiece and could never get that thing back, and it made him upset, so that's why he became aggressive," the younger Coltrane has said. "But this is one of the greatest musicians who ever played. He's not gonna divert because of a technical problem."

The rest of Coltrane's career supports this observation—he did not divert—yet we shouldn't overlook the fact that technical problems (or, more accurately, technical considerations) always inform musical expression. It is not that jazz musicians are uninterested in technology—most are just as inclined as the stereotypical rock guitarist to "geek out" over new gear. But this interest is rarely factored into an aesthetic concept, by either the musicians themselves or by those who enjoy or comment on the music. Technology is seen rather as a means to an end. When jazz is discussed, described, evaluated, and celebrated, emphasis is overwhelmingly placed on personal expression, as if it is occurring in a vacuum. And the unwillingness to go beyond that point obscures the fact that like even the most formulaic, auto-tuned, excessively multitracked, mechanically produced pop, jazz relies on technology for its existence and its meaning. Recording machinery, audio media, instrument design, and studio engineering norms are all aspects of its artistry, as are the larger dissemination mechanisms of the recording industry.

Composer Darcy James Argue makes the point more broadly in a blog post about jazz repertoire. "For reasons that I think are relatively obvious," Argue writes, "it makes a lot of jazz musicians, critics and fans very uncomfortable to think about issues of cultural significance." Instead, our conversations usually have to do with "craft—whether the rhythm section is hooking up, or whether the improvisers are listening to each other closely enough, or whether the surface qualities of the music are 'complex' and 'innovative' enough to satisfy our discriminating tastes." The dominance of these supposedly pure musical considerations suggests that most members of the community "really, *really* do not want to think about questions like 'what does this music mean?' or 'why are we doing this?' or 'how does this music relate to the culture at large?' "

Decomposition is not so much about how music relates to culture at large, but only in the sense that I frame the issue the opposite way: how does our culture at large relate to what it thinks of as music? I try to respond to Daniel Cavicchi's concern that we are missing a viable reception theory for music. In 2002 Cavicchi pointed out that the music disciplines "are an embarrassment" when it comes to a consideration of the audience, and that whatever work has been done in this area pales in comparison to similar inquiries in literature, film, and other arts. The observation is still broadly true: in 2013 Ben Ratliff described how "I have spent a lot of time with the books in my house that come to grips with listening as process and reaction and ritual, the real-time experience of it, how music might change our listening and how our listening might change music. I am always looking for books like this. There aren't that many." One possible explanation for this inadequacy is that musicology and music pedagogy have traditionally been "text-based," privileging the content and execution of a given composition over the way it is received, stressing what Richard Taruskin calls "the myth of musical autonomy." Equally problematic is "the discipline's institutional commitment to vocational training, in which the audience is secondary in all ways to the performer and the performance."

But we can, I think, go farther. In its strictest sense, even "audience" is limited as a signifier, referring as it usually does only to people listening to music in a theater, through a set of earbuds, at an arena rock concert, or in similar scenarios. A robust reception theory for music would posit "audience" as a much broader phenomenon, one that includes connections to the music that might at first seem more attenuated (e.g., the technicians who build instruments) or perhaps counterintuitive (e.g., the musicians themselves). It would assume that any performance, whether live or recorded, is the result of a network that extends far beyond performers and their immediate listeners.

Decomposition is my attempt to understand that network.

"CORPSES THAT DECOMPOSE": TRANSDUCTION

> There's a song as it exists in my mind when I write it, the words and the melody and what it means to me. And then there's the song as it exists on the tape when we record it. Then there's the song as it exists every time it's played and the way the individual standing there, receiving it, feels about it. That's never the same, it always changes.
>
> —Conor Oberst

> If one says "Red" (the name of a color) and there are 50 people listening, it can be expected that there will be 50 reds in their minds. And one can be sure that all these reds will be different.
>
> —Josef Albers

This book is divided into three parts. In the first, chapters 1 and 2, I critique authorship, vis-à-vis recognized composers Duke Ellington and Ludwig van Beethoven, and vis-à-vis technology. In the second part, chapters 3 through 6, I critique authenticity—what it is, the philosophical weaknesses of its claims, and how it is misapplied to both performance and written music. Finally, in the third part, chapter 7, I look at the modern implications of decomposition, particularly how it has informed the emergence of a digital culture for music, and how it might point toward a robust creative future.

As a whole, the decompositional argument is grounded by a second metaphor—or perhaps a conceit—a term from audiology and physics that I have taken the liberty of interpreting somewhat broadly: "transduction" (from *transducere*, to "lead across"), or the process of changing energy from one form to another. In the physiology of human hearing, transduction happens within the ear, and involves the transformation of vibrations—typically, vibrating air—into nerve impulses. In a sound system, a transducer similarly changes vibrations into electricity (through a microphone) and then back again (through a speaker). More broadly, older technologies like the phonograph etched vibrations into a material surface—whether tinfoil, wax, shellac, or vinyl—from which they would then be reproduced, usually after being transformed into electrical energy. And digital technology translates electrical current into a representative pattern of zeroes and ones, which are then read back in order to reproduce the encoded sound.

Schopenhauer once wrote that music is "quite independent of the phenomenal world, positively ignores it, and, to a certain extent, could still exist even if there were no world at all." The transduction metaphor insists on exactly the opposite: music is deeply *bound up* in the phenomenal world, the world of experience and sensation. It is a material occurrence, as suggested by Frank Zappa's reference to its "wiggling air molecules," or percussionist Evelyn Glennie's surmise that hearing "is basically a specialized form of touch," or Marshall McLuhan's synesthetic notion of the "audio-tactile." Of course sound does not *only* travel through air, as Zappa suggests—but it is dependent on material interactions, and that dependence always has a direct effect on what we understand it to be. Music by its very nature can never be pure, as posited in Schopenhauer's metaphysics; it can never be, as Lucy Green puts it, "played outside a situation"—the corollary being that "every situation will affect the music's meaning." Or, in the words of Ola Stockfelt, "One can even assume that daily listening is often more conditioned by the situation in which one meets the music than by the music itself."

We have all experienced the ways that music is "conditioned by the situation" in which we encounter it: for instance, the architecture and construction of a performance space, the means of amplification (if any), the size of an audience, where that audience is sitting exactly, the make and model of the instruments, the technique and aesthetic approach of the musicians. Also helping to define what is heard are more ambiguous factors, promoting even more individualized perceptions—your emotional state, cultural background, musical background, critical disposition, self-awareness, personality, social status, and so on.

Transduction doesn't seem terribly controversial, when laid out so plainly. Yet we routinely discount its significance when discussing what music means, how it affects us, or what it is. And therein lies the problem. Ultimately, we assume that ostensibly extramusical factors—anything that is not the "trace left behind," or the music you end up hearing—are irrelevant to the depth of musical experience. We are convinced that the quality of a musical work cannot derive, even if only partially, from its context. But this is a misapprehension. We all help to create any musical work through our perception of it, as does the context of the encounter.

Even the perceptions of so-called expert listeners are subject to the workings of transduction. It is not that underneath all the layers of mediation there is a "true" work that can be perceived accurately through the right kind of transduction. Rather, the work is only possible in the first place because of transductive transformations. Thus "the work" is never just one work, never produced by just one composer. Nicholas Cook is right, for instance, when he notes that musicological inquiry typically "bears no relationship to how ordinary people hear," and that this discrepancy means not "the difference between two sorts of listeners, but between two sorts of music." In supporting his argument, Cook alludes to Kathryn Bailey's writing on the composer Anton Webern, in which she claims that a Webern composition is actually "two quite different pieces—a visual, intellectual piece and an aural, immediate piece, one for the analyst and another for the listener." This is an essential insight that should be considered in tandem with the conceit of transduction. In any performance of an ostensibly single work there are actually as many works present as there are listeners, including the musicians themselves. Ten people listening to a solo piano piece in the same room produce eleven "quite different" pieces: the ten heard by the audience and the one heard by the pianist.

These distinctions are really where musical experience is rooted, and are ultimately what makes the art form so resilient. By asking us to think about them, decomposition points to a "quantum aesthetics"—a notion of artistic difference that works all the way down to the smallest increments of perceptual awareness. Marcus Boon finds a useful parallel in Marcel Duchamp's idea of the "infrathin," or the difference that exists between objects that, in part because of our understanding of how they were made, seem to be identical copies. Consider Duchamp's *Fountain,* a commercially produced urinal he had purchased second-hand and then labeled and offered for exhibition as his own work. Boon acknowledges the cultural resistance to seeing any difference between the commercial product and the artwork, and yet the infrathin—which "distinguishes the same from the same," highlighting an "indifferent difference," as Jay D. Russell puts it—gives us a way to unpack the single reified musical work we assume as a given every time we listen.

The CD in my stereo system right now, Michael Jackson's *Thriller,* is a mass-produced copy, but a specific one, with a scratch that prevents me from playing track 3 (no matter, I never liked that song anyway), thus altering the intended continuity of the album. At exactly 1:02 p.m., on a Saturday in January, in the year 2014, I choose to play track 4, the famous title track, listening from the plush red sofa in the middle of my living room. The music I hear, like Duchamp's urinal, is "composed of unique physical matter, occupies a unique point in the space-time continuum, and has a unique passage through that continuum." If you decide to put down this book, come to my home, and listen to "Thriller," from the same source CD, the same stereo system, and the same position in the living room, but even a few seconds later, all of those qualities will have changed: the music's matter will have changed, its point in the space-time continuum will have changed, the way its sound moves across the room will have changed, you and I will have changed. "Thriller" is "never the same," to adapt Conor Oberst's way of putting it—"it always changes." It may be broadly understood in terms of the simplistic category of the hit song and the star performer, but "hit song" and "star performer" are convenient conceptual shortcuts for the two complex and distinct listening experiences I just described—yours and mine. And they do not even begin to get at the many more listening experiences of the "same" work that neither you nor I will ever be privy to.

Transduction is thus an aesthetic double whammy, reminding us what an unstable phenomenon perception is, while simultaneously reminding us that there is no possibility of music outside of perception. It brings us closer to the decompositional goal of thinking about music in a way that gets beyond the hardened ideas of authorship and authenticity. And it reminds us that while we need not completely dispense with these reifications—since we use them to organize the complexity of musical experience—we ought not to forget what that shorthand represents and occludes.

Part I

AUTHORSHIP

1.

A THOUSAND WROUGHT LIKE ONE

It takes a thousand men to invent a telegraph, or a steam engine, or a phonograph, or a photograph, or a telephone, or any other important thing—and the last man gets the credit and we forget the others.
                    —Mark Twain, "Letter to Ann Macy"

If we would stop and attribute too much to genius, [Emerson] shows us that "what is best written or done by genius in the world, was no one man's work, but came by wide social labor, when a thousand wrought like one, sharing the same impulse."
                    —Charles Ives

My introduction to the music of Duke Ellington came in 1987, when I accidentally discovered *Duke Ellington,* a biography of the composer written by novelist James Lincoln Collier. Just out of high school, a jazz neophyte at the time, I was a callow suburban white kid with only the dimmest awareness of who Ellington was, and as I delved into this book (during lunch hours at my switch-making assembly line summer job) I had no idea what a flash point it had become for musicians, fans, and critics. But the truth was that many had railed against what William Youngren called Collier's "preoccupation, even obsession, with proving that Ellington was not really a composer." The poet and scholar Amiri Baraka exemplified the backlash when he acidly noted that Collier's "various writings give off the distinct aroma of a rotting mint julep." And critic Stanley Crouch—who I would later learn was pretty good at generating music-world kerfuffles of his own—characterized the biography as "insipid, sloppy and irresponsible."*

---

* Collier has also been accused, with some justification, of being "unconsciously racist" (Francis Davis, *Outcats,* 22). Consider for instance his comments on the Ellington band's extended concert music—that the numerous three-minute masterpieces it produced early in the twentieth century represented an artistic peak never duplicated after World War II. "I have seen this sort of thing happen,

In my naïveté, my interest in *Duke Ellington* had nothing to do with this controversy. What caught my attention instead was the idea of collaboration in the Ellington group. Ellington, I realized, did not fit the myths about composition that I had heard espoused by friends, music teachers, or professional performing artists. I remember being struck by this at the time, because it was my first encounter with a description of the creative process that bore some resemblance to my own experience. I had only recently started organizing my own bands, but I already knew that it was nearly impossible for me to write in a vacuum, with no idea of who would be performing. I required the specificity of knowing not only which instruments or voices I was writing for, but also which human beings would be involved. And coming from the pompously heroic worlds of rock and classical music, I was drawn to the depiction of collective creative labor in *Duke Ellington* as a breath of fresh air, despite the book's other faults.

Today, many years (and many Ellington books) later, I am a modestly more cynical musician, but I still see Ellington's career as an inspiring example of the importance of collaboration, an example that forcefully challenges the usual story of how music is made. In retrospect, one of my own frustrations with Collier is that he never bothered to theorize his observations. Instead, he implied that Ellington's process was an anomaly that stood out against the "regular" way great art is made. Ellington was unusual, he suggested, in that while he did produce masterpieces, he did not do so in the stereotypical manner of a Beethoven or Mozart, feverishly composing in the dark solitude of a garret. Indeed, traditional authorship is an idea whose validity Collier never really questioned. And for their part, few of his critics questioned it either. Much of the negative response to the book was driven by an insistence not only that Ellington was a great composer, but that he was a great composer in the Beethovenian or Mozartean mold.

I sympathize with that impulse. Throughout the twentieth century,

---

again and again," he scolds. "The writer of much-admired children's books abandons his method when he sets out to write an adult novel and tries to imitate Henry James; the successful advertising illustrator paints in a wholly different style when he does what he considers serious work" (Collier, *Duke Ellington*, 221). Collier's comparisons here infantilize Ellington—recalling a long tradition of white critical paternalism—and cheapen the band's music.

jazz fought an uphill battle for recognition even as a legitimate art form, let alone one capable of generating music on par with the best the classical tradition had to offer. In some ways, it is still fighting that battle. Yet Collier's critics, and Collier himself, had things precisely backwards, ignoring the possibility that we can achieve cultural parity for jazz via a different route entirely. The best response to the charge that Ellington worked collaboratively is not to argue that Ellington is like Beethoven or Mozart, but to flip the terms of the comparison: Beethoven and Mozart were like Ellington.

In other words, the collaborative model of musical creativity did not begin (and it will not end) with Ellington, or with jazz.

THE RHETORIC OF GENIUS

In coming to their problematic conclusions, Collier and his critics had bought into the Western stereotype of composition, derived from classical music's eighteenth- and nineteenth-century heyday, and most forcefully articulated in the context of Romanticism. Simply put, this idea of composition celebrates superhuman solitary geniuses who produce masterworks out of thin air. Alfred Einstein's biography of Mozart is a good example. "As an artist, as a musician, Mozart was not a man of this world," Einstein wrote. "To a certain part of the nineteenth century his work seemed to possess so pure, so formally rounded, so 'godlike' a perfection that Richard Wagner, the most violent spokesman of the Romantic Period, could call him 'music's genius of light and love.' " Such is the line on just about any "major composer." Of Bach, Wagner said he was "the most stupendous miracle in all music," while Charles Gounod opined that he "is a colossus . . . beneath whom all musicians pass and will continue to pass." Of Beethoven, H. L. Mencken wrote that "his emotions at their greatest level were almost godlike," while Scott Burnham refers to the common idea that the composer was "the hero of Western music, 'The Man Who Freed Music,' " liberating it "from the stays of eighteenth-century convention, singlehandedly bringing music into a new age by giving it a transcendent voice equal to Western man's most cherished values." Of Brahms, conductor Hans von Bülow said he was "the greatest, the most exalted of composers" (surpassed only by Bach and Beethoven); Brahms himself thought he was "in tune with the infinite."

Mozart, Bach, Beethoven, Brahms: among the usual suspects singled out for such praise. But grandiloquence about musical creativity extends beyond the boundaries of composition, too. By the late nineteenth century, the object of adulation could just as easily be a conductor or a performer. Lawrence Gilman, for instance, called Arturo Toscanini "the greatest musical interpreter who ever lived," "the priest of beauty," the "consecrated celebrant," "custodian of holy things," and "guardian of spiritual things." Today, such hagiography can be found in just about any genre, and applied to just about any type of musician. In an essay about his popular but controversial documentary on jazz, for instance, Ken Burns informs us that "Louis Armstrong is quite simply the most important person in American music," because Armstrong "is to 20th century music (I did not say jazz) what Einstein is to physics, Freud is to medicine and the Wright Brothers are to travel." Echoing the view of Beethoven cited by Burnham, Burns credits Armstrong with "liberating jazz, cutting it loose from nearly all constraints," and "essentially inventing what we call swinging." Afterward—as if liberating jazz and inventing swing were not enough—Armstrong "brought an equally great revolution to singing."

I call this language the rhetoric of genius, and studying it can tell us a lot about traditional attitudes toward composition. Note for instance how all of these examples have a quasi-religious cast. That is perhaps not surprising, since music has traditionally been thought of as being from "the celestial realm." Canonical composers, when describing their own creative processes, frequently explained it in terms of the divine. "I thought I saw all of heaven before me, and the Great God himself," Handel supposedly said, during the creative spree that produced the *Messiah*. Puccini similarly wrote that his opera *Madame Butterfly* "was dictated to me by God," the composer himself being simply an amanuensis. "To realize that we are one with the Creator, as Beethoven did, is a wonderful and awe-inspiring experience," echoed Brahms, confidently implying that a similar dynamic informed his own creativity (otherwise how would he know?), and adding, "Very few human beings ever come into that realization, and this is why there are so few great composers or creative geniuses in any line of human endeavor." Even Debussy deemed Bach "a benevolent god, to whom musicians should offer a prayer before setting to work so that they may be preserved from mediocrity." The religious dimension of the rhetoric of genius appears in considerations of popular music as well—see for instance the "Clapton is God" graffiti, or the surprising number of urban legends in which celebrated musicians (Elvis Presley and Jim Morrison come to mind) are reputed to have cheated death.

What is more, the rhetoric of genius always seems to celebrate the *isolation* of the artist. This might have something to do with gender stereotypes, since genius is usually coded as masculine. It might also be attributable to the personality and biography of Beethoven, with his penchant for solitude—a function of his poor health, and in particular his deafness. "Alas! how could I declare the weakness of a *sense* which in me *ought to be* more acute than in others—a sense which *formerly* I possessed in highest perfection," the composer wrote in the so-called Heiligenstadt Testament, a letter to his brothers. "Forgive, therefore, if you see me withdraw, when I would willingly mix with you." Beethoven had an understandable reason for wanting to be alone, but to the extent that he has become an archetype of genius, the rhetoric puts undue emphasis on solitude—and even solipsism—as a prerequisite for artistic greatness. True creativity is assumed to be self-sustaining, and the collaborative involvement of other human beings and contexts is deemed secondary, extraneous, or altogether irrelevant.

The rhetoric of genius matters because patterns of discourse affect our understanding of their subjects. Sloppy language, as George Orwell once famously noted, produces sloppy thinking. In an era of mass media and mass culture, predigested phrases and clauses can be strung together almost interchangeably, too easily producing statements that sound impressive but convey little information. These bad habits produce an automatic discourse, "partially concealing your meaning even from yourself." The rhetoric of genius works like this too, creating and sustaining ways of thinking about art that are more compulsive than compelling—ways that distract us from deeper understanding. The problem occurs every time we glibly privilege the "mystery" and "magic" of creativity, as if that is all there is to it.

I don't want to exaggerate the case here by suggesting that the rhetoric of genius is the only available mode for speaking about music in our culture. But I do see it as the dominant mode. Tellingly, it informs a good deal of modern copyright discourse, as we will see in chapter 7. It also informs a wide range of other institutions and practices related to music, from conservatory tenure, to the Grammy Awards, to journalistic "best of" lists, to grant-making procedures, to marketing campaigns, to *American Idol* and related fare. It moves effortlessly between "high" and "low" culture. For most twenty-first-century listeners, in fact, the key context for genius is the star system—the hierarchy of celebrity that emerged in the nineteenth century, with touring musicians like Niccolò Paganini, Jenny Lind, and Franz Liszt. As tropes, "celebrity" and "genius" are not as unrelated as they might initially appear, or as we have been taught to think.

The point is worth underscoring. In his heyday, Liszt, now considered a part of the art music pantheon, was so popular that he inspired a cultural phenomenon known as "Lisztomania," in which devoted listeners responded to his performances with what at the time was considered excessive enthusiasm. Liszt's "high-intensity, often frantic bravura manner provoked involuntary physical reactions—shaking, shuddering, weeping," writes Dana Gooley. "Applause for Liszt, indeed, appears less a gesture of appreciation, wonder, or joy, than a sheer corporal reflex—an outlet for great physical excitement." Gooley cautions us against taking Lisztomania out of its original historical context—at the time, it was literally considered a kind of disease, whereas today the suffix "-mania" is often used in a more attenuated sense. Yet the connection between Liszt and the Beatles, who inspired their own eponymous mania late in the next century, is too remarkable to gloss over. It suggests that the Romantic view of creativity does not derive exclusively from either high culture, where it is construed as genius, or low culture, where it is construed as celebrity. Rather, genius and celebrity are two sides of the same coin. As Simon Frith has written,

"The mass cultural notion of stardom, combining a Romantic belief in genius with a promise to make it individually available as commodity (and merchandise) derives as much from the packaging of 'high' artists as from the hype of the low."

THE COLLABORATIVE THEORY OF MUSICAL CREATIVITY

Over the last half century, the traditional view of authorship has been subject to careful critique by scholars working primarily in the field of literature. Joseph Grigely's study of the poet John Keats is a good example. Grigely looks at nineteenth-century editors who reworked Keats's poetry in order to adapt it to changing times. One of these, Richard Monckton Milnes, published a comprehensive Keats collection *(The Life, Letters, and Literary Remains of John Keats)* nearly three decades after the poet's death, ostensibly bringing greater elegance to Keats's syntax and diction, while also redacting key details of the poet's biography. The resulting text significantly manipulated the reader's sense of Keats's work, and of how the poet represented himself:

> In one sonnet, the line "The anxious month, relieving of its pains" is changed to "relieved of its pains"; in another sonnet Milnes changed "browless idiotism" to "brainless idiotism"; in yet another sonnet he added a word to correct a missing foot; in another poem he reversed word order. The previously unpublished poems were extensively repunctuated and edited.

This manipulation helped construct what Grigely calls the "canonical Keats," in contrast to the original or "embarrassing Keats"—who, Thomas De Quincey complained, "played such fantastic tricks as could only enter into the heart of a barbarian, and for which only the anarchy of Chaos could furnish a forgiving audience." In producing it, Milnes engaged in *direct collaboration,* my term for an individual's obvious involvement in an already existing work (often a work officially belonging to someone else) through editing, translation, cowriting, or other kinds of intentional interaction. Though culturally subordinate to authorship, direct collaboration is usually understood as a respectable activity in its own right. Any Shakespearean or Homeric scholar will argue for the importance of editing or translating, for instance. We understand that when done poorly, direct collaboration can destroy a work; the Italian adage "traduttore, traditore!" ("translator, traitor!") describes a worst-case scenario.

Direct collaboration, then, is the most commonly understood idea of what collaboration is. Yet there is another, equally valid if more subtle way of "decomposing" traditional understandings of creativity. A whole host of seemingly irrelevant secondary matters can quietly transform our appreciation of literary texts: design, for instance, or marketing, or different reading technologies (such as tablets, scrolls, codices, screen-based readers). Even something as simple as the choice of a font can have a profound effect on how we read: Garamond seems quaint and unassuming, say, while Helvetica seems efficient and emotionless. Each has an impact on what we understand the content of a literary work to be. (The widespread revulsion to Comic Sans, which inspired the "ban Comic Sans" movement, as well as Mike Lacher's brilliant parody "I'm Comic Sans, Asshole," is a good example of a font's capacity for conveying meaning beyond the ideas of the text itself.)

These observations suggest the importance of context, or framing. "We are traditionally inclined to think of how an artwork transforms the space it inhabits—more literally how a painting 'fills' a room," Grigely writes in a discussion of visual art, "but we must also consider how a text is transformed by that same space." The *Mona Lisa,* for instance, does not hang in pure undistracted glory in the Louvre, but is framed by the milieu of an internationally famous museum: guards, a glass case, barricades, the frenzy of tourists, the enforced propriety of the painting's reputation as "great art." It is almost impossible to view with the sort of isolated contemplation that a masterpiece is supposed to require. The *Mona Lisa,* then, "is not a mere painting, but a performance, a *mise-en-scene* in which the cultural status of the work is reflected in how it is presented and received." The work, to paraphrase Ola Stockfelt, is partly constructed by the situation in which it is met.

The same is true of music. Gene Weingarten's "Pearls Before Break-fast," an award-winning piece for the *Washington Post,* describes a solo performance by virtuoso violinist Joshua Bell—not onstage at Carnegie Hall, but in a subway station in Washington, D.C. During this unusual concert, most of the rush-hour passersby seemingly did not even hear Bell's music. Out of 1,070 commuters who came through the station that morning, only seven stopped to listen. Weingarten, offended, frames the supposed deafness of the majority as a cultural failing—"The people scurry by in comical little hops and starts," he writes, in a "grim *danse macabre* to indifference, inertia, and the dingy, gray rush of modernity." To him, the traveling workers are "ghosts," and their immersion in the chaos of modern living prevents them from hearing the celebrated violinist, who in contrast is "real."

Yet Weingarten betrays his bias (also reflected in the title of the piece, meant to echo the biblical "pearls before swine") when he adds that the compositions Bell plays are "masterpieces that have endured for centuries on their brilliance alone." The real lesson of "Pearls," as I understand it, is that *no* artwork ever endures on its brilliance alone. Bell's impromptu concert demonstrated that music depends on context—not only for whatever brilliance we find in it, but also for its very existence. I use the term *contextual collaboration* to refer to this dependence, and to distinguish it from direct collaboration. Made possible by transductive processes, contextual collaboration is frequently dismissed, assumed to be irrelevant to the deep experience of music. It is less obvious than direct collaboration, and harder to trace, involving entities that are traditionally assumed to be passive, and are even physically removed from the creative act. Yet without contextual collaboration and its transformations, *there would be no music*—as Weingarten and Bell discovered, but did not appreciate.

Both forms of collaboration (direct and contextual) work in tandem with a third category of artistic behavior, the *initiating act,* or generative burst of creativity. The initiating act might be the discovery of a theme, idea, or argument, or the production of a draft. It is associated with the euphoria of inspiration. In legal philosophy, it is imagined as the "right of paternity." Interestingly, it is that part of creativity that, true to the rhetoric of genius, often does occur in solitude (insofar as solitude is existentially possible). It's a legitimately artistic behavior, but it fosters a problematic assumption. In literature, we assume the initiating act is writing. In music, we assume it is composition. In general, we assume it is authorship, because it *feels* like authorship. But it is really part of a bigger dynamic.

That bigger dynamic—the give-and-take between initiating acts, direct collaboration, and contextual collaboration—is the essence of what I call the collaborative theory of musical creativity. This theory does not aim merely to distinguish among its components, but is also a response to the hierarchy assumed by the rhetoric of genius, in which, to the extent that collaboration is recognized at all, it always merely supports or enhances the initiating act. The collaborative theory instead posits a balance—not out of unthinking egalitarianism, but because the many trajectories that go into any creative endeavor, while seeming intuitively obvious, cannot be fully articulated, measured, or understood. The theory directs us to what is frequently skipped in discussions of art: that creativity is a process of mind, consciousness, and self; and that our understanding of how it happens is limited by our philosophical and scientific uncertainty about those things, and by the forceful boundaries of our own existence—rather than revealed by some external gauge of objective knowledge.

Consider the seemingly simple question of influence. Journalists, composers, historians, and fans love to speculate about influence—it is one of the standard features of artist biographies—but the truth is that we cannot trace or even identify many of the things that shape us, nor can we objectively know how they contribute to any work we create. Composer Milton Babbitt makes the point with refreshing candor.

> When I get interviewed by people who are not professional musicians, and above all not composers, they always ask "What things influenced you?" Well, what things didn't? All that variegated music that we've all heard; all the things that I read. I mean, I can't imagine. . . . And to be specific about it, one would almost be, I think, dishonest. So many things have crept in and determined one's thinking. I don't have to tell you, a composer. You know, as a piece germinates, the forms that it takes. If you had to go back and retrace that, it would not only be superficial . . . you've forgotten it.

This unknowability suggests that there is no reason to privilege initiating acts, however important they may *feel*. Artists, it turns out, are not entirely in control of how they create. Direct and contextual collaboration can be just as important to what they do—and conceivably, depending on the situation, even more so. By questioning what we know about artistry, the collaborative theory complicates our assumption that initiating acts are where the real art is made, while direct collaboration and contextual collaboration are mere tweaking or situational happenstance. It is an upending of the cultural habit in which "the last man gets the credit, and we forget the others."

Further, the collaborative theory is not intended as a static analysis of artistic production, in which initiating acts, direct collaboration, and contextual collaboration are each defined only one way. In the 1956 live Ellington recording of "Diminuendo and Crescendo in Blue," for example, the creation of the score might be understood as the initiating act, whereas the performance by the Ellington Orchestra might be the direct collaboration, and the response of the audience contextual collaboration. This is the configuration I will argue for later in this chapter, but there is no reason not to understand the performance itself as an initiating act, with the audience response, captured on the recording, as direct collaboration, and the audience listening to the CD at home, several decades later, as contextual collaboration. A single individual can take on more than one role in the production of any music; Ellington may have been the impetus for "Diminuendo," for instance, but he may also have directly collaborated with his own initiating act, as well as with the initiating acts of others. The various positions are not fixed. They are impossible to delineate: but delineation is not the point. Awareness of the difficulty is enough.

Keen observers have already recognized the compositional importance of direct and contextual collaboration. Sociologist Tia DeNora, in her book *Beethoven and the Construction of Genius: Musical Politics in Vienna, 1792–1803*, argues not that composer Ludwig van Beethoven lacked musical ability of a very high order, as some of her critics charged, but rather that what is commonly thought of as Beethoven's genius was in fact a complex process that was contingent upon the support of aristocratic patrons and tastemakers, advancements in piano manufacturing that worked well for Beethoven's comparatively forceful manner of playing that instrument, a historical moment that was ripe for aesthetic change, and other factors. Composer and saxophonist John Zorn also writes insightfully about collaboration. "Whether we like it or not, the era of the composer as autonomous musical mind has just about come to an end," Zorn says in the liner notes to his *Spillane* album, released in 1987. He goes on to cite several important instances of group creativity in twentieth-century music: Ellington with his band and Billy Strayhorn; John Cage with David Tudor or Takehisa Kosugi; Karlheinz Stockhausen with the Kontarsky brothers, Harold Boje, Markus Stockhausen, or Susanne Stephens. Mauricio Kagel, Philip Glass, Steve Reich, the Beatles, Frank Zappa: they all relied on collaboration, according to Zorn, to "produce a musical statement greater than the sum of the individuals involved." Note that Zorn's quick survey touches on all three elements of the theory I have just laid out: the initiating acts attributable to composers, the direct collaboration of ensembles or performers, and, in the example of the Beatles and Frank Zappa, the kind of contextual collaboration provided by the environment of a recording studio, where the state of technology helped determine what was possible in the resulting music.

My only qualification of Zorn's commentary is that the "era of the composer as autonomous musical mind" is a rhetorical construction that has never accurately described how art happens. We have always created collaboratively, even if we have mostly refused to acknowledge it.

COLLABORATING WITH ELLINGTON: SOUNDS AND FRAGMENTS

Duke Ellington—as I noted, the musician who first got me thinking about these issues in a serious way—is considered by many to be America's premier jazz composer, though he actually resisted the word "jazz" in describing his oeuvre. The individual compositions credited to him run well into the thousands—some estimates run as high as five thousand, although Jørgen Mathiasen puts the number at 1,694.

Scott Yanow recently pointed out that there are "countless" Ellington recordings on the market, and that previously unreleased material has been issued regularly since his death. Yanow is not alone in arguing that the bulk of this material is of "consistently high quality." Indeed, for decades now Ellington's fans have repeatedly used the rhetoric of genius in their advocacy of his work. And as Harvey Cohen recently demonstrated, Ellington and his manager, Irving Mills, deployed this rhetoric too, as part of a marketing campaign to promote the composer early in his career.

This passage from a 1931 *Pittsburgh Courier* article is typical of the way emphasis is placed on Ellington, over and above the musicians with whom he was associated:

> During the past year or more the name of Duke Ellington has lingered upon the lips of radio fans, dance lovers, theatregoers and the amusement public of the Nation in general. . . . Crowned "King of Jazz" last week in the National "Most Popular Orchestra" Contest conducted by the *Pittsburgh Courier,* reigning supreme and having polled 50,000 votes, the largest amount, competing with over 50 orchestras and bands all over the United States, Duke Ellington has proved that he is the most popular orchestra leader today.

Notice the name "Ellington" as fetish—how it is supposed to have "lingered upon the lips." Much writing about this music follows suit. George Avakian, in his review of *Ellington at Newport,* for example, notes that "Duke Ellington's" performance of "Diminuendo and Crescendo in Blue" was "one of the most extraordinary moments" in that festival's history. Strictly speaking, of course, Avakian isn't referring to *Ellington's* performance, but the band's—in fact, one of the things that made this performance so extraordinary, as Avakian well knew, had very little directly to do with Ellington at all, but was instead a twenty-seven-chorus solo by tenor saxophonist Paul Gonsalves, of which more later.

Richard O. Boyer, in a 1944 portrait of Ellington called "The Hot Bach," describes what seem to be scenes of effortless mastery taken right out of Peter Schaefer's *Amadeus.* Some of Ellington's best work, Boyer noted, was "written against the glass partitions of offices in

recording studios, on darkened overnight buses, with illumination supplied by a companion holding an interminable chain of matches, and in
sweltering, clattering day coaches." Stanley Crouch, in a 1988 article
describing several of the band's extended works, takes this language to
a level worthy of the Old Testament—reminding us once again that the
rhetoric of genius can have a religious character. For Ellington in the
1950s, Crouch argues, "the view from the mountaintop was as clear
and precise as that of an extraordinary hunting bird who continued to
amaze as he swooped down into the valley, got what he needed, then
started moving up higher, and higher, leaving an indelible image in
the sky." Earlier writers indulged in similar imagery. "Duke Ellington
holds a privileged position in the history of jazz," André Hodeir, one
of the first critics to appreciate the work of Ellington's band from a
musicological perspective, wrote in 1958. "Single-handed he changed
the face of a desert and brought forth the first fruit of that multidimen-
sional music which may one day supplant every other form of jazz."
Miles Davis, for his part, insisted that "all the musicians in jazz should
get together on one certain day and get down on their knees to thank
Duke."

What is interesting about these assessments is that although the rhetoric of genius is their most salient feature, they also take note of facts
that contradict that rhetoric. Yanow remarks that Ellington "always
considered his orchestra to be his main instrument," and in the rest of
his article suggests just how much Ellington depended on the people
with whom he worked, remarking that while most big bands were
lucky to have three or four good soloists, Ellington's boasted many
more. Crouch makes a similar point. "In order to do what his creative
appetite, his ambition, and his artistic demon asked of him," he writes,
"Ellington had to maintain an orchestra for composing purposes longer than any other, almost fifty years." Hodeir is more specific about
the underlying dynamic. Consider this crucial observation in his review
of "Concerto for Cootie" (a piece named for featured trumpeter Cootie Williams):

Unlike the European concerto, in which the composer's intention
dominates the interpreter's, the jazz concerto makes the soloist a kind

of second creator, often more important than the first, even when the part he has to play doesn't leave him any melodic initiative. Perhaps Cootie had nothing to do with the melody of the *Concerto;* he probably doesn't stray from it an inch; and still it would be impossible to imagine *Concerto for Cootie* without him.

Indeed. If we look at Hodeir's previously quoted remarks—Ellington was "single-handed" in the way he "changed the face of a desert and brought forth the first fruit" of jazz—and juxtapose them with this passage, the contradiction becomes clear.

What Hodeir actually identifies in his discussion of "Concerto for Cootie" is a case of direct collaboration in the Ellington group: the distinctive sound of a notable player. In other words, the reason it would be impossible to imagine "Concerto for Cootie" without Cootie Williams—even if Williams had not supplied what Terry Teachout refers to as the tune's original "snippet of melody"—is that the trumpeter, like most mature jazz players, had a unique sound, involving a combination of mutework and vocalized effects, as well as "a bright luster." As Hodeir suggests, Williams's sound opened up important expressive possibilities for a composer, to the extent that without him a work like "Concerto for Cootie" would have been harder to imagine in the first place. In this sense, Williams's sound is not merely a happy complement to the music, but rather a root cause of it.

Importantly, the dynamic between Ellington and Williams was by no means unusual in the group. In *Beyond Category,* his biography of Ellington, John Edward Hasse explains that alto saxophonist Johnny Hodges also frequently found himself in the role of featured horn player. After all, Hodges too had a unique sound—a plaintive, sweet wail, perfect for ballads like "Never No Lament," which became one of his signature tunes. For a variety of reasons, including the feeling that he wasn't being sufficiently compensated, Hodges, along with trombonist Lawrence Brown and drummer Sonny Greer (two important band members in their own right), left the Ellington organization in 1951. Hasse writes of this migration that "Hodges's sliding, passionate way with ballads, his moving blues, and his majestic melodies helped define the Ellington sound; robbed of it, how could Ellington continue his band, keep alive his sound? It was a stunning blow, the greatest professional crisis Ellington had ever faced."

Note here how the possessive case slips from Hodges to Ellington: "Hodges's sliding, passionate way with ballads, his moving blues, and his majestic melodies" is rhetorically absorbed into the implicitly more important "Ellington sound"—a shift that is particularly problematic given sound's identity-generating role in jazz. Yet Hasse also recognizes that Ellington *depended* on Hodges, going so far as to argue that during the latter's sabbatical from the band (he would return in 1955), "none of Ellington's recordings can be considered quintessential." It's a recurring, frustrating pattern in Ellington writing—this recognition that the composer needed his players, juxtaposed with the disclaimer that he didn't need them *too* much, or enough for us to consider them artistic equals. Our habitual way of resolving that tension—the rhetoric of genius—remains unsatisfying.

Direct collaboration in the Ellington group was sometimes even more concrete than the lending of an interpretive style or unique sound, however. Many sidemen created melodies, or fragments of melodies, or riffs, or other ideas, that were then incorporated by Ellington into the music for the group, often without compositional credit, and sometimes against the will of their putative inventor. The aforementioned "snippet of melody" that became "Concerto for Cootie," and "Never No Lament," whose theme is attributable to Hodges, are both well-known examples. This is the point Collier takes up so controversially in *Duke Ellington* when he asserts that "the central melodic ideas of virtually all of Ellington's best-known songs originated in someone else's head," and proceeds to make a list of eighteen popular Ellington pieces (including "In a Sentimental Mood," "I'm Beginning to See the Light," "Creole Love Call," and "Mood Indigo"), indicating which band member he believes was responsible for the main idea of each. Here Collier seems to echo the bitter words of trombonist Lawrence Brown, who, frustrated by how his own tunes were used in this way, famously told Ellington, "I don't consider you a composer. You are a compiler."

Other critics have pointed out the same dynamic—usually, to their credit, more delicately. Ken Rattenbury cites Gunther Schuller, who wondered how "Ellington and his men" were "able to create a unique kind of big band jazz, in the late 1920s and early 1930s?" Schuller argued that trumpeter Bubber Miley was crucial to that accomplishment, in part because he introduced "a rougher sound," pioneering the trumpet "growl" technique—another example of the direct collaboration of individual expressiveness—which he then taught to some of the other brass players in the group, including trombonists Charlie Irvis and Joe "Tricky Sam" Nanton. (The growl would later become part of Williams's aesthetic too.) But like Williams and Hodges, Miley also contributed tunes. Indeed, Schuller contends that not only was Miley the band's strongest soloist in the initial period of the group, but that he also cowrote—to an extent that has been underappreciated—some of its best-known pieces. Three of these—"East St. Louis Toodle-Oo," "Black and Tan Fantasy," and "Creole Love Call"—are often categorized as early masterpieces of the Ellington canon. Rattenbury judiciously points out that Miley was never recognized for his contributions to "Creole Love Call," in either the original sheet music version (published in 1926) or in the oeuvre cataloged in *Music Is My Mistress,* Ellington's autobiography. And yet, with great irony, the rhetoric of genius then reasserts itself, as Rattenbury includes a transcription of "Creole Love Call" for the reader's consideration—crediting it only to Ellington. (All of which overlooks the fact that "Creole Love Call" was actually adapted from "Camp Meeting Blues," an even earlier piece by cornetist King Oliver.)

In a more recent Ellington book, Teachout, referring to the composer's "magpielike borrowings," argues that "no more than Beethoven or Stravinsky was Ellington a natural tunesmith: His genius, like theirs, lay elsewhere." By now the point was not new: some portion of the Ellington catalog (though certainly not all of it, as Teachout is careful to remind us) was the result of his direct collaboration with the initiating acts of others. In retelling that story, Teachout, like Collier, drew his share of opprobrium. Trumpeter Nicholas Payton, for instance, responding to reviewer James Gavin's rephrasing of Teachout's point that Ellington was "no great melodist," counters that Ellington "is a central part of the 20th century melodic landscape" and accuses Teachout and Gavin of being "brainwashed to see the Black American as nothing more than lazy and shiftless thieves who are incapable of contributing anything more than entertainment or being a nuisance to society."

Teachout is certainly guilty of a gratingly superior tone—a function of the aesthetic positivism that seems to be his professional bailiwick—but he is far from seeing Ellington as "incapable." And though I have greater sympathy with the spirit of Payton's complaint, for the purposes of this chapter I must point out that he here frustratingly enacts one of the traps of the rhetoric of genius. Deconstructions of creativity are often dismissed in what Joseph Horowitz, writing about classical music, calls an "attitude of hortatory, contentious reverence," a stance that "denounces impostors and wards off agnostics." Jazz has its sacred cows too, and to the extent that the music is understood as heroic art, the idea of traditional authorship, at least when it comes to jazz composition, may be one of them. Saying so does not make Ellington's artistry any less impressive. But in the end our understandable desire to defend him from critical presumption should not come at the expense of the other musicians in his band, as if they were inconsequential to the resulting beauty.

"COTTON TAIL": SOLOISTS AND PALIMPSESTS

In his liner notes for *The Blanton-Webster Band,* a three-CD compilation of the Ellington band's music from the early 1940s, Mark Tucker writes, "In considering Ellington's rich and productive life as a professional musician, one's head spins. How did he do it? What could account for his unparalleled success?" Ironically, when discussing the origins of "Cotton Tail," one of the compilation's featured works, Tucker walks us through a beautiful example of the collaborative dynamic in the group, answering his own question. "*Cotton Tail* emerges as a simple, straightforward romp on the chords of Gershwin's *I Got Rhythm,*" Tucker says. "Ben Webster's celebrated solo forms *Cotton Tail*'s centerpiece. The later chorus for the reeds is also thought to be Webster's invention. In fact, it sounds like a harmonization of a sax solo." Tucker's analysis helps us understand the creative work in the song quantitatively; by his reckoning, eighty-four bars of "Cotton Tail" can be attributed to Ellington (seventy-six bars of ensemble playing and eight bars of Ellington's soloing), whereas 104 bars are Webster's (the sixty-four-bar main solo, an eight-bar solo break, and thirty-two bars of harmonized solo at the end). There are others who think Webster was responsible for more of "Cotton Tail" than that—Teachout notes that the piece "is solely credited to Ellington, but Webster is thought to have both composed the tune and arranged the equally celebrated *soli* chorus." In either case, the striking thing is that Webster's contributions—based in improvisation but still essentially compositional—are proportionally greater. Hence the apposite title of the CD set—*The Blanton-Webster Band*. (In addition to Webster, bassist Jimmy Blanton is featured.)

But if it is true that Webster is responsible for more than half the music that makes up "Cotton Tail," is it fair to simply assign authorship to Ellington alone, as the producers of *The Blanton-Webster Band* do—or to imply more broadly, as Harvey Cohen does when addressing the same era, that Ellington was able as a solitary actor "to produce one of the greatest periods of extended creativity in the band's history"? The technical reasons for the "Cotton Tail" credit are clear, of course—just as they were in Rattenbury's listing of Ellington as the author of "Creole Love Call." If the copyright for the piece is filed in Ellington's name, then there is some obligation to reproduce that information whenever attributing authorship. But why not more aggressively challenge that claim, or at least steer clear of the rhetoric of genius?

Indeed, we ought to steer clear of the rhetoric of genius when it comes to any music involving improvisation, given how the performers of such music are routinely denied authorship. Many observers claim that since improvisation happens "in the moment," it is fundamentally different from composition, sans editing, and sans contemplation. And yet I contend that the underlying gestures are the same. For one thing, the experience of a "moment," like the experience of time in general, is subjective. And so of traditional composition, one can say that it too is embedded in "real time," even if that is obscured by the standpoint of history. And of what we call improvisation, one can say that any one example of the phenomenon is a single step in a recursive process from which it cannot be excised. It's not that there is a lack of editing, it's just that the editing happens faster. And it's not that there is a lack of contemplation, it's just that the contemplation happens before the gig. (We will return to this subject in more detail in a moment; see "Composing Is Work.")

It is well known that the most straightforward jazz "cover" usually features a great deal of what musicians call "blowing." Typically the predetermined main melody of a tune (a standard like "How High the Moon," or "All the Things You Are") is played briefly at the beginning and end of a performance, but the intervening solo section, in which musicians take turns improvising over the song's chord progression, goes on for many choruses. John Coltrane's version of "My Favorite Things" is one of the best-known jazz recordings of all time, and most of it, as Chris Cutler points out, consists of sequences of notes not found in the original Rodgers and Hammerstein score. Improvisation is more often than not the real point of such music, adding a good deal of content that wasn't there in the first place—including not only new melodic ideas but variations on the harmony and even form of a piece. Yet for all its aesthetic impact, none of this is typically recognized as compositional.

And even once we recognize the authorial role of improvisation, in the case of "Cotton Tail" we still have not plumbed the depths of unacknowledged collaboration. We might be so bold as to ask why Ellington receives sole compositional credit for the tune, even though its harmonic source material was, as Tucker mentions, George Gershwin's "I Got Rhythm" (from the 1930 musical *Girl Crazy*). "Cotton Tail" is not the only piece ever built on this harmonic foundation—the practice has been so frequent that the chord progression has become known among jazz musicians by the generic label "rhythm changes." Yet Gershwin is never officially cited as a collaborator in this capacity. Of course the problem is much broader than that: improvising a new melody over chord changes taken from a preexisting composition is one way jazz composers create in general. The process is acknowledged by historians and musicologists, but is not usually understood as an aspect of creativity. Miles Davis's "Donna Lee" is a new melody over the chords of "Back Home in Indiana," but we do not really think of "Indiana" songwriters Ballard MacDonald and James F. Hanley as among its "authors." The situation is similar with Charlie Parker's "Ko Ko" (not to be confused with the Ellington composition of the same name), which derives from "Cherokee," by songwriter Ray Noble. In jazz theory, these are called contrafacts, and the practice of creating them stems from musicians' (understandable) attempts to avoid fees required for recording copyrighted songs. But this clever workaround should not obscure the fact that the harmonic foundation of a contrafact is still a component of its composition.

This is not to say that the composers of standards, or the tunes upon which contrafacts are based, are the unsung heroes of jazz culture. To be clear, from a historical and political perspective, the denial of authorship for African-American improvisers in general is far more troubling than the omission of Gershwin as a collaborator on "Cotton Tail." But the point of seeing authorship collaboratively is to celebrate the richness and complexity of any work's creative sources. And so, for that matter, it is odd that we assume Gershwin was the inventor of the rhythm changes in the first place, just because "I Got Rhythm" popularized that particular chord sequence. Western harmony had been developing for centuries by the time Gershwin got around to writing music. And especially since most of the music played in that time was never put on paper or recorded, it is highly unlikely that he was the very first ever to use what is essentially a rather simple set of chords.

Sometimes the kind of direct collaboration typical of pieces built on rhythm changes can be spread out widely over time, involving the work of numerous participants. Consider "'Round Midnight," originally composed by Thelonious Monk as early as 1936. When Cootie Williams recorded it in 1944, he embellished the melody with "an eight bar interlude," and when sheet music transcriptions were made of Williams's recording, they included those embellishments—though according to Williams he was the only one to play them. Later, Dizzy Gillespie added an introduction and a coda; Robin Kelley notes that

"Monk himself made them integral to the entire composition." Miles Davis is also known to have added an interlude. Each alteration, regardless of how it was received, brought another layer to the modern understanding of the song, which is determined by what has been a collective, additive process.

In a recent roundtable discussion, composer Dave Restivo explicitly advocates this sort of aesthetic layering as a creative tool, encouraging young writers to "use pieces you like as templates for creating your own works—maybe borrow elements of the form or structure, harmonic progression, time signature, groove, or just the 'vibe.'" "Don't worry," Restivo insists, "they never end up sounding like the source!" Note the interesting tension here between the blatant call to "borrowing"—what in another context might be called "stealing" (as we will see in chapter 7)—and the notion that it can lead to something that is "your own." Sometimes the process can be even more attenuated. Supposedly, John Lennon's "Because" was written as a retrograde version of Beethoven's *Moonlight Sonata*—though anyone who knows both works can attest that "Because" is actually closer to being an impression of the Beethoven piece, taking it as a fairly obvious reference point, but nothing more. Whether compositions generated this way "never end up sounding like the source" is a question of taste.

Earlier I argued that traditional authorship makes it easier to talk about music, substituting a synecdoche for a complex reality. In each of the situations I have just described—contrafacts, improvisations in the context of a cover version, extended collaborations involving multiple authors, impressionistic riffs on preexisting tunes—it is easy to understand why we resort to the shorthand of singular authorship. It is much more elegant to say that "Cotton Tail" is Duke Ellington's composition than it is to say "Cotton Tail" was a messy palimpsest, composed by Ellington, Ben Webster, George Gershwin, some unknown musician who first used the rhythm changes, et al. Shorthand in aesthetics— like shorthand in office dictation—is a practical tool. But that's also the problem. Without the reified idea of composition, a conversation about musical creativity is much harder to have. But there is always a great deal more going on than that idea will allow.

"COMPOSING IS WORK"

In a 1962 interview with *Metronome* editor Bill Coss, Billy Strayhorn offers a counterargument to the collaborative theory of musical creativity by suggesting that to the extent that Ellington's artistic role in his own group was as a manipulator of musical fragments generated by others, that role was more artistically important than the fragment generation itself. The raw materials of a composition, Strayhorn suggests, matter less than how they are arranged.

Of course, Strayhorn had unparalleled access to the creative process within the Ellington band. A remarkable composer in his own right, he met Ellington in 1938, when the younger man was just twenty-three. He would subsequently go on to become Ellington's closest musical associate (a fellow composer, a co-composer, an arranger, a sounding board, a confidant) for almost thirty years. Notwithstanding the research of Walter van de Leur, who I think ultimately puts too much faith in after-the-fact analysis of extant scores (see chapter 6 for my discussion of the pitfalls of treating written music authentically), the exact nature of their collaboration is difficult to elucidate, as is often the case in such partnerships. Some indication of how Ellington viewed it is found in *Music Is My Mistress,* in which he called Strayhorn "my right arm, my left arm, all the eyes in the back of my head, my brain waves in his head, and his in mine." (Ellington's reference to "brain waves" here is particularly fascinating, reminding us of the listener's inability to know what either Ellington or Strayhorn was actually thinking as he composed.) Although van de Leur argues from the scores that the two composers were more stylistically distinct than is usually assumed, for a long time even careful listeners heard uncanny similarities in their music and had difficulty telling where one's contributions ended and the other's began. By the time Strayhorn died, in 1967, he had composed many "characteristic" Ellington pieces, including "Take the 'A' Train," "Chelsea Bridge," and "Lotus Blossom."

Given his close involvement with Ellington, Strayhorn's comments to Bill Coss (edited though they seem to be) carry a certain weight, and are worth quoting at length:

> COSS: So many people suggest a question which, I suppose, is the kind you expect when someone gets into a position as important as Duke's. What it comes down to is that Duke doesn't really write much. What he does is listen to his soloists, takes things they play, and fashion them into songs. Thus the songs belong to the soloists, you do the arrangements, and Duke takes the credit.
>
> STRAYHORN: They used to say that about Irving Berlin too.
>
> But how do you explain the constant flow of songs? Guys come in and out of the band, but the songs keep getting written, and you can always tell an Ellington song.
>
> Anyway, something like a solo, perhaps only a few notes, is hardly a composition. It may be the inspiration, but what do they say about 10 percent inspiration and 90 percent perspiration? Composing is work.
>
> So this guy says you and he wrote it, but he thinks he wrote it. He thinks you just put it down on paper. But what you did was put it down on paper, harmonized it, straightened out the bad phrases, and added things to it, so you could hear the finished product. Now, really, who wrote it?
>
> It was ever thus.
>
> But the proof is that these people don't go somewhere else and write beautiful music. You don't hear anything else from them. You do from Ellington.

As much as I want to defer to Strayhorn's firsthand expertise, and as much as I applaud his staunch defense of Ellington from unfair assumptions, this analysis feels like an overcompensation. How exactly do we determine that one facet of collaboration should take precedence over another? By any measure I can imagine, the initial inception of a work (what Strayhorn appears to concede to the band members who claimed that Ellington borrowed things from them) and its artful arrangement (the process of finishing a piece by transcribing, harmonizing, streamlining, and expanding it) are mutually dependent. If nothing else, from a strictly utilitarian standpoint, however extensively Ellington reworked the contributions of others, the initiating acts of relevant sidemen were crucial to the resulting composition. Not just any notes would do: without these collaborators there would have been nothing to rework. So without diminishing Ellington's feat, we have to ask: if it is wrong for "these people" to think of themselves as authors, why is it less problematic for Ellington to claim authorship for himself, in those cases where he did so exclusively?

Indeed, when Strayhorn says "composing is work," he is being a little unfair, implying that "something like a solo, perhaps only a few notes" is, by contrast, *not* work. Terry Teachout makes the same mistake when he argues that "to be a facile melodist is not a prerequisite of musical greatness." The assumption is that composition is meticulous, careful, labored, while improvisation is casual, unthinking—not an unusual way of contrasting the two, as it happens. Critic Gene Santoro, for instance, argues that Ellington enjoyed a "closed feedback loop" with his band, in which players would typically "hook" a melodic idea in the course of a rehearsal, and if Ellington heard something he liked, "he'd seize it (sometimes with credit, sometimes not) and weave his rich orchestral tapestry around it." In Santoro's view, only in the tapestry-making phase would the fragment become a "total composition, something living in a fully ramified way, quite apart from the scrawl or flash that had given it birth." Again, there is a hierarchy implied here, in which composing is assumed to be difficult, complex, requiring intellectual mastery, while improvising an interesting melodic idea is simply a casual, spontaneous, serendipitous event.

Anyone who has spent any time learning to improvise will be suspicious of the idea that improvisation is mere "scrawl or flash." An effective solo may have the illusion of spontaneity, and a buoyant melody seemingly produced extemporaneously may seem "facile," but dedicated players spend long hours practicing, studying, and listening to music. Jazz musicians even have a specific term for the work Strayhorn, Santoro, and Teachout gloss over: "woodshedding," or a period of self-directed study and practice, often spent in physical isolation. Guitarist Emily Remler describes a typical experience. "At one point, I went down to the Jersey shore and locked myself in a room for a month," she says in Paul Berliner's *Thinking in Jazz*. "I lost twenty pounds, stopped smoking, and became a serious guitar player." But Sonny Rollins has perhaps the best-known woodshed story. The celebrated saxophonist "retired" from music in 1959, after becoming exhausted by the pressure of his own success and uncertain about contemporaneous developments in jazz. It took him three years of hermetic study before he released another album (*The Bridge,* named after the Williamsburg Bridge, where he practiced during this period). The woodshed ethos also explains why, in response to a woman's unfavorable comment about his playing, Miles Davis retorted, "It took me twenty years study and practice to work up to what I wanted to play in this performance. How can she expect to listen five minutes and understand it?" If what Remler, Rollins, or Davis improvised seemed flashy to some listeners, it is only because each musician had labored for years to make it sound that way.

We must also consider the extent to which Ellington's style as an arranger was itself informed (in ways that are impossible to trace) by his long association with the men in his band. It may be true, as Harvey Cohen argues, that "during WWII and afterward, Ellington composed in a more solitary manner with far less input from the orchestra"— but by that time, as Cohen also acknowledges, he had already had decades of experience in a looser, more direct collaborative relationship. "In the earliest days of the band," Cohen notes, "from roughly 1925 to 1935, the band was very tight, personally as well as musically, and ideas flowed freely. Many contributed to writing and arranging new pieces, encouraged by Ellington." Are we entitled to assume that Ellington would have developed his later ideas about arranging if he had not had the luxury of this hothouse creative environment for so long?

It is even possible that the Ellington group enjoyed a "constant flow of songs," as Strayhorn puts it, not in spite of the fact that band members came and went, but in part *because* of it. In other words, although the lineup in the ensemble was fairly consistent over time, at least for a band of its size, the periods of turnover may have kept the collaborative process fresh. New players meant new sounds, new skills to be exploited in a compositional context. New people meant new ideas, new melodic fragments to be turned into complete pieces. Perhaps it was true that "these people don't go somewhere else and write beautiful music"—yet this does not disprove the importance of collaboration, but merely suggests that those band members who did leave were unable to construct equally productive relationships in their new ensembles. Successful collaboration, as many good songwriting teams have discovered too late—that is, after breaking up—depends not merely on bringing together two or more talented people, but rather on the chemistry between specific personalities. Paul McCartney and John Lennon wrote many beautiful songs together. Paul McCartney and Elvis Costello did not.

Finally, and most important, the comparison Strayhorn is asking us to make is not testable. Weighing the importance of a borrowed melody against the way it is transformed in an arrangement assumes we can extract each and compare them side by side. But how can an arrangement be heard separately from the melody it is used to express? For that matter, how can a melody be heard retroactively, once we have been exposed to its arrangement? How do we know how much of that arrangement was or was not suggested by the melody in the first place? We are now in counterfactual territory—at best, an opportunity to misleadingly confirm our biases about which aspects of creativity we think are the most important.

"THEY'RE TAKING PART IN IT WITH US"

So far we have been looking primarily at the interaction of initiating acts and direct collaboration in the Ellington group. What about contextual collaboration?

One key aspect of this more elusive dynamic is the role played by an audience. To step away from Ellington for a moment, one can hear that relationship pretty clearly, for instance, in "Deacon's Hop," a 1951 performance by rhythm and blues tenor saxophonist Big Jay McNeely, recorded live at Los Angeles's Olympic Auditorium. The work is accompanied throughout by the sound of an enthusiastic crowd that at times is more prominent than anything the band is doing. And there's good reason for that imbalance. McNeely is known for the physicality of his show; Art Pepper once recalled how "he marched up and down the street playing his horn, he lay down on his back playing his horn,

he came into the Downbeat playing his horn." A famous Bob Willoughby photograph captures something of the McNeely mayhem on
the night "Deacon's Hop" was recorded, just at a moment when the
saxophonist is literally bent over backwards. Interestingly, McNeely is
not the focal point of Willoughby's image: he takes up only about a
third of the photographic space, and is depicted off to the side. It is as
if Willoughby really wants us to see the audience members crowding
the stage's edge. He photographed McNeely from behind, and so we
get a performer's-eye view of several fans leaning forward, clearly lost
in the throes of emotion. Fists are clenched, eyes are closed, heads are
tilted back—all gestures that would become commonplace in the ico-
nography of the rock and roll era.

  We have become accustomed to thinking about the power of live
performance as emanating entirely from the people onstage. To paraphrase Grigely, it is not unlike the way we are used to thinking of
how a painting transforms a room. So when we consider "Deacon's
Hop," our impulse is to assume that McNeely produced the audience
response through the force of his musicality and showmanship. As
Willoughby himself puts it, McNeely "created some sort of resonance

with the audience. In some weird way, he seemed to be playing them!" Yet it would be a mistake to conclude that the flow of creativity in this music was unidirectional. Pianist Vijay Iyer points out that African-American music draws on "a notion of communication as process, as a collective activity that harmonizes individuals rather than a telegraphic model of communication as mere transmission of literal, verbal meanings." It is not that the music is merely passed from point A to point B, in neat little packages of audio data, like Morse code. Rather, it is inherently participatory, created from all directions at once. The shouts of encouragement that came from the crowd were there partly as a consequence of McNeely's performance, it is true, but unless he was oblivious to the ecstatic fans, he received cues from the audience just as he gave them. Hence his telling comment, in a recent interview, that "you have to watch people close when you do this. There are some people on the aisle wearing expensive suits, and you have to play one way when you get near them. Or if you see kids, you have to let go of other types of notes. I'd stop and play differently for different people I'd see along [the] aisle." To riff on Willoughby: McNeely wasn't just playing the audience, he was being played (in the best sense of that term) by them.

Ellington too understood the importance of an audience. He valued his band's "dance engagements," believing that when the players "see people moving around the floor, they've got to put snap and ginger into their work." When there were dancers present, the music changed; the band knew it was playing not *for* the audience, but *with* them. "We like to know," as Ellington put it, "that they feel they're taking part in it with us." Think again of "Diminuendo and Crescendo in Blue," the 1956 Ellington recording mentioned earlier, featured on the live *Ellington at Newport* album. Among other things, "Diminuendo" featured an unplanned twenty-seven-chorus solo by tenor saxophonist Paul Gonsalves, which, like Ben Webster's solo in "Cotton Tail," occupies a significant portion of the piece's overall running time (just over six minutes out of a total of 14:37), and which, taken on its own, is another instance of improvised direct collaboration. With this solo Gonsalves became an icon of jazz heroism: the stereotype of the professional musician pushed to his limit, wringing every last bit of inspiration out of a performance. But Stanley Dance, who wrote the *Ellington at Newport* reissue liner notes, remarks that though Gonsalves's solo "provoked pandemonium among the festival crowd," the effect was amplified "when a blond in a black dress got up in one of the front boxes and began to dance ecstatically." That unnamed woman helped produce the pandemonium too. Her frenzy—patriarchally read as an erotic response to the music—in fact cannot be separated from the creativity of those on the stage. Indeed, in George Avakian's telling, this woman seemed to focus the energy of the festival space. ("A moment later somebody else started in another part of the audience," Avakian later wrote. "Large sections of the crowd had already been on their feet; now their cheering was doubled and redoubled.") She, and those who joined her, were thus crucial to the legacy of this album.

The incident reminds us that during the big band era that helped bring Ellington to national prominence, jazz maintained a creative connection to what Marshall Stearns called "vernacular dance." Ellington's music, particularly in the early years of his career, was often explicitly designed to support dancers, both onstage and in the audience. Again, choreography influenced what and how the band played. In fact, early jazz in general drew much of its rhythmic inspiration from dance, a detail that is often treated lightly in jazz histories. Drummers Buddy Rich and Philly Jo Jones (for example) began their careers as tap dancers, and many other jazz drummers performed with "hoofers" such as Baby Laurence, Groundhog Basie, and the Nicholas Brothers. Dancer Charles "Honi" Coles has gone so far as to insist that tap dancers were crucial in the creation of bebop, arguing that they supplied the music's basic rhythms. In a typical performance, Coles claimed, the drummer listened to the dancer, "and the rest of the musicians listened to the drummer, and a whole syncopated sound evolved. I like to tease the musicians about it, but it's absolutely true—they got it from dancers."

Coles may overstate the case a little here, but the gist of his argument is important. The first jazz audiences were, to some extent, audiences-in-motion. And that motion—the visibility of it, the sound it made, its tactility—served as a source of contextual collaboration for the music. To return to "Diminuendo": if Gonsalves's opening notes inspired an initial mayhem, that feeling from his listeners was fed back to him, providing inspiration in turn. At any point, the audience could have decided to sit back down, to cut off that feedback. In that case our sense of this recording would have been greatly altered, regardless of what Gonsalves actually played. Instead, the audience's presence on this "Diminuendo" made the composition into a radically different thing from what it had been. One need only compare the Newport recording with the 1937 studio recording—just as one need only compare the live recording of "Deacon's Hop" with McNeely's more sedate 1949 studio recording. Each is a different work, not merely in degree, but in kind.

INTERLUDE: IN A SILENT WAY

More than half a century after the Newport "Diminuendo," jazz is often performed in front of polite audiences, sitting respectfully; the music's connection to vernacular dance has become tenuous. It's a phenomenon that was already common in classical music. "The relationship between music and dance has long been lost," Paul Theberge argues, adding that "even by the eighteenth century, so-called 'dance suites' had already become autonomous and highly stylized forms of instrumental music." But we should not assume that the contextual collaboration of an audience requires pandemonium or a blond in a black dress—in jazz, classical music, or any genre. We should not assume that silence is physically nonparticipatory. We should not, in other words, rely on what Susan McLary calls "one of the principal claims to supremacy in European classical music (and other forms of high culture)": the idea that music "transcends the body, that it is concerned with the nobler domains of imagination and even metaphysics." This is the problematic Schopenhauerian notion of music as an immaterial phenomenon, and it completely misses the transductive transformations of listening bodies. After all, in order to be perceived, music *depends upon* bodies, as ethnomusicologist John Blacking reminds us. "Many, if not all, of music's essential processes," Blacking wrote, "can be found in the constitution of the human body and in patterns of interaction of bodies in society." In this sense, listening is itself a form of dancing. If your heart is beating, if you are breathing, if your blood is moving, if your eardrum is vibrating, you are dancing.

So while it is true that the etiquette of art music—which in some cases is actually codified and presented as a contract with the audience prior to a performance—usually denies the body to a significant degree, we must be careful here. We might, for instance, juxtapose the Willoughby photo of Big Jay McNeely with the palpable physicality visible in the painting reproduced on the cover of Tia DeNora's *Beethoven and the Construction of Genius*. Part of a nineteenth-century genre of paintings that featured people listening to music, marking what Peter Gay called the "ascent of inwardness" (for other examples, see Henri Fantin-Latour's *Around the Piano,* or Émile-René Ménard's *Homer*), the painting has an unwieldy title: *Ludwig van Beethoven and Intimates, Listening to Him Playing.* The artist, Albert Gräfle, depicts Beethoven, seated at the piano, surrounded by four men who listen to him perform. While Beethoven occupies the central position, in the context of the image he nevertheless appears to be just another figure. The dramatic physicality of his small audience dominates the painting, just as the audience dominated the Willoughby photo. Of the three

men who are seated, one is leaning back fully, staring at the ceiling; the second is turned away from the piano, his face completely covered by his hand; the third clutches his chin in a classic gesture of contemplation. The fourth man, standing behind Beethoven, crosses his arms and stares pensively at the pianist.

This small audience helps to make the music possible through the bodily context it creates. The men in Gräfle's painting are, in a very important sense, as much a part of the music as the notes themselves; they embody it, visually evoking its seriousness. They help to define the sound we hear when we experience Beethoven two centuries later: their body language sets a template for contemplative listening that informs the practice to this day. They are not as demonstrative as the Newport or Olympic audiences, to be sure—but that does not mean that nothing is being transformed in the space between Beethoven's fingers and their ears, or between Gräfle's fingers and ours.

BEETHOVEN AND DIRECT COLLABORATION

My case illustrates how success is always rationalized. People really don't like to hear success explained away as luck. Especially successful people. As they age and succeed, people feel their success was somehow inevitable. They don't want to acknowledge the role played by accident in their lives. There's a reason for this: the world doesn't want to acknowledge it either.

—Michael Lewis

A skeptical reader, hesitant to embrace the argument I've been making about authorship, might be tempted to respond that Ellington is a unique case in the history of music. The real reason he fits the collaborative argument, this critic might say, is that he was a *jazz* composer, and as even the most casual listener knows, jazz often involves some form of improvisation—a creative technique that because of its spontaneity is necessarily collaborative, requiring musicians to respond to each other, and to their surroundings, in real time. This critic might also buy into the stereotype that jazz musicians don't read traditional notation, and so of course again collaboration is to be expected—

because how could a single composer orally dictate the sort of nuance and multi-instrumental complexity that can be described with relative ease by a score?

In reality, the idea that jazz is never written down is a myth. Ellington himself used scores, extensively if idiosyncratically, and now, after decades of jazz's institutional intermingling with other art music and the growth of jazz education as a discipline, it is rare indeed to find a jazz musician who cannot or will not read notation. It is equally rare to find a jazz musician who will insist that jazz must always involve improvisation. Jazz, in other words, is not a special case in which collaboration is uniquely relevant, à la John Zorn's suggestion that Ellington was a new type of composer because he relied on the creative participation of others. It is easy to assume that jazz is the exception that proves the genius rule for classical music, but composition of *any sort* necessarily involves collaboration. Indeed, the collaborative theory of musical creativity helps explain even that most venerable of classical composers—by some accounts the man who defined, or whose career was used to define, the traditional notion of genius in music: Ludwig van Beethoven.

To ground our discussion of this well-loved artist, and to offer a kind of balance to this chapter, let's look in more detail at Tia DeNora's *Beethoven and the Construction of Genius,* which, like Collier's biography of Ellington, has been strongly criticized, though for different (and less persuasive) reasons. *Beethoven* is not, and wasn't intended as, musical analysis—a fact that is worth noting right away because the assumption that it should have been drove much of the controversy. That is, many readers were unhappy that DeNora had little to say about the quality of Beethoven's art. Charles Rosen, for instance, in his *New York Review of Books* piece on DeNora, insisted that a listener cannot "explore 'music's social meaning' with no reference to the music." Self-appointed critics from the lay audience, some of whose reviews can be found on the Amazon page that sells *Beethoven,* expressed similar complaints. One wrote that there "is no analysis of the music itself in this book, because she has decided it is irrelevant. I'm not kidding." Another added, "As the other reviewer of this book exclaimed, listen to the music!" Farther down on the same page, a third observer drove the point home with an urgent question: "Are we really to believe that the music of this man does not speak for itself? . . . how about a serious listen to what he actually wrote down! What I am suggesting is a serious listen."

But why fault a book that is not about musical analysis for its lack of musical analysis? The absurdity of the complaint—as if we all agree on what "music" even is—suggests that there is actually something else at stake here. Philosopher Peter Kivy exemplifies the problem in his own critique. "If one were to come to believe, as does DeNora, that genius is a political construct, Beethoven a political put-up job," Kivy argues, "then one perforce cannot experience the music of Beethoven with the sense of wonder and fervor one had when one believed in the traditional concept of genius." This extraordinary statement suggests that for Kivy, musical pleasure and the "traditional concept of genius" are strongly and inevitably linked. Yet he never explains why this should be. Instead, he asks us to assume that because DeNora does not offer a critique of Beethoven's music, she is therefore offering a negative critique, which is in turn a threat not only to Beethoven's reputation but also to the audience's experience of his music. (How fragile Kivy seems to believe that experience to be!)

As I read her, DeNora does not claim that anyone plugged into Beethoven's context would have produced the same body of work. She does not claim that Beethoven lacked agency vis-à-vis his own artistry or that he was a puppet manipulated by the political machinations of those more powerful than him. And she does not claim that we've somehow been duped into including Beethoven in the Western musical canon. What she actually addresses is the collaborative theory of musical creativity that I have been discussing in this chapter, but in different language. And her insight is all the more important for how glibly it has been dismissed. When, for instance, in response to Charles Rosen's review, DeNora rearticulated her position by stating that "Beethoven's talent was a necessary but not sufficient cause of his subsequent acclaim," Rosen was prompted to retort that "put that way, the thesis is acceptable and even bland. Who would deny it?"

But the thesis is not bland, and I submit that plenty of listeners would deny it. What popular rendering of the Beethoven legend acknowledges, for instance, DeNora's point that the composer's relationships with musicians must necessarily have informed his compositions, even after he could no longer physically hear them? "Not all Viennese-based composers had the good fortune to work intimately with respected and highly skilled performers," DeNora points out—just as not all jazz composers have had the luxury of year-round access to a big band stocked with world-class players and improvisers. There is even some indication, DeNora suggests, that Beethoven "benefited from the suggestions these musicians offered for improving his works." The cellist Antonín Kraft, for example, recommended marking "a passage in the finale of the third trio, Opus I, with *sulla corda G,*" she notes, "and that in the second of these trios the finale, which Beethoven had marked 4/4, should be changed to 2/4." Beethoven also responded to advice from friends and musicians to excise portions of the initial version of his opera *Fidelio,* eventually paring it down to two acts. And after the composer's death, pianists who knew or studied with him engaged in posthumous editing of his work, imposing what Alessandra Comini has called "separate gospels to the faithful on how Beethoven should be played"—"gospels" that may have been revised later, but that helped create an initial sense of what was meant by "Beethoven music."

Such influences were perhaps less significant or frequent or obvious or lasting than the direct collaboration or initiating acts of members of Ellington's band. And yet it feels wrong to assume so unequivocally. After two centuries of hagiography, it is all too easy to discount the possibility of Beethoven being swayed by anyone, because the forceful personality that is part of his mythos is more appealing to our sense of what creativity is. But classical composers, like all composers, have always relied on other musicians for their conception of music's sonic material—we can never know the sound of a given instrument except based on our experience of having heard it played—and always in a way informed by the idiosyncrasies of material expression. "Opera was always composed for a special occasion and for particular singers," Albert Einstein notes, citing an example that echoes the argument about the distinctive sounds of Cootie Williams and Johnny Hodges, and "the choice of singers influenced the vocal style and other characteristics as well." Why should this dynamic have been any different in other genres?

Beethoven, like Ellington, also borrowed melodies from the world around him, using them as building blocks with which to construct an elaborate "musical architecture." Olufunmilayo Arewa claims that "Beethoven reworked existing music in more than a third of his compositions"—some of it coming from other composers, such as Cherubini and Clementi. H. L. Mencken seemed to presage Teachout's comment that Ellington was not "a natural tunesmith" when he wrote of Beethoven that "it would be hard to think of a composer, even of the fourth rate, who worked with thematic material of less intrinsic merit. He borrowed tunes wherever he found them." But as with Ellington, it is misleading to assume there is a hierarchy between a reworking and its raw material—to argue that it is what Beethoven did with the melodies he borrowed that *really* counts, as if the latter had no role whatsoever in generating the former. Even if no one else reworked those melodies in quite the same way, that doesn't therefore mean we can simply dismiss a borrowed melody as a creative component of a Beethoven composition. The interaction of setting and source is greater than the sum of its parts, and we should not be satisfied with celebrating the author of one part only.

BEETHOVEN AND CONTEXTUAL COLLABORATION

One of the most intriguing moments of the film [*From Mao to Mozart*] occurs in the dialogue between [violinist Isaac] Stern and Li Delun, conductor for the Central Philharmonic in Beijing. Li proposes that the greatness of Mozart had to do with the era in which he lived, which was a time of transition from a feudal to a modern, industrial society. After listening attentively, Stern responds by saying, "Well, I'm not sure that one could argue that the genius of Mozart had anything in particular to do with the development of the social or economic stage of life at that time."

—Mari Yoshihara

The Romantics heard in Beethoven's music a representation of a limitless beyond; a result, paradoxically, of Beethoven being in exactly the right place at exactly the right time. Beethoven was already the greatest composer of an era in which it was suddenly decided that composers were eligible for greatness; he was specializing in instrumental music just when instrumental music made a worst-to-first leap in the aesthetic standings.

—Matthew Guerrieri

Beyond the details of direct collaboration in Beethoven's career, what DeNora is really interested in, it seems to me, is a more subtle understanding of the contextual collaboration that informed his work—particularly the social forces that helped it attain, even if they did not guarantee, its canonical status. In laying the groundwork for her argument, DeNora turns to sociologist of science Michael Mulkay, who has written of the social construction of scientific innovation, arguing that the "apparent temporal priority of discovery is something of an illusion." The impression we have of the surprising suddenness of a given breakthrough, Mulkay suggested, is due to our retrospective habit of overlooking the many tiny details—the unassuming, unspectacular preparatory work, if you will—that led up to it. In this sense, moments of innovation are "interpretively projected backwards upon earlier events."

Mulkay was influenced by Robert King Merton, another sociologist of science, who in discussing the phenomenon of simultaneous discovery—innovations that happen independently but concurrently—argued that "discoveries become virtually inevitable when prerequisite kinds of knowledge and tools accumulate in man's cultural store and when the attention of an appreciable number of investigators becomes focused on a problem." Matthew Guerrieri makes the connection to Beethoven when he points out the "resemblance" between the G-minor Symphony of Etienne-Nicolas Mehul (1763–1817) and Beethoven's Fifth, arguing that their similarity was "in all likelihood the product of mutual and common influence, not plagiarism." From this perspective, the (much more famous) Fifth seems less a dramatic rupture than an inevitable outcome of the coalescence of social trends and individual events. But at the very least, our inability to hear all the music of a given era means that claims of artistic originality are tricky to prove or deny. How can we *really* know a given compositional gesture had no precedent? Would we even recognize such a precedent if we heard it?

Riffing on Mulkay, DeNora posits an interactive relationship between an artist and her social context—its audiences, gatekeepers, technologies, mores, and so on. She suggests that art is not a set of fully fledged great works springing suddenly and dramatically from the minds of innately talented individuals working in isolation but is instead a cumulative phenomenon that emerges from and is "constantly renewed through the reflexive interplay, bit by bit, between perception and its object." This is an interesting turn of phrase that is worth savoring for a moment: it suggests, I think, the complex inner life of creativity.

As an artist creates, she is inevitably influenced by a set of expectations—her own, but also what she intuits about others she has observed or interacted with in the past—even as she helps to create new expectations about what art can be. While composing, artists think not only about a work but also about a whole range of issues surrounding it. As Beethoven wrote the *Eroica,* for instance, no matter how it absorbed him, he could not have been focused unceasingly on the notes alone, in some kind of hermetically sealed, purely aesthetic headspace. He must surely have been aware, even if only tacitly, of the importance his culture attached to large-scale, long-form compositions; of how his own such works had been received in the past; of the uncertainty of the marketplace; of the opinions of the cognoscenti. How this awareness affected him and his music, and in particular how consciously, is less significant than the fact that the effect occurred—and indeed, was impossible to avoid. It is not, to refer back to Burnham, that Beethoven was "The Man Who Freed Music"; it is more accurate to say that he recognized a way in which music was ready to be "freed" and that the readiness itself informed the shape that the "freeing" would ultimately take.

The complex inner life of creativity is thus an ongoing process of engagement with a cultural environment. DeNora argues that in Beethoven's case the social perception of art was tempered by shifts within Viennese culture, most notably a reorientation of musical taste among segments of the aristocracy, who used a notion of high art to separate themselves from other classes, including lesser aristocrats. This reorientation, according to DeNora, produced a system of patronage in which a coterie wielded great influence, to the point that "in Vienna it was virtually impossible for a local musician to build a successful concert career without the patronage of individual aristocratic concert hosts." For much of the last decade of the eighteenth century (things would change somewhat after the Congress of Vienna), Beethoven was "exceptionally well placed" in a time when "aristocratic connections were still crucial to a musician's economic survival," and aristocrats were actively looking for artists to champion. Prince Karl Lichnowsky, his wife, Princess Christiane, and especially Baron Gottfried van Swieten were all important patrons in Beethoven's career.

Aside from the issue of his talent, in other words, Beethoven was also a prime candidate for musical greatness because of his social context and because of how he reacted to it. "In terms of his connections and position within the musical field, Beethoven was perhaps unique among the composers of his day," DeNora concludes. Which is not to cynically suggest, as Kivy and some of DeNora's other critics do, that being "exceptionally well placed" was *enough*. But being exceptionally well placed was, it turns out, very important. Expectations fuel the act of trying to find something to fulfill them, and the aristocrats whom Beethoven became involved with in the decade DeNora focuses on "were already receptive to the notion of musical greatness." And Beethoven's awareness of that receptiveness certainly informed his capacity for fulfilling it. It was, as Guerrieri says, a classic case of "being in exactly the right place at exactly the right time."

DeNora develops the point through a comparison of Beethoven's career with that of his contemporary Jan Ladislav Dussek, a fellow composer-pianist, whose music is sometimes viewed as an anticipation of Beethoven's. During the period in question, Dussek was based in London, having recently fled the French court (his previous employer) in the wake of that country's revolution. According to DeNora, musical life in London was remarkably different from musical life in other areas of Europe, and particularly in Vienna. More receptive to entrepreneurship, London was a city in which musicians could make an independent living, and could survive economically without relying on a patron. At the same time, however, the free market of London's music scene required greater attention to the popular tastes of the general public. Most local composers earned money by teaching, creating sheet music for amateurs, or performing for audiences who were primarily interested in showmanship, virtuosity, and accessibility. These audiences were less attracted to the qualities Beethoven became most renowned for—aesthetic innovation and difficulty.

In DeNora's view, the contextual collaboration of the differing environments of London and Vienna contributed to—did not determine, but contributed to—the difference between the careers of Beethoven and Dussek. In Vienna, Beethoven was more economically dependent upon the patronage of the aristocracy yet freer to create works that were artistically experimental and challenging, at least in part because these were the musical qualities sought by those who supported him. Patronage thus not only provided Beethoven with a degree of economic stability, but also gave him access to the resources necessary to create works in genres that were becoming the exemplary forms of musical high art, such as the symphony and the string quartet. It also contributed to his sense of himself as a composer, thereby helping to drive the creation of later works.

Dussek, for the time being, lacked Beethoven's social connections. He grew up in a provincial town, where his father was an elementary school teacher, materially and socially unable to give the younger Dussek either "the exposure to visitors and teachers or the concentrated attention that Beethoven received." For all the infamy of his later run-ins with the aristocracy, Beethoven at least came from a modest courtly lineage, as the grandson of the most recent Bonn court *Kapellmeister,* or music director. He was thus, as DeNora puts it, "positioned from the start for, at least potentially, a very different type of career." Lacking similar courtly ties, Dussek was unable "to get practical experience with larger instrumental ensembles, as Beethoven could," and was thus primarily constrained to the production of piano literature:

> Unlike Dussek, Beethoven did not have to follow the route of boy soprano in a cathedral choir (the typical early path to a music career), or otherwise prolong his formal education in order to gain exposure

to potential patrons. Consequently, he could afford to devote less energy to the search for patrons (his existing patrons did that work for him) and instead conserved his time and energy for creative work.

Similarly, other contextual factors seemed, whether by accident or intention, to work in Beethoven's favor. Consider, for instance, the famous "Haydn's hands" story, a recurrent trope that began with a letter from Count Waldstein, written as Beethoven was embarking for studies with Haydn. "You are going to Vienna in fulfillment of your long-frustrated wishes," Waldstein wrote. "The Genius of Mozart is still mourning and weeping the death of her pupil. With the help of assiduous labor you shall receive the spirit of Mozart from Haydn's hands." As DeNora points out, it is hard, particularly from the vantage point of one familiar with twenty-first-century marketing techniques, not to see this story, and the way it was repeated at the outset of Beethoven's career, as having the effect of a PR campaign—not unlike the campaign designed by Irving Mills and Ellington at the outset of the latter's career. And it is hard not to see how it would also affect Beethoven's confidence as a composer—functioning as a kind of mantra of positive thinking—no matter how strong-willed his persona.

Merton is again useful here; in the late 1960s, he coined the term "Matthew Effect" (adapted from the biblical parable about the rich getting richer) to describe a phenomenon in which scientists who accrue early accolades tend to receive more of them as time goes on, while those who are similarly gifted but ignored at the outset have an increasingly difficult time getting credit for their work later. And indeed, as Alessandra Comini has shown, Beethoven benefited from a number of tropes like the one about "Haydn's hands." (Another famous story describes the radically different reactions Beethoven and Goethe had to the presence of nobility at the Teplitz spa.) Surely some of these tropes were based in truth and sprang from genuine affection for either Beethoven or his music, or even from a genuine *desire* for such affection (many listeners, after all, had to learn how to love Beethoven). But certainly some of them were more superficially motivated, either because the narrative of Beethoven's genius served some extra-musical purpose, such as flattering the listener's self-perception as a tastemaker, or perhaps because of a personal antipathy for certain tastemaking rivals. Anton Schindler, a companion and early biographer of the composer, was known, for example, to have "added and altered entries" in Beethoven's conversation books "to exaggerate his relationship with the composer and thus his authority over Beethoven's legacy." Whatever impulses produced them, at some point the Beethoven tropes attained critical mass, contributing to an emergent system of Beethoven hagiography. And today that hagiography only appears inevitable.

The point is that biographical narratives of successful musicians often invoke teleology, but they do so retrospectively, after fame has been attained. They are full of assumptions about how the personal compulsion to get from point A (failure and obscurity) to point B (success and fame) is evidence of a direct cause-and-effect dynamic. "Origin stories"—from the "Haydn's hands" trope to the image of Ellington composing on a redeye bus by the desperate light of a series of matches—become the stuff of an artist's legend, and in the retelling one is left with the impression that outcomes were fated, chosen ahead of time by the artists themselves. Yet serendipity, accident, and other kinds of contextual influence are always involved too.

2.

METAL MACHINE MUSIC

Ever since I'd been writing music I was dreaming of getting rid of the performers.

—Conlon Nancarrow

The American-born composer Conlon Nancarrow is best known for his player piano music. A collection of more than sixty pieces, these "studies," as he called them, use the instrument—popularly understood as a curiosity of late Victorian entertainment—to execute passages so intricate that they are beyond the technical ability of even the best pianists. According to James Tenney, the complexities of Nancarrow's studies are primarily rhythmic, and include quick changes in meter and tempo, and different meters and tempos superimposed atop each other, varying independently. In Study no. 42, for instance, there are ten voices that "appear to be in different tempos, and these tempos increase in the course of the piece, until—at the end—they are all moving very fast."

Nancarrow created such works in the "extreme musical isolation" of Mexico City, where he had moved in the early 1940s. He was motivated to explore the possibilities of the player piano in part by deep-seated frustration with the limitations of human musicians—a feeling more than likely exacerbated by a series of concert mishaps early in his career. For instance, while preparing for a 1941 performance of his septet—not an easy piece of music—Nancarrow had been unable to get all of the musicians to show up together for even a single rehearsal. Not surprisingly, the performance was a disaster. "A couple of instruments lost their place right at the beginning," he would later remark. "All through the piece, they were playing in some other place." (Note Nancarrow's muted hostility in his reference to these musicians as "instruments.")

Nancarrow's experience here is a good example of how sometimes, despite mutual good intentions, musicians and composers approach performance differently. Disagreements about purpose or execution can quickly become heated. According to Robert Jourdain, Bach was capable of verbal tirades that belied his pious reputation, Handel "once lobbed a whole kettledrum across the stage," and Mahler was regularly challenged to duels—all because of contretemps with players. In the last century, singer Anita O'Day described Nancarrow's contemporary, Raymond Scott, as "a martinet" who treated musicians like "wind-up toys." Charles Mingus too was reputed to be a difficult bandleader, who in one instance "actually reduced a promising young saxophonist to tears, before an audience, with a running commentary of 'Play something different, man; play something different. This is jazz, man. You played that last night and the night before.'" Mingus's abuse could also be physical, as when he punched trombonist Jimmy Knepper in the mouth, knocking out a tooth and permanently ruining his embouchure.

Thankfully, Nancarrow dealt with his own artistic demons by turning to the player piano instead of fisticuffs. To be clear, however, he was not the first "art" composer to write specifically for the instrument. Igor Stravinsky, Paul Hindemith, Nicolai Lopatnikoff, and others had already done so in the 1920s. Perhaps the most ambitious of these early "classical" player piano works was George Antheil's controversial *Ballet Mécanique,* a large-scale fantasy scored for, among other things, sixteen synchronized player pianos and three airplane propellers. Antheil's description of the *Mécanique* revealed a skepticism about musical humanism to rival Nancarrow's: "All percussive. Like machines. All efficiency. No LOVE. Written without sympathy. Written cold as an army operates. Revolutionary as nothing has been revolutionary."

More than half a century later, Frank Zappa, who like Nancarrow was driven by an impulse toward impossible music, and a similar frustration with musicians, turned to a modern descendant of the player piano: the Synclavier. In his autobiography, Zappa praised this powerful synthesizer for its ability to do what human musicians could not. "Anything you can dream up can be typed or played into the Synclavier," Zappa wrote. "Any group of imaginary instruments can be invited to play the most difficult passages, and the 'little guys inside the machine' play them with *one-millisecond* accuracy—every time." For Zappa, the fact that the Synclavier allowed relatively precise renderings of complex note sequences, tempo shifts, dynamics, and articulation meant that it was finally possible to bring an "idea to the audience in a pure form, allowing them to hear the music, rather than the ego problems of a group of players who don't give a shit about the composition." It was, he suggested, as close as one could get to the pure expression of the mind's ear.

From our perspective in the twenty-first century, Zappa's enthusiasm for the Synclavier seems almost quaint. Nowadays even the cheapest, most consumer-friendly music software—Garageband, for instance, which comes standard with new Mac computers—offers similar capabilities. But there is a functional continuity between Garageband, the Synclavier, the player piano, and related technologies of automatic music. In Garageband's software instrument mode, for instance, notes are represented as dashes across a horizontal timeline—like the holes punched in a player piano roll. This is also how music is visualized in MIDI, a communication specification used by the Synclavier, and by most other modern synthesizers as well. With poetic symmetry, conversion to MIDI is now one of the means by which original piano rolls (many of which have suffered significant deterioration over the last century or so) are archived. In an important sense, then, the language of the player piano has been foundational for subsequent forms of automatic music. The player piano may even be considered the first "digital" keyboard, as some have argued, in that it relied on a system of discrete values—holes or no holes, punched into paper—instead of the continuous signal flow that is at the core of analog recording and instrument design.

So by choosing to compose almost exclusively for the player piano, Nancarrow had tapped into what was to be an important gestalt for modern keyboard- and computer-based automatic music production. And he did so with a dedication that was impressive. Years after the player piano fell out of favor with the American public—the Great Depression virtually destroyed the market for the instrument—

Nancarrow quietly and persistently continued to explore its potential, intrigued by composer Henry Cowell's suggestion that it invited the creation of a new kind of music, one that could "not be played by any living performer," and that could potentially capitalize on "some of the advantages gained by removing the personality of performers from the performance." Nancarrow would earn his place in the modernist pantheon by remaining "fascinated," for the rest of his life, "by this thing that would play all of these fantastic things by itself."

Indeed, if we stopped the narrative there, Nancarrow would seem to be a compelling counterexample to everything I have said so far about collaboration. Like a musical Emily Dickinson (another American artist whose creative isolation was legendary), he would, at first glance, fit the stereotype of the rhetoric of genius, and particularly its emphasis on solipsism. Virtually unknown until the end of his life, Nancarrow was cut off for most of his career from audiences, from other composers, and, needless to say, from performing musicians. No wonder Charles Amirkhanian described him as a godlike figure, arguing that "what the computer now is beginning to make possible for ordinary mortal composers, Nancarrow has been able to accomplish with his bare hands, guided by an innate musicality and intelligence as well as an ornery persistence which would make Sisyphus blush." Composer Gyorgy Ligeti went further, calling Nancarrow "the most significant composer of the twentieth century. In complete musical isolation in Mexico, he created astonishing music" that was "thoroughly original."

The argument that Nancarrow was a solitary musical genius seems airtight. But is it?

THE MEANING OF MUSICAL MACHINES

Igor Stravinsky referred to himself as an inventor of music, rather than a composer.

—John Oswald

Before we assume Nancarrow's music is truly noncollaborative, we should look more carefully at cultural attitudes toward music technology—for these attitudes have influenced how we understand the art such technology makes, and no less so in Nancarrow's case. To begin with, though many early-twentieth-century critics feared that the player piano would alienate human beings from music making altogether, and though there has been a broad current of musical technophobia in the wake of that fear, if we look further back in history, we see that music technology was not only tolerated but even embraced as a fundamental part of the creative processes of music—and in a way that seems somewhat surprising to us.

In the preindustrial era, instrument makers were "musically gifted" members of their communities. Some were even professional musicians themselves. Conversely, many of the composers we revere today (thanks to the rhetoric of genius) weren't even viewed as "artists" in their own time, as Bruce Haynes points out. They were instead perceived—and they perceived themselves—as "clever craftsmen, rather like building contractors." Knowing technology intimately was part of the composer's job. Albert Schweitzer tells us that Bach, for instance, had "the open mind of the self-taught man for inventions." He was deeply interested in how instruments were made, and "whatever related to practice," however insignificant it may have seemed to an outsider, was considered "important enough to be worthy of his serious attention." It is tangentially interesting in light of this observation to note Bach's categorization of one group of his keyboard pieces under the heading "inventions," a label used by European composers throughout the sixteenth, seventeenth, and eighteenth centuries, although its currency probably had more to do with classical rhetoric than with machinery. More relevant is the commonly encountered critical opinion that Bach's music is "architectonic," expressing structure in a way that is scientifically or mathematically appealing, presumably because of its clarity, elegance, symmetry, and logical arrangement of lines and forms.

Mozart too had a technological muse, underappreciated in modern appraisals of his talent. Despite the fact that he dismissed the playing of his keyboard rival, Muzio Clementi, as "mere mechanicus" (drawing on technology as a metaphor for artlessness), Mozart shared Bach's practical understanding of the mechanisms powering the instruments he wrote for. In praising the piano manufacturer Johann Andreas Stein, for instance, Mozart noted the "splendid advantage" of Stein's "escape action" with what seems an engaged and knowledgeable analysis, especially if we allow that at the time the piano was only just beginning to emerge as a legitimate instrument. "Without an escapement it is impossible to avoid jangling and vibration after the note is struck," Mozart observed. "When you touch the keys, the hammers fall back again the moment after they have struck the strings, whether you hold down the keys or release them."

More intriguingly, Mozart evinced what Alfred Einstein called a "pleasure in playing with figures," and in particular a fondness (as in his K. 516f) for the eighteenth-century fad of formulaically created dance music. This genre, *Musikalische Würfelspiele*—"musical dice games"—enabled even the musically untutored to compose by selecting from a database of short melodic chunks that could be mixed and matched according to the chance operations of a pair of dice or some other random number generator. Haydn too displayed an interest in this fad, which, one is tempted to say, predated by two hundred years the more celebrated chance composition techniques of John Cage.

Even Beethoven had a practical interest in musical machinery. The developments in piano manufacturing he both prompted and responded to—the instrument became heavier and louder over the course of his lifetime—clearly affected the things he wrote for it. The *Hammerklavier* Sonata, for instance, would have been "obscured to the point of meaninglessness on the shallow, precise, clean yet more sensitive Viennese pianos of Beethoven's youth," as Bernard Holland points out. Beethoven was also one of many musicians of his era to write, apparently without existential conflict, for automated performance, as he did for Johann Maelzel's diorama of the Battle of Vittoria—the so-called Battle Symphony, scored for Maelzel's Panharmonicon, a gigantic self-playing organ. Maelzel, best known as the first manufacturer of the metronome (an invention he actually stole from Dietrich Winkel), had mounted similar projects with Haydn, Handel, and Cherubini.

And so Western music's earliest composer-heroes had a healthy artistic appreciation for musical machines. Of course, their openness about this appreciation had something to do with the relative technological innocence of the time in which they lived. With the rapid spread of industrialization in the nineteenth and especially the twentieth century, there would be a gradual shift, as many observers began to imagine that mechanical processes might someday on their own end up dominating the creation of music, supplanting human influence entirely. Knowing technology as it related to music was still part of the composer's job, of course, but gradually composers became less willing to openly own that knowledge. Music's reliance on technology was tempered by a new awareness of technology's capacity for displacing, demeaning, or even damaging human beings, especially in the workplace.

Edwin Votey created the first player piano prototype in 1895, just as these concerns were reaching a particularly fevered pitch. Ambivalence about the instrument's arrival was abetted, no doubt, by the more general unease of the fin de siècle. But the criticism leveled at Votey's device also had to do with the fact that the player piano enabled the broad dissemination of automatic music (even before the phonograph, which did not hit its stride as a musical medium until electrical recording techniques were introduced in the 1920s). Easily accessible "self-playing" music, it was feared, might make traditional forms of music making obsolete. The latter had become a mainstay of Victorian domesticity: most middle-class (and many working-class) households in nineteenth-century America had a piano, and in most families at least one person, usually a daughter, could play it. But with the player piano, writes Craig Roell, increasingly "music, like clothing, was 'consumed,' not 'made'; the experience was becoming instantaneous and easy, requiring no investment of time." Many models of player piano did not even require someone to sit at the keyboard. The Link Piano Company made a "photoplayer"—a player piano designed for film accompaniment—that, according to a rather emphatic advertisement, "REQUIRES NO MUSICIAN." As one theater manager glibly reported, "We simply turn on the current in the morning and shut it off at night and the instrument does the rest." Many manufacturers of player pianos eventually produced consumer models that functioned similarly: the music was generated by the mere flip of a switch. For the pessimist, the symbolism could not have been more obvious.

And the pessimists certainly made their views known. Responding to audiences who enthusiastically purchased player pianos in order to hear popular music at home, John Philip Sousa seemed to speak for the naysayers when he warned, in an infamous 1906 essay titled "The Menace of Mechanical Music," that by replacing musicians, the player piano and related technologies would cause "a marked deterioration in American music and musical taste," reducing "the expression of music to a mathematical system of megaphones, wheels, cogs, disks, cylinders, and all manner of revolving things." To help make his point, Sousa coined the pejorative term "canned music," most likely in reference to the canisters that cylinder recordings came in. He felt that mass dissemination would result in the shortening of the typical listener's attention span, and, more important, replace the nineteenth century's vibrant amateur musical culture with an aloof class of gadget-obsessed dilettantes.

Interestingly, Sousa's reputation as a founding father of twentieth-century musical technophobia is more complex than is usually acknowledged. His concerns, that is, were not entirely selfless. In part he was irritated by the fact that composers were not yet paid royalties for recordings of their works—a logical enough concern, given that he was himself a popular composer and recording artist at the time. (Sousa's music appeared in both piano roll and phonograph form, and he once famously told recording executive Eldridge Johnson, in a promotional spot, "Your Victor Talking Machines are all right.")

More important, Sousa's complaints were not unprecedented. In fact, earlier critics had expressed similar misgivings about the traditional piano itself. "The piano exempts a pupil from learning music," Louis Pagnerre claimed in his *On the Evil Influence of the Piano upon the Art of Music,* published in the 1880s. "A pupil, be he the most refractory toward any artistic feeling, be he the least apt to understand differences of pitch, their blend or their combinations, will succeed by a more or less obstinate mechanical labor in acquiring what is called 'a pretty talent on the piano.'" The argument was echoed by Vernon Lee in her *Studies of the Eighteenth Century in Italy,* cited in an 1890 essay in which three fictitious "amateurs" debate musical issues of the day. One quotes Lee's comment that the piano would foster that wholesale ignorance of music in general which is inevitable where a performer need aim only at mechanical dexterity; arranged pieces, pedals, and tuners having relieved him from the necessity of learning harmony, of studying expression by means of the voice and of obtaining a correct ear by tuning his own instrument; where, above all, everything has been done for him by others, and he has been educated to a total want of musical endeavour.

In the amateur's view, the piano threatened to reduce music "to a question of such dexterity as is shown by a first-class operator on Remington's typewriter."

However snide this comparison may seem to us, at the time it was not entirely unpersuasive, even to some nonamateurs. Composer Hector Berlioz actually boasted of his lack of piano-playing ability—a technical weakness that helped him, he felt, avoid "the appalling number of miserable platitudes" to which the instrument had "given birth, which would never have seen the light had their authors been limited to pen and paper." Pagnerre, Lee, Berlioz, and Sousa helped to establish a pattern for the coming century, one that would inform our understanding of Nancarrow many years later: keyboard instruments would be subjected to the lion's share of musical technophobia. That fear may have had something to do with the great complexity of the piano's machinery—anyone who has ever looked inside the instrument can attest to how visually arresting its internal mechanisms are. Or perhaps it can be attributed to the piano's capacity for mimicking the sound of an ensemble, potentially rendering other instruments irrelevant. ("The trumpet can blare, but not sigh, contrariwise the flute; the pianoforte can do both," as Ferruccio Busoni put it.) Whatever the reason, the player piano was not the last keyboard to be chastised as a "menace of mechanical music." In the late 1960s, for instance, Robert Moog would have to deal with similar complaints directed at his earliest keyboard-based synthesizers. "Anything that didn't come out of wood, or a brass instrument, or from a string," Moog recalls, "was considered somehow suspect at least, and downright harmful at best. People were very suspicious of electronic instruments producing musical sounds." This is easy to forget now, a mere fifty years later, when Moog synthesizers are highly prized for their retro charm.

Even in the solitude of his Mexico City studio, Nancarrow lived and worked against the grain of this keyboard-centric technophobia. And it is in this context too that we have come to understand him as "the greatest composer you've never heard of" (as Michael Roddy put it). Not only did he create as a socially and intellectually isolated expatriate, but he did so by using an instrument that many assumed was inherently *un*creative. Again: how could his work have been anything but noncollaborative?

TECHNOLOGICAL ANONYMITY

But technophobia has a way of provoking the rhetoric of genius. In the narrative of music history, the putative monstrousness of technology provides a convenient and tempting foil for the heroic composer—Nancarrow or Antheil or Zappa or whoever—willing to face and subdue it. According to this view, each new machine can, in the right hands, be made into a mere tool, a static object that exists only to be acted upon. Indeed, the machine's very existence is sometimes posited as merely a function of the will of the composer. "I dream of instruments obedient to my thought," Edgard Varèse once wrote, "which with their contribution of a whole new world of unsuspected sounds, will lend themselves to the exigencies of my inner rhythm." Thus the composer, as Charles Rosen explained, need not be intimidated into writing "only for the instruments available to him." Innovations in music technology sometimes occur because composers demand them.

Yet while composers are often involved in technological innovation, that's hardly the whole story. Clearly some composers *do* write only for the instruments available to them—or even, as in the case of Nancarrow, for instruments that are, for all intents and purposes, obsolete. And sometimes inventors invent instruments—the theremin might be a good example—that no composer was asking for, however popular they might later become. Compositional desire, in other words, is not the sole wellspring of music technology. More important, the simplistic assumption that technology exists, lifelessly, either to be controlled or to exert control, overlooks the fact that every machine has a history and a relational status in the world. Technology is not primarily a static thing or device, but a *space* in which human interaction takes place, however asynchronously.

The claim that Nancarrow surmounted the problem of unreliable real musicians by turning to the player piano is thus both misleading and incomplete. In truth, Nancarrow replaced one set of collaborative artists (performers) with another (inventors and technicians). This is the decompositional view: each machine is a rich site for the direct and contextual collaboration of those who create, design, implement, or maintain it, and who make its music possible through that collaboration. In our culture, with its technophobic legacy, we usually miss the importance of this work, even in cases where we acknowledge art's dependence on technology. That is, technology is rarely integrated into a deeper, more organic concept of creativity. When they are recognized at all, inventors and technicians are typically lower in the compositional pecking order than any of the collaborators we examined in chapter 1—assumed to be less creative than improvisers, band members, patrons, and even audiences.

Note for instance how Philip Carlsen discusses the practical details of Nancarrow's involvement with the player piano. We learn that the composer originally punched all of his rolls by hand, but after becoming frustrated by the laboriousness of that task, he returned to New York to find a punching machine, which, it turned out, had to be borrowed from legendary roll arranger and pianist J. Lawrence Cook and then duplicated—that is, recreated from scratch—by a local machinist. Later, another technician altered Nancarrow's player so that it would advance the roll paper continuously, allowing for music with subtler rhythms and tempo changes. In both cases, the collaboration was crucial, as it enabled Nancarrow's compositional goals, which depended on properly executed nuances of tempo and rhythm. But in Carlsen's account very little is said about either of these collaborators. In fact, both remain anonymous.

Jürgen Hocker frames the issue much the same way, despite first-hand experience with the technological challenges of bringing "live" Nancarrow performances to Europe in the 1980s. Since Nancarrow's pieces were written for customized player pianos, Hocker first had to find a potentially suitable instrument for these concerts. Then he had to find a way to adapt it. It took his friend Jörg Borchardt, an expert in player piano restoration, two years to complete the necessary adjustments to the Ampico Bösendorfer Hocker eventually located. Hocker then discovered that Nancarrow's pieces for two synchronized player pianos had never been precisely performable, even by the composer himself. That synchronization problem was solved for the first time by a computer control system created by Horst Mohr and Walter Tenten.

Yet in Hocker's account we learn very little about Borchardt, Mohr, or Tenten, aside from their names and a brief mention of what they did. (Indeed, Hocker underplays his own importance in this collaborative relationship.) All are treated respectfully but tangentially. This is in stark contrast to the obsessive, loving attention lavished on the composer. Hocker's website is a true fan site, featuring a good deal of Nancarrow-related correspondence, reminiscences about him from family and friends, an exhaustive chronology of his work and life, and detailed images of his cluttered workshop. It's a fascinating collection of material. But in terms of understanding the music, its emphasis is skewed.

Nancarrow himself was ambivalent about his relationship with technologists. Here he is in a frank moment with William Duckworth:

> People think that if I can write for player piano I must have much mechanical ability. In fact, the one man in Mexico who was really good and kept my pianos in shape died not too long ago. So I don't know what I'm going to do. Since he died there have been only a few minor things, which I could do. But a serious repair, I can't do it. The mechanisms are as complicated as a Rolls Royce engine, or more maybe.

It is astonishing that "the one man" goes unnamed, given how vital Nancarrow suggests their collaboration was. It is possible that he was here referring to Octavio Santibanez, a piano tuner and restorer of player pianos, or perhaps Jesús Acosta, a piano technician—these men are at least briefly identified in the liner notes to the Nancarrow CD series released by Wergo. According to Amirkhanian, Santibanez assisted Nancarrow in ways that were both "invaluable" and "indispensable," yet his contribution is curtly addressed in only three sentences of a seventeen-page booklet devoted to musical analysis of Nancarrow's work.

It's not clear what criteria are being used to justify the cursory attention—or, worse, outright anonymity—accorded Nancarrow's technical collaborators. When weighing the cultural value of the composer's ability to conceive of a piece, and his ability to translate that conception into a piano roll, how do we understand those accomplishments in relation to the technological skill of an expert in obscure machinery, who has been asked to draw on a lifetime of experience to accomplish a difficult task for which there may be no clear precedent, which might take years to accomplish, and which was clearly beyond the ability of even the composer himself? Why should one achievement be considered so much more *extraordinarily* creative than the other? After all, without a functional customized instrument, Nancarrow's music could not have existed.

Santibanez, Acosta, Borchardt, Mohr, Tenten, and their cohorts, named and unnamed, point quietly to the long history of labor-intensive craftsmanship traditions in automatic music, even preceding the player piano. We have already seen Maelzel's Panharmonicon, but there were many other such instruments. "Until records and radio shut them up," Evan Eisenberg notes, for instance, "music boxes were everywhere," including such unlikely places as "scent bottles, beer tankards, fans, chairs that sang when sat on, even bustles like Queen Victoria's which played 'God Save the Queen' when she sat down." Part of what made player pianos seem more threatening than bustles that played "God Save the Queen," of course, was that they were, to an extent, mass-produced—an easily stereotyped detail that could make the resulting music seem robotic and sinister. Yet even the mechanistic context of modern manufacturing afforded opportunities for collaboration. An inventor somewhere devised every feature of every menacing musical machine. Someone had to imagine each player piano's hole-punch system—indeed, the idiosyncratic hand of a human designer is obvious in many of them, as rolls manufactured by one company often cannot be played on pianos made by others. Or consider the spark chronograph, a mechanism invented and developed by Charles Stoddard and Clarence N. Hickman and used in a special kind of player piano called a reproducer (of which more in a moment). The spark chronograph calculated the force of a pianist's keystroke by measuring the time it took for the hammer to travel between two contacts—information that was then used to "recreate" the pianist's unique touch in the roll. Given how essential the "pianist's unique touch" was to the aesthetic of the reproducer, Stoddard and Hickman should be understood as direct musical collaborators. But like Santibanez, Borchardt, Mohr, and Tenten, they are treated as marginal figures even in considerations of player piano music, let alone broader musical discourse.

Again, how do we explain this kind of neglect? To some extent, our Cartesian inheritance prevents us from even asking the right questions when it comes to player piano authorship. Technological collaboration is perceived as mere grunt work—the menial labor of amateurs, enthusiasts, or hobbyists—compared to the composition it enables, which is assumed to come from the more noble realm of the soul. Of course musicians can be similarly overlooked. But even an unrecognized musician's status can be recouped (usually posthumously) by the rhetoric of genius—think of the unsung folk musician, rediscovered and canonized many years after her accomplishments. Technologists are rarely that lucky. Many are simply forgotten, even though we use their inventions all the time.

The point is not limited to player piano music, then. Choose any recording from your collection, and you can instantly identify which artist it is attributed to. It is far less likely that you possess similar knowledge of those who created the media itself, or the machine that plays it: most of us have to look up the people responsible for the CD, the MP3, the headphones—or else we fall back on the rhetoric of genius. ("How Steve Jobs Built the iPod," as one chapter in Steve Knopper's book about the music industry, *Appetite for Self-Destruction*, is misleadingly titled.) The same discrepancy occurs at a concert. We acknowledge those onstage usually with no trouble. Often, we possess excruciating detail about their lives and careers. But what do we know about the people who created their instruments, the mixing boards that help them achieve an effective blend, the lighting systems that illuminate them so dramatically? What do we know about those technologies at all, beyond the manufacturing logos with which they are adorned?

There is thus an important caveat to the argument that technology will dehumanize music. A player piano is not "a thing that would play all of these fantastic things by itself," nor does it remove "the personality of performers from the performance." At the moment, outside of futurist fantasy, no musical machine, no matter how sophisticated, is capable of the self-actualization assumed by these statements. Rather, each is space visited over time by many collaborators, each offering something crucial to whatever beauty is ultimately heard.

THE ART OF THE PLAYER PIANO

The contextual collaboration in Nancarrow's work is a result of the many people who worked on his pianos. But other types of collaboration obtain in player piano music in general, and are worth mentioning here even if they do not always factor into Nancarrow's oeuvre. Given the player piano's foundational status in the history of automatic music, they help us better understand similar creative relationships with respect to other kinds of music technology.

Consider, for instance, how player piano music often involved the direct collaboration of a performer—someone who sat at and operated the instrument according to its design, usually involving a combination of foot pedals and hand-operated expression controls. It is true that some player piano manufacturers downplayed the role of performers, insisting that though the instrument depended on the presence of a human being, it was nevertheless childishly simple to operate. The Gulbransen company even had as its trademark the image of a baby crawling up to the instrument's pedals, accompanied by the tagline "Easy to Play." Another company's advertising claimed the elimination of the hard work usually associated with the production of good music. "The amount of practice necessarily required to become a finished, artistic pianist is discouraging," the copy ran. "Before [Ignacy Jan] Paderewski [the Polish pianist and composer] could attain the high position which he occupies today in the musical world, and accomplish what now comes to him with ease, he was obliged to toil unceasingly day after day in practice." At the time, Paderewski was the very symbol of the almost maniacally dedicated musician. But the player piano, this ad implied, made Paderewskian results possible to anyone, more or less instantaneously.

Yet the idea that player pianos were easy to play is an oversimplification that, like the dismissive take on improvisation that I critiqued in chapter 1, prevents us from seeing work by asking us to look for work in the wrong place. And this oversimplification could lead to a rude awakening. "Playing the player piano properly takes years," writes Rex Lawson. "You don't get anything for nothing, despite the advertising." Lawson imagines the "disappointment people must have felt when they got their new player piano home, and found that it didn't sound like it did in the showroom." To be fair, player piano advertising occasionally complicated its own claim of easiness. While some argued that the instrument provided a ready substitute for human dexterity, the brain, it was also asserted, "remains unfettered and is still the controlling influence." The driving force of the performance was "taste and temperament." As an advertisement for a Baldwin Manualo player piano defiantly stated, "You *do not* operate the Manualo—you play it."

There is a relatively nuanced idea behind this statement, even if it was being used to sell more Manualos. Musical creativity has not been *eliminated* by the easy-to-use mechanism of the player piano, but rather, freed from a certain set of corporal limitations. The distinction between "playing" and "operating" depended on how the machine was used, but playing—producing something musical—was at least possible. It was not that those who understood and pursued this distinction—often referred to as "player pianists," "playerists," or "pianolists"—did not rely on technique to bring out the aesthetic potential of the resulting music. It was just a different sort of technique. "It is no good anybody sitting at the instrument and just pumping the pedals up and down," writes Eric Townley, hinting at one theory of good player piano playing. Rather, the pianolist "must know both the instrument and the music intimately." Artis Wodehouse, who "realized" (her term) the popular

Gershwin piano roll CD series put out by Nonesuch starting in 1993, similarly notes that "the pianolist can play with expression by skillful foot-pumping and manipulating the expression levers."

"Skillful foot-pumping"? However odd this might sound to the uninitiated, it merely suggests that player piano technique requires the same marriage of physical and mental ability that goes into the effective operation of any instrument. Composer Gordon Nevin wrote about skillful foot pumping, too, with respect to the pedals of a more conventional keyboard—the organ. One should "sit quietly in the middle of the bench" before beginning, Nevin advised in a 1923 text on the subject. When actually pushing the pedals (Nevin, confusingly, also refers to them as "keys"), one has to do much more than *just* push the pedals. There is, rather, an art to it. The "touch should be firm, quick in application and release, and full of nervous energy." Without the appropriate feel, the "resulting effect will be 'mushy,' slovenly, and lacking in all the desirable crispness. A slowly attacked key is undesirable, and a slowly released key an abomination!" Even with something as seemingly simple as the operation of the swell pedal—an expression pedal that allows for differences in volume—Nevin offered an analysis so detailed it eventually had to be collected in a separate volume, appropriately called *Swell Pedal Technic*. Clearly Nevin believed that organ pedaling, seemingly simple to even a novice, involved much more than "mere mechanicus."

Like the organ, the player piano requires careful foot placement, not to mention stamina and timing. According to one method, most of the effort should come from the ankles, not the legs, and the best approach is to provide only enough air to control the suction power of the player action. "Let the feet caress the pedals and make a conscious effort to break any semblance of rhythm," Arthur W. J. G. Ord-Hume advises. Instead of keeping the beat, the feet should "sense the resistance of the bellows." Yet Ord-Hume's instructions, like Nevin's, suggest the mystery and ambiguity of an art. "Give short dabs with one foot if you like," Ord-Hume continues, "and long, languorous presses with the other," or "give the occasional double-dab in mid-stroke," or "put one foot on the floor and pedal adroitly with the other during soft passages." These movements are somewhat counterintuitive, going against the beginner's—or indeed the trained musician's—tendency to pump in a regular pattern, alternating the right and left foot in sync with the beat of the music.

Further, once the pianolist has mastered a given instrument, it should not be assumed that she is ready for *any* player piano—idiosyncratic manufacturing styles mean that there are challenges specific to each. "When you sit down at a strange player," Ord-Hume warns, "accept that you must play it for half an hour or more to get the feel of it." A mechanic, he suggests, "can with confidence drive just about any car that comes in for servicing," but "pianos with paper rolls are a different matter." Many mechanics would object to that comparison, as cars too can be temperamental beasts. But the point is that even "automatic" musical machines are subject to the influence of human interaction. In preparation for her Gershwin Pianola performances, Wodehouse tells us that she "played the rolls over and over again, maybe a hundred times." It is hard to imagine the point of such meticulous rehearsal if the player piano really was the unthinkingly easy, self-actualizing "menace of mechanical music" it was assumed by its critics to be.

PAY ATTENTION TO THE MAN BEHIND THE CURTAIN

As we saw earlier, some models of player piano really did operate with the flip of a switch, after which it was no longer necessary for a human being to sit at the controls. It would be a mistake to overlook how this feature provoked concern: surely there is brutality in the erasure of the human pianist, who is after all a customary feature of piano performance. Yet even when the pianist, or pianolist, disappeared, other forms of collaboration filled the emptiness suggested by the instrument's unoccupied bench. Again, human creative interaction occurred, however asynchronously.

Rolls that made a musician unnecessary in the parlor were often produced, for instance, with the help of a real piano player at the factory. There, the performance would indicate where the holes were to be cut into the paper, via a series of pencil markings made by the depression of the keys. Sometimes the pianist's keystrokes would actually do the cutting. With the reproducing piano, companies tried to incorporate into the roll as much as possible of the factory pianist's personal style, claiming for the instrument a level of sophistication that had eluded previous player piano models. The reproducer could record not only a human pianist's notes, but also her dynamics, articulation, and other more elusive aspects of style.

But for all their attention to verisimilitude, and despite the "hand played" label, reproducers still relied on additional technical assistance. For one thing, whatever the skill of the human player, errors were unavoidable. Mistakes had to be fixed before the roll could be issued. An editor would be expected to tape up wrong notes and then correctly repunch them. Even a musician as formidable as Paderewski relied on this practice. "I do not play these passages evenly," he observed in a note scribbled in the margins of one of his master rolls. "Can you even them out for me?" As with Nancarrow's technical collaborators, the unnamed "you" here is interesting—particularly in light of Paderewski's massive fame as a live performer. Some of Nancarrow's rolls have been "fixed" this way too—see for instance the recent recordings for the German Dabringhaus und Grimm label. "The original perforated paper rolls were copied and fitted with new, exact holes," notes Invar Nordin. "In some cases the holes were slightly corrected, in the cases when the original holes had been punched a little off the intended places."

Other kinds of direct collaboration enhanced a roll that already had its holes in the right places. The dynamics and accents to be performed by the reproducer were not only captured by its recording mechanism, but also added by editors, who listened to the pianist's performance while it was being recorded, monitoring complicated dials, punching relevant information onto the roll in real time, or taking careful notes on the interpretation, so as much of it as possible could be added to the roll later. Generally, technicians finished the work from their desks, checking the notes against the score. Often dynamics had to be "put on the note roll and then holes punched in the paper by hand at the beginning and end of each note." The resulting "trial roll" was reviewed, played for the pianist, and, if met with approval, signed and released. James M. Edwards puts the complexity of this process more concretely when he notes that one Ampico roll of "The Blue Danube"—an eight-minute piece of music—was the result of 71,235 operations, completed by several technicians over the course of five days. (The process is comparable to the painstaking techniques used in hand-drawn animation.) And so while reproducing rolls may have allowed for more naturalistic expressivity, in the end the pianist's interpretation of the music was still subject to the technicians' interpretation of that interpretation.

In other scenarios, arrangers created a master roll completely from scratch by cutting all of the holes themselves by hand. This was the method used by Nancarrow, who, like Berlioz, was not a pianist. If you were an arranger, you did not necessarily need to slavishly copy a source score; sometimes what the composer had written on the sheet music was "merely a starting point." Liberties involving the addition of octaves, contrapuntal melodies, or other embellishments eventually rendered the music humanly impossible to play. But the most skilled arrangers could make what was an entirely "artificial" performance sound, at least to some ears, "real." Such densely reworked pieces, which influenced the pyrotechnics of the novelty piano style that developed in the 1920s, and which provided an unacknowledged popular precedent for Nancarrow's work, became known as "orchestral arrangements." One of the best-known artists in this genre was J. Lawrence Cook, who continued to produce rolls for the QRS company well after the player piano industry's demise (up until the early 1970s), perfecting a layered sound that, as Bob Berkman put it, drew "color and variety from a seemingly monochromatic palette." Frank Milne was another, who worked for the Aeolian Company and, like Cook, outlasted the player piano vogue. Milne's arrangement of Gershwin's *An American in Paris* is so sophisticated that in order to justify advertising it as "hand played," Aeolian had to attribute it to "Milne and Leith"—since the arrangement seemed to require four hands, Milne was forced to create a pseudonym for a fictional partner.

Pianist and composer Zez Confrey, who also worked as an arranger for QRS, and who was one of the most popular practitioners of the novelty piano style (of which the exemplar is perhaps his own composition, "Kitten on the Keys"), adapted the aesthetic norms of player piano music—no matter how antihumanist they seemed—to more conventional modes of music making. Confrey delighted in the obviously mechanical qualities of the player piano—the moments when the illusion of human performance began to break down. His work for traditional piano frequently seems to be the expression of a human imitating a machine imitating a human poorly. David A. Jasen discusses a performance routine that Confrey and his brother developed in Ottowa during the first years of the twentieth century:

> Automated player pianos were in vogue during this time, and Twaify's, a favorite hang-out in La Salle, had an especially out of tune and partially broken, coin-operated machine. Zez heard this piano so many times that he was able to imitate it exactly on a regular piano. . . . He would start by pumping the pedals, dropping a coin and then going into his imitation of that broken-down nickelodeon. This version of "TWAIFY'S PIANO," unfortunately never published, became a standard part of his performing repertoire.

Jasen's assessment that Confrey could imitate Twaify's piano "exactly" is misleading, given the absence of any extant version of this piece. But I cite this anecdote because it exemplifies the tightly interwoven relationship between technological and musical authorship. "Twaify's Piano" had a complex provenance: Confrey may have put it together, but he owed a lot to the arrangers and editors whose piano rolls he was imitating. Confrey and these arrangers and editors were situated in a complex relationship, in which they not only influenced but also were influenced by each other, in an intertextual web that is ultimately too dense to untangle.

THE PLAYER PIANO AND THE RHETORIC OF GENIUS

Just as the rhetoric of genius has obscured the collaborative complexity of the music associated with Ellington, Beethoven, and other composers, so it obscures the technical creativity without which player piano music could not exist. The reproducer, for instance, is often framed spiritually, as if pianists and composers suffused the instrument with an otherworldly power—the "Living Soul of the Artist," as one advertisement put it. Various publicity stunts symbolically enacted this transfer. In November 1917, pianist Harold Bauer performed live in Chicago while his reproducing piano roll simultaneously performed on the East Coast with the New York Symphony. The gimmick encouraged the audience to entertain the idea that "Bauer" could be performing in both cities at once—thereby downplaying the technical artistry that had helped create the music as it was being heard in New York.

Bauer was not the only famous pianist to get involved with reproducing pianos. Welte, the first reproducing piano company, released rolls featuring the playing of Grieg, Debussy, Respighi, Bartók, Leschetitzky, Granados, Paderewski, (Richard) Strauss, and others, whose photographs and logotypes were also used as endorsements. Of course, some pianists were skeptical of the reproducer's charms, at least initially. When told that it could capture sixteen musical nuances in its rolls, Artur Schnabel explained his reluctance to record by wryly noting, "I am sorry, but I am capable of seventeen." But Schnabel too eventually relented. And it is likely that much of the public discomfort with automatic music was assuaged by the involvement of celebrated musicians like him—for listeners, it was easier to think of the reproducing piano in terms of individual artistry, rather than in terms of the collaborative complexity we have briefly considered here. The artist's already established genius credentials made the task of selling the instrument easier.

Thus sales personnel were never to refer to the instrument as an "electric piano." The reproducer, one Ampico script ran, was "an instrument which reproduces so faultlessly the playing of eminent concert pianists that the artist seems to *play again*. The reproduction is not distinguishable from the public performance of the artist himself." This commercial patter evoked a ghostliness that has been associated with all kinds of mechanical reproduction, from phonographs to photography to moving images. But whereas photography, once seen as an almost supernatural activity, now seems routine and unremarkable—cameras, after all, are everywhere, from the shopping mall security desk to the smartphone—the player piano has preserved the ghost trope down to the present day, partly because it is now also seen as a historical artifact. In her description of the preparations that led to the Nonesuch recordings of Gershwin rolls, for instance, Wodehouse writes that the Disklavier, the modern reproducing piano that was used in the final stages of that recording, "played Gershwin's rolls from a floppy disk for the microphone, as if Gershwin's ghost were present at the session." The ghost trope reminds us of traditional authorship's religious affinity—clearly Gershwin is here being imagined as a benevolent spirit presiding over the Nonesuch sessions. Yet the true ghosts of these recordings are the music's mostly unknown or forgotten technological collaborators.

Indeed, the rhetoric of genius suffuses the marketing of most anything having to do with the player piano. Consider the 1993 Biograph CD *Scott Joplin: Elite Syncopations,* a compilation that claims to feature "Classic Ragtime from Rare Piano Rolls." Joplin is the textual focus of that title—his name, written in all capital letters, is prominently featured on the album cover—and seems in that sense to be the "author" of the recording. Yet the credits that appear on the back of the jewel case specify that although most of the rags were in fact composed by Joplin, the second one was composed by W. C. Handy, and a later piece, "Lily Queen," by Joplin and Arthur Marshall. The final track, "Silver Swan," though considered Joplin's composition, was never published or copyrighted by him (its score, apparently, had been lost until 1970).

Looking at the liner notes more closely, we learn that the first three rags were "played by Scott Joplin"—an assertion that can only be partially true, given the inevitable collaboration of technicians in player piano music. But the thirteen remaining rags have no listed performers, and it is only by carefully perusing Michael Montgomery's commentary that we are able to discover their origins. Montgomery informs us that Hal Boulware, a private collector, produced all but two of the remaining rolls—in the 1960s. Boulware had been unable to find many of Joplin's best rags issued in roll form, and so he made his own (whether by arranging them only, or playing and arranging them, is unclear). Ralph Mullen, a piano roll maker from California, created one of the others, also recently. Even more confusingly, we are told nothing about how "Silver Swan" was made. That roll is attributed only to QRS.

So there is a complex web of authorship in *Elite Syncopations*—a tangle of popular composers and pianists, obscure player piano enthusiasts, and completely anonymous technicians and pianists. But the chaos of collaboration is almost entirely obscured by the way the CD advertises itself. The cover strives for "ragtime era" authenticity, featuring late Victorian graphic design and Joplin's name rendered in a nostalgic saloon font, inferring that the words "Classic" and "Rare" in "Classic Ragtime from Rare Piano Rolls" mean that the rolls are all from the appropriate historical period, or are at least old. By placing the three Joplin-played rags first in the program, the CD packaging misleadingly suggests that all of the rags on the CD were simply played by the composer, when in fact many of them were constructed in a much more complicated way, half a century after his death. It's good marketing, but bad aesthetics.

SOUND AS THE SIGNATURE OF TECHNOLOGY

When we looked, in chapter 1, at "Deacon's Hop" and "Diminuendo and Crescendo in Blue," I argued that the sound of the audience was a form of contextual collaboration on those recordings, an artistic component of what the listener ultimately perceives as the composition. Like those cheering crowds, recording technology leaves a sound

behind, an aural signature embedded in every artifact it is used to produce. That signature too is evidence of contextual collaboration, in
this case by the technicians and inventors who worked to create the
recording medium and its playback devices.

In the player piano the signature is especially hard to miss. "All
of these movements—of pedals pumping, of paper unrolling, of air
rushing in and of notes being activated from within—represent a different kind of ambient 'noise' than you may be used to on other CDs,"
Michael Montgomery writes in the liner notes to *The Greatest Ragtime of the Century,* a Biograph disc consisting entirely of piano roll
performances, ostensibly hand played by such well-known pianists as
Fats Waller, Jelly Roll Morton, James P. Johnson, and Jimmy Blythe.
Montgomery helpfully describes the complex mechanical operations
that make up a player piano performance, but as one reads, his remarks
begin to sound less like an explanation and more like an apology. Possibly in an effort to prevent these unfamiliar sounds from turning listeners away, he invokes both traditional authorship and authenticity,
telling the reader that "we felt you would want to experience these
almost-live performances as if you were personally sitting at the controls pumping the rolls and watching the notes play. It's the next best
thing to having been there, watching and hearing these giants of the
keyboard while they performed live."

The "next best thing to having been there"? As enjoyable as *The
Greatest Ragtime of the Century* is, I suspect few listeners will hear it
this way—though Montgomery's motivations for making the claim are
understandable, given the modern preoccupation with audio fidelity.
In part, his words evoke the ghostliness that we saw in descriptions of
the reproducing piano. But the bigger issue is that the "ambient noise"
in these recordings is not merely, as Montgomery assumes, a technical problem that has not been solved, but an artistic sound in its own
right, even if it was not intended as such. And our eagerness to hear
around or through that sound means we are overlooking the contextual collaboration it is a marker of.

So far in this chapter, we have been thinking of music technology
in terms of the player piano. And with good reason: as I noted earlier,
the instrument established a gestalt for later generations of keyboard-

and computer-based automatic music production. Yet the descendants of the player piano—devices like the Synclavier and its MIDI-based cousins—have primarily been of interest to musicians. As twenty-first-century fans of recording, we should remember that the player piano eventually lost out to another instrument, the phonograph. And given our modern preference for phonograph-like devices on which to listen to music—a laptop equipped with iTunes has more in common with a Victrola than it does with a pianola—for this discussion of the aural signature of recordings I want to shift emphasis, focusing on the phonograph's rise to prominence, from the earliest forms of acoustic recording, through the glory days of the 78, and until roughly the end of World War II. ("Phonograph," by the way, was originally a brand name referring to a specific type of "talking machine." But as the twentieth century went on, the word was increasingly used in the United States in a generic sense, which is how I employ it here.)

Inevitably, contemporary perception of the aural signature of the phonograph was influenced by its marketing. Faced with the same technophobia that dogged the player piano industry, phonograph manufacturers tried to make their products seem more human and less threatening—tried to get us to ignore the sound of the machine, and even to forget that a machine was at all involved in the music. While the earliest phonographs had intentionally revealed their mechanism—not unlike early jukeboxes, which "always provided a glass window through which the patron could watch the internal workings of the machine," since "it was part of the entertainment that one purchased"—that novelty soon wore off, and the industry instead began hiding its technology. The Victrola, for instance—introduced by the Victor Talking Machine Company in 1906—was the first phonograph to offer "Victorian camouflage for the industrial machine," concealing its mechanics and even its horn in an attractive wood cabinet, almost like a piece of furniture with a record player inside. (Perhaps ironically, this phonograph may have taken its name from the "pianola"—another name for the player piano—though William Howland Kenney argues that "Victrola" was a contraction of "Victor's viola.")

Other phonograph companies attempted to soften the hard technological edge of their products too. One creative designer tried to make the mechanism less intimidating by obscuring it beneath a flower-shaped playback horn. Another included cords through which a listener was supposed to be able to imprint her emotions onto a recording. Later, anthropomorphic brand names like the "Golden Throat" loudspeaker system and the "Magic Brain" automatic turntable served the same humanizing purpose, going to almost ridiculous lengths to claim a natural quality for the machines. Yet the evidence of technology was pretty hard to ignore. Consider the phonographic equivalent of the player piano's pedal, paper, and air noise—the instrument's much-bemoaned scratchiness, a sound caused by the stylus wearing away the recording's surface. The material used to manufacture the disc or cylinder (typically shellac, vinyl, or wax) determined the character of that scratchiness, which contemporaries described in a variety of ways—most memorably, it was compared to the sizzle of a heated frying pan. And then there was the medium's limited frequency range. In acoustic recording, for instance, the sound was constrained to frequencies of between 168 and 2,000 cycles per second—a mere fraction of the range of 20 to 20,000 cycles per second that can be heard by the average human ear. Timothy Day puts that more practically, pointing out that acoustic recordings were "unable to reproduce all the frequencies of notes below the E below middle C and of notes higher than the C three octaves above middle C." It is not that the notes higher or lower than those limits were inaudible, but rather that all sounds were distorted, an effect that was observable even after the invention of electrical recording. Both surface noise and frequency range, then, contributed to the unique sonic character of early phonographs—what we could call a phonographic *timbre*.

In yet another idiosyncrasy, early phonographs could only feature so much sound. Before 1947, restrictions on the size of a disc's or cylinder's grooves meant that commercial recording typically could not accommodate more than three or four minutes at a time (five minutes in the case of twelve-inch records). Longer compositions—most classical music, for instance—had to be significantly truncated when issued in recorded form. Often the result seemed a horrible disfigurement of the original, as when the *Firebird Suite* and *Till Eulenspiegel* were each cut by half their original length so they could fit together on a single recording. Sometimes longer works were recorded in something closer to their entirety, but only after they were broken up over numerous discs. A 1927 rendition of Wagner's *Tristan und Isolde*—not even the entire opera, but merely a "sizable chunk"—was thirty-eight discs long.

These characteristics of early phonographs are easy to dismiss as by-products of technological crudity. The machine wasn't good enough, and we listen in spite of its shortcomings. But what if we turn that formulation around and try to hear those "shortcomings" more generously? The length restriction, for instance, led music in some interesting directions. Consider Fats Waller's 78s. Making them was a process fraught with challenge. A single microphone captured each three-minute take, which could not be edited or enhanced. Playback options were minimal; the master disc could not be used for that purpose, since it would be destroyed in the process, and though a backup disc was recorded simultaneously with the master, it would yield only one or two replays. In effect, Waller had to get his recordings right the first time, distilling everything he wanted to say on a given tune into the space of a few minutes, sans revision.

But while Waller was certainly restricted by this limitation of 78 technology, he also used it to his advantage. And in a sense, that technology—or, more accurately, its inventors—used him creatively too. In this period extended jazz improvisations were rarely (if ever) recorded in their entirety, chopped up over a series of discs like *Tristan und Isolde*. But Waller approached the problem from the opposite direction, evolving a sonnetlike style of playing and composing specifically for the temporal limitations of the medium. As Eric Hobsbawm has written, jazz musicians in general responded to phonographic brevity by inventing a form of the music that used concision as a strength, doing a lot with a little. And they did so much more effectively than their classical peers. It is not that classical composers completely *ignored* the possibilities of phonographic form: Puccini, for instance, had tailored some of his arias to the length of the 78. And it is not that jazz musicians were uninterested in longer phonographic forms: Ellington was one of the first to explore that possibility, as early as his 1930s twelve-inch recording of "Creole Rhapsody." But Ellington, Waller, and other jazz artists were also much more adept than any "orthodox composer" in their aesthetic exploitation of phonographic brevity, creating what Hobsbawm called "marvels of unity and shape."

The point here is that contexts are transformative, inspiring creative adaptation by those who act within them. Like the contextual collaboration of a cheering audience, or of a silent group of listening bodies, the work of those who devise and manufacture recording technology cannot simply be wished out of the resulting music or written off as an unfortunate distraction. Instead, it forces new kinds of beauty, prompting musicians to explore artistic paths they might otherwise have ignored. Would Waller or Ellington or any other pre-LP jazz musician have been as driven to come up with "marvels of unity and shape" if they had not needed to keep their recorded performances within the limit of a few minutes? How indeed would modern popular music in general have developed without that limit? One could argue that the three-minute "pop symphony" that set a standard for commercial music in the latter half of the twentieth century had its roots in the time constraints of early recording technology, and that in this sense there is a clear formal line from Waller and (early) Ellington to rock and roll and Motown.

The academic term for the connecting thread here is "bricolage," or "making do"—that is, using the tools at hand, however imperfect they may be, to one's advantage. "In popular movies," writes Stephen Nachmanovitch, "the power of *bricolage* is symbolized by the resourceful hero who saves the world with a Swiss army knife and a couple of clever tricks. The *bricoleur* is an artist of limits." That too is a way of describing the contextual collaboration informing early jazz recordings. A medium hampered by a technological restriction may not at first seem capable of producing a new kind of art. But if a new kind of art is produced anyway, we may have to reconsider whether we are talking about a "restriction" at all.

Phonographic timbre—the scratchiness and limited frequency range I mentioned a moment ago—had a similarly creative function. Singer Enrico Caruso might never have enjoyed a recording career otherwise. "For years in the minds of nearly everybody there were records, and there were Caruso records," Compton Mackenzie, founder of *Gramo-*

phone, an early British audiophile publication, wrote in 1924. "He impressed his personality through the medium of his recorded voice on kings and peasants." But by framing Caruso's records as impressions of the singer's personality—another way of assuming the "telegraphic model of communication" Vijay Iyer critiqued in chapter 1—MacKenzie overlooked that they were actually produced by a symbiosis between art and technology. Whatever his ability as an artist, Caruso's voice, particularly its frequency range, was exactly the sort of sound that contemporary recording machines were good at picking up, and thus tended to come across with vitality and warmth, even on the least sophisticated record players. Like Beethoven, Caruso was "exceptionally well-placed"—not by being close to supportive patrons, but by his propinquity to a technology that was well suited to his talent.

And like Dussek, some of Caruso's contemporaries were not so fortunate. Tim Gracyk and Frank Hoffmann remind us that the capabilities of a given technology determine who is able to use it. With the earliest phonographs, certain artists, no matter how musically skilled, were discouraged from recording at all. Soprano voices were not suited to the frequency range of the instrument—they tended to sound shrill—hence the underrepresentation of female singers on contemporary discs and cylinders. And before the 1902 adoption of the permanent master, which allowed a single good take to be used as the basis for commercial copies, recording artists required endurance, even more than musical talent. That is, they had to be willing to record and rerecord the same song, in take after take, in order to generate enough copies to justify commercial release. Those who lacked the stamina (or single-mindedness) to do so were effectively denied a recording career.

In other words, it is not that Caruso's many fans simply put up with the faults of the phonograph out of deference to the singer's talent. Though they clearly appreciated that talent, they also appreciated the *sound* of his records. Even today, a hundred years later, Caruso fans by and large still prefer the original Caruso recordings when given the opportunity to hear versions "fixed" by modern technology. Hence the uproar when RCA's *Caruso 2000* project removed the original accompaniments from sixteen Caruso recordings and overdubbed Caruso's voice with a new orchestra, producing an asynchronous hybrid of some of his best-known songs. The release frustrated the listener's desire for the sound of Caruso's voice in its original technological habitat. "If Caruso can be made to sing with a newly recorded orchestra," Allan Kozinn sarcastically asked, "why can't he sing with Elvis Presley, another RCA mega-seller whose catalog the label is forever raiding?" Indeed, Kozinn wondered, why stop there? Through the magic of digital editing, Luciano Pavarotti and Placido Domingo could be made to sing with Caruso "as an alternative for those who think that Jose Carreras isn't quite up to the level of the rest of the Three Tenors." One could go so far as to catalog all of Caruso's recorded utterances into a database, Kozinn joked, reassembling them at some point in the future for the ill-advised but inevitable *Caruso Sings the Andrew Lloyd Webber Songbook in Italian* album. Of course what Kozinn really wanted was for RCA to stop fiddling with Caruso's work altogether and just "let its great recordings speak for themselves, on their own terms, as they always have." Part of what made those recordings "great" in the first place, he suggests, was their original technological expression.

It's a bias Kozinn shares with other modern listeners: the sound of old technology speaking for itself is artistically valued in our culture. In the late 1990s, for instance, an article in *Musician* magazine described a digital plug-in (for use with recording software) that could

> provide any computer-based recording with the grooves and grit of all your favorite 78, 45 and 33 1/3 records. Want to control how warped your recording sounds? Easy. Want to alter the quality of the turntable's surface, or turntable rumble? Done. Want to dictate the stereo width or compression of your samples? Hah! Controls for dirt, hiss, static, wear, warp and scratches are all there. Sorry—record sleeves not included.

Soon after, Steinberg released its "Grungelizer" plug-in, which featured a timeline dial that allowed users to set the sound of a track to the technological norm of a particular year, regardless of when that track had actually been recorded. The virtual dial (itself a visual representation of technological nostalgia) went all the way back to the year 1900.

The existence of tools like the Grungelizer suggests that even today there are listeners who prefer the sonic qualities of older forms of sound reproduction, whether they feature the voice of Caruso or not. "Devotees of acoustic recording can be found all over the world," Andre Millard writes, "playing their 2- and 4-minute records on well-oiled phonographs. Allen Koenigsberg's *Antique Phonograph Monthly* has a subscription list of over 2,000." In North America, there are active phonograph societies in Michigan, California, Indiana, Massa-chussetts, Oregon, and elsewhere. The listeners who belong to these groups, or who independently share their affinities, are not motivated primarily by the quality of musicianship or even by the compositional content of the records they love—after all, at the time these records were made, many aspects of musical performance eluded the technol-ogy altogether. Some may appreciate phonographs from a historian's perspective, but fans listen to them because *they like to listen to them*. And that pleasure is evidence enough that the technological collabora-tion at work here is both creative and artistic.

We have already seen how Montgomery wrote apologetically about the "ambient noise" of the player piano on the *Greatest Ragtime of the Century* CD. Mike Lipskin, in his liner notes for *Turn On the Heat*, a collection of Waller 78s, also seems self-conscious about the audio quality of the material he describes. As he puts it, "Listeners should be aware that the method by which these selections were recorded is a far cry from today's multitrack digital technology." Ward Mar-ston, the reissue producer for Naxos's Caruso series, assures us, with a similar tone of regret, that for certain Caruso discs "the recording apparatus was defective, causing the speed to decrease as the disc was being recorded." Apology is a common theme here, and the implica-tion is that if only Waller, Caruso, and other early recording stars could remake their records in a modern, state-of-the-art studio, the result would be better recordings of the same works. But that implication misses the point. If Waller and Caruso could remake their records in a modern, state-of-the-art studio, the result would be not better or worse versions of the same pieces, but a new oeuvre altogether. "The work," in other words, is not the pure composition as perceived through the neutral filter of a given performance, and in turn through the neutral filter of a given recording technology or media. Those filters are never neutral, but rather are always integrally creative components of the music, helping to bring it into being in the first place.

"SOUND PHOTOGRAPHY"

The phonograph's aural signature is also due to another kind of collaborator—the studio professional, a descendant of the player piano's roll arrangers and editors. In the Ellington discography, for instance, the "Ellington sound" referred to by scholars, critics, and fans is an outcome not only of the initiating act of the band's performance, and the contextual collaboration of the medium's materiality, but also the direct collaboration of engineers and producers. While Ellington himself was "very, very fussy about recording," and thus played an important role in creating the sound that bears his name, without these latter individuals the band's recordings would not have been possible.

Hasse makes the point when he praises "the recording engineers at Victor"—like Nancarrow's player piano technicians they remain anonymous—arguing that by the 1940s they "managed to capture the Ellington sound with a richness and fidelity unprecedented in its previous recordings." By articulating the dynamic this way, however, Hasse evokes an "Ellington sound" that existed before producers and recording engineers "managed to capture" it. For our purposes, that's imprecise. It is not that an "Ellington sound" did not exist outside of the context of recording. But clearly, too, *that* sound is not available to us, and is not what we actually mean by "the Ellington sound." Today, we know only the records. The best modern Ellington repertory bands—from the Jazz at Lincoln Center Orchestra to the high school ensembles that compete in the annual "Essentially Ellington" competition—know only the records too, having learned the music in part by dissecting, studying, and emulating the same Victor releases Hasse discusses. And yet the modern Ellington repertory sound, good as it is, is worlds away from what we are familiar with as "the Ellington sound"—the sound on the records—because each exists in a different material context. All of which is to say that "the Ellington sound," as we use the term, did not precede, and is not extractable from, the "richness and fidelity" of the band's recorded works, but was in part created through them. Engineers and producers did not so much "capture" it as they helped to generate it.

Habitually, we invert that paradigm. Indeed, Hasse's view of production has deep and stubborn historical roots. As Brian Eno puts it, recording was initially "regarded as a device for transmitting a performance to an unknown audience, and the whole accent of recording technique was on making what was called a 'more faithful' transmission of that experience." It was assumed that the only real creative input a producer had was "over the relative levels of sounds that went onto the machine," which, Eno reminds us, were simply a function of each instrument's distance from the microphone. Fred Gaisberg, who in the first half of the twentieth century worked as a producer for both His Master's Voice (HMV, the European branch of Victor) and EMI, exemplified this assumption by referring to recordings as "sound photographs."

This phrase is unfortunate, implying an objectivity not present in either photography or sound recording. It is true that the typical studio of Gaisberg's day lacked much of the fancy gadgetry that would be proactively used by later generations of producers to explicitly manipulate recordings. Even at the height of his career, Gaisberg knew nothing of splicing techniques that would eventually allow for the creation of an edit compiled from different takes, for instance. He did not have access to sophisticated audio processing tools such as equalization or compression. His successor at EMI, second-generation producer Walter Legge, would use such technology to stake out a modern conception of the producer's role, in which raw recordings were edited into finished works, ostensibly more "perfect" than any live performance. (Of course, even the modern conception of production is often overshadowed by the rhetoric of genius, which is typically reserved for the artist. Eno, for example, is more renowned because of his work with superstars like U2 and David Bowie, whose reputations have in some sense legitimated him, than he is for things done under his own name.)

Yet although Gaisberg worked before these significant developments in the history of production, he too was an active, technologically engaged producer. The direct collaboration he provided was extensive and important, even beyond the "relative levels of sounds that went into the machine." He was, for instance, one of the first record producers to work with classical musicians, many of whom had previously scoffed at the idea of making phonographs at all. He saw the potential in Enrico Caruso, agreeing "to pay him by far the largest fee accorded any recording artist up to that time—the princely sum of one hundred pounds for ten recordings." The gamble paid off when the records became hits, motivating other well-known opera stars to follow suit and opening up a new market for records.

In the studio, Gaisberg offered performance advice, seeing aesthetic possibilities where the musicians did not. This too was a form of direct collaboration. It was Gaisberg, for instance, who recommended that the Russian opera singer Feodor Chaliapin record the "Volga Boat Song," which would go on to become another hit. And he explicitly helped to plan its performance. "Together," Gaisberg explained, "we conceived the idea of beginning the number softly, rising to a *forte* and fading away to a whisper, to picture the approach and gradual retreat of the haulers on the river banks." It was also Gaisberg who in 1932 masterminded the collaboration between Yehudi Menuhin and Sir Edward Elgar, producing an influential recording of Elgar's Violin Concerto in B Minor that is still in print today. Gaisberg and his peers coached performers in new and unusual musical techniques in order to better meet the peculiar demands of the recording process. Musicians had to learn to play or sing at a constant loudness, for instance, avoiding the subtle dynamic nuances they might have employed in other performances. Recording was also physically uncomfortable, and sight lines were obscured, necessitating new and awkward forms of ensemble cuing, which producers helped invent and oversee.

And so while Hugh Griffith writes that "in a single afternoon on the third floor of a Milan hotel, Caruso had made recording respectable," it would be more accurate to say that recording's respectability had come about through rigorous collaboration between Caruso, the composers whose works he sang, the musicians who backed him, the technicians whose machines recorded him, and Gaisberg, the producer who saw his potential in the first place.

"TRANSPARENCY HAS BEEN ACHIEVED"

One branch of musical aesthetics, traceable to Lutheran cantor Nicolas Listenius and his 1537 book *Musica,* holds that sound is a secondary consideration of music. Music, in this view, is essentially the score (the written composition)—the "musical text which endures after the composer's death"—whereas the performance, even by a virtuosic star performer, is a subordinate expression of that essence, and the recording, presumably, a mere document of that subordinate expression. "In the more extreme forms of this discursive polarity," Paul Theberge writes, "the actual physical sound of music, as produced by musical instruments"—or by recording technology—"is considered to be little more than an unfortunate though necessary medium for the presentation of the 'pure' structure of the music manifest in the score." This, of course, is a variation of the Schopenhauerian argument we saw earlier. My own skepticism about it derives from my sense that it bears little relationship to how most people actually listen to music. If modern listeners heard only "the 'pure' structure of the music manifest in the score," separating that from sound itself, instrumentation would be irrelevant. We would, for instance, be able to imagine Bach's Brandenburg Concertos played entirely on kazoos, and not be bothered by the grating, raspy sound, as long as the pitches and rhythms adhered to our inner, score-derived sense of the ideal composition. And yet for many if not most listeners, this would be not merely absurd but offensive. Although instrumentation in Bach is not always specified, the ideas of the Brandenburg Concertos are wedded, in their expression, to a certain timbral palette—and so when Wendy Carlos performed them on synthesizer, they were dramatically remade.

More to the point of this chapter—and particularly the argument about the collaboration of a technological sound signature—if only the score mattered, if music were a truly ideal phenomenon, listeners would never develop media allegiances. Audiophiles would not argue endlessly about the superiority of vinyl, or tubes, or one brand of speaker over another. Yet anyone who has any familiarity with the world of recorded sound knows how easy it is to get caught up in such arguments. The aforementioned Compton Mackenzie, one of the first professional audiophiles, lived that temptation—and also its caprice. Mackenzie was one of the more vocal critics of electrical recording when it became commercially available in 1925. The sound, he complained, suffered in comparison with that of its acoustic predecessor. "The music itself is a jangle of shattered nerves," he wrote in a review of an HMV recording of Tchaikovsky's Fourth Symphony, "and even where there is any attempt to rid the music of the exasperation which sets us on edge the recording steps into the breach and sees that our nerves are not allowed any rest." Apparently this particular recording had been a "symphonic debut in the latest methods of recording"—not only electrical recording but also an attempt at a stereo effect. MacKenzie was skeptical, arguing that "we must at once dethrone this stereoscopy at the expense of everything else." Many of his readers expressed a similar disdain. "Mellowness and reality have given place to screaming," wrote one, referring to the music's "peculiar and unpleasant twang." The music "is completely spoilt by the atrocious and squeaky tone," the critique continued, and the "din is ear-splitting," with "a continual humming roar pervading everything."

Again, MacKenzie was an audiophile, so these complaints were not, like Sousa's, motivated by a critique of mechanical reproduction as such. Rather, they derived from a championing of the acoustic recording sound over its descendant, electrical recording. From a twenty-first-century vantage point, that argument seems especially odd. For us, all of recording history appears to lead inevitably to the current technological moment. But according to R. W. Burns, a hundred years ago the modern idea of high fidelity was not a foregone conclusion. After decades of exposure to acoustic recording, listeners had developed certain expectations about recorded sound, many of which the new technique violated. The national debates over the issue were "so antagonistic at times that some gramophone companies queried the wisdom of adopting such a radical system."

Ironically, after listeners learned to appreciate the sound of the first electrical recordings, many of them became equally loyal to *that,* shifting their disdain to even later technological developments. Thus the same Compton Mackenzie would by the late forties be arguing *for* the "superior listening experience" of 78s, against the new sounds of the next latest development, the LP. (He was not alone among music professionals who preferred the 78 over the LP: pianist Alfred Brendel expressed a similar bias decades later.) Mackenzie justified his position by asserting that, as Simon Frith puts it, "the collector of 78 recordings had to be an 'active' listener, had to use her imagination to hear the sound that was buried in the 78's bumps and crackles, had to keep jumping up to change the record, which could never be, then, background music." But this idea that a listener had to hear "through" the noise of the 78 to get to the real work inside is on some level a rationalization for the fact that, in a certain context and for a certain set of ears, 78s simply sound *good.* The same thing could be said for any media format: each has its loyal fans, who are attracted because of what it sounds like. Even when unconscious, such affinities are significant: those of us who do not self-identify as audiophiles nevertheless develop attachments to the sound of specific media too.

Over time recording technology has seemingly evolved to eliminate its aural signature. The invention of microgroove records (and then CDs) allowed for longer running times. The invention of full frequency range recording allowed for a broader spectrum of recorded sound. And the incorporation of less scratchy vinyl compounds into disc manufacturing eliminated much of the phonograph's frying pan sizzle. These and other developments would lead many listeners to assume the machine noise had disappeared. Consider Paul Elie's comment on Yo-Yo Ma's first recordings of the Bach Cello Suites, made in the 1980s: "The sound of the record is the sound of the cello, full stop. A hundred years after the advent of recording, transparency has been achieved." But the truth is that the signature of technological collaboration is always apparent for those who are willing to listen for it. In fact, the highest-fidelity recording, played on the best stereo system, will still always bear audible traces of the technology that produced it. Notwithstanding the famous Memorex ads, in which listeners could not tell the difference between live and recorded sound, even casual music fans can in most situations easily distinguish between a recording (of whatever quality) and a live performance. At the very least, it is in that distinction that recorded sound continues to function as the signature of technology—the marker of its direct and contextual collaboration—even if it does so "silently."

In a discussion of film sound, John Belton argues that "the work of technology can never quite become invisible. Work, even work that seeks to efface itself, can never disappear." This is an astute observation, and a fitting close to our discussion of the collaboration that occurs through technology. It is not that modern, cleaner recordings are any less technologically produced—indeed they are for the most part far *more* technological, despite their desire to call less attention to themselves. Every time we marvel at the clarity or fidelity of a given recording, we admire it *as* a recording, and implicitly note the work of the machine that was used to create it. In this sense, Ovid's dictum, *Ars est celare artem* ("it is art to conceal art"), is only partially true. Art cannot be concealed; its obviousness can only be missed by those willing to overlook it.

Part II

AUTHENTICITY

3

AN INTRODUCTION TO AUTHENTICITY

It's so obsessed with the real that it's unrealistic, atavistic, and just silly.
—Sarah Nicole Prickett

In 1983, composer and percussionist Art Jarvinen commissioned a piece from his friend Frank Zappa. "While You Were Art," the coyly titled work Zappa submitted, was to be debuted by the California EAR Unit, a new music ensemble Jarvinen belonged to, as part of the Monday Evening Concerts series at the Los Angeles County Museum of Art—a regular haunt for new music audiences in Los Angeles. Yet as the performance date drew closer, Jarvinen began to suspect that

> Frank never did intend to give us a piece we could actually play. We could have played it, and intended to eventually, but he delivered it late enough that we could not possibly have learned it well enough in the time left before the scheduled performance. So he asked us if we would be willing to "lip synch" it. And we said yes. Then several people got cold feet, but we did it anyway.

By "lip synch," Zappa meant that he would give the group a digital tape recording of an electronically sequenced performance of the piece—created with his beloved Synclavier—which, he suggested, could be played through the PA system while the ensemble pretended to play their instruments.

On the evening of the concert, the trappings of a live performance were supposed to complete the illusion: complicated-looking equipment was arranged onstage, wires were dangled from the instruments, mics were set up without being turned on. "Any sound the audience hears that might be deemed 'synthesized' will be overlooked" because of these accoutrements, Zappa told the musicians. But as soon as the

concert began, David Ocker, Zappa's copyist and assistant, noticed
a problem—what he later described as "a wall of hiss." Previously,
Zappa had recorded a version of the piece to a cassette tape, which had
been provided to the group as a learning reference, and it was this tape,
not the high-quality digital recording, that was mistakenly being used
for the performance. Ocker was chagrined. "I slunk down in my seat,"
he writes. "I was sure that everyone in the audience would instantly
know what was going on. I mentally prepared myself for a disaster."

But disaster never came—or at least not the disaster Ocker was
expecting. He continues:

> Much to my surprise the audience sat quietly throughout. And there
> was polite and extremely unenthusiastic applause afterwards. The
> Unit trudged out for a bow and then went right on to the next piece.
>
> After the concert I went on-stage to talk to Art. He was standing
> in a small group—one of whom was the composer Morton Subot-
> nick—a former teacher of mine whose music is frequently performed
> by the EAR Unit. I told Art "It sounded awful!" Bad-mouthing a
> performance directly like that is a "no-no" in the chamber music
> world and this comment was greeted with some surprise. When it
> was explained that the "awful" comment referred to the quality of
> tape-reproduction, it became immediately clear that the audience had
> not understood the pantomime quality of the performance.

Zappa's recounting of the event, featured in his autobiography, is
positively gleeful at the resulting confusion. In his view, the incident
justified a long-term grudge against classical music institutions and
audiences, proving the ignorance of both. "The man who ran the concert series didn't know the difference," he scoffed. "The two classical
reviewers from the major Los Angeles newspapers didn't notice anything either. Nobody in the audience knew, except for David Ocker."

Zappa did not attend the performance and thus was basing his
interpretation of what happened on secondhand information. But
he was right to conclude that the incident "produced quite a scandal." According to Jarvinen, Subotnick was particularly offended, and
because of his close relationship with the EAR Unit, some people in the
group "were made to feel very ashamed." In the media coverage of the
story, these more contrite EAR Unit members "put their tails between

their legs and basically apologized for the error of our ways, on behalf of the group," as Jarvinen puts it. "That pissed me off, but Frank was livid." Zappa vented in his autobiography: "Several members of the ensemble, mortified by all the hoo-ha, swore they would never '*do it again*.' (Do what again? Prove to the world that nobody really knows what the fuck is going on at a contemporary music concert?)"

But what really *was* the "hoo-ha" here? Was it simply a matter of the audience having been fooled? Or is it problematic to assume, as Zappa did, that *nobody* had any idea what was "going on"? What about the listener who, as Ocker notes, sat near the stage and was overheard wondering about the lack of direct sound from the instruments? What if the ignorance Zappa described was actually disinterest, or even a muted expression of scorn? Or what if, more generously, the audience actually took as a given the possibility of electronics, tape, or a performance art element? (The Monday evening series, after all, was a forum for experimental music.) From these perspectives, it is quite possible that at least some people in the audience did recognize the virtual nature of the performance and quietly assumed it was intentional.

On the other hand, perhaps Zappa was right, and the LACMA audience did not know what was happening during "While You Were Art." But then how much do any of us ever "know" about what we experience during *any* musical performance? Zappa's remarks, amusing as they are, only make sense if we assume a rigorous epistemology of music that we can compare "not knowing what the fuck is going on" *to*. Yet we have no basis for such an assumption. Sound's relationship to knowledge is convoluted at best. It is true that in some fields—medicine, for instance, with its stethoscopes and sonograms—listening is a viable method of inquiry. Yet most of the words we use to describe intellection come from sight—"focus," "point of view," "overview," "insight," "envision," "enlightenment." Listening is typically assumed to be more mysterious, interior, and intuitive, not a domain of reason and rationality.

And while whole disciplines are now dedicated to understanding listening scientifically—psychoacoustics is a good example—audiences remain flummoxed by persistent philosophical questions, like "What is music for?" or "What does music mean?" or even "What *is* music?"

One can sample a wide range of the scientific literature and come away feeling informed but still oddly unsatisfied. Every answer leads to more questions, and ultimately we continue to know only what we like. In that sense, the most lavishly trained conservatory violinist is no closer to "getting it" than the earnest amateur moonlighting in a bar band. That is, whatever musical understanding we are capable of is phenomenological—a kind of personal "embodied knowledge," and not the Kantian *Ding-an-sich* (thing-in-itself). The ambiguity of our conclusions—the range of idiosyncratic perceptions that we will explore in more detail in the next chapter—means that it's not merely that "nobody really knows" what's "going on at a contemporary music concert." Nobody really knows what's going on when it comes to music, period.

Perhaps, in a roundabout way, that was Zappa's point too. Interestingly, despite the sarcasm he directed at those who did not know what to make of "While You Were Art," his career had been and would continue to be an exploration of the deceptions we all experience in music, and the agnosticism of listening. Zappa was simply obsessed with fakery: from the pseudo-porn audiotape that briefly landed him in jail as a young man, to his willingness to overdub putatively live recordings, to his later experiments with "xenochrony" (his own term for a compositional technique in which tracks recorded for different pieces were randomly merged into a new recording), to his work with the Synclavier, he consistently troubled the listener's expectation that a sound should actually *be* what it sounds like.

Everyone else at the "While You Were Art" concert cared about musical fakery too—obviously, they cared a lot. The strong emotional reactions—Zappa's scorn, the embarrassment of Ocker and the members of the EAR Unit, the anger of Subotnick—suggest that the incident was much more than a mere prank perpetrated by a wealthy rock star on a hapless avant-garde music scene. What was at stake was something bigger, a vested interest in a more important debate. No one seemed comfortable with the deception, whether they were in on it or not. And that discomfort marks deception as a key problem for modern music—one usually encountered under the broad category of "authenticity."

ORIGINS

You put together two notes, and you hope that it's not casual, as in, "Those two notes will do, but any other two would also do." These notes represent this fight and this struggle and this eternal truth. And that's what makes us feel like composition is a noble pursuit.

—David Lang

With things that go together, I never got to the point of what Cage says: someone asked him about putting notes together according to the I Ching, "What do you do if you put them together and it sounds terrible?" He said, "You get used to it."

—Conlon Nancarrow

At the beginning of this book, I defined musical authenticity in its peculiar modern sense as the quest for a singularly true, ideal (that is, optimal, replete) experience of music (whether a recording, live performance, score, or transcription) that both supersedes and ignores the multiplicity of an audience's perception and is only accessible to those with the "proper" understanding. The goal of listening, in this formulation, seems simple enough: it is just to comprehend the authenticity. But that's the problem, too, as we will see; each listener is inclined to make a different assumption about the "singularly true, ideal experience of music" she is after. Indeed, our experience of music today has a lot to do with the incompatibility of these different assumptions.

Where does this yearning for authenticity come from? Certainly one of the usual suspects when discussing its origins is the "Early Music" movement, a subgenre of classical music that dates from the late nineteenth and early twentieth centuries, achieved its greatest popularity after World War II, and is still with us today, though in a less strident form. Early Music practitioners initially took as their mission the excavation and reperformance of works from the medieval period through the Baroque. But the synonym of "historically informed performance" gives a better sense of what the movement has actually been about. In the West, while there have always been those willing to reperform music from earlier generations—Bach reperformed Palestrina, for instance, just as Mendelssohn reperformed Bach—it was rare before the nineteenth century for musicians to *commit* to historical repertory. Early Music changed all that. More than merely revisiting old compositions, its practitioners sought to revisit old musical contexts. They advocated the use of period instruments and performance practices, and claimed to adhere to whatever was known of a composer's intentions. At their most insistent, they brandished authenticity as a mark of status—the word was even, for a while late in the twentieth century, employed as a marketing term.

At roughly the same time as the emergence of Early Music as a category, a group of European composers—Stravinsky, Milhaud, Respighi, Reger, Hindemith, among others—sought another kind of revival, a "neoclassical" compositional response to the excesses of Romanticism and modernism. This reactionary trend influenced the development of musical authenticity too, however obliquely. One of its first works was Stravinsky's 1920 ballet *Pulcinella*—actually his rewrite of commedia dell'arte music attributed to Giovanni Pergolesi (later revealed to have been composed by some of Pergolesi's contemporaries). *Pulcinella* demonstrated how twentieth-century composers could look to models from the eighteenth century and before, integrating antiquated aesthetics into contemporary works and rejecting the progressivism so prized by the avant-garde. However successful the results—and I disagree with Zach Wallmark's suggestion that the neoclassical enterprise was, in Stravinsky's hands, inherently ironic, a "dark, sly, distancing maneuver"—the output of this group complemented the conservatism of Early Music. The main difference is that neoclassicism was not a repertory movement, but a loose compositional genre.

The revivalism that drove both Early Music and neoclassicism did not develop in a vacuum, but drew on new perspectives from musicology and music history—inchoate disciplines that had begun to construct a rigorous and comprehensive relationship to the musical past. One of the most important figures in early-twentieth-century musicology, for instance, was Heinrich Schenker, whose forceful articulation of what he saw as the "immutable laws of music" dovetailed nicely with the emergence of an authenticity-based worldview. But it was the broader social context that dispersed the concerns of musicology, music history,

Early Music, and neoclassicism into areas of music making that at the time existed outside the ambit of high art. Authenticity seems to take hold where there is an existential crisis, as there was in the West during the transition to modernism (and in some ways ever since). In the early twentieth century, many "experienced an inner emptiness and a sense of unreality in a swiftly industrializing and urbanizing society," as William Howland Kenney puts it. People "longed to be 'liberated' from sterile repression and hungered for an 'intense experience' of 'radiant, wholesome living.'" Many were alienated by contemporaneous technological developments—the industrialization Kenney mentions, but also the growth of mass production and the depersonalized, packaged commercial culture it enabled. Persistent political unrest, including the specter of global war, only added to the unease. As one example of how this matrix of factors informed the music of the period, Milan Kundera makes the fascinating claim that Stravinsky was influenced in his own neoclassicism in no small measure by his forced departure from Russia. Having lost his geographical homeland, the composer metaphorically "resettled," Kundera asserts, in the aesthetic comforts of the tonal, absolute music of the European tradition.

Miles Orvell observes that the quest for authenticity is linked to the possibility of fraud, a by-product of an increasingly atomized and disconnected society. In this sense, it has been a desire to establish what could be known, understood, and counted on in the face of a growing potential for untruth. The emerging recording industry soon accommodated—even stoked—this desire, by "providing redundancy and therefore stability," as R. Murray Schafer argues. In Schafer's view, music was often treated "as a sensory anchor and stabilizer against future shock." David Suisman describes how music publishers in the first decade of the twentieth century favored comforting lyrics about domestic and moral order, similarly mitigating the anxieties produced by rapid cultural change. (Much popular music has been put to this purpose ever since.) In the same vein, recall manufacturers' and marketers' efforts to humanize musical machines: the attempt to make the reproducing piano more familiar and "lifelike," for instance, or the promotion of playback devices like the "Magic Brain" turntable, with its charmingly awkward anthropomorphism. Marketing language complemented these efforts, claiming devices that achieved "a spiritual transcendence of the sterility of modern life."

Authenticity in music did not only function as a palliative for turn-of-the-century cultural stresses, however. In some ways, it made things worse, not better. Perhaps most obviously, its rearview sensibility complemented the often virulent nostalgia of early-twentieth-century nationalism. In that context, music took on political significance, beyond the concerns of musicology or of private listening pleasure. In contemporary France, for instance, neoclassicists rebelled against the Germanic influence of late Romanticism (Wagner in particular). And in Germany, Early Music drew sustenance from the *collegia musica,* institutions that were in turn susceptible to the contemporaneous German longing for music of "a simpler past, and a life at one with nature or with God." These *collegia* demonstrated a disturbing political affinity with Nazism and other forms of fascism, which of course also celebrated an (imaginary) idyllic history.

Indeed, it is impossible to understand the rise of musical authenticity in the early 1900s without also thinking about the rise of totalitarianism. "The period from the mid-thirties onward," writes Alex Ross, "marked the onset of the most warped and tragic phase in twentieth-century music: the total politicizing of art by totalitarian means." Paul Elie similarly observes that "the countries most invested culturally in music"—Germany, Italy, Russia—were most responsible for the hostilities that led to World War II. Thus the racial purity sought by the Nazis was to be expressed through "authentic" Aryan culture, codified by the Third Reich's compulsive specificity about art. As Mike Dash has shown, this did not always mean the complete exclusion of American popular music, which the Nazis felt could be co-opted for propaganda purposes when necessary. But that co-optation, when it occurred, was contrived at best, and betrayed a cultural naïveté that would have been laughable if it wasn't so dangerous. Czech dissident and writer Josef Škvorecký, remembering state-sponsored Nazi regulations, recalls that "pieces in foxtrot rhythm (so-called swing)" were "not to exceed 20% of the repertoires of light orchestras and dance bands" and that "so-called jazz compositions" could not contain more than "10% syncopation." Drum breaks were not to exceed "half a bar in four-quarter beat (except in stylized military marches)." And so on. Later, the Communists too imposed strict musical limits, as Škvorecký also observed. The young Dmitri Shostakovich, who unlike Stravinsky remained in Russia after that country's revolution, came face-to-face with the aesthetic narrow-mindedness of Stalin when *Pravda,* the state-run newspaper, reviewed his opera *Lady Macbeth* and menacingly hinted that if the composer continued to ignore Soviet aesthetic mandates, his career might "end very badly."

Of course, not all examples of musical authenticity have been as egregious as those imposed by the Soviets or the Nazis. Indeed, before rushing headlong into accusations of aesthetic oppressiveness in our own time, we should acknowledge that the yearning for authenticity seems hardwired into the human psyche. To some degree, if only for our own sanity, we have to believe in the objective integrity of the world, of knowledge, of our relationships, of ourselves. In the discourses of identity politics, authenticity has a potentially recuperative role to play, too, depending on who is exploiting the term. But things seem to work best when we acknowledge that while we want to live authentically, truly doing so is impossible. When we yield to compromise, taking whatever approximation of the concept we can get, we attain authenticity at its healthiest, situated within the complex realism of everyday life.

On the other hand, our culture is often accused, with good reason, of an obsession with the *in*authentic—of treating fakery with opportunistic cynicism or ironic reverence. This too is an important caveat. Witness the superficiality of Hollywood entertainment, the cavalier disengagement of the poststructuralist intellectual, the sociopathic cunning of the lying politician—all instances of what Orvell calls the "culture of the factitious," a world awash in simulacra. Las Vegas kitsch, Disney World theme parks, reality TV, Burning Man, the faux internationalism of the suburban mall food court: we are surrounded by cultural expressions so obviously and purposely contrived that it is hard to believe they could be taken seriously by anyone. Indeed, sometimes, in such cases, the play of surfaces is the point. But the larger observation here is that, taken together, both the idea of balance and the embrace of the patently unreal strongly qualify the occasionally encountered conviction that authenticity is "the foremost spiritual quest of our time." Inauthenticity, it appears, is at least as important, whether we live with it as a hard, inescapable truth or intentionally turn to it as a source of postmodern nirvana.

MUSICAL MORALISM

A rockist is someone who reduces rock 'n' roll to a caricature, then uses that caricature as a weapon.

—Kelefa Sanneh

Still, my interest is not with those who compromise, or who reject authenticity in favor of its opposite. Instead, I want to think about a different phenomenon as it occurs in the global music ecosystem—the act of pursuing authenticity as an existential imperative and demanding it be taken seriously, even literally. I want to think about how authenticity in this context is not only invoked, but also followed to its logical extreme, promoting aesthetic arrogance and even brutality.

As it turns out, we don't have to look too far in our own culture to find all-too-familiar "dos and don'ts" reminiscent of Škvorecký's list of Nazi musical rules, and ranging in severity from the deeply disturbing to the merely asinine. Consider the laws and mores historically segregating black and white musicians and audiences in the American South, for instance. Or the viciousness of the "Disco Sucks" campaign, with its frenzied destruction of disco vinyl at Chicago's Comiskey Park during "Disco Demolition Night" in 1979. Or Max Roach allegedly punching Ornette Coleman in the mouth to protest the latter's reimagination of jazz. Or pianist Keith Jarrett's infamous proclivity for berating his audience at the slightest disturbance. Or the long history of booing that has been an important part of the culture of opera, and has been directed at many of the genre's best-known stars at one time or another—from Enrico Caruso to Maria Callas to Placido Domingo. Or similar dynamics during Amateur Night at the Apollo, where future stars like James Brown, Luther Vandross, and Lauryn Hill were all once booed. Or the murders of Brian Deneke and Sophie Lancaster, killed a decade apart because of their identification with musical sub-cultures (punk and goth, respectively). Or, more recently, the death threats received by Los Angeles DJ Fei-Fei Wang—for playing dubstep at a rave. And so on.

All of these examples assume a link between aesthetics—concerned as it is with what is beautiful or ugly—and ethics, the delineation of what is morally good or bad. The dissonance of the blues contributed to its classification as the devil's music. The sleek and funky rhythms of disco were assumed to hint at sexual "deviance" (in this case, code for homosexuality and blackness). Detractors still complain that Ornette Coleman's free jazz is crude, and so accuse him of self-indulgence. Fans of Keith Jarrett, on the other hand, laud him for an exquisitely emotional musicality, which is used to ethically rationalize his can-tankerousness. Opera's high cultural status—taken as evidence of an advanced society—becomes a justification for shutting out new inter-pretations of its works. The Apollo's onstage musical amateurs—so identified by the Apollo's seated musical amateurs—are at the mercy of an impenetrable set of criteria, enforced by intimidation. Punk and goth, claimed the classic rock kids, was too moody, the sound track of self-pitying delinquents who ought to get real jobs. And dubstep's increasing reliance on laptop processing was read as evidence that it had become too hip for its own good.

Pianist Brad Mehldau, describing the aesthetic confrontations of his youth, argues that with music, ideology always lurks in the shad-ows, surreptitiously asking us "to suspend our aesthetic judgments and acquiesce to its claims." I take that to mean we are always in danger of ceasing to understand music as a personal, idiosyncratic experience and forcing it into an external, objective hierarchy, pushing it onto oth-ers through what Alex Ross calls the "politics of style." The listener, in other words, is always at risk of jumping to the conclusion that not only will her favorite music lead to an individually "meaningful life," as Andrew Potter puts it, but also that her taste is "good for society." And that risk points to a fine line between loving music and becoming an ideologue about that love.

Sometimes it is hard to even see where that fine line is. Affections can be unpredictable, leaning either toward or away from ideology and violence. Witness, for example, swing, a danceable subgenre of jazz, created in the United States in the early twentieth century. In the context of the rise of Nazism—when, as we have seen, non-German music was mostly banned—it provided a means of protest for the *Swingjugend,* or "Swing Kids," young Germans who resisted the authoritarianism and propaganda of the Hitler Youth. Young people involved in this movement adopted a hip style of dress and grooming, held clandestine dance parties, and generally forged a subculture that, but for the Nazi context, had a lot in common with other youth movements of the twentieth century. Clearly, for the *Swingjugend,* swing was a survival technique. It is hard to imagine how the desire for authenticity in that context could be a bad thing; it is even harder to imagine how the Swing Kids' dedication to their music could be called "ideological."

Yet the resurgence of swing roughly half a century later shows how the legacy of totalitarianism has sharpened aesthetic debate for us. Note the urgency when an anonymous writer of an online essay about the revival asserts that

> East Coast Swing is more of a purer, faster, real Savoy Ballroom type of swing, while the West Coast Swing Style is a sultrier, slower variation of the Savoy Lindy Hop. The East Coast Swingers find West Coast overly sexual, while West Coast aficionados find New York's traditional Lindy as too wild. There is some bad blood flowing between the two styles because each fears losing dancers to the other side.

The competing interpretations of the dance, one "purer" than the other, and made more dire by the threat of "bad blood," indicate that for some of its adherents, swing revivalism was more than a fun weekend diversion. But with the Nazi context removed, what, we wonder, is the harm of losing dancers "to the other side"? What does it mean to say (as the Nazis also did of the original *Swingjugend*) that other dancers are "overly sexual," or "too wild"? Unlike "Disco Demolition Night," this violence is merely implied. But what is implied violence doing in a discussion of art?

One somewhat uncomfortable answer is that implied violence is a way of showing love. Clearly the writer wouldn't be making these distinctions between East Coast and West Coast swing if she didn't *care* about the music. And isn't caring the point of being a music fan in the first place? Presumably we could say the same thing about Keith Jarrett's temper, or the rudeness of opera fans. Perhaps all are merely expressions of people so committed to the music they love that they are willing to do ridiculous, selfish, and even hurtful things to prove it. In principle that seems admirable. But on the other hand, why should proofs be necessary? Music is not a social problem to be solved, and musical taste is not a scientific theory, whose veracity or falseness can help or harm us. So why are we motivated to back up our opinions with rotten tomatoes or harsh words—or worse? Why can't we just love what we love, and allow other listeners to do the same?

Why, for instance, does Christopher Lydon, in a recent episode of the *Radio Open Source* podcast, feel compelled to argue that the Ellington Orchestra's performance at Newport (the same performance we looked at in chapter 1) helped define what he presumptively calls "the American century, the Jazz century"? Lydon cites a blog commenter, Shaman, who takes swing revivalism to an absurd extreme by asking whether "the rise and fall of America has anything to do with the rise and fall of Swing." Lydon and Shaman both privilege the connection between art and power—the lurking ideology Mehldau had warned against—but for Shaman, it is not enough merely to idolize swing. That idolization must also involve a putdown. "I think the messages of Rap," he later argues, "may come uncomfortably close to the uniquely French intellectual movement known as Existentialism, which, among other things, offered the world 'No Exit.'" This, ostensibly, is a bad thing, because "the Rap and Hip-Hop sound speaks first and foremost to the futility of its world. Don't you think? And futility don't swing." It is both an opinion and a call to arms.

The same lack of generosity permeates an otherwise interesting essay on Sharon Jones and the Dap-Kings (among other artists), by critic and composer George Grella:

That's perhaps the word of the current era, authenticity. It matters, but few people seem capable of evaluating it. The mass media exists for the most part to promote falseness as authenticity, and the damage it does would be minor if the political media had not embraced those values. . . . Recently, there was the spectacle of Helene Hegemann, plagiarist, declaring that "there's no such thing as originality anyway, just authenticity," completely unaware that she was damning herself as both unoriginal and inauthentic. Is it really so hard to judge? No, it's just those who get to do so in public forums are mostly unqualified.

A thoughtful observer of the contemporary music scene, Grella nevertheless indulges numerous qualities of the music ideologue in this post: hyperseriousness (authenticity "matters"), an appeal to authority (the qualified judges implied by the last sentence), a moral conviction (Hegemann "was damning herself"), a branding impulse (the career-summing pronouncement chucked at "Helene Hegemann, plagiarist"—all of eighteen at the time), a link between music and politics ("the danger it does would be minor if the political media had not embraced those values"), and a stubborn traditionalism (earlier in the same piece Grella had dismissed pop star Beck as "gestural and insincere"—presumably because while both Beck and Sharon Jones borrow from African-American popular music, Beck does so more experimentally). Demonstrating how easily this stance can fall back on itself, there is an odd moment at the end of Grella's piece where, after discussing two new classical recordings, he declares one authentic and the other not, and concludes with a curt "true dat"—an awkward appropriation of street slang that, given his conservatory training, makes his insistence on authenticity elsewhere ring a little hollow.

The issue here, as I hope is obvious, is not that Grella, Shaman, Lydon, and the anonymous writer on swing express passion for music. Rather, by assuming a link between aesthetics and ethics, and by offering a one-dimensional response to the epistemology problem—our frustrating uncertainty about musical purpose, meaning, and definition—they misrepresent that passion. What is really at stake is not conviction about any loved work itself—after all, we love what we love—but existential anxiety that uses musical opinion in an attempt to establish the listener's identity, self-worth, and place in the world. And while such concerns do not always lead to actual violence, in the West they are situated in a context of competitive commerce. Authenticity discourse thus informs a social Darwinism for music—violence of a different sort, which we will look at in more detail in chapter 7. And it does so everywhere: in the polished writing of music marketing and PR; in the informal conversations that occur between musicians (I have personally had more than one friend proudly describe himself to me as a "jazz Nazi"); in new media, such as the *Pitchfork* blog, or the local alternative weekly, or the work of independent music bloggers, or the music Twitterati. Perhaps least surprisingly, it is found in old media—whether in *Rolling Stone* or the music pages of the *New York Times,* both understandably obsessed with hierarchy, given their own histories of cultural dominance. Eavesdrop on any of these contexts and you will become privy to heartfelt conversations about musical authenticity that are materially motivated by economic competition, philosophically motivated by urges to purism and ideology, and psychically motivated by the angst of self-definition—even when they are expressed in snarky, ironic prose.

Again, the extremism I've described does not account for the musical experience of all listeners in our culture. It may not even completely account for the musical experience of the critics I just examined, beyond their public personae. Yet even if what Dane Rudhyar once called "musical fascism" doesn't quite capture what's going on here, something akin to it exists today, and that is troubling enough. Indeed, Grella's idea that "few people" are "capable of evaluating" authenticity is nonsensical. Anyone with an opinion is "capable" of evaluating, proclaiming, or denying authenticity. That is precisely the problem. Many do so, loudly and daily—often parroting Grella's claim to exclusivity.

COMPARATIVE AUTHENTICITY

The Big Question: What is the most influential song of all time?
—*The Atlantic*

And so the yearning for musical authenticity is a broad phenomenon in our culture. Let's consider some of its more specific forms.

Authenticity is often claimed, for instance, in conversations about relative value—I call this usage *comparative authenticity*. One good example is the middlebrow impulse to identify "great music"—an impulse that informed the twentieth-century music appreciation movement, epitomized by recording anthologies issued by Time-Life or *Reader's Digest*. Comparative authenticity is also a standard motif of music reviews and their inherently posited hierarchies. "Music critics love to make lists," as Tom Moon puts it. "Given a few minutes, we can crank out a roundup of All-Time Best Singles, or Greatest Beethoven Symphony Performances, or the Most Mind-Bending Guitar Solos." Interestingly, when pressed, most critics will simultaneously disavow this practice, even as they participate in it. "Lists are ridiculous, but if you're going to vote, you have to play the game," Roger Ebert once wrote in the introduction to his own list of the "Greatest Films of All Time." That tension is typical.

Musicians and fans like to make lists too; *Rolling Stone* online, for instance, recently asked readers to rank the "Best Drummers of All Time." Though the project started out casually, almost as a joke—that is, with Ebert's notion of ridiculousness intact—it quickly devolved into something more heated and earnest. The crowdsourced results generated intense disagreement, at least as measured by the hundreds of comments appended to the post. "How the shit Danny Carey didn't end up on this list is beyond me," complained one commentator. "Ringo? Give me a freaking break. He isn't even in the top thousand," added another. "Go to YouTube and check out some Derrick Roddy, then let's think about it," grumbled a third. With such a divergence of opinion, it seems the main beneficiary of the list was *Rolling Stone,* which had capitalized on an effective way to drive eyeballs to its website.

While the passion on display here was admirable—and it is important that it was literally on display, given the online context—"The Best Rock Drummer of All Time," as *Rolling Stone* knew full well, is a meaningless, impossible category, a cartoonish simplification of ambiguous perceptual phenomena. It posits authenticity as a binary, relational quality, dependent upon its inverse. It suggests that a thing can only be called authentic if we assume the absence of authenticity in the things it is being compared to. (Think of Shaman's impulse to belittle rap and hip-hop as a way of validating swing.) None of the three musicians just cited—Ringo Starr, Danny Carey, Derrick Roddy—can be "the best drummer of all time" until it is proved that all other drummers are unworthy of the title, proof that is impossible for practical if not aesthetic reasons. Who among us has heard all of the world's rock drummers? And of the rock drummers we *have* heard, who among us has heard everything they have ever played?

The catch—and the other facet of authenticity revealed here—is that exchanges like this have a certain social value. (Again, the extensive comment stream is instructive.) Ultimately, the criteria by which we measure drumming greatness—playing "in the pocket," say—are not inherently meaningful, but derive their importance from how they are deployed in the context of a community. They provide a set of shared claims for like-minded listeners. And that alone makes comparative authenticity tempting and easy to engage in, despite the fact that, like Ebert, many of us who do so simultaneously recognize the silliness of the enterprise. In a way we assume that claiming comparative authenticity is the price we must pay for sharing our musical passions. Trying to discover the best drummer of all time may be an empty exercise—on some level we don't really care to have an answer—but we enjoy it anyway because it helps define us as a community of musicians and fans.

Still, in the end that enjoyment is superficial. No matter how you look at it, comparative authenticity is a tricky concept to sustain on its own terms. If we take it literally, as it demands, it cannot be spread across instances of a thing, lest the original designation be diluted. We can't "agree to disagree" about the best drummer of all time—there has to actually be one for the label to have any value. Further, a thing cannot be *partly* authentic in the comparative sense—that is already a dilution. (Ringo Starr cannot "sort of" be the best drummer of all time.) When we praise an individual recording as "definitive," then—as many CD reissue marketers love to do—we should understand the impossibility of what we are actually saying: that there is a quality of truth that that recording possesses to the exclusion of all other examples of the music it contains. We cannot say any other performance or recording could also be authentic (or definitive), because that would undercut the point of making the comparison in the first place.

TAXONOMICAL AUTHENTICITY

Why are you bent on destroying the classical music of America with watered-down something else?

—Albert Reingewirtz, in a comment left on NPR's *A Blog Supreme* website

Ultimately, comparative authenticity is used to organize musical experience, serving the production not just of lists, but databases. For that slightly different emphasis, we could devise a slightly different name: *taxonomical authenticity*. Typical statements in this mode might be, "Green Day is an authentic punk band" (or not), or "*Nashville Skyline* is an authentic country record" (or not), or "This is an authentic performance of Hildegard von Bingen's *Scivias*" (or not).

The immediate problem here is that it takes a bit of willful intellectual laziness to make any such categorization stick. In order to gloss over the many contradictory traits any work might evince, we have to rationalize. What kind of music did Ellington make? Was it blues? Was it jazz? Was it a new kind of classical music? Was it pop? Was it avant-garde? Fans and scholars have described it in all of these ways. Ellington himself complicated the issue by famously declaring his own resistance to any label at all—his mantra was to get "beyond category"—and by insisting that there are only two kinds of music, good and "the other kind." And yet if we took Ellington at his word, refusing to categorize him, we'd be hard pressed to ever find his music in the local record shop, let alone on iTunes. Perhaps we could solve this problem with a simple alphabetical scheme—perhaps that would enable us to organize music without imposing genre—yet if we did not already know what we were looking for, the chances of finding Ellington's music in an alphabetized array of hundreds of thousands of titles would still be rather small. Not surprisingly, taxonomical authenticity remains a more appealing solution.

But it's a solution that also generates problems. Consider the category in which Ellington is usually placed: jazz. Audiences not immersed in this music may only be familiar with its beret-wearing hipster stereotype, born of the beatnik era—for many, that's the taxonomically authentic category. But the truth is that in jazz's short history, it has developed along rather volatile lines, changing significantly every decade or so—in part through the influence of recording technology, which disseminated each subgenre with unprecedented speed. Given this constant change, plus the layman's accusation (however unfair) that jazz is inaccessible, not to mention the concern for audience growth expressed by many younger market-savvy musicians, it is not surprising that the "jazz community," such as it is, would periodically seek stability by defining an "authentic" form of the music. In fact, jazz has already gone through two revivals, both driven by this impulse. In the post–World War II era, traditionalists—mocked as "moldy figs"—prompted a return to early styles, in a reaction to the (then) provocative and aggressive new stance of bebop. Ironically, in the 1980s, bebop itself became a repertory style, prompting jazz's own neoclassical movement (a riff on the Stravinskyan neoclassicism we looked at earlier).

The tensions caused by the development of neoclassical jazz were quickly subsumed under the rubric of the so-called Jazz Wars. Composer Darcy James Argue neatly summarized that conflict in 2008:

> One side—the traditionalist faction—was spearheaded by Wynton Marsalis and his *consiglieri,* writer, and critic Stanley Crouch—both tireless defenders of the essential virtues of swing, blues, and standards, both deeply suspicious of outside influences, especially those they saw as coming from popular culture or "modern European concert music." The other side, a ragtag coalition of those left excluded by this narrow view, lacked a unifying figurehead of comparable stature and influence, but they are perhaps best described as "those who don't think Miles Davis was a sellout for going electric, and who don't think Cecil Taylor's whole style is merely derivative of the European avant-garde."

This summation can be distilled even further: at their most intense, the Jazz Wars were driven by a fundamental disagreement over what exactly constituted "authentic jazz," and the Ellingtonian question of whether "jazz" was even the right label for the music (a version of the debate most recently raised by trumpeter Nicholas Payton, who proposed a new label altogether: "Black American Music," or "BAM").

Marsalis and Crouch may have "spearheaded" late-twentieth-century neoclassicism in jazz, but the movement had plenty of other spokespeople. In 1990, for instance, writer Tom Piazza penned "The Shock of the Old," an essay on the Classical Jazz at Lincoln Center series, one of the best-known jazz repertory programs. In it, he describes a (then) recent performance of "Diminuendo and Crescendo in Blue":

> For the second year running, twenty-three-year-old tenorist Todd Williams, who plays with Wynton Marsalis's septet, hit the ball out of the park on a Paul Gonsalves feature. Last year, Williams took on Gonsalves's role in the series' performance of "Diminuendo and Crescendo in Blue." Gonsalves caused an uproar at the 1956 Newport Jazz Festival by playing 27 blues choruses on tenor at a rocking medium tempo in the middle of the extended piece. At Classical Jazz last year, Williams truly recreated the moment—not by playing Gonsalves's solo note for note, but by playing something original that fit idiomatically with what Gonsalves had done. As a result, he generated the same kind of excitement Gonsalves had.

It's a confusing paragraph. Although Piazza ostensibly recognizes Williams's originality, he also imposes the burden of a specific recreation. In fact, when Piazza says that what Williams played fit "idiomatically" with Gonsalves's 1956 performance, he is being inexact. It is true that by 1956 Gonsalves had established a recurring role in "Diminuendo"—an "idiom" of sorts. But when Piazza says Williams "truly recreated the moment" of Newport, he means that Williams matched *a specific recording of a specific solo.*

One could argue that "a specific recording of a specific solo" is an unreasonable standard to which to hold a later improvisation, or that it is absurd to define jazz with respect to specific solos (rather than to improvisation in general). But at least Piazza absolves Williams of having to play the 1956 Gonsalves performance note for note. Critic Francis Davis, describing a 1988 concert by the Mingus Big Band—a posthumous repertory group, consisting at the time largely of former Mingus sidemen—points out how taxonomical authenticity could be taken even that far, writing with disappointment that "it was painful to watch the great Jaki Byard tentatively reading passages that he probably made up from scratch (at the composer's angry urging) twenty-five years earlier." It is hard to imagine why anyone would even want to attempt such a feat, except out of a paranoid concern for shoring up a threatened notion of "real jazz."

To be fair, from the perspective of the new century, some of these tensions have dissipated. It is easy to hold Piazza and his ilk up as extremists: "The Shock of the Old" is emblematic of a particularly vivid phase of the taxonomical authenticity polemic in jazz. Today, the mention of "Jazz Wars" is as likely to produce an exasperated sigh, particularly among younger musicians, as it is to bait engagement on one side or the other. In part this is because, as time passes, it has become increasingly clear that the neoclassicists have hardly been the only ones to invoke taxonomical authenticity to buttress their claims. In 2009, when *Jazz Times,* a mainstream jazz publication, temporarily went out of business, Chris Rich, the effusive advocate of left-leaning music, scoffed at its demise, implicitly accusing it of helping to make jazz too commercial, accessible, and predictable. Rich coined a memorable phrase—"the Middle Mind mediocrity of NPR fern bar jazz"—to describe what he saw as the watered-down quality of this form of the music, implying that it wasn't "real" jazz. But as fellow blogger and journalist David Adler objected (fairly, I think), "This sort of self-righteous, us-versus-them, marginalized-and-proud-of-it blather is as suffocating as any hegemonic corporate jazz I've come across." (Rich later softened his stance.)

Yet the fact that Adler demonstrated an admirable evenhandedness here does not mean that the tension he was responding to no longer wields any influence over jazz discourse, even today. Argue may have concluded that the Jazz Wars were "officially over" in his 2008 piece, but his own survey of the contemporary scene suggested more of a limited rapprochement. For every member of the jazz community who seems done with the issue—one might argue for the mellowing of Marsalis, for instance—there are others who continue the fight. Argue cites the example of "most college jazz programs," which have ignored "the vitality and diversity of developments in jazz since the '60s—which, at this point represents more than half of jazz's recorded lifespan." Things have certainly changed since those words were written—thanks in part to the pedagogical efforts of musicians like Argue himself—but some notion of authentic jazz (and some resistance to same) still informs jazz education. And given the fact that most upcoming jazz musicians are institutionally trained, the possibility of future skirmishes should not be dismissed.

In fact, two years after the publication of Argue's piece, Jason Marsalis (Wynton's younger brother) recorded his infamous "Jazz Nerds International" video, a comic rant that spread quickly through the community, thanks to the networking power of YouTube. "Jazz nerds" was Marsalis's satirical term for the primarily young musicians—students in their teens or early twenties—who had ignored what Marsalis assumed should count, categorically, as jazz. Ironically, such students were the direct beneficiaries of the surge in jazz education that the Marsalis family helped to inspire in the first place, during the earliest phase of the Jazz Wars. But with his video, Marsalis reignited what had seemed only minutes before to be a cold debate, over the protests of many who continued to maintain that the issues it raised were no longer pertinent to jazz culture.

The pattern would be repeated in 2013, with the appointment of pianist Vijay Iyer as a MacArthur Foundation Fellow. That appointment generated a heated backlash from more straight-ahead players, exemplified perhaps by pianist Kenny Drew Jr., who took to Facebook and posted videos of his own playing, framed with comments like, "Here's some real swing for your ass MacArthur Foundation & Vijay Iyer!"

EXPRESSIVE AUTHENTICITY

I wish we lived in a time when there wasn't such a premium put on things being real.

—Mike Doughty

Taxonomical and comparative authenticity are complemented by what Andrew Potter calls *expressive authenticity*—what he defines as "a true expression of the artist's *self,* her *vision,* her *ideals,* or perhaps her community, culture, or 'scene.'" More simply, expressive authenticity is the conviction that an artist can, and ought to, speak in her own voice. For our purposes, it is a corollary to traditional authorship: the idea of one's "own" voice requires both a denial of collaboration and an assumption that voices can exist independent of one another.

Expressive authenticity can be found under other names too; consider the honest signal theory of biology, or the facial action encoding system of psychology—both attempts to correlate the external expression of an organism with its inner state. Also relevant is psychologist Roger Watt's idea that listeners personify their music—as though it has emotions, a gender, or personality traits—holding it to standards of truthfulness expected from other human beings in daily life. Expressive authenticity may even be seen as a defense against aesthetic formulae, an implicit critique of algorithms as diverse as Irving Berlin's list of "nine inviolable rules for writing a successful popular song"; the "cultural technology" claimed by noted K-pop impresario Lee Soo-man; the computer-driven music of Emily Howell (David Cope's composing software); or a recent *Wall Street Journal* article that pseudoscientifically claimed to reveal the "anatomy of a hit."

Some of the loudest authenticity scandals of recent years—Mike Daisey's interview with *This American Life,* James Frey's book *A Million Little Pieces,* the *lonelygirl15* videos posted on YouTube—have been more specifically violations of expressive authenticity. In these examples, the controversy arose when the work was accused of being an untruthful representation of its author—his research, his biography, her online presence. And yet a problem should already be apparent here. Who gets to decide what is or is not a "truthful representation" of another human being? To make that determination, we have to presume to know the essence of another mind or soul. And that, at the risk of stating the obvious, is an absurd proposition. Who am I to say when you are or are not being true to "you" (whatever that is)? If we are honest, most of us have a hard enough time answering this question even when we apply it to ourselves.

Yet we are tempted to make claims about another person's "true self," Potter suggests, because of our facile willingness to link expressive authenticity with the more quotidian question of a work's material provenance (what Denis Dutton refers to as its "nominal authenticity"). In the process we muddy the question of honest self-expression by confusing it with the work of art historians, who are professionally concerned with keeping track of who created what. Is the painting I just paid a few hundred million dollars for really a Picasso? It is an understandable inquiry for the collector, but it is a leap to go from that question—which it seems to me has a relatively straightforward, if philosophically incomplete answer—to a contemplation of whether Picasso was being true to himself if and when he painted it.

And yet we fall for the expressive authenticity claim with frustrating regularity, particularly in music. Potter remarks that

> virtually every artist of note over the past fifty years has had their expressive authenticity called into question. Elvis was just a white boy stealing from the real blues musicians, and the Monkees were just aping the Beatles. The Sex Pistols didn't emerge organically out of the London punk scene of the 1970s but were created out of whole cloth by fashion impresario Malcolm McLaren. And so on, down to bands such as the Jon Spencer Blues Explosion and The Strokes, who were both dismissed by some critics as consisting of trust-fund babies who hadn't earned the gritty street cred advertised by their music.

Already this is an impressive list of artists, never mind similar controversies in other genres (in classical music, Joyce Hatto comes to mind). But the gold standard of expressive authenticity betrayal was Milli Vanilli, the late 1980s pop duo whose lip-synching scandal led to their becoming a stubborn cultural metaphor for insincerity. Indeed, we still use the qualifier "the Milli Vanilli of" pejoratively. Geoffrey Dunn recently called Sarah Palin the "Milli Vanilli of American politics," and Graham Filler referred to ESPN as the "Milli Vanilli of Sports Coverage," while Kathleen Schmidt advised writers not to pay for reviews, for fear of becoming the "Milli Vanilli of book publishing." It is the metaphor that refuses to die.

At the time of the original scandal, group members Rob Pilatus and Fabrice Morvan had enjoyed a very successful year, with a hit album, *Girl You Know It's True,* that had gone platinum six times, spawned three number one singles, and earned a Best New Artist Grammy, as well as a few American Music Awards. But we know the rest of the story. In 1990 producer Frank Farian revealed that Pilatus and Morvan did not actually sing on *Girl,* an admission followed by almost universal condemnation, as the group found itself up against a zeitgeist that was in no mood to compromise with inauthenticity. The Grammy was revoked. Numerous lawsuits were filed on behalf of "deceived record buyers." Angry fans were prompted to send in for a rebate. Milli Vanilli songs were removed from radio playlists. The album was deleted from Arista Records' catalog. Even politicians became involved in the controversy, as when a New Jersey congressman tried to prohibit unacknowledged lip-synching.

Faced with this precipitous turn of events, Pilatus and Morvan resorted to play as damage control—call it their postmodern defense—by making fun of themselves in a chewing gum commercial. But the scorn only intensified. The real Milli Vanilli singers (Brad Howell, John Davis, Jodie Rocco, Linda Rocco, Charles Shaw) garnered little public sympathy—unlike Martha Wash, a later victim of lip-synching injustice. Morvan and Pilatus responded to charges of audience betrayal by calling the agreement to use other singers "a pact with the devil"—a not wholly illegitimate defense, given that both had escaped relative poverty through a lucrative contract with Farian, who in turn had insisted that they lip-synch. Both continued to work in the music business, with little success. Pilatus eventually died of a drug overdose, an outcome of abuse exacerbated by the situation, and an uncomfortable reminder of how the implied violence of authenticity discourses can occasionally be realized.

Decades later, we have to wonder: Was the outrage really warranted? Did it make sense? Why, in particular, were former *fans* so unforgiving? Did the music suddenly sound different once the Grammy was revoked? Or was the audience merely lashing out, embarrassed by their own unrealistic desire for artists who could sing, dance, and look good at the same time? There was an unpleasant whiff of retribution about the whole affair, as if the band was getting its just deserts for having become too popular too quickly. (Admittedly, Pilatus didn't make any friends when he claimed to be "the new Elvis.") More important, the retribution seemed manufactured; the anger about authenticity itself seemed inauthentic. After all, Milli Vanilli did not single-handedly destroy the integrity of the music business, as so much of the criticism suggested. What happened was made possible by a context.

Long before Milli Vanilli, such important music-oriented television programs as *American Bandstand, Soul Train,* and *Top of the Pops* had all relied on lip-synching, eliciting little complaint from their large audiences. MTV and the emergence of music video as a commercial force merely capitalized on and exploited that dynamic. When Michael Jackson famously lip-synched "Billie Jean" at a Motown anniversary concert in 1983 (the same year as the "While You Were Art" concert, by the way), he marked what Jaap Kooijman called a "shift from live performance to the re-enactment of the imagery of the music video." Subsequent pop performers—Madonna, Britney Spears, Janet Jackson, Justin Timberlake—all came to rely on lip-synching to execute increasingly complex stage presentations, following Jackson's lead. For these artists, and many others, lip-synching has been "largely uncontested," Kooijman argues, because "contemporary audiences prefer to see their superstars present a visual spectacle that re-enacts the music video, rather than hear them sing a live rendition of their hit songs." In fact, Milli Vanilli too was initially given a pass when their playback technology malfunctioned during a 1989 show. The band was embarrassed, but MTV's Julie Brown reported that the audience hardly noticed or cared.

Perhaps the assumption that artists like Jackson were at least capable of "really" singing, even if they didn't always choose to, made them less susceptible to the sort of criticism that ultimately destroyed the careers of Pilatus and Morvan. But the situation was not so simple. Importantly, the industry's interest in expressive authenticity had ticked upward in this period. MTV's *Unplugged,* for instance, which premiered in 1989, featured artists associated with electrified music (Rod Stewart, Bon Jovi, Nirvana, and others) performing stripped-down versions of their material, on mostly acoustic instruments. The conceit was intended to capture something more genuine about the performers, but the show's title was misleading, as, regardless of the instruments used, these performances, by virtue of the fact that they were broadcast on cable television, still required amplification and electricity. Instruments and vocals were miked, and except for a small live audience, most listeners could only experience the music through the speakers of their (plugged-in) television sets and, later, in CD releases of the same material, played on their (plugged-in) stereo systems. Indeed, seen in the context of the Milli Vanilli backlash, the *Unplugged* phenomenon recalls the paradoxes of the 1960s folk movement, whose audiences infamously booed Bob Dylan for playing electric guitar during his set at the 1965 Newport Folk Festival—even though they had gladly accepted electrical recording as a way for Dylan to disseminate his material in the first place.

The point is that the "scapegoating" of Milli Vanilli (as Ted Friedman so nicely put it) conveniently ignored the fact that in the modern music industry, the group's failure to sing on *Girl You Know It's True* is merely one morsel plucked from a veritable smorgasbord of deceptions music technology routinely makes possible, even inevitable. Nor are these deceptions endemic to pop. The classical pianist Glenn Gould annoyed a lot of people in 1966 by openly acknowledging the value of audio splicing, the tape-based forerunner of today's digital cut and paste. Splicing produced a performance that was not "real" in any way the listener was traditionally used to, even though when done well it could *sound* real. Irked by that slippage, many of Gould's peers treated the technique with the same repugnance that would later be directed at lip-synching. In fact, in 1952, a Milli Vanilli–esque uproar followed the revelation that soprano Elisabeth Schwarzkopf had sung a high C for Kirsten Flagstad on a recording of Wagner's *Tristan und Isolde*. When Gould criticized the antiediting camp for being defenders of "aesthetic morality," he used the *Tristan* recording as an example. "Elisabeth Schwarzkopf appends a missing high C to a tape of *Tristan* otherwise featuring Kirsten Flagstad," Gould grumbled, "and indignant purists, for whom music is the last blood sport, howl her down, furious at being deprived a kill."

Music technology, from the purist's perspective, interferes with expressive authenticity, forcing the dissociation of a voice—whether it comes out of a throat or out of an instrument—and its producing body. And while by the twenty-first century many listeners may have become inured to splicing and even lip-synching—after all, both practices have been around for decades now—this underlying fear of technologically produced dissociation is still with us. Auto-tune, a software tool designed to fix bad intonation, but also one of the distinctive production sounds of the last ten years, is a more recent variant of the problem. Auto-tune is simultaneously popular and despised, but the latter reputation comes from its ability to deceive—a kind of musical cosmetic surgery, it creates an artificially perfect performance, depriving a singer of her natural voice. This explains why critic Neil McCormick called it "a particularly sinister invention," and why in 2010, *Time* magazine named it to their list of the "Fifty Worst Inventions," a distinction it shared with more obviously horrific technologies like Agent Orange and DDT. The software's capacity for artificiality is also exploited in the "Songify the News" video series (formerly known as "Auto-Tune the News"), where comedy issues from the juxtaposition of the seriousness of current events, the self-importance of the typical newscaster, and the striking effect of auto-tune, blatantly used. This juxtaposition suggests the insincerity of television journalism—yet it can't help but also remind us of a similar dynamic in the music industry.

I'm no fan of auto-tune. Looked at strictly in terms of expressive authenticity, however, there is no reason why it should be singled out for ridicule or scorn while other studio technologies, like chorus effects or distortion, are overlooked. Distortion is even named after its own lack of authenticity—a distorted sound is by definition not an "original" sound, but one that has been intentionally corrupted by machines. Yet a distorted guitar is hardly ever accused of lacking expressive authenticity—if anything, it epitomizes the concept, seeming to convey a greater communicative vitality than can be accessed with more subdued timbres. The popular stereotype of the air guitarist, with her flamboyantly emotive grimace and arched back, merely underscores that connection—imitation being a form of flattery—in a way once exploited by Guitar Hero, a video game in which the goal was to mimic someone *else's* expressive authenticity, the more precisely the better. "I truly feel like the Guitar Hero games gave players some tiny, almost allegorical sensation approximating what being a real rock star feels like," enthuses Darren Franich, describing his initial experience with the game. And yet Guitar Hero was no less fake than auto-tune. We can only marvel at the cultural ironies that allow one of these technologies to be labeled "sinister" while the other is treated as an allegorical approximation of reality.

THE AUTHENTICITY PARADOX

What the Milli Vanilli case finally demonstrates is authenticity as a knee-jerk response, an unbalanced obsession with the impossible. To riff on the popular definition of insanity, we keep reaching for something that isn't there, realizing it isn't there, and then reaching again (and again). Going on anyway requires a willing suspension of critical disbelief—and so coexisting with our capacity for outrage at every violation of truthfulness is a kind of apathy about the deceptions that are now possible. Listeners, after all, can no longer convincingly claim to having been duped by technological manipulation: technological manipulation is everywhere. Popular software—consider Garageband, or MultiTrack DAW (for the iPhone)—has dispersed the multitrack aesthetic to an extent that even Zappa and Gould would probably find surprising. Children's toys, like the "Paper Jamz Kids Microphone," offer crude approximations not only of auto-tune, but various chorusing and harmonic effects. All sorts of digital tools, from Microsoft Word to Photoshop, allow users to cut and paste, taking the fundamental logic of the audio splice and writing it large across culture. And at one time or another, most people have attended amateur drama and dance productions that make uncontroversial use of canned music.

Indeed, listeners can no longer claim to having been duped in general; being duped is part of what makes the global music ecosystem work. Assuming otherwise, we hover in the realm of hypocrisy. In 2005, *Pitchfork* celebrated the success of indie band Clap Your Hands Say Yeah, arguing that they proved "it's still possible for a band to get heard, given enough talent and perseverance, without a PR agency or label," and adding disingenuously, "Damn, maybe this is how it's supposed to work!" The purported insight here was that Clap Your Hands had succeeded entirely on their own merits; unlike other hip bands, they were not at all manufactured by the discursive organs of the industry. But that argument assumed the reader wasn't aware that *Pitchfork* was itself one of those discursive organs; that it had an interest in being seen as a convincing bellwether for indie rock; that it had helped construct the band in the very piece that celebrated its lack of construction.

Sometimes these contradictions evoke not only hypocrisy, but absurdity, and perhaps a little sadness too. The tribute band phenomenon, for instance—the rock version of Jazz at Lincoln Center—is stuck in a world of mixed messages. At their most endearing, these bands seem to playfully epitomize *in*authenticity, often involving elements of camp and parody, as in the example of We Got the Meat, the all-male tribute to the 1980s girl group the Go-Gos. But the fact that tribute bands have become big business—in some cases selling millions of dollars' worth of tickets annually and earning their practitioners a better living than peers recording original music for major labels—suggests that something more is going on. Tribute band fans are like art collectors who settle for prints because they are cheaper, and because from a distance sometimes it is hard to tell the difference anyway. But is this philistinism, or something else?

Even with the explicit understanding that tributes are not "the real thing," it is striking that many in the scene take the experience seriously. "If we dare attempt this tribute to Rush," says Chris Nelson, a member of a band called Lotus Land, "we better do a really good job." The Return, based on the early period of the Beatles, claims that they stand out in the field because of their "truly authentic" performances— "the very essence of the Beatles themselves." ("Seeing the Return is like traveling back to Liverpool in the early 1960s," muses Jim Weiss, quoted on the band website.) Ruth Newell notes that tribute bands even have "groupies with their cell phones held high in the air videotaping the performance as if it were really Guns n' Roses on stage."

David Suisman, writing about the rapacious early years of Tin Pan Alley, suggests that contemporary listeners may have realized they were being taken advantage of by the hard-sell marketing of the typical song plugger, "but if they liked a song enough, they did not mind going along as willing accomplices." And that may be the best explanation of the literal stance toward authenticity as well. Our love of the music invites our complicity in the received idea that it could be authentic—and maybe that complicity periodically requires a purge. That, I think, is ultimately what happened to Milli Vanilli. As Friedman points out, the band became "the recording industry's sacrifice meant to improve the integrity of the rest of their product—as if the music marketed under the names U2 or Janet Jackson weren't every bit as constructed and mediated, just because the voices on the records matched the faces in the videos."

Authenticity, it seems, is a fickle master.

4

DO YOU HEAR WHAT I HEAR?

Every act of perception is to some degree an act of creation.

—Gerald Edelman

An old friend of mine once defined tragedy as when two people are right. In art, everybody is right. Systems are right. Tonality is right. Functional harmony is right. It's all right.

—Morton Feldman

In his book *Tone Deaf and All Thumbs?* neurologist Frank R. Wilson cites a sharp disagreement between two critics writing about the same performance of César Franck's Symphony in D Minor. In Wilson's telling, the contrast is almost comical. While one critic appreciated the "fine, resonant, splendidly balanced interpretation that was elicited from the players," noting that "the little answering phrases between strings and woodwinds in the first movement, for example, were neatly done, the brass accomplished throughout," the other was far less generous, complaining wryly that "the conductor waved his hand in the direction of pianissimo every now and again, but nothing came of the gesture. He asked for more sound when the men of the brass section were already red in the face and, worst of all, he let the orchestra play out of tune."

The contrast is an object lesson in, among other things, the perils of taxonomical authenticity. Each of Wilson's critics had a different conviction about how Franck's symphony should have been rendered in order to count as a truthful example of that work. Yet their disagreement is hardly anomalous, for it parallels discrepancies in many areas of musical discourse, not just newspaper concert reviews. Even arguments cloaked in the robes of academic sophistication fall prey to this sort of head butting. As ethnomusicologist John Blacking has pointed out, music scholarship is "full of contradictory explanations of the same music. Everyone disagrees hotly, and stakes his academic reputation on what Mozart really meant in this or that bar of one of his symphonies, concertos, or quartets." Nor is the dynamic limited to classical music. Consider, for instance, the fundamental incompatibility of the notoriously cantankerous Frankfurt School intellectual Theodor Adorno, with his avowedly antipop aesthetic, and his postmodern descendant Richard Shusterman, who sought to recuperate popular music from Adorno's scathing critique.

Importantly (and yet frustratingly), such disagreements are rarely random or unfounded; often they are well argued and engaging. Wilson points out that in the case of the two Franck critics, the disagreement was not merely a "casual difference of opinion." Instead, "either one of the two was guilty of malpractice, or they heard separate and contrasting fragments of the same performance." I would go further: these critics—like all critics, and like all listeners—heard different works. And they were, as Feldman would put it, "all right." The point is that while we readily admit there is no one way to understand a work of art, no one manner of perceiving—"all art is subjective" is one of the great clichés of aesthetic dialogue—we ignore the consequences of that statement: that there is, as far as perception goes, never a singular work to agree about in the first place. Instead, we cling to the reified idea of music, using it, in the worst-case scenario, to police the responses of others, or else, more kindly, to prioritize the overlap in our perceptions—as with, for example, the concert protocol that calls for simultaneous group applause, and the impression of consensus it produces by eliding complexly differentiated responses into a symbolic burst of ostensible mass agreement.

The situation is complicated by the fact that as listeners and performers, many of us *long for* consensus. "Collective music making may encourage social cohesions," neuroscientist Daniel Levitin writes, following Clifford Geertz, because "humans are social animals, and music may have historically served to promote feelings of group togetherness and synchrony." The phenomenon of entrainment suggests that there is even a physiological basis for these feelings. Yet there is more going on here. It is not enough for most listeners that music making evokes "feelings of group togetherness"—many of us also, on some level, want our experience of music to be *knowable* by our fellow listeners, and even transferable to them (which is why most critics attempt to persuade rather than report). When it comes to art, "not only do we dislike physical isolation," as Leonard Meyer points out, "but we want to share our emotional life with others." That desire is commonly expressed by the platitude that music is the "universal language." And it's a sentiment, not incidentally, that has deep connections to the history of the music industry—for instance, in the way Tin Pan Alley–era publishers and songwriters often repressed their own musical biases in favor of the presumed general taste of "the music-buying public." The irony is that despite Tin Pan Alley's material successes (and the successes of the music industry it helped spawn), it is misleading to suggest that even the most accessible pop song can ever be understood the same way by all listeners.

It is not that audiences lack common perceptual ground. It seems intuitively true that some sort of affinity is established when two or more people self-identify as fans of a given artist or work. The problem is in understanding what that really means—and what it cannot mean. We jump to conclusions about the replicability of our personal listening biases, but it may ultimately be that, as Blacking put it, the most we can expect of musical experience is to be "alone in company."

As the Greek philosopher Heraclitus had it, one can never step into the same river twice. That observation stemmed from the fact that, technically speaking, the water molecules that make up any river are always moving and never consistently in one place. Heraclitus may as well have added that two people can never step into the same river even once—though you and I may cross at the same geographical point, we will still be immersing ourselves in different manifestations of the river itself. In either case, the Heraclitean river argument is useful because it problematizes certain assumptions about our experience of the world as we imagine it to exist beyond our senses. Indeed, Heraclitus's observation is germane to a multitude of experiences. Gourmands, for instance, may share an affinity for a favorite recipe, but it would be absurd to suggest that any two diners could ever eat the same food. Friends may enjoy a mutual walk in the rain, but we wouldn't necessarily say they walk in the same rain. Whether we embrace, smell the roses, enjoy a sunset, or make love, in each case we share these experiences without literally sharing them. We might say, more exactly, that we coexperience them, but that we each do so from an exclusive, individuated standpoint.

The perception of music has this same paradoxical dual quality—it can be shared without really being shared. In the end, Wilson's quibbling critics inadvertently reveal this truism about listening, which is too often hidden by the will for collective agreement. Music is not the universal language, but rather, as I suggested at the outset of this book, an extensive network of individuated aural perceptions. This does not mean that it is "powerless to express anything," as Stravinsky infamously put it (echoing Cocteau before him, and Wilde before that), nor that it is the dreaded site of postmodern meaninglessness. Rather, music "expresses" prolifically, abundantly, flexibly—a feat achieved anew every time it is perceived, and as a function of each listener's perceptual involvement. It is, in a sense, an aural Rorschach test, containing at once the many meanings and emotions different listeners invest it with. As we listen, we produce a string of recompositions—or, in the metaphor of this book, *decompositions*—that continually undercut the assumption of authenticity with its stipulation about a single, pure work that is greater than and immune to the multiplicities of perception. In this sense claiming musical authenticity is the most misleading thing a listener can do.

In turn, the best response to the claim of musical authenticity—whether we're talking about the comparative, taxonomical, or expressive varieties—is to look carefully at perceptual variance. In his writing on tone deafness, Levitin muses that if between 3 and 10 percent of listeners (maybe more) "cannot distinguish musical tones a semitone apart, what are these people hearing when they listen to music?" That's the sort of question we should be asking with respect to *all* listening, whether it is done by a "normal" ear or not. Given our idiosyncrasies—the differing end results of mediation—what do each of us hear when we listen to music? The more possibilities we can demonstrate—and particularly if we can show that variance affects *everyone,* not just the listeners we happen to disagree with—the less support there is for the argument that music can ever be authentic in any of the ways I detailed in the last chapter. The challenge for the lover of authenticity is to explain why any of the many decompositions we habitually group under the heading of the "single work" are less true, simply because they have not been experienced as such by that individual.

Many books have been written about the variability of auditory perception. In the rest of this chapter I will trace merely the broadest outlines of how I think it functions. I remind the reader again of the metaphor of transduction, which describes the trajectory between a musical sound's source and its destination, allowing for vast possibilities of transformation and perceptual idiosyncrasy along the way. Theodore Gracyk gets at the complexity of this dynamic when he argues that authenticity, to the extent that it can be found at all, "can only be determined on a case-by-case basis, by inspecting the complex interplay of cultural processes, musician's intentions, and listeners' activities." I will look at the problem even more fundamentally, breaking the trajectory of listening into three distinct phases: the mediation that occurs as the sound is produced, the mediation that occurs as the sound travels outward to a listener, and the mediation that occurs as a listener's brain processes the sound. Let's examine each phase in turn.

PHASE ONE: THE MEDIATION OF SOUND GENERATION

Musical sound physically begins with vibrations originating from some source, whether an instrument or a playback technology. These vibrations are affected by the source's material properties, as well as by the unique way it is used to produce the sound. Thus music comes not merely from a particular instrument, but a particular instantiation of a particular instrument, played in a particular way. In other words: not merely a guitar, but my acoustic-electric Takamine guitar, manufactured in 1989, and played with my hands, my aptitude for mind-body coordination, and my own musical sensibility, in early 2014, at a moment when I am feeling melancholy. Levitin notes that he can tell the difference between his 1956 Martin 000-18 acoustic guitar, his 1973 Martin D-18, and his 1996 Collings D2H "very clearly; they sound like different instruments, even though they are all acoustic guitars; I would never confuse one with another." Quite right: they sound like different instruments *because they are different instruments.* Different instances of each model are different instruments too. And each becomes a different instrument yet again in the hands of a different player.

If I were to play the introduction to "Stairway to Heaven"—that showpiece of beginning guitarists everywhere—on my Takamine, given the particulars I mentioned above, the song would exist in a unique way during that performance. If Jimmy Page, to my astonishment and delight, were to show up at my house, grab the Takamine out of my hands, and play that same introduction, it would exist in another way altogether (a much better way, I'll grant). While listeners who compared the two would more than likely recognize an identical (or very similar) series of pitches and rhythms, and, for convenience's sake, would probably categorize each as an example of "Stairway to Heaven," the material expression of the piece would have changed. But convenience be damned; each performance would actually be a remaking—a decomposing—not "again," but "anew." Each would be a different bite of the same meal.

The generative phase of music highlights the relevance of absolute processing, one of two types of perception that inform aesthetics. "Decades of research on music cognition," Levitin points out, "have shown that humans process music using both absolute and relational processing—that is, we attend to the actual pitches and duration we hear in music, as well as their relative values. The extent to which we use this dual mode of processing appears uniquely human." Relational processing is akin to what psychologists call "perceptual constancy"— the sense of cohesiveness we have about an object, regardless of the context in which we find it. Observing a car passing us on the street, we assume that it is the same vehicle before it reaches us as it is afterward, even though it looks and sounds rather different up close than it does from far away. And this form of understanding is of course essential for living in the "real world." Knowing that the "tiny" car you see from a distance will be "larger" when it gets close is all the incentive you need to step out of its path.

Yet we should not dismiss absolute processing, just because it is a less efficient way of experiencing the world, or because it more accurately describes what is happening as the sound is produced (before we have a chance, that is, to map its relations). And we also have to take the idea of absolute processing further than a consideration of mere "actual pitches and duration" if it is to be useful for the argument about perceptual variance. We need a concept of "quantum aesthetics"—again, something akin to Duchamp's "infrathin"—because what we are appreciating in absolute terms are often the smallest details of a sound. To the extent that each new performance of "Stairway to Heaven" is different, in other words, we must be prepared for the fact that the differences can be rather subtle. Relationally, we may detect a contour common to each instance of the song's melody, a general sequence of its harmony, a set of patterns established by its rhythm, and so on. If those perceptions are similar enough to what we understand "Stairway to Heaven" to be, then we will say the song is the same each time we hear it. But absolutely, we may perceive an endless array of differences. And philosophically, there is no reason to privilege relational perception over the absolute differences that obtain during the initial generation of sound, simply because the former makes it easier to talk about listening.

Indeed, in some ways, the problem of authenticity may arise from a desire to treat relational perception—which is after all a kind of "rounding off" of sensory experience—as if it is absolute. In our hypothetical example, most listeners (and rock fans in particular) would say that Page's performance of "Stairway," as compared to mine, was the authentic one. This is logical enough, given that Page is one of the official composers of the tune, and performed it on the original recording, as well as many times in concert. But what if we compare Page to himself? If authenticity is, as I have defined it, a singularly true experience of music, one that ignores perceptual variance—if we take the concept literally, on its own terms—how are we to choose which of Page's performances is authentic? In this *Gedankenexperiment,* there is no way for even Page himself to reproduce the exact same "vibrations originating from some source" that characterized any one of his performances. Even if he had used the same guitar in the writing, recording, and concert history of "Stairway," and brought it along to the hypothetical meeting at my house, the instrument would have been subject to the changes brought on by use and time: new strings (many times over), the wearing of the fretboard, the gradual decay or warp of the wood, the gradual oxidation of the metal. Page's operation of the instrument would have changed too. Aside from the new interpretive nuances that would enter each performance (some consciously, some not), his body, as all bodies inevitably do, would have continued to age. Any performance would always occur at what for him was a different point in his own biography, influencing the resulting music in some way.

What about the recorded version of "Stairway"? Couldn't we say that the officially released track, featured on the album *Led Zeppelin IV*, qualifies for authentic status, at least at the generative level? Admittedly, it is tempting to make that claim—as Levitin argues, "Recording introduced the idea of a 'master performance,' a single canonical, iconic version of a song," and thus "the standard way of thinking about popular music for the past fifty to a hundred years has been that a single 'official' version of the song exists." For most rock music, anyway, the "official" recording is what informs our idea of the reified song. But while such perspectives tell us something about listeners' respect for the commercial system of music, and about the perceptual habits that lead to the reification of music, they don't tell us much about authenticity. Even the least self-aware consumer recognizes that in a market context, qualities like popularity, commercial success, and critical acclaim—the qualities that help define Levitin's idea of a "master performance"—can be almost entirely unrelated to the music itself. And even if we could set aside the variances that obtain with remixes, rereleases, compilations, and cover versions, we would still have to recognize that copies of the same recording—like my scratched *Thriller* CD, described at the beginning of this book—are each unique in an absolute sense. As Colin Symes puts it, "Records are dynamic artifacts that have, after leaving the factory, 'careers' of their own as well as distinctive profiles of ownership and possession." Further, each individual recording becomes something new whenever it is played. (We will look at the problem of authenticity in recordings and live performance in more detail in chapter 5.)

Nor can we make the argument that is often made in classical music, that the performance of "Stairway to Heaven" that most conforms to the score is therefore the most authentic at the generative level. I own a volume of *Led Zeppelin Classics,* a compendium of sheet music published by Warner Brothers under the "Authentic Guitar Tab Edition" rubric. Despite this title, an interested student will quickly discover that there are multiple published sheet music versions of the tune, each with its own claim to legitimacy. Even more important, the music was not composed on paper in the first place: any available sheet music version is actually a transcription of the recording, a fact that disqualifies it as an authentic urtext. Interestingly, but not surprisingly given its claim of authenticity, the Warner Brothers volume makes no mention of the fact that it consists entirely of transcriptions. (We will look at the problem of authenticity in scores and transcriptions in more detail in chapter 6.)

Thus we are frustrated at every turn by the attempt to identify the one authentic generative performance of "Stairway to Heaven." In fact, we are unable to consistently identify what "Stairway to Heaven" even is. Is it a single, authentic performance? If so, how do we choose which one? Is it the sum total of all performances of that song? (One wonders if anyone has ever heard them all.) If so, does that include performances by guitarists other than Jimmy Page? And if so, which ones? Is it, more abstractly, some supposed ideal of the song, the song's metaphysical essence? And if so, how do we understand that essence, or transmit it to others, in a way unaffected by its material expression?

PHASE TWO: THE MEDIATION OF VECTOR

> Every single one of us, depending on where we're sitting, will experience this sound quite, quite differently.
>
> —Evelyn Glennie

And so there are numerous variations that occur at the moment of a sound's physical origin, numerous ways that material expressions of a composition—what we think of culturally as the reproduction of an unchanging, reified work—are altered with each iteration, before the performance's sound waves have traversed a given space and reached their first listener. But these issues become more complex once we take into account the changes wrought by the second stage of mediation. As they travel outward from a source, sound waves are dynamically altered by the materiality of an acoustic medium.

One way to get at what this means is to recognize that it is impossible for any one listener to have an overview—or, if you will, an "overhearing"—of the total sound produced in any environment. Listening always relies on a particular "point of hearing." (It is telling, by the way, that in English we lack a specific vocabulary to describe auditory perspective.) Moreland Perkins, in *Sensing the World,* asks us to imagine an explosion loud enough to be heard in all directions for many miles. "Do persons five miles from the explosion hear the same sound as those located one mile from it?" he asks. In one sense the answer is obviously yes, in that both groups of listeners are within earshot of the same sound waves, which Perkins describes as stretching in a train over the total area of its sounding. But these listeners don't hear each wave simultaneously, because it takes time for the sound to travel from a person who is a mile away to a person who is five miles away. Listeners at different places along that path actually perceive only a portion of the total sound. "The sound," Perkins writes, "must be said to last not for only a part of a second, as it appears to those who hear it to do, but for about twenty-five seconds, the period of time during which it is traveling to the most distant point at which it is audible." The result is that "the auditory impression that everyone who hears the explosion will have, that the sound lasts for only one second, will be egregiously mistaken."

This is a simplified example of the kind of variance that affects sound as it moves outward from its source. In practice, the situation is much more complicated. As sound issues from its locus of generation, its waves become differentiated. Some reach the listener unimpeded— imagine a pool ball that travels directly to a pocket on the table following an opening break. But some—to continue the pool analogy, think of the stray balls that ricochet off bumpers or other balls before arriving at the desired destination—bypass our ears at first, instead reaching walls, ceilings, counters, windows, other people's bodies, and so on. The latter are either reflected, with some alteration of sonic character, or absorbed, coming to the end of what George Wang describes as the sound's "life cycle." The first reflections to reach the ear from these other surfaces (instead of directly from the sound source itself) may come very quickly, and are often consciously perceived as direct sound by the listener. But there is also the more delayed arrival of sound waves that bounce off these surfaces later—what is usually called reverberation.

Thus when considering the movement of sound in a space, it is more than a mere "point of hearing" that we need to consider. That idea still suggests a one-to-one transmission between a sound source and a listener. But in a sense, sounds are always multiplied in the process of being transmitted. How that happens, and its effect on the sound, is determined in part by the architectural design and construction materials of the performance space. Concrete walls typically cause harsher reflections than wooden walls, and increase both the volume and the intensity of the sound. Carpeting, on the other hand, is more absorptive than wood, and has a dulling effect. Composers, aware of these distinctions, often write for specific spaces. Thurston Dart distinguishes between the brass consort music of Giovanni Gabrieli, written to be heard in a cathedral, and Hans Leo Hassler's music for the same instrumentation, written, in contrast, for the open air.

Like listeners within a five-mile radius of an explosion, listeners at different locations within a performance space will perceive the behavior of sound differently. At one seat, sound waves might arrive at a listener's ears in phase, moving together, synchronized and thus intensified. In another, they might go out of sync, and the effect might be very different—by moving at different speeds, waves have the potential to cancel each other out, and to hide or obscure aspects of the music. A striking example of the latter phenomenon is the offstage trumpet in Beethoven's Leonore Overture no. 3 (from the opera *Fidelio*), which can sometimes sound out of tune to an audience because curtains or the proscenium can mute its higher frequencies without similarly affecting the rest of the orchestra. The trumpet may sound just fine to the conductor or orchestra, but that's because they are both much closer to the source.

Producer Bob Margouleff calls this feature of sound "vector"—what we could also describe as music's directionality and physical movement. Importantly, the effect is not always obvious, because the idea of a spatial dimension to music comes very naturally to us—indeed, the ability to localize sound is an important part of our evolutionary inheritance. Thus we typically only notice vector as a characteristic of music when our expectations about it are frustrated—as was the case at the 1962 opening of the original Philharmonic Hall (now Avery Fisher Hall) at Lincoln Center in New York City, for example. The initially implemented design was acoustically disastrous. Severe echoes occurred at certain seats, and were so strong in some places that, as Robert Sekuler writes, they "caused a single note to sound like two notes." The acoustics failed to diffuse enough sound to adequately reach other seats. Because the stage was close to the ground, the bodies and clothing of the people in the first few rows absorbed much of the direct sound, producing a quieter experience for those in seats farther back. The orchestra too had difficulty hearing itself, because the backstage wall acted as a giant acoustic sponge. The general lack of low frequencies meant that the bass instruments were muted.

All of these were problems of acoustic design that were happily learned from and remedied. Yet even though the revised space better conformed to the audience's expectations of how music should sound, the bigger point is that the new listening experience was no more or less mediated than that of the original hall. The mediation of vector, in other words, is not endemic to "bad" spaces. No performance space, no matter how it is designed, can eliminate it, or the many different listening outcomes it produces. Even when we don't notice what is going on spatially, every seat in every venue participates, by virtue of its location, in the creation of a unique work with respect to each performance. Most modern recording studios are equipped with signal processors that mimic vector, enabling engineers to create an artificial space—and even a specific listening location within that space—for any recording. You can thus make your bedroom rendition of the introduction to "Stairway to Heaven" sound like it was played in a highly reverberant cathedral or a cramped nightclub. That the makers of these tools provide a range of choices speaks to the fact that, to paraphrase Feldman, they are all right. Some may be preferred over others, of course, depending on the style of music, the size of the ensemble, the listening preferences of the engineer, and so on. But questions of taste aside, such tools are appealing mostly because of the possibility of choice itself.

And so to return to our thought problem: imagine Jimmy Page performing the introduction to "Stairway to Heaven" in some hypothetically optimal hall—a location we'll consider because of the assumption that vector would no longer be an issue. The idiosyncrasy informing the initial generation of sound as it emerged from Page's guitar would in turn be processed in numerous ways as it traveled around the hall. The effects would be different—the piece would be different—depending on where one was sitting. Assuming Page stood exactly stage center and only faced forward during his entire performance (a big assumption, but one we can make for the purpose of argument), those seated on either side of the hall would experience differently emphasized characteristics of his instrument. Even controlling for motion, the sound of an acoustic guitar in a large concert hall does not emanate in all directions equally, from a single finite point. It is instead generated across most of the instrument's surface. The guitar strings vibrate along their entire length—a distance of a couple feet—as does the body of the guitar. (When recording the instrument, engineers place microphones at different spots in relation to its neck and sound hole, depending on the desired sound.) The sound of the strings being manipulated—the abrasiveness of the pick, or the softness of the fingertips, or the more acute tone created by the fingernails—would be more audible on the side of the hall closer to Page's picking (right) hand. On Page's left, fingers sliding along the fretboard from position to position would make another sound—a squeak very characteristic of acoustic guitar—which would be more audible on the side of the auditorium that was closer to his fretting hand. If the guitar were amplified, additional distinctions would occur, depending on the number of channels a listener could hear from her location, the "coloring" added by the mixing board and the speakers, and any effects that were added along the way.

So here we are, sitting in the audience. The sound hasn't even arrived at our eardrums yet, and already it has undergone two major transformations. Indeed, we have introduced even more confusion as to what the song in question actually *is,* beyond the fact of its physical complexity. What happens next?

PHASE THREE: THE MEDIATION OF SUBJECTIVITY

A delicate, sensitive ear is otherwise affected than that of a stronger, rougher nature. The tumult, the whistles, and the shrieks in which the latter delight, would throw the other into the highest state of alarm or discomfort.

—Dr. J. Mainzer

After reaching the eardrum, the already twice-mediated sound will be mediated a third time, processed by the psychological phenomenon of subjectivity—a word I am using in the general sense to describe how the acoustic information that arrives at a listener's eardrum is further shaped by consciousness and other activity of the mind. And here we arrive at the most complex form of mediation. What exactly do we do with all the data bombarding our ears? Science can tell us some things about this process, of course—and we do know more about how listening happens now than at any point in the past. In her research on musical perception, for instance, psychologist Isabelle Peretz has gone so far as to map a "modular model of music processing"—a sort of flow chart describing the pathways of audio information in the brain. Today we also understand more about how different regions of the brain—different cortexes—process specific parameters of music. Still, at a more abstract level, the question of subjectivity—what Steven Pinker calls "the raw sensation of toothaches and redness and saltiness and middle C"—remains "a riddle wrapped in a mystery inside an enigma."

It doesn't help that subjectivity is often discussed in terms of equally idiosyncratic (and equally elusive) concepts like taste (the impulses that lead us to the music we like), emotion (how music makes us feel), attention (what we choose to focus on when listening), and desire (what we want music to do for us). More helpfully, philosophers of mind use the word "qualia"—what Daniel Dennett calls "an unfamiliar term for something that could not be more familiar to each of us: the way things seem to us"—to describe this aggregate mental state, usually with the caveat that "the way things seem to us" cannot be articulated completely and objectively. It would, to take a clichéd example, be impossible for you to describe the color "red" to another person; ultimately, you would simply have to show them an instance of the color, as a way of demonstrating how red seems to you. But even that gesture would be of limited semantic utility, since we have no way to determine whether "the way things seem" is the same from person to person— whether the "red" you show me is the same color for both of us, even if we both agree we are seeing red. As far as we know, "redness" is not a quality of an object, but rather a function of how the object is perceived. The same is true of many musical concepts: pitch, volume, and key, for instance, are all psychological constructs, not things that already exist in the world—or, more specifically, in a given musical work. Indeed, a musical work is itself a psychological construct. As Bruce Smith puts it, in listening, "the physical facts of time and space become the psychological experience of time and space. In the listener's ear, frequency becomes pitch. Pressure becomes loudness. Noise, timbre, inharmonics, and vibrato become roughness, brightness, warmth, and quaver."

Unlike physical facts, however, psychological experience is notoriously resistant to articulation. What exactly *are* "pitch," "loudness," "roughness," "brightness," "warmth," and "quaver"? This problem of communicating "the way things seem"—the way music seems—means that the decompositional effect of subjectivity can be easy to miss. In fact, subjectivity rarely seems subjective to the person it belongs to. From my point of listening, a given performance of "Stairway to Heaven" seems unlikely to be very different from the way you, a fellow Led Zeppelin fan, hear it, especially if we both applaud enthusiastically when it is over. We assume there is nothing to discuss, because we assume we are hearing the same thing. But in some ways that may be a trick that our own subjectivity plays on us. The distinctions in our listening do not depend for their significance upon our conscious recognition or articulation; indeed, their importance to our aesthetic life may have nothing to do with whether or not we even know that they exist. As ethnomusicologist Kay Shelemay notes, in reference to musical intervals or gestures that at first blush appear to be identical across cultures: even when we assume of each other a similar perception, we may actually be conceiving things "very, very differently."

Science does raise an interesting point about authenticity, however. With its goal of objectivity, it seems to introduce the possibility of an authentic sound—a sound that is singularly true, regardless of our perception of it—something along the lines of what is revealed by an oscilloscope, or an electronic tuner, or an EEG of the listening brain. But many listeners who accept authenticity as a concept resist it when framed this way. That is, when it comes to aesthetics, the impression of qualia is strong enough to override the findings of science. "When we watch TV," Pinker writes, discussing a different sense (vision) in a way that has implications for the perception of music, "we stare at a shimmering piece of glass, but our surface-perception module tells the rest of our brain that we are seeing real people and places." Pinker calls this masking of reality a "cheat-sheet" and argues that it is "so deeply embedded in the operation of our visual brain that we cannot erase the assumptions written on it." The same dynamic applies to listening. We may rationally know, for instance, that a sound is a wave of vibration, but that's not how we experience it. Indeed, the idea of a "wave" of sound does not at all match how sound seems to us, certainly not in the way that other kinds of waves (ripples in a pool, for example) appear to be what they are.

Aural illusions are fascinating for this reason: they highlight the cognitive dissonance between what the ear hears and what the rational mind understands as "true." In the 1960s, cognitive scientist Roger Shepard created an aural illusion known as the Shepard scale, in which the seven notes of a major scale, played repeatedly within a single octave, appeared to infinitely ascend or descend, depending on the direction in which the scale was played. (The illusion was due to the fact that the scale was composed of computer-generated sine tones, which lacked any overtones—information that normally contributes to our understanding of which octave a pitch resides in.) The Shepard scale, which has also been referred to as a "sonic barber pole," raises a key question: what does it mean that our perception of continuous ascent or descent does not match up with what we know is "actually" happening? Try as we might, we can never hear the Shepard scale authentically. In other words, it will never sound like what the performer tells us it is—the same seven notes played over and over. Yet we accept and enjoy the aural illusion, even though we know it is not "real" (and even though we resist other aural illusions, like lip-synching).

If we were to make a list of different kinds of subjectivity, the most obvious place to begin would be with the perceptual variations that have been recorded across cultures—the stereotypical view of ethno-musicological inquiry. One clichéd example is the idea that Western listeners are not culturally inclined to understand microtonal music. With such comparisons, differences in musical perception are perhaps easy to spot. But by considering the issue so broadly, we tend to overlook the subjective differences that occur *within* cultures as well—indeed, even within subcultures, between professed fans of the same work. "Men of the most confined knowledge," as David Hume observed many years ago, "are able to remark a difference of taste in the narrow circle of their acquaintance, even where the persons have been educated under the same government, and have early imbibed the same prejudices." In this book I am interested in this latter, less obvious form of subjectivity. That is, I'm interested in the idea that two supporters of an Early Music ensemble, for instance, who might even explicitly agree that a performance was authentic, always to some extent hear different things when they listen, whether or not they outwardly articulate or are consciously aware of those differences.

In fact, we can get even more particular here, pointing out the differences in subjectivity as it occurs within a single individual. We often speak of personal subjectivity as if it is a static, unchanging phenomenon. But actually it is organic and responsive, a function of what neurologists call "plasticity of mind," and constantly evolving, however slowly, in relation to the environments in which it occurs—both the external environment and the inner, neurological environment. It is also affected by the attentional choices we continually make as listeners. Of course, with hearing it may not seem like we make such choices at all. In discussions of aural perception it is common to point out that, unlike the eyes, the ears lack lids—the assumption being that, barring a pair of industrial-strength earmuffs, we cannot control what we hear, but are instead helplessly immersed in a sea of sound whether we want to be or not. Yet subjectivity complicates this assumption. Even in our immersion, we home in on individual bits of sonic flotsam and jetsam, processing each according to our own peculiarities as listeners.

Over the course of a lifetime, "we change, correct, or reverse our opinions," as Josef Albers puts it in reference to visual art. Indeed, such metamorphoses apply to any qualitative experience (art, food, sexual attraction, political affiliation). "Doth not the appetite alter?" Benedick asks in *Much Ado About Nothing*. "A man loves the meat in his youth that he cannot endure in his age." As listeners, we are like Lucy Lowell, who as a mature concertgoer found herself wondering, with respect to Wagner's *Siegfried Idyll,* "how I could have not liked it the first time I heard it." Or perhaps we become the stereotypical curmudgeons who can't stand any bands adored by the kids today. But even that calcification of taste is a shift from an earlier, more open perspective. Our experience of music grows, develops, and sometimes contradicts itself. In that welter, it is virtually impossible for a single individual to maintain the same aesthetic biases from birth to death.

SENSES WORKING OVERTIME

Don't you wonder sometimes about sound and vision?

—David Bowie

One of the things that makes subjectivity or qualia so complex and difficult to discuss is that it is a holistic concept, a function of the fact that any one sense always interacts with and is influenced by sensory input from elsewhere in the body. This interaction is a source of even greater perceptual variance, as the combinatorial pell-mell of incoming data creates a unique experience of each work in the mind of each listener. Oliver Sacks casually hints at the phenomenon when he supposes that we all may "use visual and tactile cues along with auditory ones to cre-ate the fullness of musical perception."

As in all matters neurological, I defer to Sacks's expertise here, but I would cavil with his tentativeness. We *certainly* use visual, tactile, and other sensory cues to "create the fullness of musical perception"—or to compromise it, for that matter. And in each of us that multisensory creation is unique. Some people are synaesthetes, for whom the senses are clearly linked in daily experience. Others can selectively emphasize senses, based on desire, cultural tradition, or biological imperative. A musician, for instance, has learned to emphasize hearing. But even in musicians, hearing can never truly be an isolated phenomenon, the mental equivalent of the sound system that can be removed from your car when parked in a dicey part of town. It is, rather, embedded in a broad and complex bundle of perceptual activity, sometimes referred to by both neuroscientists and philosophers as the "sensorium"—what Walter Ong defined as "the entire sensory apparatus as an operational complex." Ultimately, our senses collaborate, whether we want them to or not. Whatever emphasis we place on a particular connection to the outside world (and every sense is such a connection) always occurs in relation to other such connections, even if it does so without our awareness. Each sense provides an additional "layer" of mediation, an additional filter, in turn affecting the functioning of the sense you are at that moment nominally emphasizing.

In effect it is impossible to speak of the subjectivity of listening as if it can be sequestered. "Musical subjectivity" is always a much bigger problem, describing the interaction of numerous sensory subroutines: it is a synthesis of the subjectivity of listening, plus the subjectivity of seeing, plus the subjectivity of touch, and so on. Each "local" form of subjectivity feeds into the broader "general perception" or qualia of music. And along the way, each is also an additional variation or idiosyncrasy introduced into that general perception.

Let's simplify the problem a little by looking in more detail at one point of intersection between the senses: the relationship between hear-ing and seeing. Clearly, the potential for variation, even at this one intersection, is huge. Visuality, after all, is not a monolithic experience: some of us are nearsighted, some farsighted, some have better than

20/20 vision; some of us are sensitive to color; some are stereoblind. Each of these categories can be broken down further: it is not merely that some of us are sensitive to color, for instance, but rather that those who are sensitive are sensitive to *different* colors. And that diversity is complicated by how differences in color perception also exist between societies, even down to the fact that the words we have for color affect our ability to perceive it, as Jonathan Winawer and others have recently shown. More generally, all of us who are sighted develop a familiarity with a personal vocabulary of images, built up over a lifetime. Each image in that vocabulary can have a variety of associations.

And so even the most iconic juxtapositions of sight and hearing are subject to multiple interpretations. Recall *Ludwig van Beethoven and Intimates, Listening to Him Playing,* the Albert Gräfle painting we discussed in chapter 1, which so dramatically articulated the classic pose of the serious listener as we think of it today. One of the central "intimates" in that scene covers his face with his hand, in an apparent attempt to shut out visual stimuli—seeming evidence that sight distracts from or otherwise influences listening. "We all sometimes block out the visual world to focus on another sense," Sacks notes, sharing memories of his music-loving father, who often closed his eyes when listening, believing he could hear the music better that way, because "he could exclude visual sensations and immerse himself fully in an auditory world."

But while it is easy to understand how closing one's eyes makes for better listening, it may be impossible, at least for listeners who have had the capacity to see for some portion of their lives, to ever "exclude visual sensations" entirely while listening, or to achieve purely auditory immersion—even if that goal *seems* attainable. Headphone guru Tyll Hertsens goes further, suggesting that "the listening system is used primarily as an alert and support system for the visual sense," which in turn implies that sight can never entirely be ignored by hearing. Even the act of covering your eyes while listening does not "exclude" sight from the sensorium as much as it replaces a visual image of the space you are in with a dark field. And that dark field too is a kind of image. It is mentally visible, in the same way that the imagery of dreams is mentally visible—and usually just as subconsciously. How could it fail to influence the music you hear? And more important, how could that influence fail to vary from listener to listener? What, after all, does darkness "mean"? For some, it might impart a sense of musical gravitas; for others, loneliness, drama, peace, danger. One can perhaps imagine tens or even hundreds of other possibilities.

Today, our pervasive multimedia environment teaches us, in thousands of ways and on a daily basis, to reinforce the connection between seeing and hearing. Anyone who has ever taken a road trip with an iPod full of music will have noticed the possibilities. Once taken out of its "natural habitat," Beethoven's Ninth Symphony undergoes a metamorphosis—actually, a slate of potential metamorphoses—depending on whether one is driving in downtown Chicago, for instance, or out on one of the American Southwest's seemingly endless desert highways. And each of these connections is itself variable, so that the Ninth can be many things even in a single context. In the desert, it may be a hopeful affirmation of life, a narrative of human ingenuity for overcoming limitations. Or it may be a frightening expression of human insignificance. It may even—if, say, one has recently viewed *A Clockwork Orange* (in which the piece has an important relationship to narrative violence), or if the desert one is driving through is near Alamogordo, New Mexico (close to where the first atomic bomb was tested)—evoke the human capacity for evil. Or it may seem to be a simple exercise in incongruity—how often does one get to hear a symphony orchestra in the desert? It is hard to imagine a more divergent set of interpretations than these. Yet each is justifiable.

The same complex interaction of sight and sound occurs in live music. On one level, the point seems obvious: an audience's view of an ensemble (or individual performer) affects its understanding of the performed music. "It did me good," poet Walt Whitman once wrote of his experience at a concert, "even to watch the violinists drawing their bows so masterly—every motion a study." But taken to its logical conclusion, that observation greatly disrupts our most basic assumption about what music is—that it is a purely sonic phenomenon. Evan Eisenberg notes anecdotally that in orchestral listening, when audiences are "positioned Janus-wise, those facing the stage say the balances are fine, while those facing away say they can't hear the second violins." For the former group, a certain arrangement of players is presumably convincing "evidence" that we are hearing the sound that an ensemble that *looks like that* would naturally produce. Levitin adds that as we listen, we "are exquisitely sensitive to the physical gestures that musicians make." We pay attention (with whatever degree of consciousness) to a musician's body movements, and through them we detect—or assume—certain "expressive intentions." Experimental subjects pick up on what Levitin calls "an emergent quality"—something "that goes beyond what was available in the sound or the visual image alone." This "emergent quality" seems to be the result of a synergy between visual and audio stimuli, and consequently informs listeners' understandings of the music.

But "emergent quality" is an open-ended term. The same gestures can have rather different significance for different listeners. For some, the electric guitarist's grimace I referred to at the end of the last chapter convincingly signifies expressive authenticity. For others, it seems hopelessly pathetic. Why shouldn't the same range of interpretation arise from the visual aspects of any performance? Saxophonist Greg Osby recently complained about musicians who perform with "prominent holes and stains in/on their jeans, wrinkled and tattered t-shirts, dirty sneakers, visible underwear, greasy, unwashed hair (or bodies), dirty fingernails, or worse." He cited an old adage—"They SEE you before they HEAR you"—in support of his argument that musicians who dress this way do a disservice to their music by encouraging audience disrespect. But Osby also failed to identify who "they" are, or to acknowledge the variance in how audiences hear, or to consider how that variance could be connected to what they see. More than likely, Osby's personal sensitivity to visual cues—or, to put it more precisely, his own visual expectations of live music—had some connection to the cultural meaning of dressing "up," with its connotation of professionalism. But the truth is that some audiences have little concern for either dressing up or professionalism—as saxophonist Chris Kelsey suggested in a response to Osby—and may even respond more favorably to casual or sloppy attire, regardless of the music being played. The point is that people listening to the "same" performance can potentially hear different things based on a single extramusical factor: how a musician is dressed.

We can believe ourselves above such considerations, arguing that as sophisticated, experienced listeners, we are capable of concentrating on only what can be heard. And indeed, some of us may come closer to this "pure" listening state than others. But if we can see, or have ever been able to see, then we can never completely escape visuality's influence on music. If we could, it literally wouldn't matter what a musician wore. I sincerely doubt that any sighted listener can make that claim; all of us find some form of attire distracting. And indeed, as listeners, all of us are distracted—or, to put it more generously, influenced—in multiple ways by visual cues in general.

WHAT DO YOU KNOW?

Is the distinction between "thoughtful" and "thoughtless" music—or "thought-filled" and "thought-free" music—coincident with that between good and bad music? If not, it is probably not too far removed from it.
—Jerrold Levinson

Greg Osby, I should note, is an expert musician, a professional who has studied his instrument for many years and knows how to use it proficiently in a performance situation. And here we come to one of the more stubborn and tempting counterarguments against the critique of authenticity presented by subjectivity. With expertise, the counterargument suggests, we *can* overcome the bias of qualia, getting humanly close to the objectivity of the oscilloscope, or the electronic tuner, or the output of the EEG.

Yet as Daniel Cavicchi suggests, "objectivity" is itself a construction of the Enlightenment, and, in music, of the idea that "one's ability to distinguish good from bad sound was directly related to social class, morality, and character." Without that imposed framework, we are left with the elusiveness of musical epistemology. Unlike the epistemology of science, musical knowledge cannot convincingly be placed in an evolutionary timeline. It is not that scientists don't argue too—and there is a legitimate philosophical question about just how objective or truthful the products of scientific inquiry can ever be. But for the most part science enjoys a common purpose and methodology, which has over time contributed to a convincing impression of its progress. Isaac Asimov noted that our understanding of the shape of the earth has moved through degrees of lesser and lesser wrongness: it was once thought to be flat, then a sphere, then an "oblate spheroid" (a sphere with a slight bulge in the middle), then, most recently, more "pear-shaped" (in the sense that it bulged slightly more south of the equator). "Once scientists get hold of a good concept," Asimov wrote, in describing the underlying pattern here, "they gradually refine and extend it with a greater and greater subtlety as their instruments of measurement improve."

We can't similarly talk about the history of music in terms of "greater subtlety" or gradual refinement over time. Is polyphony more refined or subtle than monophony? Is the CD more refined or subtle than the LP? How about the electric guitar as compared with its classical progenitor? It is true that critics, fans, and artists often imply that particular works or schools are "progressive"—a term that suggests an advance over what came before, based on an assumption of improved knowledge. So-called progressive rock, for instance, assumes more complex harmony, rhythm, song structure, and so on. But equating greater complexity with objective progress is a trap. In music what we think of as expertise is really just another form of mediation.

Typically, expertise is contrasted with naïveté—a tension Meyer reminds us can be described as a relationship between formalism and expressionism, or, in other contexts, between intellect and emotion. Yet though we may intuitively identify with one side of this model or the other, the comparison is forced. John Lennon, for instance, seemed to eschew expertise and to champion naïveté and emotion when he said that "rock 'n' roll music gets right through to you without having to go through your brain." Yet no one would deny that Lennon was himself an expert on rock and roll. Conversely, pianist Glenn Gould once claimed that rock and roll was boring because there was nothing to think about. But surely there is never truly "nothing to think about" in *any* music—there is no "thought-free" music, to put it in Jerrold Levinson's terminology. At worst, there is a lack of interest in having certain thoughts. Listening can never be purely emotional, can never bypass the brain (or intellect), even if only in the sense that emotion takes its import and its shape from the thoughts we have about it. We recognize and are aware of—that is, we think about, however vaguely—what we feel. Yet listening can never be purely intellectual either, never only a thing to think about. The sort of cognitive engagement Gould longed for is desirable precisely because it is pleasurable, and its absence is decried when that pleasure is denied (and the denial of pleasure is itself a kind of emotion).

It is thus odd that such a conflicted and vague musical concept as "expertise" should be used to enforce hierarchies of listening. Musicologists and conservatory-trained musicians, for instance, tend to assume that "expert" musicians are "better" listeners. Ironically, this view is frequently supported by the collusion of the so-called naïve, who all too willingly aver their own insufficiency, expressing it in terms of the clichéd disclaimer "I don't know anything about music. I just like to listen to it." When nineteenth-century feminist writer and intellectual Caroline Healey Dall reflected on her qualifications as a regular concertgoer, for instance, she admitted embarrassment that "loving music dearly as I do, I cannot become an adept in the science." As if loving music did not itself grant one the authority to speak knowledgeably about it.

To make things more confusing, "naïve" listeners are sometimes also imagined as being closer to the natural, gut-level expression of music—often by the same musicologists and conservatory-trained musicians I just described as claiming expertise, who use that credential to speak assertively about who or what should go in each category. For instance, consider composer Kyle Gann's 2001 essay "Naïve Pictorialism: Toward a Gannian Aesthetic," in which, without the slightest self-consciousness, Gann uses his expertise to claim his naïveté. He argues that his opera *Custer and Sitting Bull,* which exploits nearly every avant-garde trick in the book, including microtones, shifting meters, nested tuplets, and "chord progressions that have never been used before," is nevertheless saved from the elitism he assumes these strategies to imply by various naïve "narrative signs": a military snare beat, a Native American flute, and so on. Embracing naïveté as a virtue, he claims that even a ten-year-old child—his quintessential inexpert listener—could not miss the import of these signs. And yet Gann misses how the conscious act of mixing naïve devices into a work of art music could itself be taken as a marker of expertise, a knowing act of technique-pastiche that has clearly been turned to in an effort to escape academically imposed boredom. The bigger problem is that we can't unilaterally assign the descriptors "naïveté" or "expertise" to any work or listener. Those qualities are not inherent in a composition, but are momentary, site-specific effects of the way listeners and works interact.

Of course, emotion and intellect, or naïveté and expertise, or biases toward formalism or expressionism, do create *differences* in listening. But they don't create the assumed distinctions between *good listening* and *bad listening*—or, more dramatically, between *listening* and *not listening*—that are so regularly inferred from the terminology. The problem is that intellect, emotion, formalism, expressionism, expertise, and naïveté have all been used to claim both musicality and authenticity.

SPEAKING OF MUSIC

Martin Mull's dictum that "writing about music is like dancing about architecture" is rightly famous (though often misattributed), and is a succinct way of demystifying our expectations about the expression of musical opinion. Mull reminds us that even the most complex, scholarly, sophisticated aesthetic discourse is ultimately reducible to a simple choice between two rather vague statements: "I liked it" or "I didn't like it." Everything else is a rationalization for one or the other of these options. Some rationalizations are more eloquent, or entertaining, or engaging than others, of course—but a rationalization is a rationalization. How could it be otherwise? Musical perception, as Meyer has pointed out with respect to emotion, is "much more subtle and varied than are the few crude and standardized words which we use to denote" it. That is, while there are numerous ways we can *express* the experience of listening, none of them really gets at what is significant or meaningful (or not) about it.

Consider the range of statements that Peter Kivy suggested might be generated in response to a single well-known folk tune, "Greensleeves." A listener versed in music theory could follow the piece's development, note the contour of the melody, analyze the harmonic progression, discern the time signature, observe aspects of form or instrumentation, and so on, describing all of these things in natural language. Kivy imagines one reviewer: "I like the suggestion of the Dorian mode given by the B natural (when the melody starts on D)." Recording engineers, on the other hand—especially those who claim a "golden ear," or the supposedly exquisite ability to hear fine details that escape most listeners—could describe a recorded version of "Greensleeves," or its sound reinforcement in live performance, in a highly specialized technical jargon, noting aspects of EQ, compression, or microphone choice and placement. Musicians with absolute pitch could describe "Greensleeves" directly in the semiotics of musical notation, telling you what key it was in, and what pitches it utilized, without the help of an external reference. Music historians could write about the song's original context in Renaissance England. Neuroscientists could tell us how some listeners are more attuned to the tune's pitches, and others its rhythm. "Ordinary," nonexpert listeners could track their listening too, as Kivy notes, revealing that "I like that kind of archaic, ecclesiastical quality it has" or simply that "it sounds sort of old-fashioned." Affection for the work could be expressed even more vaguely, without explanation at all: "I just like it; I don't know why."

But even if all of these responses could be completely translated from the mind to the page, they would still tell us almost nothing about what each listener was actually hearing. Verbally describing a piece in terms of its use of the Dorian mode simply tells us that a listener knows how to identify the Dorian mode. The same thing is true of the technical jargon of the recording engineer, or the transcriptive powers of the listener with absolute pitch. Even the reticence of the noncommittal listener doesn't tell us everything it seems to. Is that reticence evidence of a lack of musical awareness, or, rather, of an unwillingness to engage with a pushy interrogator? The point is that identifying the Dorian mode, or noting the EQ curve of a mix, or transcribing a performance, or failing to articulate a response at all, brings us no closer to understanding the philosophical, existential questions raised by the music. Each response is self-referential, or at best referential to the community from which it is derived. What is music for? What does music mean? What is music? The Dorian mode, or the way the tune is recorded, or the key it is in, or a listener's silence, says nothing about these bigger concerns.

We thus have to be careful of confusing the impulse for certain kinds of critical articulation—born as they may be out of the desire for community, or out of other good intentions—with the ability to derive a more meaningful impact from a piece, or to connect with it more effectively. Indeed, no listener fails on account of her perceptual idiosyncrasies to connect with what she hears. We *all* connect with music, constantly. The very act of listening is by definition a connection—again, the listener is always on the other end of a transductive transmission. It follows that if you like to listen to music, you "know" about music—at least insofar as music can be known by anyone. And what you can *say* about that knowledge does not in the end matter. Ultimately, the only honestly "authentic" option as fans, critics, or practitioners is agnosticism about our own experience and generosity toward our fellow listeners.

GOLDEN EARS, TIN EARS

The problem with the cultural and psychological assumptions attending "expertise" and "naïveté" is that they are very hard to override, and indeed often appear normative. Depending on our background or biases, most of us believe that some ways of listening are truer than others. When Robert Jourdain points out that "many people are essentially deaf to complex harmony," adding that they "find only a spattering of tones where a keen ear would unearth gorgeous patterns," he taps into preconceptions established by social constructions of listening, which in turn pertain to social constructions of music. Is complex harmony, one wonders, *inherently* gorgeous? And is a "keen" ear closer to the putative truth of music? (After all, in Jourdain's usage, the word links perception of musical detail with deeper knowledge.) Conversely, is deafness inherently as it seems when discussed—that is, a zone of amusicality—a kind of void? (Note that the Old English form of the word simply meant "empty" or "barren.")

What does it really mean to be deaf, or to possess a keen ear? In terms of decomposition, neither is the monolithic state so often assumed. A 2008 Johns Hopkins study suggests that hearing impairment is "approaching epidemic proportions" in the United States, affecting a third of Americans (the World Health Organization estimates that the worldwide figure is 275 million). But there are many types of hearing impairment. In *loudness recruitment*—a condition that affected Beethoven before he lost his hearing altogether—cochlear hair cells become less sensitive to low-intensity sounds but remain normally responsive to those expressed at high volume, which in turn seem to "jump out." In *paracusis,* the cochlea, or inner ear structure, shrinks slightly with age, raising the perception of pitch, sometimes by as much as a whole step. *Presbycusis* is a loss of high-frequency hearing that, according to one source, affects 83 percent of the population over fifty-seven. *Hyperacusis* leads to an extreme sensitivity to certain sounds (a sensitivity not necessarily related to volume), while *diplacusis* causes a single pitch to sound like two. *Tinnitus,* which according to Katherine Bouton affects "between 30 and 50 million Americans" and is perhaps the best known of these conditions, produces a variety of inner-ear sounds, including hissing, ringing, whistling, roaring, chirping, screeching, or even musical tones. *Amusia,* a poorly understood phenomenon more commonly known as tone deafness, covers a wide range of neural processes, including the inability to perceive specific qualities of music (a rhythmic pulse, for instance), the inability to sing back a melody, even if it can be perceived, or the inability to remember music after hearing it. And there are other, less clinical ways of thinking about deafness. Some may not be typically categorized as "deafness" at all: consider research suggesting that boys have less acute hearing than girls.

"Keenness of ear" also has a wide range of possible expressions, as we saw in our discussion of expertise. Perfect pitch, a background in music theory, an ability to focus more on pitch or rhythm, the "golden ear" of a recording engineer, and even the social science knowledge of an ethnographer, anthropologist, or historian are all different manifestations of what could generally be described as musical intelligence. But none of these possibilities—either of deafness or of keenness of ear—is necessarily as limiting or empowering as it seems. The assumption behind absolute pitch, for instance, is that those who possess it are "blessed with much 'better' ears than other people," as Ernst Terhardt points out. And there is no doubt that absolute pitch can be useful to the musician. But its benefit is inconsistent. Typically learned in childhood, absolute pitch must be exercised regularly, and its effectiveness may depend on a work's genre, length, and complexity—indeed, it may be more observable in response to music with which its possessor is already familiar. In a worst-case scenario, absolute pitch can impart a rigid perception to music, making it sound wrong when transposed to another key. "Sometimes when a piano is a whole tone flat or a half tone sharp," wrote pianist Josef Lhévinne, who had absolute pitch, "I become fearfully confused, as it does not seem that I am playing the right notes. I instinctively want to transpose the sounds to where they belong and thus get mixed up." Frank R. Wilson writes that musicians with this gift "may end up feeling cranky a good deal of the time since almost everything but their own playing usually sounds out of tune to them."

More important, those with absolute pitch experience the same subtle variations in perception that affect all listeners. They come no closer to escaping their own subjectivity. They come no closer to hearing sound as "waves," or the length of a big sound like an explosion as lasting for as long as its sound waves do. They come no closer to hearing through the aural illusion of the Shepard scale, or through the problems of out-of-phase sound waves. They come no closer to escaping the fact that pitch and other musical details are psychological constructs.

Instead of obscuring or revealing a work, deafness or keenness of ear—like the idiosyncratic quirks of an instrument or the acoustics of a room—*mediate* it, making it a different thing for different listeners. If we are in the putative mainstream of ear health, we have probably overlooked how that mediation affects us too. And most of us have overlooked how listening modalities generate their own forms of music. But our ecosystem of genres and styles was not born in a vacuum; rather, it was directly informed by the variegated ways we experience music. More than one observer has speculated that Beethoven's music may have been affected by changes to his hearing—the decreased ability to perceive high frequencies, for instance, may have led to the production of music that focused on lower, darker registers. Loudness recruitment, on the other hand, was a problem for Beethoven because his music is full of carefully wrought formal intricacies and great dynamic contrasts—itself a function of the fact that he lived in a world that was, on the whole, quieter than ours. But loudness recruitment could actually be useful for the fan of noise, black metal, doom metal, or any of a number of other styles of music in which the physical vibration of sound, played at a high volume, is of paramount importance, and the music is supposed to be perceived primarily *as* vibration. In a review of American duo Sunn O)))—a band named, incidentally, after a brand of amplifier—George Grella echoes Evelyn Glennie's concept of listening as a haptic sense (and Japanese musician and writer Merzbow's argument that "noise is the most erotic form of sound") when he writes that the band's music "literally touches the audience," in a way that "what they play doesn't only reach the skin and the ear, it enters the body and vibrates it from the inside out. When they hit certain frequencies this vibration can produce a reactive sound that is heard from inside the body." During the show Grella experienced, "there were moments when a distinct, buzzing hum was clearly audible to my inner ear and clearly coming from inside my body." Simon Reynolds summarizes the aesthetics of noise as a fascination with "the materiality of music." That materiality is surely intensified by a condition like loudness recruitment.

We could go to the other extreme. Many have pointed out the philosophical implications of John Cage's composition, "4'33"," in which the performer is asked to be silent for four minutes and thirty-three seconds. The piece, then, consists of whatever the listener perceives. The listener with tinnitus, who, as I noted earlier, hears "hissing, ringing, whistling, roaring, chirping, screeching, or even musical tones" as a matter of course will immediately take "4'33"" out of the realm of Zen meditation so often assumed to be the point when it is programmed. That is, tinnitus's sounds—or the influence of other forms of deafness—do not automatically interfere with the enjoyment or appreciation of this music, as they would for so many other works in the Western high art tradition. Their idiosyncratic mediation is instead the *point* of the work (indeed, George Prochnik argues that Cage himself had tinnitus). I should note that "4'33"" was partly inspired by Cage's visit to Harvard's anechoic chamber, a specially designed room in which all sounds are absorbed rather than reflected. The composer had gone there in search of silence, only to discover that it could not exist for him, or for any hearing human being. "I heard two sounds, one high and one low," he later wrote. "When I described them to the engineer in charge, he informed me that the high one was my nervous system in operation, the low one my blood in circulation." Whether or not Prochnik is right that these sounds were actually tinnitus, what the composer discovered in that room was the inevitability of transduction.

Similarly, listeners of different skill sets are no more or less qualified to experience composer Pauline Oliveros's "Tuning Meditation," which, as Michael Carroll points out, simply asks performers to sing a random note, sustaining the sound "for a comfortable length of time," and then to sing another, or else try to match a pitch produced by someone else in the ensemble. As a result, "Tuning Meditation" is a work for a community in which the binary of "expertise" and "naïveté" does not make sense. Since the performer is asked to sing a random note, it does not matter which one is chosen or how it is sung. Instead of a continuum of authenticity that corresponds with a continuum of skill, we are left with a continuum of listening styles and biases—a continuum of mediation and subjectivities and, in the postmodern cliché, a play of difference.

We need not posit a tepid egalitarianism for musicality, pretending that differences in listening do not exist or do not matter. On the contrary; my argument is that to some extent the differences are the whole point. Clearly they exist, clearly they matter, and clearly they impact our understanding of music. But they can never lead us to authenticity, because none of them is singularly "true."

CRITICAL EMPATHY

Isn't it wonderful? We color deficient people have understood Gogh's true wonderfulness. But color normal people do not understand it well, seemingly.

—Asada Kazunori

As a professional musician, whose livelihood is in some degree dependent upon a clear distinction between the expert and the nonexpert, I find much of this counterintuitive. My impulse, frankly, is to insist that a listener like pianist Alicia de Larrocha, with her great memory and her sensitivity to pitch—her Mozart-like ability, upon hearing a given work, to "say exactly the notes, chords, intervals, everything"—hears "more" and hears "better." I want to insist that she is an "authentic" listener—indeed, given the competitive marketplace in which I am professionally situated, and the complicated music I enjoy making, I have a vested interest in the idea that such listeners exist. Alternately, in speaking of a continuum of listening styles and biases, I don't want to romanticize hearing that does not meet the usual standards of ear health, as measured for instance by audiology's Weber and Rinne tests. "I may truly say that my life is a wretched one," Beethoven wrote, bitterly summarizing his feelings at impending deafness. I myself have mild tinnitus, and even at a low level I find it annoying and would prefer not to have it at all. Technology theorist Michael Chorost's quest to find a scientific solution to his own hearing loss, so he could once more enjoy the beauty of Ravel's *Bolero,* a piece that had special importance to him, is a memorable, somewhat heartbreaking read. (Chorost eventually got a cochlear implant, but so far this technology has been unable to completely recreate the functioning of a healthy ear.)

Yet a deaf person might say that such observations betray a "hearie" (or "audist") bias. It is too seductive, apparently, to make the leap from the mechanics of hearing, which are at least measurable, to the subjectivity of listening, which cannot be evaluated in the same way, or perhaps at all. It is too easy, that is, to think of hearing impairment as listening (and thus musical) impairment, or hearing precision as listening (and thus musical) precision. But if all sound is mediated in the process of being heard, as I have been arguing, then *no* sound is ever listened to in a way that is singularly true, or musically precise—we don't even know how to describe what singularly true or musically precise listening would be. The expert, who can transcribe a work, situate it historically, or reproduce it on another instrument, impresses with those skills, but it is a big leap to go from that impressiveness to saying that she hears it more authentically, in any of the ways I identified in the last chapter. More important, while she is undoubtedly capable of hearing something beautiful, we have no way of knowing whether it is more or less beautiful than the thing heard by the listener with the so-called impairments.

Many listeners simply defy the assumption that various kinds of deafness are amusical. I once taught a guitar student, an adolescent boy with a hearing aid, who had great difficulty reproducing basic melodies or rhythms, and who made little progress learning any of the beginner's songs I tried to teach him. Still, he possessed and passionately displayed an encyclopedic knowledge of punk, folk, and outsider music. He was in fact one of the more demonstrably enthusiastic students I have ever met: always on time for lessons, always wanting to stay longer than the allotted period. He persistently stuck with the instrument, by his own choice, despite what seemed to me to be excruciatingly slow progress. He reminded me of how the word "amateur" once meant, literally, "lover," and was only defined downward over time. We were obviously different kinds of musicians, but in the end he was far more qualified than I to make claims about the music he cared about. And his experience of that music seemed every bit as "authentic" as the experience of someone with extensive training and conventionally valued aptitudes—in some ways even more so. (Historically, listeners with institutionally approved skill sets are often unable to even recognize as "music" any sound that falls outside the purview of their training.) In short, he was the sort of listener who, as Sacks has observed, is "almost tone deaf yet passionately sensitive to music."

We should not assume that this particular listening profile is limited to the population of adolescent guitar students with hearing aids. As Sacks points out, hearing loss in musicians may be more widespread than we know, due to underreporting that may in turn be a function of professional shame. (Conversely, there may be many listeners who possess a core aptitude for music yet lack a real interest in it.) "I don't have an ear for music," John Cage once told William Duckworth. "I don't hear music in my mind before I write it. . . . I can't remember a melody." In recent years, Evelyn Glennie, Brian Wilson, Neil Young, Eric Clapton, Pete Townshend, Ben Luxon, Sean Forbes, Isaiah Jackson, Bono, Richard Einhorn, Will.i.am, Mandy Harvey, Jay Alan Zimmerman, Beethoven's Nightmare, Beverly O'Sullivan, Signmark, and others have made music professionally, in a variety of genres, despite forms of hearing loss or "inability." YouTube is dotted with videos of popular songs that have been annotated with sign language. As of this writing, there is a beautiful one for Michael Franti's song "Everyone Deserves Music"—renamed "Everyone (Even Deaf) Deserves Music." (The wording of this title, incidentally, may appear odd to hearing people, but that is due to syntactical differences between American Sign Language and "standard" English—evidence of the fact that the Deaf are "a distinct cultural group with its own language, traditions, and values.") The Deaf are drawn to music too, and can enjoy and celebrate and argue about it like hearing people. Why would a deaf person seek a music career in the first place—why would she even be interested in music—if she were not deriving some pleasure or meaning from it?

The historical context for this question is important. It is only recently that Deaf education and Deaf civil rights have been taken seriously in Western culture. Katherine Bouton notes that "the stigma of deafness dates back to at least 1000 B.C.," and for a long time deafness was associated with mental impairment, linked with the word "dumb" and its pejorative connotation. But contrary to preconceptions, the Deaf are not people with "diseased ears," but rather, as Sacks puts it, people "adapted to another sensory mode." And that sensory mode has its music too.

"Authenticity" is often a label we hang on music we love. It can be a code, a shorthand, usually meant as praise—calling something authentic is a way of saying you like it, while inauthentic works are assumed to be bad. But if what matters most about music is the pleasure we take from it, there is no necessary correlation between that pleasure and a particular mode of listening. Some, in fact, completely invert the usual paradigm, positing the superiority of the deaf experience of music. Unlike Beethoven, whose artistic success is usually understood as occurring in spite of his deafness—though the struggle it involved was also a form of contextual collaboration—Glennie owns her biology as a part of her art, and indeed suggests that it allows her to hear more, and hear better. "We can feel this," she tells a deaf girl in *Touch the Sound,* a documentary about her life and work, while striking a drum:

> For an audience member, for a listener: I strike it, they may hear it, and then they may no longer hear it. For us, however, we've got our hand on the drum, we strike it, we can see, we can feel, we've had the process of striking it, meanwhile we're hearing the sound, because we're feeling the sound, far longer than an audience member. Do you see what I mean? So in fact, we're hearing more.

In one of the great ironies of the music industry, the man who is often associated with the invention of the phonograph, Thomas Edison, was deaf too—a lingering effect of having contracted scarlet fever in childhood. He "often listened to recordings," as Emily Thompson points out, "by biting into the wooden case of a phonograph to conduct the sound directly to the bones of his inner ear." It's a striking, memorable image; Edison's teeth, jaw, and skull became the transductive intermediaries that allowed him to perceive his own recordings. Ever the curmudgeon, Edison later claimed that what others understood as an infirmity actually gave him an auditory advantage. "I have a wonderfully sensitive inner ear," he wrote. "For more than fifty years it has been wrapped in almost complete silence. It has been protected from the millions of noises that dim the hearing of ears that hear everything."

In other words, we need not ever listen in the conventional sense at all, and our critical empathy as listeners should keep us open to the unconventional listening of others. Again, to paraphrase Levitin: what do we hear when we listen to music? It could be anything.

5

LIVE TO TAPE, AND BACK AGAIN

Within the cultural field of music, there is a continual struggle over who or what belongs, or does not belong. In the early twentieth century, this clash concerned what kinds of musicians and musical activity would be validated and included within the field. Through opera and Red Seal, Victor expanded the prevailing definition of musicians to include those who made commercial musical recordings. At stake was whether the cultural value that already accrued in music could legitimate the business and technology of sound recording as well.

—David Suisman

One of the most remarkable musical developments of the twentieth century was what I call the "megaconcert"—a new category of performance event in which audiences, thanks in part to the extended reach of electronically amplified sound, were routinely measured in the high tens and even hundreds of thousands. From Woodstock (with an audience estimated at five hundred thousand) to the New York Philharmonic's 1986 performance in Central Park (with an audience estimated at eight hundred thousand), these concerts drew fans in numbers that just a few years before had seemed unimaginable—although similarly large political rallies dated back at least as far as Nazi Germany. They built on the biggest concerts of the previous century, whose venues—the Metropolitan Opera House, the Royal Albert Hall, the Cirque d'hiver, for instance—typically counted their audiences in the "mere" thousands. Indeed, the closest megaconcert antecedents from the Victorian era may have been the "Peace Jubilees" given in the late 1800s by Boston's Patrick Gilmore, which at their peak drew as many as fifty thousand people—exact estimates differ—to hear an ensemble of eleven thousand musicians. Some contemporary critics referred to Gilmore's jubilees as "monster concerts," though it is worth noting that the term was not originally meant pejoratively.

In any case, megaconcerts pose an interesting philosophical problem for both performer and fan. More often than not, given their sheer size, they impede the very communication that many would argue is the reason for music in the first place. Take, for instance, the Beatles' infamous Shea Stadium show. The record-breaking audience of fifty-five thousand overwhelmed the PA system to the extent that the band could not hear itself play. Indeed, band and audience were separated by such a long stretch of empty baseball field that one is entitled to wonder whether we can consider this a "concert" at all, or whether it contradicted that word's etymological suggestion of togetherness. Such extremes had been typical of live Beatlemania, but the magnitude of the problem at Shea contributed to the group's 1966 decision to stop touring and become a studio entity. After their final official concert, at Candlestick Park in San Francisco, there would be only the impromptu Apple rooftop set the group played shortly before their breakup—a performance that was as casual, intimate, and free to the public as Shea was intense, alienating, and commercial. "It was a very strange location because there was no audience except for Vicki Wickham and a few others," Paul McCartney later noted of the Apple show. "So we were playing virtually to nothing—to the sky, which was quite nice."

I suspect many contemporary musicians and fans would identify with the wistfulness McCartney expresses here. I know I do. I went to my first megaconcerts in high school—late-night jaunts to Madison Square Garden and Giants Stadium to hear acts like Genesis, Billy Joel, Boston, and McCartney himself. The experience was routinely disappointing, not least because I could never afford the good seats and often found myself watching the entire performance on a gigantic TV screen from an uncomfortable spot thousands of feet from the stage. From my already jaded teenaged perspective, the music usually seemed unnecessarily loud, or uninspired, or annoyingly mingled with the extramusical preoccupations of an uninterested audience. Yet I got the appeal too. It was not just that megaconcerts afforded an attractive social environment for young people looking to cut loose. The thing that really drew the audience, I think, was the promise of authenticity.

Modern megaconcerts, even those for the most "manufactured" pop stars, still depend on an underlying cultural assumption that it is more aesthetically truthful—more ethical, even—to experience live music from the great physical distance of the nosebleed section than it is to experience canned music from the even greater philosophical distance of recorded media. Of course the sanctification of live performance characterizes many genres that rarely make it to the megaconcert stage too—jazz, for instance, or classical music—and often in a more intense way. But the point is that for many audiences, live music is "real" music. "Listening to records is generally less gripping than hearing a concert or playing oneself," as Charles Rosen put it—appealing to Walter Benjamin to draw a parallel between records and cinema, and arguing that both are designed for "an audience in a state of distraction." "If played beautifully at a concert," Rosen contends, by way of example, "the introduction to the last movement of Mozart's Viola Quintet in G Minor can bring tears to my eyes"; conversely, he admits, "I have never wept at a recording."

Ironically, the record-making process is itself usually informed by an idea of what music ought to sound like when performed live, and the resulting artifacts are judged by the degree to which they approach the "real thing," through some permutation of the concept of high fidelity. Even genres that are not typically associated with "live" performance in the conventional sense—electronica, for instance, or acousmatic music—are expected to be, and are derided when it appears they are not, expressively authentic snapshots of some real-time moment of compositional intent. Such works may not seem to emerge organically from a guitar or a horn, but they are often performed onstage as if they did, and are often treated (by their fans anyway) with the same gravity. The mashup artist Girl Talk spends most of his performances hovering over a laptop, reproducing samples from already existing recordings—yet something about his physical presence elicits the sort of fan response that is usually reserved for acts with more traditional pop and rock instrumentation.

In fact, it is pretty obvious that notwithstanding Rosen's commentary, some people do weep at recordings—or respond to them with other strong emotions that are stereotypically associated with live performance. "Listening now to the Pablo Casals recordings of the Bach Cello Suites, made half a century ago in the mid 1930s," writes Stephen Nachmanovitch, "I feel a quality to the sound itself that goes right through me. It vibrates my whole body like a leaf in a storm. I don't know what to call it—power, the life force." It's hard to imagine a less distracted statement than that. And there are good reasons for listeners to engage so forcefully with a record. Just as the record-making process is informed by an idealized notion of "live sound," so too have recordings gradually become a standard against which live performance is measured. Again, as Levitin puts it, "Recording introduced the idea of a 'master performance,' a single canonical, iconic version of a song." But it's more than that—we have learned to hear live music in terms of the recorded music with which our environment is suffused.

And so, for instance, while it is true that at a typical megaconcert fans sing along with the artist—seemingly evidence of the event's authenticity—one would be hard pressed to sing along without an already existing knowledge of the music being sung, usually developed through experience with recordings of it. Blogger Ben Smith points out that "it seems hugely preferable for me not to hear a real live piece until I've listened to it a bunch of times in the comfort of my apartment. I want to understand the piece first, instead of trying to piece together the themes in the concert hall." Yet the synergy between records and live performance is generally overlooked in our culture. When writer Ben Cohen went through a period of self-imposed auditory denial for his *Vice* magazine article "Life Sans Music," he neglected to mention that he was not living without music, as his title claimed, but without recordings, or the contexts in which they could be found (films, video games, parties, and so on). At one point he had to stop his girlfriend from singing, but on the whole he didn't have to worry about a friend sitting down at a piano to pick out the melody of the latest pop hit, or his family harmonizing together after dinner, or itinerant street musicians congregating outside his window.

We can extrapolate some broader points from these observations. In chapter 3 we addressed some of the problems that arise when authenticity is invoked in specific contexts. We considered individual listeners, behaving pompously with respect to particular works, or artists, or genres—for instance, in the context of the Early Music movement, the swing revival, the Jazz Wars, or the Milli Vanilli scandal. But authenticity can be invoked less specifically, as a general feature of how we think about performance. That is, listeners who avoid the trap of authenticity when it comes to an artist or genre they admire are often willing to recuperate it for a grander purpose. For these listeners, the authenticity quest is rearticulated as a contest between different ideas of performance: music becomes a choice between recordings and live concerts, only one of which can be the "singularly true" experience stipulated by that quest, thereby providing a "correct" answer to the broader taxonomical question "What is music?"

The problem, as we have just seen, is that neither answer is sufficient, and that the question itself is circular. The distinctions between "live" and "recorded" have never been completely clear, but today they are impossible to sustain. For us, live music and recorded music are inevitably bound up in one another, and the pure independence that authenticity assumes about each is impossible. We can make an analogy to similar assumptions about digital culture, and especially social media, which is often unfavorably compared to more conventional forms of human interaction, as Nathan Jurgenson recently pointed out:

> We have been taught to mistakenly view online as meaning not offline. The notion of the offline as real and authentic is a recent invention, corresponding with the rise of the online. If we can fix this false separation and view the digital and physical as enmeshed, we will understand that what we do while connected is inseparable from what we do when disconnected. That is, disconnection from the smartphone and social media isn't really disconnection at all: The logic of social media follows us long after we log out. There was and is no offline; it is a lusted-after fetish object that some claim special ability to attain, and it has always been a phantom.

We could substitute "live music" and "recorded music" for "offline" and "online" everywhere in that paragraph and the point would be the same. The logic of the record follows us long after we turn it off.

The last hundred years have been shot through with this unacknowledged overlap. For all the neoclassicist sympathies of Respighi, did his use of a phonographic nightingale in *Pines of Rome* disqualify it from ever being a truly live performance? Were the different musical personas Bill Evans conjured on his series of overdubbed piano albums (*Conversations with Myself* and its follow-ups) really examples of his improvisatory art? (Improvisation, after all, is usually assumed to happen in the unpredictability of real time, and not in relation to something you have just played and have the power to stop and revisit.) Is my own megaconcert memory of watching Paul McCartney's performance on a large TV screen, even though I was putatively "at" the McCartney concert as it took place, a memory of a recording or a live concert? Even in cases where there is no material overlap between these two modes of performance, the perceptive habits each engenders—their respective "logics"—are not as easily disentangled as we think.

Today we still tend to ignore or explain away these complexities. But the truth is that recording and live music are deeply and conceptually interrelated. Just as, in Derrida's famous dictum, "there is no outside the text," in music, there is no outside the recording. And so it is wrong to assume that recording is an authentic artifact and to rely on it as the basis for modern conceptions of what music is—but it is equally wrong to treat it as a corruption, to confine it to the perspective of what I call the antirecording critique, as a foil to "prove" the authenticity of live music.

Indeed, now that we have had more than a hundred years to live with recording technology, we need to see that it did not represent a radical break in music history but, rather, an organic development in the continuum of human performance.

WE'RE ROLLING: THE ANTIRECORDING CRITIQUE

No matter what may be your mood, I am always ready to entertain you. When your day's work is done, I can bring the theater or the opera to your home. I can give you grand opera, comic opera, or vaudeville. I can give you sacred or popular music, dance, orchestra, or instrumental music. I can render solos, duets, trios, quartets. I can aid in entertaining your guests. When your wife is worried after the cares of the day, and the children are boisterous, I can rest the one and quiet the other. I never get tired and you will never tire of me, for I always have something new to offer.

— "I Am the Edison Phonograph," 1906 promotional recording

It is easy to forget the number of ways recorded sound informs our lives today—ways that were unforeseen even in the first decades after the technology was invented. Without recorded sound, radio, television, film, commerce, medicine, forensics, and many other areas of modern life would be dramatically different. Some of these fields might not exist at all. Without recorded sound, it is hard to imagine the experience of shopping, or riding in a car, or jogging, or hosting a party, or waiting on the phone. It's not that we can't do any of these things without canned music. But we have become so accustomed to having it there—it has become such a thoroughly integrated environmental phenomenon, a realization of Erik Satie's prescient and malleable term "furniture music"—that in the daily routines of the twenty-first century, silence is more the exception than the rule. Recording has even given us a way to understand environmental noise as a kind of music.

Recording technology is not only pervasive, it is powerful. It allows us to experience music in ways that were formerly never possible in "reality," ways that defy the limitations of time and space. Try as you might, you will never be able to fit an orchestra into your Volvo station wagon—but you could have the recorded sound of an orchestra anywhere you choose to put a device that can play it back for you. (For a more extreme example of this technologically enabled freedom, think of the spacecraft *Voyager*'s Golden Record, currently hurtling through deep space and inscribed with a variety of sounds, including Glenn Gould playing Bach, field recordings of Pygmy groups, and Chuck Berry.) You can listen to music performed by people who died many years ago. You can listen to music that comes from parts of the world that you may never visit, or on instruments that you may never actually see in person. You can stop any piece of music in mid-playback if you suddenly decide you don't like it—and you don't have to worry about offending the musicians, because they don't even have to know of your interruption. On the other hand, you can repeat a recording many times if you do like it. You can make Ana Vidović's classical guitar as loud as a heavy metal band. Or you can listen to Black Sabbath with the volume turned way down, to avoid waking the baby sleeping in the next room.

Yet despite all this power—or perhaps because of it—many of us continue to harbor a deep unease about recording, barely acknowledged today even though it was a major theme earlier in the history of the technology. We recognize that all of the above-mentioned capabilities of recorded sound are literally untrue. The orchestra is not really playing in your Volvo, the dead musician is not really performing again, Black Sabbath is not really soft enough to allow the baby to sleep. Each scenario, rather, involves a copy or facsimile that is doing this work at the behest of the listener. There is thus assumed, however obliquely, a certain underlying illegitimacy to recorded music—a certain lack of authenticity—and this is the root of what I call the antirecording critique.

In academic discourse, the antirecording critique is often described in terms of the destruction of "aura," a quality Michael Chanan defines as a work's historically "intimate unity with the time and place of performance." The argument about aura, of course, was made famous by Walter Benjamin in his influential 1936 essay "The Work of Art in the Age of Mechanical Reproduction"—although we should note that Benjamin there addressed the mechanical reproduction of music only tangentially. Still, Benjamin's argument has been interpreted to mean that in the twentieth century, music making and musicians were separated for the first time—music became both "literally disembodied," as Chanan puts it, and decontextualized, producing a syndrome that R. Murray Schafer calls "schizophonia" (a pejorative term that clearly riffs on the notion of disease). In a more recent instantiation of the argument, Carolyn Abbate claims that in the process of being recorded, music loses its defining temporal and material qualities.

Ted Gioia has suggested that the destruction of aura is a by-product of the abundance of music—a function not merely of mechanical reproduction, but of an industry savvy enough to exploit it—which in turn "appears to lead inevitably" to music's "devaluation." Gioia thus gets at the moral dimension of the antirecording critique, helping to articulate its connection to authenticity. "Just as the photograph has led to the trivialization of the visual image," he writes, "and the spread of printing has lessened the dignity of the written word, so has the easy accessibility of inexpensive recordings led to a devaluation both of the musical performance and the performer." Chanan concurs that the ubiquity of recordings has threatened to turn music into so much random, worthless noise. This moral argument hinges on the idea that too much music—the musical profusion problem I identified in the introduction of this book—not only overwhelms the listener's capacity to process it, but also creates intense competition for professional musicians, so that it becomes harder for "good" music to be heard in the first place.

Lest it seem that the antirecording critique is merely an academic exercise in dystopian fantasy, consider how artists themselves have participated in it over the last century. From the earliest days of the recording industry, many composers shared John Philip Sousa's mistrust of the new medium—though often, interestingly, with the same equivocation, so that like Sousa they participated in the very system they were critiquing. "In a time like ours, when the genius of engineers has reached such undreamed of proportion, one can hear famous pieces of music as easily as one can buy a glass of beer," Claude Debussy despairingly wrote in 1913, the same year he recorded some of his own piano pieces on Welte-Mignon piano rolls. "Should we not fear this domestication of sound, this magic preserved in a disc that anyone can awaken at will?" the composer wondered. "Will it not mean a diminution of the secret forces of art?" According to Timothy Day, many other musicians also feared that recording would unleash an ear-numbing, soul-destroying deluge of music. Arnold Schoenberg, Day informs us, had a fatalistic antipathy for both recordings and radio, arguing that they would inevitably produce "a 'boundless surfeit' which would wear music out"—but also that opposition was "a hopeless prospect."

Benjamin Britten in turn picked up the schizophonia theme, bemoaning the fact that a sacred work intended to correspond with a particular day in the church calendar—Bach's *St. Matthew Passion*—"was now being used to provide a discreet accompaniment to the conversation of guests at a cocktail party." And Roger Sessions, in a 1969 lecture at

MAKING
MUSICAL
MINCE MEAT!

BIFF, bang, crash! . . . The wheels turn
. . . the cogs mesh . . . Canned Music
fills the air!

Harvard, complained that recording drained music of its power to surprise and astonish, describing the feeling of frustration a certain disc created in him. "What infuriated me," Sessions explained, "was my fully developed awareness of having heard exactly the same sounds, the same nuances, both of tempo and dynamics, the same accents, down to the minutest detail, so many times that I knew exactly—and I emphasize exactly, to the last instant—what was coming next." Aaron Copland too cited repetition as a significant grievance against the technology. "The very great drawback of recorded sound," Copland wrote, "is the fact that it is always the same."

The resistance to recording had a practical as well as a philosophical dimension, though the two were most likely mutually reinforcing. Matt Novak has written of the Music Defense League, an organization of the American Federation of Musicians, which in 1930 published a series of dramatic print ads designed to alert audiences to the dehumanizing (and, not incidentally, job-destroying) onset of recorded sound. The ads, featuring imagery that would have been well suited to the Flash Gordon comics that became popular later in the decade, depicted the phonograph industry as an army of giant, unfeeling robots run amok over American culture.

Meanwhile, recordings found their way into radio, where they also tended to replace live musicians, causing such tension that by the next decade, the AFM, now under the leadership of James Petrillo, went on strike twice (in 1942 and 1948). Such efforts could also be more geographically focused, as was the case later in the century, with protests by New York's Local 802, designed to stop the use of prerecorded music at Lincoln Center; or the Council for Living Music, whose project has been to ensure the viability of live music on Broadway ("the thrill of seeing and hearing a live orchestra at a Broadway musical is one of the few remaining authentic live musical experiences in American society," the organization notes on its website). According to the CLM, Broadway producers have repeatedly violated a 1993 good-faith agreement with the musicians' union, turning to canned music instead of live musicians as an ostensibly cost-cutting measure. By 2003, the union had had enough and went on strike. Yet incidents with prerecorded music have continued to affect productions of *Sweeney Todd* (2005), *Tony and Tina's Wedding* (2009), *West Side Story* (2010), *Swan Lake* (2010), and, most recently, *Priscilla, Queen of the Desert* (2011).

The different elements of the antirecording critique are perhaps best summed up by Neil Young's song "Union Man," with its mandate to issue "Live Music Is Better" bumper stickers. And they have all informed music's death cult, described in the introduction of this book. Recording technology, the critique suggests, may have created the music industry we know today, but it also contained the seeds of its own destruction, by forcing music's domestication, decontextualization, inundation, and redundancy.

THE WAY WE LISTENED

Whoever has approved this idea of order . . . will not find it preposterous that the past should be altered by the present as much as the present is directed by the past.

                                                 —T. S. Eliot

One of the problems of the antirecording critique is that it depends heavily on assumptions about how music was experienced before the arrival of the technology it decries, positing a listening past that the habits of the recording-era audience can be compared to. Yet as we saw in chapter 4, we have a hard enough time understanding the complexity of listening in our own historical context—a hard enough time merely appreciating the mediations that impact our own listening. No matter how diligently we attempt to reconstruct past listening from contemporary accounts, historicism folds in additional mediations: from any present, understanding the listening of the past inevitably requires putting "the past" through our own temporal filters.

Old music is a special case of this general historical problem. When considering the musical past, even something as seemingly basic as timbre is obscured by an unbridgeable distance. "A present-day musician's idea of harpsichord tone-color," writes Thurston Dart, "is a mixture of the various sounds produced by different players and different instruments, and it is overlaid by a mesh of associations of oldness and strangeness and general quaintness which simply did not exist for Bach. If the harpsichord is an eighteenth century one, it is old to us, but it was new then, and its sound was not the same." Unlike a painting, or sculpture, or treatise, we have no primary document of a pre-recording era performance. We cannot hear those sounds for ourselves. Moreover, surviving secondhand accounts—newspaper reviews, diaries, letters—suffer from the inadequacies of language. And scores, where they exist, merely anticipate the music that was actually heard.

Thus the history invoked by the antirecording critique is selective, and we must be careful. If musical aura has really been "destroyed," how do we, so many years after the advent of recording, know what it was when it existed? In what way is the term meaningful for us? "The aura of listening," as Leon Botstein puts it, "is so remote for us now that it's very hard even to try to understand what people in the nineteenth century were doing with music." In other words, we have nothing to compare "auralessness" to—just as we are unable to look at a medieval painting without doing so through our contemporary experience of photography and film.

Responding to the antirecording critique on its own terms, then, how do we know that before recording, sound was not in some ways already domesticated, already decontextualized, already available in "boundless surfeit," and even already subject to certain kinds of repetition? We can argue, for instance, that the "domestication of sound" that Debussy feared as a result of recording had happened long before he uttered his concern. In the Victorian era, the piano became an accoutrement of bourgeois life; most middle-class homes—and indeed many working-class homes as well—had one, particularly after developments in piano design enabled manufacturers to produce the instrument cheaply and so that it required little maintenance by the user. Piano ownership was not an empty status symbol; the instrument was, rather, a well-used domestic device. Members of a household (usually daughters) could and were expected to play it.

Among other things, these nineteenth-century domestic pianists performed piano reductions of ensemble works—operas, symphonies, choral pieces—all of which were being realized outside of their intended context, like the *St. Matthew Passion* Britten regretted hearing under cocktail party conversation. At the same time, this "schizophonia" had begun to occur in concert life as well, as when Boston's Handel and Haydn Society programmed Handel's *Messiah*—perhaps the exemplar of a sacred work—in a secular performance space. But the Victorian decontextualization of music was not merely a question of out-of-place genres; it also had to do with vector, with the "territory" that music occupied. Increasingly, private music penetrated public spaces. Nineteenth-century pianos were significantly louder than their Enlightenment forebears—they had been fortified with cast iron frames and heavier action—so it was easier for the sound to reach beyond the parlors and living rooms where they were typically housed. By the mid- to late 1800s, city dwellers were complaining of the domestic piano's capacity for disrupting the peace. Discontent eventually swelled to a "painful outcry," as the instrument increasingly became associated with what Eduard Hanslick called an "offensive power and offensive character."

The nineteenth-century piano thus contributed not only to the growing "footprint" of musical sound, but also to music's general profusion, anticipating the deluge of records that Schoenberg and others would later scorn. But even before the domestic piano added to the noise pollution of the Victorian era, more intentionally public forms of performance were everywhere in European culture. As early as the sixteenth century, Schafer notes, street music was a despised feature of urban life, "a continual subject of controversy." By the nineteenth, the situation had become more extreme. Charles Babbage referred to street music as an "instrument of torture." Thomas Carlyle, confronted with a persistent organ grinder, wondered whether the correct response was to "assassinate him" or merely "call the police." In 1864 some two hundred British petitioners, including Carlyle and other cultural luminaries, like Dickens and Tennyson, voiced their support for a bill to ban street music, arguing that they were "daily interrupted, harassed, worried, wearied," and indeed "driven nearly mad" by it.

Suisman shares a remarkable Stateside account from a few decades later, a complaint that is representative of the overload many listeners felt at the turn of the century, before the commercial viability of recorded music (the bracketed remarks are his):

> "One afternoon, when I was watering flowers in the backyard, a boy in the street whistled a tune that I had not heard before," a typical jeremiad began. "The infliction of that tune on my unwilling ears [infuriated me], not only because of its offensive vulgarity, but because there was something in the nature of that mephitic air [that is, song] that made me feel certain I should hear it a thousand times during the summer. And my prophetic soul divined the truth. In the course of a week or two every boy in town was whistling that tune, every other man humming it, and every tenth woman playing it on the piano."

Except for the absence of recording technology, there seems to be little difference between this description of a song being whistled or sung "a thousand times" and the "boundless surfeit" Schoenberg would soon attribute to phonographs. Yet the whistling boy of Suisman's anecdote is just one example of how pervasive (and premeditated) the prephonographic deluge actually was. The music publishing industry, as Suisman also points out, came by its first burst of economic growth not through records, but through the diligent efforts of an army of "song pluggers"—musicians in the pay of a given publisher, who performed songs in order to advertise sheet music. Pluggers—the name comes from the idea that any available silence in the landscape should be filled (that is, "plugged") with sound—could be found in a wide variety of venues, from theatrical events, to sports competitions, to department stores, and even nudist colonies and prisons. "We'd sing a song to them thirty or forty times a night," claimed publisher Louis Bernstein, describing the techniques of the profession. "And the result was that when the people walked out of there they'd be singing the song. They couldn't help it; it was forced down their throat. They'd cheer, and they'd yell, and they'd boo, but we kept pounding away at them. We made songs that way." Clearly recording technology was not the only source of musical inundation.

PUT ANOTHER NICKEL IN: ON REPETITION

What about the antirecording critique's complaint that recordings are always the same—the repetition decried by Copland, Sessions, and others? For one thing, the point is misleading to the extent that it conjures the foil of a past in which listeners were not able, or did not desire, to hear music again. Of course, at the most basic level, there has never been any music anywhere that does not repeat itself in some way. Musicians and listeners have always experienced performance as the reinstantiation of elements of melody, or harmony, or rhythm, or other musical characteristics. Thematic material in sonata form, motivic devices of late-nineteenth-century composers like Wagner and Bruckner, the steady pulse of marching music, the recurring intervals of Alberti bass, and the refrain of popular song are among the more obvious examples.

But repetition in the time before recording was not a mere aesthetic tool for composers. Particularly in the nineteenth century, with the rise of concert culture and the entrenchment of Romantic aesthetics, many audiences and critics were more than willing to attend repeat performances of the same work; they *wanted* to hear compositions again. Indeed, in its original context, a nineteenth-century piece may have had a greater chance of being reheard as a live performance than is most of the art music composers write today. "Romantic theatergoers," writes Judith Pascoe, describing a theatrical phenomenon that was not untrue of music, were willing to attend "performances over and over and over again. In fact, the intensity of their pleasure seemed to stem partly from the repetition, which allowed for a deep familiarity with the lines and gestures associated with particular plays." Such practices were partly spurred by the cult of celebrity, which, as Daniel Cavicchi points out, encouraged listeners to seek out "repeated encounters with the same performer," and even inspired pilgrimages for that purpose. But listeners were also after multiple hearings of a given piece. Lucy Lowell, describing her experience at a Wagner Festival in Boston in the 1880s, wrote that "I should like to hear just the same thing over again every week for months." "I never can satisfy myself about music till I have heard it more than once," noted George Strong, "and have ruminated on it, marked, learned, and inwardly digested it." Schoenberg "recalled a listener who had attended a performance of Beethoven's Fifth Symphony fifty times," and many others who had attended other works as many as ten, fifteen, or twenty times.

Even within a single concert, it was not uncommon for an audience to express its enthusiasm for a piece by calling for encores, sometimes before the piece was actually over. Importantly, the word "encore," in this setting, was taken literally. It was understood as a request for the reperformance of a specific work, or even a specific movement, not the performance of an additional selection in the performer's repertoire, as is the usual definition today. And for at least some listeners, calling for an encore assumed a very specific kind of repeatability, as if different performances would automatically conform to a single score.

The antirecording critique is further compromised if we look at the issue of repeatability from the other direction. That is, although recordings can be played again, the effect of that repetition is another question altogether. It certainly does not mean there is never anything new to hear. Rather, recordings are remade as they are reheard. "There is music that I have listened to for years and years," guitarist Pat Metheny once remarked, in a statement that could serve as a direct rebuttal to Sessions et al., that "sounds different to me every single time I put it on." Lydia Goehr distinguishes between "cold repetition" and "constructive repetition," indicating in the first case that "we end up in the place where we began because we keep doing the same thing over and over again in the same way," while in the second, "development takes place, where even in doing the same thing over and over again, in each instance we do something different and thereby show a change in our understanding." Yet though I appreciate Goehr's distinction, I suspect that truly "cold repetition" is rarer than she allows, in part because constructive repetition can sometimes go unnoticed by the listener herself, and in any case is impossible to measure.

In the terms of this book, contextual collaboration is the underlying dynamic here. As we saw in chapter 1, any work is inevitably transformed by the situation in which it is met. There is no reason that that transformation should not apply to recorded sound the way we earlier saw it applied to live performance. Listeners help to *create* recordings as they are perceived, through transductive processes determined by the variables of the playback device, the listening environment, and the specifics of a listener's subjectivity. In order to exist, recorded music, like all music, requires a body to detect its vibrations—a fact undercutting Chanan's claim that with recording, music "has become literally disembodied." When someone experiences a recording, the performing body may be missing, in one sense, but the listening body is not. Indeed, the listening body is *a kind of* performing body. And sometimes these listening/performing bodies work together; as Timothy Day suggests, the experience of "a familiar record in fresh company" can provide a new perspective "through another's ears and responses." But even in solitude, new perspectives emerge. Jazz critic Francis Davis, writing about the pieces included on the *Smithsonian Collection of Classic Jazz,* suggests that "these are works so rich they reveal new detail on every hearing." That is quite a claim. Yet it's true, even though for dedicated music fans "every hearing" might amount to a lot of hearings indeed.

Consider how Davis's colleague Eric Nisenson describes his relationship with Miles Davis's *Kind of Blue*. Initially resistant to jazz, Nisenson came to love it after discovering his brother's copy of Davis's most famous recording. With that discovery, the work gained "increasing profundity and value for me, something I could not say about many of my other youthful pursuits":

For instance, some of the books that I had read and loved as a teen-ager, like the novels of Thomas Wolfe, Sinclair Lewis, or Herman [*sic*] Hesse, lost their meaningfulness when I got older. The works of other writers I read at this time—Faulkner, Hemingway, Fitzgerald, and Ellison—took on new layers of depth as I experienced more of life. Jazz was like these novels; even though I lost my romantic images of the jazz musician and the jazz world itself, the music became increas-ingly meaningful and inspirational. I still got goose bumps when I listened to Kind of Blue, but as I got older, it seemed to gain emotional and spiritual resonance and become even more a central part of my life. And I discovered the same thing to be true of the best albums that I first discovered in my early years with jazz.

Note here, by the way, how Nisenson collapses "jazz" ("jazz was like these novels") and "jazz albums" ("I still got goose bumps when I lis-tened to Kind of Blue")—another example of how recording and live performance have become conceptually entangled.

But what Nisenson leaves out of this account is his own role in cre-ating the richness of *Kind of Blue*—richness that, for all the album's popularity, surely some other listeners declined to perceive, just as Nisenson declined to perceive it in the novels of Hermann Hesse. The contextual collaboration he enacts is one of the main ways a recorded, repeatable work can in fact "gain emotional and spiritual resonance"—and can, in the process, become a new work. Day cites Leonard Bernstein's view that while "a recording might not change," a "listener does"—but even that's not quite right. Through contextual collaboration, the music on a recording actually does change as the lis-tener changes. Listeners do not merely link "unchanging sounds with personal and ever-developing associations and memories." Rather, the sounds are changed as they are contextualized (and recontextualized) through different media, listening spaces, social situations, sensory ratios, and subjectivities. All the while, the music is never "in" the recording, but is produced by the listener's interaction with it.

If a recording did not change with each successive listen, we could not really be said to "listen" to it at all. Even a fan with highly conser-vative tastes cannot experience exactly the same thing when she returns to that greatest hits collection for the umpteenth time. Perhaps she had fallen in love with the album after her third listen. At that point it had changed from a confusing series of sounds into something beautiful. If, returning to it later, she merely notices the same musical details, the work becomes a confirmation of past listening. And the confirmation that occurs on the tenth listen is different from the confirmation that occurs on the fiftieth, even if only in the sense that in the latter the perception is strengthened. If, somewhere along the way, she stops noticing details, but continues turning to the work out of habit, as a source of comfort, it has been transformed from stimulus into anodyne. If she begins to find it boring, the work has changed even more dramatically, almost into the opposite of the thing that initially attracted her. In a sense, the work dies for her. But if, conversely, she continues to notice new details "on every hearing," even at this advanced stage in the relationship, then the work clearly has a capacity for reincarnation.

That possibility of an extended relationship with a recording, and of its reincarnation through listening, comes from the different kinds of attention we bring to music. Though listeners limited to a single listen can be generally aware of how a work's harmony, rhythm, melody, and other musical attributes coalesce, more detailed understandings require following Metheny's lead and putting the record on again. So the repeatability of recordings is not necessarily the experiential cul-de-sac that its critics make it out to be. Rather, it allows for perceptual depth. Charles Rosen is thus precisely wrong when he claims that "recording tends to dilute and disperse the attention necessary for difficult music." Recording actually enables unprecedented appreciation of the sonic complexities of performance. To some extent it makes those complexities possible in the first place. Citing Milton Babbitt, Evan Eisenberg notes that "the increased 'efficiency' of modern musical language" requires "increased accuracy from the transmitter (performer)," and so benefits from "purely electronic media of performance," which makes that accuracy more attainable. To put that another way: the fact that a recording can be analyzed over repeated listens means that composers are now free to write music that rewards that sort of obsession, and that assertively demands something more than a first impression. With recording, a bemused audience has one less excuse to "hand down a verdict at first hearing by applauding or failing to applaud or hissing." Instead, a confused listener ought to feel obligated to play the piece again.

Gottfried Rabl, who worked on the *Caruso 2000* project described in chapter 2, shares an anecdote about how a recording can continue to surprise, or even confuse, no matter how many times it is heard. If the antirecording critique is right in claiming that the repeatability of recordings means they are the same with each listen, then Rabl's task should have been simple enough—the process of hearing Caruso's solo voice a few times should have been all he needed to follow the singer while recording the overdubs. But Rabl had the exact opposite experience. During the recording sessions, he found himself disoriented, describing a feeling of being adrift in the cosmos, unable to detect a solid temporal reference point against which to measure the music as it went by. "The obvious lack of any form of contact with the soloist," Rabl writes, "brought us astonishingly close to Karl Popper's statement, 'We do not know, we guess.'"

Repeatability thus generates a sizable array of musical works—an ever-growing repertoire that accumulates as the listener reperceives. But the contextual collaboration of recording also occurs "spatially," through audio propinquity. Music is always heard in relation to other sound—other recordings or performances, for instance, or human speech, or environmental noises. That can be an effect of chronology— the work I'm hearing now is influenced by the work I heard a minute ago, or a year ago, just as my memory of the work I'm hearing now will be influenced by, and will influence, the work I hear next. Or it can be an effect of simultaneity—the work I hear now is influenced by the work you insist on listening to in the next room, or by your desire to start a conversation with me the moment I press play. In each of these cases, the other sound is a source of contextual collaboration, even if it is unwelcome.

In stipulating that recordings are always the same, the antirecording argument ignores this fact of audio propinquity, or sonic juxtaposition, assuming that each work is hermetically sealed, a completely isolated experience whose significance is dictated by self-contained form. The key organizing principle for recorded music in the last half of the twentieth century, the album, contributed greatly to this impression. For many, the album implicitly argued that recordings were structurally determined, made up of an inviolable sequence of tracks, expressly chosen by a producer or artist to serve a larger aesthetic point, like movements in a symphony. (Indeed, the rise of the album in the first place may have had something to do with the way it mimicked the qualities of lengthiness and weight so prized by the nineteenth-century European high art tradition.)

Most professional musicians still strive to make albums, and the critical culture around the music business is still built on the album review and the album discography. But from a twenty-first-century perspective, making albums is an ambivalent gesture at best, since today we assume an album's sequence of tracks is anything but inviolable. This is the age of iTunes and Spotify, which encourage the creation of customized playlists whose individual tracks have often been obtained or accessed without their accompanying full-length recordings. These technologies also allow listeners to subject large databases of music to the random effect of the shuffle function. There have been complaints about this feature, based on the question of how random it really is—some listeners observe that, depending on the size of the database being shuffled, certain tracks seem to get left out or emphasized. But whether or not these complaints indicate a genuine conspiracy, or are traceable to some underlying law of probability, they reveal a deep desire for "real randomness," which in turn is evidence of listeners' resistance to predetermined sequencing.

Of course, listeners have always been able to resist the preset sequence of the album—or of any other organizing principle, such as the implied linearity of "side A" and "side B," which characterized the disc format almost from the beginning. John Corbett, writing in the mid-1990s, waxed rhapsodic about his CD player's shuffle feature, referring to it as a "miraculous button" that in its own time circumvented "the logic behind decades of music industry packaging." For Corbett, shuffle meant that a recording could "renew itself virtually every time it's played" because it helped the listener to assemble "unforeseeable combinations, segues, connections, and leaps of faith." That renewal was a result of contextual collaboration, where context was the work that came before or after. But even CD shuffle was not as revolutionary as Corbett makes it sound, unless we assume that commercial products have always been used according to how they have been materially structured. To make that assumption would be to ignore what Michel de Certeau called the "tactic": a discreet consumer advantage gained through "the cracks that particular conjunctions open in the surveillance of the proprietary powers." Fans of recording, Certeau would suggest, have always been poachers on the lord's estate, quietly subverting official expectations for how goods should be consumed.

In other words, shuffle need not be technologically enabled at all. With LPs and 78s, there was never anything to stop a listener from simply lifting the needle and playing a track again. The insert of a 1966 Columbia recording lists, as one of the seven ways that "records give you more of what you want," that "it's easy to pick out the songs you want to play, or to play again a particular song or side. All you have to do is lift the tone arm and place it where you want it." Much earlier, a 1915 Victrola ad suggested that listening to recordings at home "has these advantages: You can make your choice of artists and selections, and have as many encores as you desire."

Tape may have been a little harder to navigate, in that it required the patience of rewinding or fast-forwarding (one reason video rental stores used to plead with customers to "please be kind: rewind"). But it made up for that hassle by spawning the mixtape, a fan-devised art form that in turn inspired the digital versions we know today (the mix CD, the iTunes or Spotify playlist). "Often I don't like the sequence of musical numbers on an LP record," Hans Fantel once wrote, in a description of mixtape making. "Some numbers I like better than others, and when I copy I simply skip the ones that bore me." As the sort of listener who eschewed surprise, Fantel preferred to group similar pieces together, instead of mimicking the typical producer's technique of varying selections. "I rearrange the program sequence when I copy records on tape," he wrote, "regrouping the slower and faster numbers to avoid an emotional jolt at the start of each new selection." When applying this technique to the slow movements of the four Brahms symphonies, "the emotional effect is marvelous—a gradual intensification of a deeply contemplative mood—something no concertgoer or record listener who hears these works in their normal context would ever experience." Elsewhere, Fantel combined excerpts from Haydn symphonies with Sousa marches, with results that, for him, were both "hilarious" and "musically effective." Again, the recontextualization of each piece was its remaking—its decomposition.

Fantel insisted that creating mixtapes was one of "the most rewarding and creative aspects of taping," recommending it as a way of opening "new perspectives on music." Note that even in a mixtape, recordings have not been directly acted upon, except in the sense that they have been copied to a new medium. But the music has nevertheless changed, revealing "something no concertgoer or record listener who hears these works in their normal context would ever experience," simply because of the new music around them—and it does so even without the benefit of a shuffle button.

Resourceful and motivated listeners, in other words, have never been beholden to implied or explicit rules about how a piece should be heard. Recordings have always been random access and mixable, and thus always subject to renewal through repetition.

NOT FADE AWAY: PERMANENCE VERSUS EPHEMERALITY

Not only does the antirecording critique espouse dubious history, but it has also too easily accepted at face value some of the assumptions about listening that were propounded by the public relations experts of the music industry itself. Perhaps that shouldn't be so surprising—as David Suisman points out, that industry helped pioneer modern marketing so effectively that its claims have been hard to escape. From the beginning, ad after ad celebrated the durability, indeed the permanence, of recordings. Such claims may have been patently ridiculous, but the intensity with which they were made has since helped construct our understanding of the ephemerality of sound in the era before recording. And that construction has in turn been picked up by the antirecording critique as a way of "proving" the destruction of aura. "The phonograph," as Michael Chanan puts it, "prompted the idea that sound recording was a means of preserving truth for future generations." Of course, the phonograph itself didn't prompt anything. But the phonograph's marketing culture recognized and responded to the fact that media in general elicits certain expectations from its users. Stone tablets and ancient scrolls, fragile but safely ensconced in museums, set a standard that we like to imagine we can surpass with our advanced technology.

And so even before the phonograph was adapted for explicitly musical purposes, one of its proposed uses—and presumably one of the sources of its nickname, the "talking machine"—was as a technique for preserving the voices of loved ones, which could be memorialized in a kind of family album of sound. For recordings to be used as markers of memory, consumers naturally expected them to be durable. Marketers fed that expectation by claiming they were *extremely* durable. In a 1900 industry handbook, a man describes how his wife made several records of their son's first sounds, and how these records might even outlive the boy: "I fancy him listening to those 'talks' twenty years from now! But should he be taken from us in the meanwhile, I know I'd hold them as my most highly-prized possession." (One wonders how many of these early homemade records lasted even a decade.) Edison, who early on saw the phonograph as a sophisticated dictation tool, also imagined, in an item published in *North American Review* in 1878, that it could be used to record telephone messages, which would then be kept as "permanent and invaluable records." At least publicly, Edison seemed to believe that recording technology by its very nature guaranteed longevity.

But the marketing of permanence really took off after music became the machine's raison d'être. Roland Gelatt refers to one remarkable example: the ambitiously named "Indestructible Cylinder Record." Elsewhere, a gramophone ad claimed that records could "withstand any amount of rough handling without danger of injuring them"; another that they would last "indefinitely." It is as if customers were expected to believe that the machinery and its media overcame decay and death, making true immortality achievable at last for great artists whose performances had previously been lost to history. A later Victor ad claimed that the Victrola "made the opera and the concert more than a fleeting pleasure. It brings them right into your own home, there to be enjoyed as your permanent, priceless possession." Yet another ad compared the fates of singers Jenny Lind and Nellie Melba. Melba benefited from her career's propinquity to recording technology, but Lind was not so lucky:

> Jenny Lind is only a memory, but the voice of Melba can never die.
> Two voices of finest, purest gold.
> One is gone forever.
> The other lives for all time.
> There was no Victrola to capture the fleeting beauties of Jenny Lind.
> But Melba's voice will still be heard in centuries to come.
> To-day Melba herself thrills and entrances vast audiences throughout the world. Happy singer and happy public, that her flawless, limpid notes will flow forever in undiminished beauty from her Victor records!
> Practically every great singer and instrumentalist of this generation makes records only for the Victor—thus perpetuating their art for all time.

Of course, there are complexities worth addressing here. It is true, as Russell Sanjek argues, that some consumers treated records merely as "fleeting documents" designed to advertise sheet music or live performance. "For all the grandiloquence about messages to future generations and hearing the voices of the dead," Jonathan Sterne similarly writes, "most recordings have been (and I would argue, are still) treated by their makers, owners, and users as ephemera, as items to be used for a while and then to be disposed of." Yet Sanjek and Sterne miss how some listeners may have wanted to read against the grain of the marketing, may even have wanted to enact the fragility of recordings as a way of humanizing them, in response to the relentless rhetoric about permanence. (In becoming susceptible to decay—a susceptibility their listeners shared—recordings would have seemed more "real," and less intimidating.) Alternately, perhaps more casual record fans assumed the objects were so well made that they could withstand domestic carelessness. In either case, even cavalier consumer behavior would have been informed by a larger view that the technology had achieved material permanence.

More important, many musicians, rather than being flattered by the idea that a fan would use a recording to "awaken their music at will," were terrified at what they believed was the prospect of permanence. The idea of committing their art to the medium was a source of great anxiety; audio documentation of an embarrassing performance could be preserved for future generations, maybe even for the rest of time (or so it was assumed). Colin Symes adapts the term "phonophobia" to describe the fear this idea generated, pointing out how self-consciousness led many respected artists—even today, despite the possibility of unparalleled editing control—to "commit more errors" during a recording session "than they would in a concert." Pianist Ferruccio Busoni hated recording; he claimed it made him "conscious the whole time that every note was going to be there for eternity." This fear of the "immortalization" of even the smallest flaw sometimes served as an impediment to recording at all. In other cases it led to an obsessive perfectionism that drove many artists to use record making as an excuse to disappear into a studio, sometimes for years on end.

In the final analysis, the marketing of phonographic permanence helped to reify music. Whether or not you were a fan of recording, the discourses that surrounded it helped focus your attention on the putative indestructibility of the disc, or cylinder, or tape. Even today, antirecording arguments often begin with the assumption that these advertising claims are based in truth, that recording really does last.

And of course in one sense such claims *are* based in truth. Historical reissues and compilations of all types, some dating to the acoustic recording era, can still be found in CD form in most any good record store or online retail site. Indeed, many of the oldest recordings are now out of copyright and can be downloaded for free from the Internet Archive or elsewhere on the web. My own music collection lacks any Nellie Melba recordings, but no matter: a quick search of Archive .org reveals that a number of her 78s have been digitized there, and will presumably wait until such a time as I should ever desire to listen to them. In that sense, the aforementioned Victor ad's claim was true: Melba's music really did, it turns out, outlive her far into the future.

But the situation is more complicated. For one thing, the life of any recording is dependent upon the life of playback devices. "The sound recording," as Jerry McWilliams points out, "is an extension of a machine, a part designed to fit into a large, often highly complex mechanical or electro-mechanical system"—what Suisman notes could be called a "machine ensemble," adapting a term coined by historian Wolfgang Schivelbusch. Whether or not that mechanical system is working well—or at all—has a direct effect on the life of the media it is designed to play. A significant prerequisite for any recording's longevity, then, is the maintenance of its playback device.

And playback devices, it turns out, are hard to maintain. Whatever kind of home stereo system you own, it is made of delicate parts that are subject to even mild environmental wear and tear. "When we wake up and cruise into our studios," sound engineer and *Mix* magazine columnist Stephen St. Croix once observed, "everything is a little worse than we left it the night before." This goes for "every connector, every switch contact, every sliver of metal, every inch of wire, every solder joint on our circuit boards, every pin or every socketed chip and even every transistor junction." Things wear out. Metal oxidizes. Electrically powered devices are at the mercy of electromigration (which inhibits the reliability of microchips), parameter drift (in which the specified values of a system change over time), transient electrical stresses (high current produced by electrostatic discharge, lightning, or bursts of energy related to power supply), changes in temperature, electromagnetic interference, mechanical failure, humidity, dust, sand, vibrations, and so on.

And of course, as playback devices decay, so media decays. Most recordings, whether commercial releases purchased by consumers or the master media from which they are made, are inherently fragile. Indeed, Kurt Bollacker goes so far as to argue that new media is even shorter-lived than its predecessors, even though we tend to assume the opposite. Compare, for instance, the stability of a wax cylinder with the gossamer flicker of an audiotape, or with the strange fragility of the hard disc, which must continually be backed up in case of arbitrary crashes, and which may be more susceptible to water, dust, and heat than old-fashioned discs ever were. Yet even from the beginning recordings were compromised by their physical existence. Early discs were self-destructive—the frying pan noise of the 78 was caused by the needle wearing away its surface. CDs, while not abused by physical contact with a stylus, have been much more susceptible to scratching, rusting, and dirt—and digital error correction can actually make the problem worse by adding data that wasn't there in the first place. Tapes, in turn, were easily erased by the magnetic fields in common household appliances like vacuum cleaners and televisions. They were also occasionally destroyed (euphemistically, they were "eaten") by the very devices that were supposed to play them.

For professionals, the National Academy of Recording Arts and Sciences recommends treating the problem of media impermanence by diversifying. Each project should have an original master, two backup masters in different media, and Broadcast Wave Format versions of all components of a session, which should be stored in multiple locations—preferably state-of-the-art climate-controlled facilities. But even if a label or artist can afford these preservation methods, none is foolproof. Samuel Brylawski of the Association for Recorded Sound Collections wrote in the early twenty-first century that "no medium has proved stable enough to be called permanent," and argued that "the well-planned repository presumes media obsolescence, plans for it, and, according to its supporters, frees the archive community of the futile search for an affordable permanent medium." Consumers face more quotidian but no less serious storage risks. Physical recordings are typically kept on shelves (where they can fall), in drawers (where they can become dusty), in plastic or paper sleeves (where they can become scratched or sticky), in piles on desks or on floors (where they can be knocked over or stepped on), in boxes (where they can be lost or forgotten). More digitally inclined audiences may prefer cloud computing as a storage solution—but despite its ethereal, seemingly benign name, the cloud is not a fail-safe either. Somewhat infamously, in 2012, Mat Honan's "entire digital life was destroyed" by hackers when he entrusted it to remote systems. That was a worst-case scenario, but the threat remains real enough.

Yet even more important than playback and media vulnerabilities in themselves is what happens to a recording once we understand it in terms of contextual collaboration. The thing we assume is *Thriller,* or *Kind of Blue,* is not the aggregate of all its copies, so that any damaged or destroyed disc or tape can simply be replaced with another. Rather, each copy is a unique work in how it has been acted upon by its listeners. Think of the scratched copy of *Thriller* I referred to in the introduction to this book, or Nisenson's copy of *Kind of Blue,* serendipitously borrowed from his brother. Each recording's uniqueness came from the situation in which it was met and the personal subjectivity it was processed through. So I will never again own the *Thriller* I own now. That CD is marked with my experiences, gained as I listened at a particular time in my life. Should I lose it and replace it with another, the new one will never have the same valence for me. And this is also true of playback devices. Even with the wear and tear St. Croix noted, boomboxes have not gone extinct—yet I will never again own a boombox like the one on which I first heard *Thriller.* My father gave me that machine when I was in junior high, and before it broke down I adorned it with stickers and scuff marks. I used its tape deck to record some of my first original songs. And I perceived in it an idiosyncratic personality that derived from the way it reproduced sound. Like the media we own, then, our playback devices bear the traces of our use, physically and associatively. Listening to the same *Thriller* CD on another system now, the music I knew dies, and is reborn as something else.

Nor, finally, is physical deterioration the only thing interfering with the supposed permanence of recordings. Independent of the "health" of the device or its media, the life of a machine ensemble is affected by how popular it is with consumers, how it fares in relation to competing technologies, and how its availability is manipulated by manufacturers. The phonograph, for instance, was not originally intended for the dissemination of music, yet when its potential for disseminating music was discovered, it replaced an instrument that was designed for that purpose—the player piano. Material factors certainly contributed to this change—the invention of electrical recording meant that the phonograph could reproduce a broader range of timbres than the player piano, while it was also cheaper and more compact. But the shift was not effortless, and certain social forces resisted it. After all, consumers had invested in player pianos in the first place because they expected to be able to continue using them for a long time.

And so media currency is always in flux. It is easy while in the middle of a period of apparent stability to assume that the popular format du jour will always be around. In the 1990s, CDs felt very much like the natural culmination of a century's worth of technological development. Not many music fans predicted that they would be challenged by MP3s (and related formats) in the new century—particularly as the first kinds of digital compression compromised sound quality so significantly. Yet looking at the history of audio recording, the decline of the CD—a fate seemingly now sealed by the fact that disc drives have become optional on some brands of personal computer—should have been assumed, just as currently popular formats will presumably be replaced too, after their moment in the sun.

It is true that devoted listeners have always kept older formats alive, even past the point of their greatest popularity—consider the phonograph societies mentioned in chapter 2, or the story Bollacker tells about the NASA archivist who squirreled away outmoded tape drives in her garage in the hope that one day the public would be interested in the information they were designed to read. Any object will always attract people willing to fetishize or honor it. Yet such specialized communities are mere stopgaps of decay, and do not ensure the limitless preservation of individual recordings or the personal machines on which they are played. I own a piano roll that I prize because it was a gift—but it is also musically useless to me, because it is too much of a hassle to maintain a working player piano amid all the other music technology I own. As each day passes, it seems a little less likely that this artifact will ever be heard again.

It is not just a matter of the investment necessary to own a particular piece of gear; every machine also calls upon a relevant body of operational knowledge. In time, the specialization required to use older media—understanding the various styli employed by 78s, for instance, or the many equalization curves relevant to recordings made before 1955, or how to clean tape heads—can be harder to come by, even when the devices themselves still exist. Thus older recordings can become *functionally* ephemeral, not because there is anything technically wrong with them or even because the machine ensemble of which they are a part is no longer extant, but because their relevant culture has dissipated or sometimes disappeared completely.

"The political economy of the recording industry," as Colin Symes points out in a discussion of the phonograph, is "predicated on periodically staging its own extinction, thus requiring its participants to invest in new equipment and new types of disc every quarter century or so and to accept that the logic of this is compelling and necessary." In the twenty-first century, these periodic staged extinctions—like so many other extinctions in our culture—may be coming more quickly. The material forms of music are more glibly euthanized now, victims of a momentum in which there are increasingly more of them to choose from. Arguably, the LP enjoyed a longer period of currency than the audiocassette, which enjoyed a longer period of currency than the CD, which enjoyed a longer period of currency than the digital download, which no sooner gained a foothold before it was threatened by streaming. A single consumer who has lived through all of these developments increasingly perceives what seems to be a revolving door of media and devices, a sad parade of planned obsolescence. Whether or not this perception is accurate, each technology that fades into obscurity takes with it many individual recordings—many individual, personally meaningful, decompositional *Thriller*s and *Kind of Blue*s.

The point is that recordings, understood as deteriorating artifacts, are fragile and fleeting, like live performances. They simply decay more slowly.

HIGH FIDELITY

Fans of recording often associate the music industry's permanence marketing with the medium's putative expressive authenticity, attained through high fidelity. The idea that "the voice of Melba can never die" assumes that Melba recordings actually captured the voice of Melba in the first place. Yet "high fidelity" contains a hidden compromise with authenticity (for which the word "fidelity" is of course a synonym)— an uncertainty suggested by the fact that the fidelity in question is merely "high," not "total." This is telling, and it points toward a deeper problem with the word "fidelity" and the authenticity it attempts to establish.

Emily Thompson argues that fidelity existed as an evaluative criterion from the very beginning of recording technology. At first it was a function of the phonograph's role as an office dictation machine, and referred to little more than "intelligibility." Later, when the phonograph was marketed as a device for playing music, "fidelity" meant "quality of tone," a concept that referred to a recording's overall "sound," including the kinds of noises (surface noise, motor hum) produced by the machine itself—what I earlier called the "signature of technology." Later still, "fidelity" would refer to the elimination of "tone"—the definition that would become most familiar to twenty-first-century listeners.

Yet the latter meaning, according to Thompson, emerged as early as 1915, when the sound of the machine was still clearly audible by today's standards. In fact, while we might imagine that even the most ambitious marketing strategy would have been forced to posit "high fidelity" as a goal that would be attained *eventually*, advertisements repeatedly suggested that the goal had *already* been attained. As Andre Millard puts it, "The manufacturers of talking machines had always made exaggerated claims about the technology of their products." By the middle of the century, for instance, they spoke of the "new miracles of war research," even though they were essentially reproducing the same 78-rpm players with fancier, fresher labels. Indeed, the term "high fidelity" was used so recklessly that it eventually lost much of its semantic force—much like the word "authenticity" itself.

One early instance of how the concept of high fidelity was used in a marketing context appeared in a National Phonograph Company publication called *The Phonograph and How to Use It*, published in 1900. In a fictional scenario, "Mr. Openeer" arrives at a Christmas party with his wife:

As we fumbled with wraps and gloves in the silent hall of the house, our feelings were divided between personal discomfort and wonderment that no one was there to greet us. Suddenly there piped up a thin little voice seeming to come from nowhere. It grew louder and stronger, and we heard "Merry Christmas, merry, merry Christmas. Welcome, Mr. Openeer, we are glad to see you. Welcome, Mrs. Openeer; how is the baby? How did you leave Ponjo?" (Ponjo is our dog.) We looked around bewildered. The voice continued: "Take off your wraps; lay them on the table. James will see them safely laid away." Astonishment gave way to curiosity, and we drew aside a curtain and found the cheery speaker to be—a Phonograph. Then through a half-open door we heard whisperings and merry laughter as the uncanny little machine went on to sing for us a Christmas glee. Before it was finished the children of the house came running in laughing, followed by our hostess and the other guests; and we saw and felt heartily the double welcome that had been prepared for us.

Although Openeer does not go so far as to explicitly say that the phonograph recording is indistinguishable from actual voices—though that is clearly the conclusion we are to draw—the narrative is remarkable for the surprise and confusion he and his wife experience. Note, incidentally, the protagonist's unusual name—it is as though we are to believe he is an inherently reliable listener because of his "open ears," and thus that we should expect to be fooled by the machine too.

A similar point was made by the famous "His Master's Voice" logo used by Victor. Adapted from a preexisting painting by Francis Barraud, the logo depicted a small dog (nicknamed "Nipper") apparently confusing a gramophone recording of his owner's voice for the real thing. Kenney describes variations on this logo, in which other listeners (children, monkeys, women) were similarly duped. The copy for one ad—"A Man's Voice, Anyhow"—snidely suggested how easy women were to fool. Another version featured a well-to-do young white couple observing as their African-American and Irish-American domestic servants listen to the machine, unable to escape its thrall. In analyzing this image, Kenney argues that "the phonograph's power, wielded by white middle-class and upper middle-class owners, transfixed the weak and disenfranchised," while the logo tried to downplay the hierarchy of race and class by claiming, "One touch of harmony makes the whole world kin." Yet it seems just as likely that the record companies actually wanted everyone to hear recordings as if they were the real thing. It is not that the young couple in this scenario are in on the trick, like the children in the Openeer story. They too are transfixed. Their social power comes not from a secret knowledge of the truth of the sounds the machine is making, but merely from the means to own and operate it.

In fact, the industry went to great lengths to demonstrate that no one was immune to the phonograph's magic. This at least seems to have been the purpose of the thousands of public "tone tests" conducted by the Edison company between 1915 and 1925. These events, which mimicked similar displays simultaneously happening in the player piano industry, occurred in both high-art and middle-of-the-road performance venues, and featured musicians and phonographs performing side by side, in a pseudoscientific effort to "prove" that no one could tell them apart. A typical tone test resembled the Openeer scene described above. Portions of the program were given over to completely live performance, followed by demonstrations of the latest recordings. Eventually the live musician and the phonograph would perform together, and at a predetermined point the live musician would drop out, demonstrating the machine's lifelike quality. As one pamphlet put it, "The purpose of this hearing is to illustrate that Mr. Edison has realized his ambition to re-create the correct tonal quality of music."

Perhaps what is most astonishing about these tone tests—and it has been remarked upon before—is not the exaggeration per se, but the fact that to modern ears acoustic-era phonographs sound nothing like "live" music—they are almost completely lacking in what we would call fidelity. Yet if there were no extant acoustic recordings for us to examine from a twenty-first-century vantage point, it would be nearly impossible to discern this failing simply by reading contemporary accounts, which uncritically trumpeted the industry's claim that sonic accuracy had already been obtained. According to Peter Copeland, for instance, "admirers of Edison's tinfoil phonograph are on record as saying that it was impossible to tell the difference between the recording and the original." And Evan Eisenberg concludes that "the common ear of the day really was gulled by records. Under the right circumstances, and with the right music, the effect was trompe l'oreille." Even so seemingly reputable a source as *Scientific American* could write, in 1877, the same year that Edison's device was patented, that "a strip of paper travels through a little machine, the sounds of the latter are magnified, and our grandchildren or posterity centuries hence hear us as plainly as if we were present." In 1913, another writer for the same publication would praise the Edison Diamond Disc player in similar terms: "The sound was lifted clear of the machine. The singer or musician was in the room, not in the box."

How to explain what seems like hopeless credulity to us? To some extent, the disconnect may be related to our inability to understand aura: the explanation has simply been lost to history. Possibly also contemporary listeners were swayed by the novelty of the talking machine. As Michael Chanan argues, the phonograph in its early years was such a source of "fascination" that its shortcomings were often ignored. Perhaps that was easier to do when singers learned to mimic the sound of their own recordings, as they often did. And perhaps some tone test audiences merely wanted to be seen in the vicinity of the latest technology, grateful for the social cachet it might bestow—the same dynamic that drives some early adopters of new technology in our own era. Others may not have been interested in the question of acoustic fidelity at all, but may simply have wanted to enjoy an evening of music, regardless of how it was produced.

Whatever their appeal, the tone tests' claims of fidelity seem outlandish to us because we assume we know how recorded music should really sound. And yet for us "high fidelity" has been no less contrived. Thompson points to the similarity between the Edison tone tests and Memorex's "Is it live or is it Memorex?" marketing campaign of the 1970s, used to sell both audio- and videotape. But unlike the tone tests, the Memorex ads never even offered the opportunity for a comparison—the ad itself was always situated within the already patently unreal listening environment of the television, or (worse) the mute environment of the magazine page. The real question the ads posed was not "Is it live or is it Memorex?" but "Is it Memorex or is it some other recording media?" Indeed, some of the ads played with this paradox quite openly, repeatedly subverting the viewer's expectation that the next image or sound would be the "true" one—which of course it never could be, since each image or sound was always part of the ad. More important, the campaign obscured the fact that if high fidelity really existed, one shouldn't have to argue for it. It should be transparent: so effective that it is both obvious and no longer noticeable. That is, the very act of having to convince someone of the existence of fidelity is itself a symptom of fidelity's failure.

In retrospect, the tone tests offered a premonition of the shape of sound to come. They set a template for how recorded performance and live performance would overlap, becoming fundamentally confused, mutually influencing perceptual experiences. From private gramophone society "recitals," to the early use of phonographs as instruments in avant-garde (and not so avant-garde) classical compositions, to "live" radio broadcasts that were actually prerecorded—the terminology of "live" and "recorded" was at least modestly corrupt from the beginning, and only became more so as the century went on and a truly multimedia landscape emerged. But the problem has never been whether one or the other was more authentic. There are differences between live music and recorded music, to be sure, but the modes of listening they engender are entangled. Today, live music is, properly, an extension of recording, and vice versa. That overlap makes authenticity in either realm impossible.

6

DOTS ON A PAGE

Unless sounds are held by the memory of man, they perish, because they cannot be written down.

—Isidore of Seville

Though the distance between Grammar and Rhetoric is great enough, the distance between musical notation and the art of playing well is infinitely greater.

—François Couperin

The text of music is a performance.

—Carolyn Abbate

In the West, we habitually celebrate the written word. The retelling of early modern history is usually marked by a special emphasis on the invention of the printing press. The story of our arts usually includes a chapter on a rich literary legacy. And advocates of our civilization usually point to its primary documents—the Bible, the Magna Carta, Luther's theses, the Constitution and the Declaration of Independence, the Gettysburg Address, *The Communist Manifesto,* and so on.

This propensity for text has persisted in the face of all kinds of criticism. One of the great theorists of the demise of print culture, Marshall McLuhan, has been posthumously marginalized, after a few years of being in vogue, and the revolution he foresaw—a post-print world ushered in by television and its corollary technologies—did not, it turns out, make text irrelevant. In fact, in blogs, Twitter, Facebook, e-mail, and other postmodern technologies, the digital revolution has seemed an extension of print culture rather than a repudiation of it. The discourse communities that the Internet is used to navigate—politics, current events, sports, entertainment, relationships, technology—still employ the written word for that navigation, even when they do so in the context of multimedia, and far away from paper or ink. What McLuhan called the "Gutenberg Galaxy" and its "spectrum of effects"—linearity, objectivity, uniformity, boundary creation—is still with us. Terence McKenna's gloss of McLuhan, that print is "just a convulsive, 500 year episode in the Western mind," has not yet been borne out.

Of course, when it comes to the nonlinguistic arts, the historical persistence of text has always seemed beside the point. Dance, painting, sculpture, and instrumental music are valuable precisely in how they presume to escape the limitations of language. They are cherished for an ability to connect directly to the human heart and soul. Yet I only know this, as a general experience, because I have perceived it in other people's verbal and written confessions about the ballets or portraits or sonatas or symphonies they love most. The fact is that we cannot really know what dance or visual art or music "say" until we actually articulate it. The frustrating paradox, then, is that writing and conversation are mechanisms for validating our experience of nonlinguistic art—making that experience into something we can share and "prove"—even as we long to escape the mediation of language and to enjoy each work more directly.

In music, ironies abound. Today, in order to have a career, a musician usually has to generate, or hire someone to generate, copious amounts of text—résumés, artist biographies, liner notes, newsletters, grant proposals—all of which run counter to Martin Mull's nagging dictum, well known and frequently quoted by musicians, about the futility of writing about music. Reviewers regularly contribute critical assessments to newspapers, magazines, and blogs. And then there are the hundreds if not thousands of books (like this one) that are generated every year by the academy and the broader literary culture. Musicology, ethnomusicology, music history, and other disciplines use the written word to establish legitimacy for both the writer and her subject matter, linguistically analyzing an art form that is popularly assumed to be above linguistic analysis. Thus these texts too are subject to ambivalence.

In the end, what Carolyn Abbate calls the "drastic" quality of music—its expression as a live performance that is "ephemeral," "phe-nomenal," and, in Vladimir Jankélévitch's word, "ineffable"—may indeed be the most appealing thing about it, but in our culture that quality is repeatedly subsumed within the unavoidably *effable* phe-nomenon of written language. To draw a parallel to the last chapter: we seem no more able to understand music outside of writing than we are able to understand live performance outside of recording.

One of the consequences of our historical emphasis on writing is that it gives clout to other textual systems. Hence the hoary reputation of music notation—the symbols, or "dots on a page," that are used to graphically denote (or connote, depending on your perspective) a complete musical utterance, typically referred to as a score. Michael Chanan cites what may be the first philosophical binding of score and work, initially referenced in chapter 2:

> The authority of the score was first mooted theoretically by a German church cantor, Nicolaus Listenius, in his treatise *Musica* dating from 1537. Distinguishing *musica practica,* or performance, from *musica poetica,* or the work itself, Listenius defined it as the task of the com-poser to produce an *opus perfectum et absolutum,* the musical text which endures after the composer's death. By the end of the century, in accordance with this new conception of their function, composers began to give their works opus numbers.

In Western musicology, this authority of the score came to be known by the German word *Texttreue.* In the nineteenth century it informed the concept of "sacralization," an attempt to elevate "the work" over the performance. But from the perspective of the twenty-first century I think it is more accurately signified by Eric Edberg's adaptation of a term from constitutional law: "textualism." In its original sense, textu-alism refers to a strict, document-based interpretation of the Constitu-tion. But for Edberg, following an insight offered by Gregory Currie, textualism is a way of saying that in music "work and text are one," that the essence of the composition can only be known in how it is written down. This denotational extreme assumes that when a score is carefully made, it instantiates, or at least "contains," the music it (more accurately) merely predicts. Advocates say the score *is* the music, or the music is "in" the score.

For a long time now, music textualists have been everywhere. Albert Schweitzer epitomized the view when he wrote in the early twentieth century that Bach's Fantasia in C Minor was "the despair of every organist" because "it is almost impossible to reproduce its ideal beauty in material tone"—as if it were not in the first place "almost impossible" to reproduce the work's material beauty in the dots on the page. According to Joseph Horowitz, conductor Arturo Toscanini similarly espoused an "ideal of self-effacing textual fidelity," a sentiment that in turn was adopted as one of the banalities of the music appreciation movement—see for instance B. H. Haggin, who made the pat argument that a musician "must produce what the printed score directs that he produce." Also in agreement with Toscanini were composer-conductor Felix Weingartner and pianist Artur Schnabel, both of whom linked textual fidelity to musical objectivity. Later, philosopher Nelson Goodman, in his *Languages of Art,* claimed that, as Ted Gioia puts it, "the musical score, and not the performance, *defines* the work." According to Russian pianist Sviatoslav Richter, when a musician reads music, "You've got how it has to be in front of you and you play exactly what's written." Conductor and composer Gunther Schuller has expressed textualist affinities too, as when he insisted "the composer and his score *have* to be respected, especially when that composer is a Beethoven, a Tchaikovsky, a Brahms, a Stravinsky, or any of the other fifty to a hundred composers whose masterpieces make up the bulk of our repertory."

This is not to say that textualism has been the only way of understanding the relationship between performance and score, ever since people first started putting musical marks on paper. The open-endedness of most Baroque music is by now well known (it's a subject we will look at in more detail in a moment). Even in the late nineteenth century—a great mythmaking period for classical music—performance practice continued to draw on conventions often ignored (and in some cases contradicted) by the dots on the page, as Thurston Dart and others have pointed out. And today, as we enjoy the benefits of MIDI, sequencers, samplers, and other affordable recording technologies, many musicians have redefined "writing" music altogether as the more immediate process of going directly to tape (in a manner of speaking) with a work in progress. For many, recording has replaced notation as a basic tool of composition—it has become a technique of both idea creation and revision, rather than merely a way to document a finished work. Our habit of making the ineffable effable through writing is thus more problematic than it seems at first; it is not a tradition we all blithely accept. We speak, after all, of writing music "down," as if inscription is inherently belittling.

Many composers of acoustic concert music, or any music that requires the organizational control allowed by notation, have taken these developments as more evidence for music's death cult, described in the introduction of this book. Richard Taruskin has gone so far as to claim that we have entered a "post-literate" age for music—suggesting that the movement away from notation is permanent. But I'm not convinced that we are witnessing the "collapse of 'print culture'" (or the "passing of a musical style," or "the extinction of a musical medium"), as John Halle dramatically puts it, summarizing Taruskin's position. There are still those who in composition, performance, and listening treat the score "piously" (to borrow Robert Levin's term). Even without that reverence, notation remains an important skill set of the professional journeyman musician. It makes it much easier for her to participate in an impromptu recording session, for instance, or to sit in with an out-of-town ensemble. When Amanda Palmer recently tried to supplement her touring band with local musicians willing to play for "beer and hugs," the resulting outrage was driven by a professionalism that assumed formal musical training, with a concomitant mastery of sight-reading, painstakingly and expensively attained through many years of practice and study. At roughly the same time, Palmer's peer Beck Hansen released a collection of songs not as a recorded album but as a set of sheet music. Part marketing gimmick, that move nevertheless assumed at least some Beck fans were notationally literate.

Notation, in other words, is still with us. It is still an efficient way of doing musical business. And its modern reputation as a specialized language—as opposed to the lingua franca it was closer to being for much of the nineteenth century—still gives it cultural cachet. To the present-day musical neophyte, the musician's skill in transforming dots on the page into music in the air can seem almost magical, the work of a priestly class possessing arcane knowledge of a sacred semiotic system. (To the musician, this credulousness is frustratingly unconnected to financial reward.) And that cachet may be why written music remains a last resort of the authenticity quest.

If we can finally dispense with the personal authenticities of the individual listener (as we did in chapter 4) and the false binary between recorded and live performance (as we did in chapter 5), I suspect there is nowhere else for the debate about authenticity to go but into this domain of musical text.

PRESCRIPTIVE NOTATION

In the last analysis we cannot be quite sure that the scores represent anything but themselves.

—Bertrand Russell

The problem of authenticity in a score—unlike the problem of authenticity in listening, or, as we will see in a moment, authenticity in a transcription—is not a specifically auditory problem per se. One could argue, I suppose, that it is difficult to know whether any score really represents the "sounds" a composer claims to have in her head. On the other hand, those interior sounds can now be more easily and directly represented by digital score-writing software, programs like Sibelius, Finale, LilyPond, and others, which seek to streamline the material interface between a raw compositional idea and its expression in notational form. At their most efficient, these programs come close to removing one mediating compositional step—the data-entry function traditionally performed by the hand and pencil, or, more recently, by the computer keyboard and mouse. They replace it with mediation of a more performative variety: simply playing the music into the computer via a MIDI keyboard or guitar.

Even so, we have no way of knowing the exact relationship between the composer's mental conception of a work and the dots on the page—

whether one really "inscribes" the other, or whether the work can even be said to exist before it is written down. (And if it does not exist before it is written down, in what sense can it be inscribed?) In general, authenticity in a score is not understood in these terms, but is applied after the fact, to the interaction between a material document and its context. Recall Joseph Grigely's unpacking of the authorship assumptions critics and readers attached to John Keats's poetry (discussed in chapter 1). There, the question was: which words, in which order, and linked to which thoughts, did Keats actually write? The same type of inquiry guides the seeker after authenticity in written music. Was a given score—a physical document inscribed with notational symbols—really produced by its putative composer, with the intention of being a definitive statement of her work? If so, the seeker after authenticity will claim that the text is the true work—will make the textualist assumption that text and work are one.

The first problem here is that the assumption that text and work are one overlooks the fact that there is always more than one text associated with any "one work"—just as there is always more than one performance associated with any one work, as we saw in our earlier discussion of "Stairway to Heaven." It is not enough to say, as Walter Emery does, that "there is no such thing as an 'original text' of any piece of old music, unless either there is only one source, or all the sources give identical readings." The truth is more complex: with both old and new music, it is impossible for there to be "only one source," or for multiple sources to give "identical readings." Instead, texts multiply, and differentiate, in their composition, in their publication, and in how they are read.

What does this mean? We rely on the idea of an authoritative or reified text—we speak of "the score" of Stravinsky's *Le Sacre du Printemps,* or Libby Larsen's *Sonnets from the Portuguese,* as if each is a single thing. But each text takes at least three different forms—a rough draft, a manuscript (sometimes called a final draft, a fair copy, or a proof-sheet), and a published edition. In turn, none of these categories is discrete or clean.

What is a draft, for instance? The word's etymology has to do with the act of drawing, or retrieving—in this case, getting a musical idea from the mind. (We see a connection in the writer's adage about going back to the well.) It suggests that drafting is a sequence of actions, not an isolated inscription etched in a sheet of paper. What is important, to refer back to an earlier metaphor, is the myriad of footsteps—not the map. If we hold in front of us the prototype of a piece, we have no way of knowing for sure how many attempts preceded or will follow it—if the composer has been writing for years, how do we even know where to start counting the attempts that led to the prototype? Similarly, we have no way of knowing all the influences that fed it. (Recall Milton Babbitt's comment, cited in chapter 1, that "to be specific" about one's influences "would almost be, I think, dishonest.") With modern technology we may be able to trace the order of inscriptive acts on a given page—to determine, for instance, which markings were made first, or to trace the evolution of an idea by studying places where things have been erased or crossed out. But that does not mean that the markings we cannot immediately see, whether or not they were willingly cast aside, are not also significant. Revealed by a keen eye, or scientific analysis, they become additional texts.

Published editions are subject to the multiplying effects of contextual collaboration too. Nineteenth-century domestic pianists, for instance, decorated their sheet music with personal annotations, ranging from captions jotted under the fanciful illustrations that were a staple of the medium, to reflections on the quality of the composition, to signatures marking ownership. The published works were turned into palimpsests of a sort, and decomposed through handwriting into new works. I can attest to the transformative power of such writing—I too marked up my sheet music (or had it marked up for me) when I was a student. Sometimes I drew obscene pictures in the margins. Sometimes my teacher added the words "edited by Andrew Durkin" near the title page—his way of saying I was playing the song incorrectly. In both cases, the score had been fashioned into something unique, unavailable to the thousands of other students working out of the "same" book.

"The score," then, is always a *collection* of texts. The problem with authenticity here, as ever, is that it assumes we can pick the one that possesses what Schweitzer called the "ideal beauty" of the work. And yet the criteria for this choice are partly established by working backward from the choice itself. "The challenge for the lover of authenticity," I wrote in chapter 4, "is to explain why any of the many decompositions we habitually group under the heading of the 'single work' are less true, simply because they have not been experienced as such by that individual." The "many decompositions" of that sentence is a phrase equally relevant to the multiple texts of written music. We may pick what we think is the authentic text, assuming it is the truest version of the work. Yet that assumption, useful as it is for organization, overlooks that each individual draft, manuscript, or published edition is actually a *new* text, a new work of "ideal" beauty.

SO WRONG IT'S RIGHT

> One should not be so like a god as not to have to correct something here and there in one's created works.
> —Ludwig van Beethoven

Suppose a scholar discovers a previously unknown autograph manuscript of a piano sonata, squirreled away in a Beethoven archive. (As it happens, there is a real-world analogy to this hypothetical example in Cees Nieuwenhuizen's 2012 "reconstruction" of a sonata from a set of early Beethoven sketches.) Common sense tells us that the autograph manuscript—a document written in the composer's own hand—is indeed the urtext. How could it not be the authentic work we seek? Yet with that conclusion, we have already made two assumptions. First, we have assumed that the visual attributes of musical handwriting are self-evidently enough to affirm the identity of the composer who created it—even though handwriting analysis is maddeningly imprecise as a discipline, and the perception of handwriting itself is subject to the influence of numerous contextual factors, such as the type of writing implement or paper. Barry Beyerstein has written of the professional "questioned document examiner," who operates under the considerably higher burden of proof of a legal setting and is "asked only to rate the probability that a given person wrote the document in question," not to definitively determine guilt or innocence. In aesthetics we should be equally careful. Even if we obtain our lost Beethoven work from a reputable source, and even if we have other examples of Beethoven's handwriting to compare it to, we can't categorically rule out the possibility that our document is a forgery, that it was perhaps given to Beethoven by another composer, or that it has some other provenance. At best, we are still dealing in probabilities.

And even if we do allow that the handwriting is Beethoven's, we still have to be careful of our other assumption: that there is a necessary and transparent correlation between a passage written in that handwriting and the composer's *intention* in writing that passage (this of course does not even get at the degree to which composer intention should matter aesthetically). Seeing the handwritten score, we assume a privileged window into what the writer meant—as if it is not just as likely that the idiosyncrasies of penmanship could obscure that intention. A scene from Woody Allen's *Take the Money and Run* nicely illustrates the point: during a bank robbery, a teller is confused by a holdup note, which reads, "I have a gub." Of course, the robber (played by Allen) meant to write "gun." The humor of the scene, however, is that the robber's intention is irrelevant. The teller can only see what was actually written—or, more accurately, what appears to him to have been actually written. (We will come back to this problem in a moment.)

Even more important, we have to consider that in order for our hypothetical sonata to be performed, to be musically functional, it must be copied and printed—both to safeguard the original for historians and to make the document's content legible for a modern pianist. For simplicity's sake, we can say that this process of copying a manuscript—either by hand, by creating an engraving, or by entering it into a computer—requires an editor to approach the written work as a series of "cells." Think of these as musical units of varying length and content—the specific dimensions don't matter as much as the idea that each cell requires some kind of editorial response. In our hypothetical case, then, the editor has to decide what Beethoven "meant" at every moment in the work. Even when she assumes she need do nothing except reproduce the content of a given cell "as is," that act is never as transparent as it seems—regardless of how completely the musical information is transferred, one immediately loses the idiosyncrasies of the handwriting, the topographical impressions of the ink sitting on the paper, the precise hue of each stroke. Still other changes, as Peter Schillingsburg notes, can creep into a score because of "scribal errors, 'Freudian slips,' and shorthand elisions" on the part of the copier.

Indeed, sometimes the content of a cell may appear from the beginning to be an accident or mistake of the composer's: a "gub" instead of a "gun." Phillip Brett describes the "patent errors" of Arnold Schoenberg's autograph score of *A Survivor from Warsaw,* for instance. Julie Scrivener Nemire similarly points to the things left out of Conlon Nancarrow's handwritten scores—rests, accidentals, ties, meter markings, clefs—even though they can be heard in his piano rolls and recordings. Of Béla Bartók, László Somfai notes the composer's mistaken metronome markings, often left in the proofs. And according to Charles Rosen, Beethoven too "was quite capable of making mistakes in manuscript, as well as in reading proof." Actually, given Beethoven's reputation for sloppiness—his apartment was notoriously untidy, and Stephen Nachmanovitch refers to the "impulsive scrawls and hen scratches" of his penmanship (as compared with "the flow and clarity" of Bach's pen)—he was capable of far more serious mistakes, such as losing the original score for his opera *Fidelio,* and having to ask Count Moritz Lichnowsky to loan him a copy when it came time to revise it.

It is true that modern notation technologies attempt to minimize composer error by making the inscription process itself far more automatic. With the notation software Sibelius, for instance, it is impossible to accidentally add an extra beat to a bar, or to forget to repeat a key signature at the beginning of a line, or to leave out rests. Software also regularizes the appearance of notational symbols, purportedly for clarity's sake. But it can create unintended noise, depending on the reader. The very regularity and artificial cleanness of a computer-produced score can work against its legibility in practice. Uniformly drawn note stems, perfectly even spacing, and forced placement of everything from accidentals to articulation marks can, paradoxically, induce eyestrain. So even if the computer-generated score technically reflects the composer's intent, the potential for misreading in performance has to be understood as yet another musical variation lying in wait, yet another strike against the possibility of authenticity.

The bigger problem here is that we can't ever know if a "mistake" is really a mistake. Subjectivity can alter the terms of our understanding dramatically. Anything unusual or remarkable on the page can be accounted for in a variety of ways. Imagine, for instance, that you are copying an autograph score and you come across a seemingly extraneous and vaguely note-shaped black blob on a music staff. You might see it in a variety of ways. Perhaps it appears as the unanticipated wrongness of an "accident," merely a drop of spilled ink. Or you might conclude that it is the more personal failing of an "error"—the blob was intended as a note, yes, but the composer has overlooked how it doesn't belong in a 4/4 bar that already has four beats. Perhaps you treat the cell as an "innovation," an aesthetically successful attempt at something new—the blob is supposed to be the fifth note in what was an unmarked bar of 5/4, perhaps a new feature of the composer's changing style. Or you might relegate it to the category of "experiment," an aesthetically *un*successful attempt at something new—the blob/note is supposed to be there, all right, but in performance it sounds incongruous. All of these interpretations result from shifting subjectivities around this one cell.

There is an analogy with live performance here. "One of the tricks is that if you play something that you didn't really mean to play, play it again," pianist Kenny Barron has said in a discussion of improvisation. "If you repeat it, it sounds like that's what you meant to play." Nachmanovitch agrees: "I can adopt the traditional attitude, treating what I have done as a mistake: don't do it again, and in the meantime, feel guilty. Or I can repeat it, amplify it, develop it further until it becomes a new pattern." It is telling that Barron refers to a "trick" and Nachmanovitch to a "traditional attitude": both suggest that for some listeners (either those in on the trick or those who espouse the traditional attitude) the mistake is still a mistake. But for others, something in the perception shifts. Nothing has literally changed, at the generative level, about the content of the cells themselves, but by focusing on them—indeed, by amplifying them—the subjective context through which they are perceived is nudged away from the conclusion of "wrongness."

In the end, something similar happens in written music. A composer's rumination of an interesting cell, like Barron's or Nachmanovitch's mistake played again, can shore up an unintended perception. Consider an anecdote about Beethoven's changing opinion of what he initially thought was an error discovered in one of his scores. "The more he looked at the misprint," Rosen tells us, "the more he was taken with it, seduced by its dramatic character." And the "patent error" label Brett uses for the Schoenberg work referenced above is thrown into question when we learn (also from Brett) that Schoenberg "was mistrustful of a mechanical approach to his method, and 'learned to treat his "mistakes" with respect as the product of intuition.'" Like Beethoven, Schoenberg allowed himself to be seduced by the unanticipated.

Audiences can be seduced too. A cell unrecognized as an error can slip through the editing process, go to press, gain exposure to a group of listeners, and become accepted—even if the composer never actually intended to write it. The "famous and controversial A-sharp" (as Rosen calls it) in the first movement of Beethoven's *Hammerklavier* Sonata is a cell that, like our hypothetical ink blob, contains a single note. The note's fame and controversy derives from the fact that it violates classical harmony (according to Rosen, an A-natural is "the note we would expect"), even though for some listeners it is audacious in a way that is aesthetically interesting. Rosen points out that although the A-sharp was rarely performed in the nineteenth century, in the twentieth, "modernism and the hope of establishing a difficult reading have naturally given rise to the adventurous project of justifying" it. Without necessarily embracing that project, Rosen empathizes with it, concluding that this particular cell can be interpreted in multiple ways.

While he is willing to leave the *Hammerklavier* controversy open, however, Rosen takes the opposite approach in his reading of the Chopin B-flat Minor Sonata. This work features a similarly intriguing cell, in which a repeat sign appears at the fifth bar of the exposition instead of the first. The difference has to do with whether one is willing to include the slow introduction of the piece in the repeat. In this case, Rosen defines the cell as a "gross error," claiming it would be "patently idiotic" to repeat back to the fifth bar. "There is no way that Chopin—

or anyone else—would proceed from an interrupted cadence on D-flat directly into the key of B-flat minor," he argues. The fact that the cell has been broadly reproduced in its "patently idiotic" form—it was reprinted throughout the twentieth century, and has been defended by other musicologists, notably Anatole Leikin—is merely a sign, Rosen believes, that those involved in the dissemination of this work were unable to perceive it authentically. He implies a kind of obviousness to the score, as if it will inevitably reveal its essence regardless of who is looking at it.

And yet the only thing preventing us from flipping Rosen's interpretation of the *Hammerklavier* and Chopin cells—substituting "error" for "innovation," and vice versa—is the question of taste. We need not dismiss Rosen's opinions on the Chopin matter altogether—whether or not we agree with him, his commentary enhances the discourse around that work. But we cannot treat that commentary as the authentic reading he seems to believe it is unless we can establish a good reason to be so stingy in the case of the Chopin, and so generous in the case of the *Hammerklavier*. Indeed, starkly juxtaposing Rosen's responses to these cells makes both seem arbitrary. But subjectivity cannot be subjectively applied, toward Beethoven but not toward Chopin. It is an all-or-nothing proposition.

Interestingly, in another context, Rosen admits that "taste is, after all, a matter of will, of moral and social decisions." Here he entertains the possibility that we like the things we want to like, or that conform to our self-perceptions, or, in some cases, that we feel we should like. Confessing his own distaste for the music of composer Olivier Messiaen, for instance, he goes on to say that "when I reflect that some of the finest musicians today like Peter Serkin adore Messiaen, I realize that I too would learn to love his music if I decided to put my mind to it. The admirers of Messiaen are clearly right: what they hear in his work is really there." But the incongruence of his position becomes apparent if we substitute "Chopin" for "Messiaen." Surely the editors of the B-flat Minor Sonata were admirers of Chopin? If one admits up front to personally disagreeing with both sets of admirers, why are the admirers of Messiaen "clearly right" but the admirers of Chopin are not?

The claim of obviousness assumes that a reader who knows how to look at a problematic cell the "right" way has the key to unlock its authenticity. But which readers have access to this recondite knowledge? Those willing to assert it seem unable to avoid self-contradiction. Schweitzer, for instance, describes how certain of Bach's clavier works were severely editorialized by copyists, and how those editions were later certified as "authentic Bach" by nineteenth-century scholars Forkel, Hilgenfeldt, and Bitter. Despite what he suggests is the unimpeachable expertise of these men, Schweitzer dismisses their conclusions in fairly harsh terms, scornfully declaring it "almost incredible" that they accepted the edited editions as if they were

> the authentic ones, and energetically maintained their superiority over those generally accepted. The children of Bach's muse slink along in the most miserable shapes—they are merely skin and bones; and the man who knew Bach's son's, who had heard them play, and in whom one might presuppose some breath of the Bach spirit, fell a victim to this clumsy deception!

Like Rosen, Schweitzer relies on the notion of textual obviousness. Each cell, he assumes, can be read transparently. Yet elsewhere, Schweitzer too is forced to contradict his intimations to objectivity, recognizing that in the continuing process of historical research "it is possible that this or that 'original' work of Bach will prove to be a transcription"—a score adapted for new instrumentation from another composer's work. Schweitzer is rather forgiving, for instance, when he refers to three clavier sonatas thought by another biographer, P. Spitta, to have been composed by Bach, but afterward demonstrated to have been the work of Johann Adam Reinken, "whom one was not exactly accustomed to regard as a striking composer." Schweitzer also seems surprisingly open to the possibility of misinterpretation when he remarks that of all the works in Bach's keyboard oeuvre, the *Goldberg Variations* "come closest to the modern pianoforte style." The final variations especially would be easy for "anyone" to confuse with "works of Beethoven's last period," he notes.

In other words, in the Reinken and *Goldberg* cases, at least, Schweitzer admits that the score does *not* self-evidently reveal its true origins. And yet why isn't he as magnanimous about the altered Bach editions authenticated by Forkel, Hilgenfeldt, and Bitter? What justifies the exasperation directed at these victims of "a clumsy deception," compared with the empathy accorded the mistaken scholars in the Reinken and *Goldberg* examples? The discrepancy suggests we cannot evaluate interpretations of a given cell (much less of an entire score) by a standard of obviousness or authenticity. The real choice is whether or not to empathize with alternate ways of listening.

ANYTHING GOES

In addition to the possibility that a single cell could be understood, in its reception, as an accident, error, innovation, or experiment, there have always been composers who have deliberately left portions of their written music "open." It is easy to forget this in the wake of our proclivity for textualism, but in practice intentional notational openness works against authenticity as powerfully as the interpretive variance we have just considered, because it similarly frustrates the quest to choose a single authentic work.

Such openness dates back to the earliest written music. With the first scores of Gregorian chant, for instance, readers did not get much more than the general contour of a melody—missing were time signatures, keys, tempo, and sometimes even a music staff or clef. The relationship between the performance and the score was like the difference between the utterance and the written word, with all the variants of inflection, accent, and vocal timbre left out. By the Baroque era, several centuries later, notation had become "like shorthand," as Bruce Haynes puts it—demonstrating "a quality known in the trade as 'thin' writing." It is somewhat ironic that Bach, the compositional exemplar of the period, is today popularly lionized as a genius composer in the textualist mold. For when one studies his scores, one quickly finds that, true to his era, many compositional details that we would consider evidence of that genius—including articulation, dynamics, tempo indications, ornaments, and even sometimes information about timbre or instrumentation—were often simply left up to the good taste of the performer.

We know from contemporary aesthetic treatises and other accounts that Baroque performers were taught to extemporize, to engage with the framework of a score and create something greater than the sum of its parts. Later, performance culture even allowed for a completely improvised introduction to a written piece (a practice that would come to be known as "preluding"), or else a space set aside for virtuosic display and, often, improvisation, usually toward the end of a score (a device that would come to be known as the cadenza). Many composers assumed a performer's interpretive freedom, her right to manipulate the content of a piece to her own liking, within "living conventions of performance." "In repeating the Air," wrote singer and composer Pier Francesco Tosi in 1723, "he that does not vary it for the better, is no master." Such practices, Haynes stresses, thrived not because the seventeenth- and eighteenth-century culture in which they existed did not know any better, or was unable to develop more detailed symbol systems for music. Rather, the practices themselves were considered inherently rewarding.

Of course, notation has developed a lot since the Baroque period. A textualist would point out that modern scores are more specific and exacting, in both intent and execution. Stefan Kostka, in his *Materials and Techniques of Twentieth-Century Music,* makes this point by comparing Bach's *Well-Tempered Clavier,* an early-eighteenth-century work, with Debussy's *Preludes,* written two hundred years later. The Bach seems barren, sans tempo, dynamics, or articulation; but the Debussy is "full of detailed and descriptive instructions." Both could be usefully compared with the still more detailed descriptiveness of integral serialism, in which the serial method is applied to musical parameters other than pitch alone, so that even dynamics and articulation could be predetermined for every note. Later still, "New Complexity" self-consciously took the idea of written difficulty—more generously, controlled subtlety—to similar extremes.

In other words, the Western system for writing music has continually approached an ideal of comprehensive detail. One might assume that a modern score thus more authentically communicates a composer's work. Certainly comprehensiveness is one of modern music's celebrated features, most likely because of this assumption. "In the award-giving and commission-granting sectors of the music community, heavily nuanced notation is still reflexively equated with professionalism," Kyle Gann wrote in 2000. "Composers who sit on panels have admitted to me that when a score comes through that doesn't contain new dynamic markings in nearly every measure, with interpretive crescendos and decrescendos and slurs and verbal directions, it is automatically tossed into the rejection heap." It is worth asking, incidentally, whether this mania for micromanagement contributes to the possibility that these pieces will never be performed outside of an institutional setting.

In any case, what has been attained here is at least partly illusory. It is not that modern scores represent some high point in the evolution of notation, or that we can now finally capture the true work on the page in a way that Bach, lacking our language, couldn't. Greater notational detail does present new challenges for the performer, but does not translate into greater authenticity. Of course, the limitations of our notation have always shown up pretty starkly when applied to non-Western music. In 1867 the editors of a collection of slave songs, for instance, pointed out with mild frustration that the singers from whom the songs were transcribed, and for whom an African musical influence was discernible, "seem not infrequently to strike sounds that cannot be precisely represented by the gamut," or diatonic scale. Presumably this was a reference to microtonal deviations from what the editors understood as a definite and immutable pitch system. And yet even today there are plenty of sounds made by Western art musicians that also "cannot be precisely represented" (and indeed may not even be "fully subject to the performer's conscious control," as Chanan puts it).

Musicians can change the intensity of an instrument's timbre or tone color, for instance, but there is no commonly accepted way to prescribe this feature of sound in a score, except linguistically—and linguistic instructions return us to the "dancing about architecture" problem. Or consider the word *accelerando,* which indicates that the player is to speed up. While that instruction may be situated between two metronome markings, it says little about *how* the speeding up is to be performed. (Is it to be perfectly evenly distributed throughout the period in question? Or is it to be weighted at one end or the other?) A *vibrato* marking—another example of the problem—does not prescribe the speed of its fluctuations. Even if it could, it is unlikely those fluctuations would be consistently and exactly performable, at least by unaided human players.

Modern notation's problematic claim to greater authenticity has generated some interesting and revealing responses from musicians themselves. One is humor. Consider the strange sadism of Satie's *Vexations,* a piano piece framed by these cryptic instructions: "To play this motif 840 times in succession, it would be advisable to prepare oneself beforehand, in the deepest silence, by serious immobilities." Or Peter Schickele's gentle send-up of the framing devices of the classical score in his "The Short-Tempered Clavier: Preludes and Fugues in All the Major and Minor Keys Except for the Really Hard Ones." Or the excessive bravado of Frank Zappa's "The Black Page," which posits unplayability as an aesthetic strength (the title refers to an imaginary sheet of music completely covered in notes). Or the more literal black page of music engraver John Stump's parodic "Faerie's Aire and Death Waltz," a document that has to be seen to be believed. By producing a score of such incredible, obfuscating density—a page of music that would take hours to decipher, and that would ultimately shut down the possibility of performance—Stump's point, as Mark Samples argues, was that by the late twentieth century, "notation has been so overburdened with meaning that it can become, well, silly."

The other response to that overburdening—sometimes taken as parody too—was to treat notation itself as an art, almost independent of the sounds it was used to prescribe. *Vexations* can be read this way, given its odd instruction. Is the text meant to be followed literally? And if so, what is its literal meaning? Or: is it less literal, and more literary? Is it a poem? An aphorism? Is it offered, as John Cage had it, "in the spirit of Zen Buddhism"—a "musical koan"? Note that the instruction is expressed as a conditional statement—saying that "to play x, one should do y" is not the same thing as directing the musician to "play x." Is it merely a provocation, then? A joke? Conceptual art? Because the work demands to be considered, at least in part, as text, perhaps one does not even need to actually hear the music to "get it."

Some of the music that resulted from this emphasis on text for its own sake would come to be called "indeterminate" or "aleatory," in reference to the fact that the composer was deliberately leaving out key details, which could be filled in by the performer. In a way, then, these developments bring us full circle to the openness of the Baroque and other early music. Now, instead of unspecified tempos, dynamics, or cadenzas, we see symbol-based notation—as in Cornelius Cardew's *Octet '61 for Jasper Johns,* which utilizes hybrid and ambiguous signs. We see graphic notation—as in Martin Bartlett's *Lines from Chuang-Tzu,* one part of which consists of a series of differently sized dots on an otherwise blank page. We see purely textual notation, as in Karlheinz Stockhausen's *For Times to Come,* which includes instructions like the following:

> Overtake the others
> Hold the lead
> Allow yourself to be overtaken
> Less often

We also, of course, see greater commitment to improvisation as an aesthetic, in both jazz (especially) and rock (less so, but not insignificantly). Although some forms of jazz have taken on aspects of textualism, others, like the genre of free jazz, have foregrounded improvisation perhaps more than anywhere else in music.

It is hard to imagine how any performer of *For Times to Come,* or Ornette Coleman's "Free Jazz (part one)," or works like them could convincingly claim the music had been realized "authentically." And yet it is not that these works are open-ended, while a piece of integral serialism is not. Ultimately, *no* score can help being open. Consequently, no score is entitled to authenticity.

DESCRIPTIVE NOTATION

I can't tell you what a joy it is to have these songs resurrected after having forgotten about them for so long! As always, where my recordings aren't great quality, you have managed to create something that recreates the feel of the original. In fact, I can't even tell which bits you were able to hear and which bits you had to make up!

—anonymous customer quoted on
John Zechiel's transcription site

There is one more direction in which the quest for authenticity can lead us—what could be called notation after the fact, descriptive notation, or, more typically, *transcription,* the reproduction of a musical work in written form. ("Transcription" has other meanings, even in a musical context, but they are less important to us here.) Transcription is useful for documenting or studying music that has not previously been written down, or for which no score is extant. And it need not always culminate in a text. Jazz musicians often study peers' or mentors' solos by learning them from a recording and then reperforming them. A garage band playing covers of punk tunes usually has to figure out by ear the part each person is to play. Both can be considered forms of transcription.

But most of the time, the text is the point. *The Real Book,* a popular "fake book," contains hundreds of tunes compressed into lead sheet format—a basic statement of each song's melody and chord progression. Initially an underground phenomenon, *The Real Book* was created by a group of anonymous transcribers, reputedly students at Berklee College of Music, in the 1970s. Its emphatically contradictory title—a fake book called *The Real Book*—revealed a philosophical (and perhaps legal) anxiety over the question of how authentic any transcription could ever actually be. And no wonder. As it turned out, the original *Real Book*—the collection has since been revised, licensed, and expanded many times over—introduced its share of errors into the jazz repertoire. These "errors," of course, were read variously, like the *Hammerklavier* note we examined earlier in this chapter. For at least some musicians, then, the original *Real Book,* even with its compromised and uncertain provenance, was a kind of urtext of jazz standards.

This issue of "errors" in the original *Real Book* highlights two significant problems confronting the transcriber. First, transcription, like score writing, is stymied by the limits of what music notation can actually express. Second, transcription cannot help but embody the mediations we discussed in chapter 4—sound generation, vector, and subjectivity. Thus, claiming authenticity in a transcription, unlike claiming it in a score, is also an auditory problem. The claim is qualified by the variability of what different transcribers hear. As composer and arranger Bill Dobbins recently put it, "Any music, no matter how perfectly it's recorded and mixed . . . if it's chromatically complex, or uses the sections and instruments of the ensemble in any except the most standard ways . . . at least 10 to 15 percent of any transcription is just going to be guessing."

We should thus be careful when, as occasionally happens in music history, we come across stories of superhuman transcription feats— many of which pertain to long-dead musicians, whose impossible-to-verify accomplishments we must process through the double haze of time and the rhetoric of genius. Mozart is the exemplar. There is a famous anecdote that is repeated in many biographies of the composer, and that has certainly had some role in the construction of his genius: at fourteen, he is reputed to have transcribed Gregorio Allegri's *Miserere* by memory after a single hearing (with some adjustments made a few days later, after a second performance). At the time, the *Miserere* was well known not only by musical reputation, but also because the papacy had forbidden its dissemination. Earlier attempts to circumvent that interdiction by transcribing the work as it was performed had failed because it featured an improvisational component that was difficult to reproduce on paper. But apparently this was no obstacle to young Mozart.

Mozart's transcription, however, has never been found, and so we have no way of knowing for sure what he wrote, nor of comparing it with the versions of the piece that were published later. Even if Mozart's transcription could be located—assuming it still exists—we have no way of comparing it with the specific performance it described (it would be a mistake, as we have seen, to assume that every performance of the *Miserere* was precisely the same). No modern scholar can ever know what there was to be heard during that performance. We have to take the story on faith, then, and in the context of other, more easily examined claims about the composer.

Still, perhaps one wants to assume the Mozart *Miserere* anecdote is genuine, and the young composer really did capture this famous piece on paper, practically in one hearing. We should at least juxtapose a similar anecdote from our own era, about which we have more information, in order to demonstrate how easily music biography can accrue the exaggerations of urban legend. A few years ago, on a musician listserv, I first read the breathless tale (posted by a smart and talented musician) of how pianist Zita Carno had transcribed all of John Coltrane's solos during one of his performances. Coltrane's solos, it is worth pointing out, were long and dense—famously referred to as "sheets of sound" by *Down Beat* critic Ira Gitler. Supposedly, Carno left her transcriptions—her sheets of the sheets—in a bundle on Coltrane's doorstep the day after the concert, much to the saxophonist's surprise. Except that didn't really happen. Coltrane scholar Lewis Porter provides the obvious corrective, noting that "nobody could transcribe even one Coltrane solo while he was playing it." The truth, according to Porter, was that during the (multiple) performance(s) Carno attended, she merely transcribed the "head" of each tune—the opening and closing statement of the theme and its accompanying chord progression. (Given the chordal repetition during the solos, she would have had plenty of opportunities to get the basic harmonic structure of each piece, if not the melody.) Separately, she also transcribed and published Coltrane's solo on his piece "Blue Train"—but she did so by listening to the recording over and over. It took her a long time.

Somehow, the separate facts of Carno's real-time head transcriptions and the published "Blue Train" solo transcription were conflated into the single fantastic tale that Carno had transcribed an evening's worth of Coltrane improvisations in real time. Not insignificantly, that claim drew on both the rhetoric of genius and the yearning for authenticity. Its retelling posits Carno's transcribing prowess (her genius), yielding a singularly true documentation (an authentic text) of what was in reality a fleeting and unrepresentable event, surely heard differently by everyone present.

But even in the corrected story, and even in the published transcription, Carno's undoubted musical skill, like Mozart's, does not mean she has attained authenticity. Again, the "best" transcribers are limited by "relative sensitivity to different features of music—harmony or rhythm or melody," which "distinguishes interpretations," as Paul Berliner points out. In the end, "details that some players hear in the music simply elude other players." Discrepancies are to be expected, Frank Tirro adds, because of "the tremendous difficulty in obtaining an 'accurate' copy of sound on paper." Actually, Tirro's scare quotes around the word "accurate" suggest that the task is not merely difficult, but impossible: it does not matter how authoritative the transcribers are. To his point, Tirro examines three different transcriptions of a 1940 Victor recording of "Ko-Ko" (performed by Duke Ellington and His Orchestra), by William W. Austin, Gunther Schuller, and Ken Rattenbury. He discovers that they "differ noticeably," even though all three men are "truly superlative musicians." According to Tirro, Austin leaves out a saxophone, Schuller adds a trumpet, and Rattenbury misinterprets some rhythms.

But how do we know that Tirro's evaluation of these transcriptions is itself accurate? It is odd that he understands the elusiveness of transcriptive authenticity in general, while laying claim to a corrective position with respect to "Ko-Ko" in particular. Apparently, one can be seduced by textualism even as one critiques it. Indeed, as a musician I am seduced by it too. I want to argue, for instance, that there are several errors in Tirro's own transcription of Louis Armstrong's solo on "Struttin' with Some Barbecue." On the second half of the second beat of the sixth bar, for instance, Tirro has Armstrong playing a (concert) A-flat; to my ear the note on the recording sounds very much like a G-natural. Similarly, at the last eighth note of bar twelve, Tirro's D-flat sounds a half step off to me; I think it should be a D-natural. And finally, the last eighth note of bar twenty-six is, to my ear, a whole step off—instead of an E-flat, it should be a D-flat.

But my corrective of Tirro is no more authentic than Tirro's corrective of Austin, Schuller, and Rattenbury. Another transcriber would surely hear this piece differently, and would pick apart other details.

HEARING NOTES

How can notes be so elusive to an experienced transcriber? They are, after all, an elemental feature of music. Part of the problem is that each "individual" note contains a fundamental frequency—associated with its letter name—but also numerous additional frequencies sounding simultaneously, though more faintly. These are called "overtones." In a sense, as Robert Jourdain puts it, there are "many sounds in every musical tone," so that "every note is actually a chord." The note C, for instance, has a fundamental frequency of C, but overtones at the octave (also C), a fifth above that (G), a fourth above that (C again), a third above that (E), and so on. The varying strength of these additional frequencies helps to create the unique character of an instrumental timbre—the quality that distinguishes a saxophone from a trumpet (say), even when they are playing the "same" note.

More important, overtones can be enhanced or muted by different acoustic contexts. James Dapogny is revealingly frank about this problem in a book of Jelly Roll Morton piano transcriptions, most of which he made from recordings of Morton's solo piano performances from between 1923 and 1939. For one thing, the early technology used to record these works added to the difficulty of Dapogny's task (surely also a factor in the "Ko-Ko" and "Struttin' with Some Barbecue" transcriptions mentioned earlier). But more to the point, the large pianos found in the recording studios of Morton's time were highly resonant. Accrued reflections in the recordings make it difficult to differentiate between notes that were actually performed and notes that are heard because of strong overtones—"implied" notes, if you will. That confusion is particularly problematic in denser sections of the music—whenever Morton pressed multiple keys simultaneously.

There is a philosophical and perceptual dilemma here. To the extent that an implied note (say, the overtone G on the fundamental of C) can be heard on these recordings, it truly "existed" during the performance. But if Morton had somehow been able to reperform the exact same piece, note for note, with another recording setup—a different piano, a different room, a different recording machine—it is possible that the implied notes, which depended on how the acoustic properties of the music manifested in a given context, would have been different, or would have disappeared altogether. The paradox is that although implied notes are in one way just as "real" as the performance itself, in another, they are not. In the Morton performance, it is not that implied notes were somehow falsely inserted into the recording, but rather that they didn't consistently correspond with the keys Morton pressed when performing the piece. And yet there is no way, based on the audio alone, for the transcriber to tell the difference between heard notes that correspond to keys pressed and heard notes that don't.

Overtones also generate the opposite problem of "actually performed" notes that get lost in the rest of the sound happening on a given recording. Dapogny gives the example of "relatively weak upper octave doublings of strongly played lower notes," which "are somewhat fainter and 'hide' in the upper partials"—that is, the higher overtones—"of the lower pitches." Such dropouts also occur in midrange left-hand chords. Dapogny's response is understandable enough, given his task: he fills in missing details based on what Morton is "known" to have done in other, similar cases—based, that is, on a historical analysis of Morton's style, itself largely a construction of recording technology. For instance, because Morton frequently doubled his right-hand melodic lines at the octave, Dapogny repeats this stylistic device in some of his transcriptions, even if that octave doubling was not immediately apparent to him in the recorded version. For midrange left-hand chords, Dapogny again follows established analyses of Morton's work, interpolating "what I know Morton played in other, more audible, instances when he used the same harmony," and warning us that "such notations are not identified as conjectural" in the transcription. Of course, if the point of transcription is to describe the notes that are actually heard, unheard notes cannot be anything but conjectural.

Overtone-induced confusion is certainly not limited to old recordings of piano music. Ensemble music of any size or any era, regardless
of the fidelity with which it has been recorded, or the nature of its
performance, can be similarly resistant to exact transcription because
of the way its overtones interact. "In final (third-less) chords, such as
those which end several movements of Mozart's *Requiem*," Anthony
Storr writes, "one sometimes distinctly hears a major third overtone,"
even where none is written. That "sometimes" is important—the effect
can be inconsistent. Yet it can also be employed deliberately, as in barbershop quartet music, Georgian choral singing, and other types of a
cappella performance. In a post on the subject, one blogger notes of
the Harborlites, a women's chorus, that "the final big chord they hit
had a vibrant high note that sounded different, almost alien. As we all
applauded, a knowledgeable woman in front of me turned around and
said, 'That high note wasn't a sung note; it was an overtone!' "

Composer Bill Russo, in a text on arranging for large ensembles,
describes how certain combinations of instruments can have a decep-
tive or masking effect because of the behavior of overtones. Weird
timbral metamorphoses result. For instance, Russo argues, combining
alto and tenor saxophone in octaves produces the sound of an alto
saxophone, while combining alto and tenor saxophone in unison produces the sound of a tenor saxophone. Similarly, combining tenor and
baritone in octaves produces a baritone sound ("especially if the figure
is heavy and low for the baritone")—but alto and baritone playing the
same notes together sound like a tenor. Of course, some listeners would
argue that combining alto and tenor in octaves produces not the sound
of an alto, but the sound of alto and tenor in octaves, or maybe the
sound of something else altogether. How could it be otherwise, given
perceptual variability? The bigger point is that just because something
sounds one way to the ear, it does not follow that that was what was
performed at the generative level. A sound that sounds like a tenor
saxophone may well be something other than a tenor saxophone. We
cannot assume—ever—that transcription will authentically identify
and document a sound as it existed at its point of origin, or even that it
will authentically identify and document whatever sound there is to be
heard. The skill and meticulousness of the transcriber merely records

what the transcriber hears. But what that transcriber hears may not necessarily be what was played, or what another transcriber hears.

In pondering "a sound that sounds like a tenor saxophone," we could turn to Barry Kernfeld's *What to Listen For in Jazz,* in which he addresses "Outer Nothingness," a bracing collective improvisation recorded by an eleven-piece version of the Sun Ra ensemble. "A mystery surrounds the solo that begins one minute into the piece," Kernfeld writes. Was it performed by John Gilmore on tenor sax? Or was it Robert Cummings on bass clarinet? In Kernfeld's opinion, one can only make educated guesses. "The timbre of the mystery instrument sounds more like that of Robert Cummings's bass clarinet than of Gilmore's tenor sax," he argues. But later in the same solo "there are honking sounds that could have been made only on a tenor sax." Kernfeld turns to the analysis of Ekkehard Jost, who transcribed the solo and who, after listening to the recording "some 20 times," was convinced that the player is Gilmore. Yet Kernfeld remains skeptical. "Is Gilmore making an otherworldly sound on the sax, in keeping with the spirit of outer nothingness?" he asks. "Is he doubling instruments, beginning the solo on bass clarinet and then at some unidentifiable point picking up his tenor sax? The answer is not clear."

HEARING RHYTHM

In terms of the human organism itself, mechanical time is even more foreign: while human life has regularities of its own, the beat of the pulse, the breathing of the lungs, these change from hour to hour with mood and action, and in the longer span of days, time is measured not by the calendar but by the events that occupy it.

—Lewis Mumford

The problems of transcribing rhythm may be even more vexing. When a transcriber writes rhythm, she is attempting to stop time, to capture something that is naturally experienced as a constantly shifting present, what psychologists call "flow." Typically, rhythm is understood as a pattern of alternating sound and silence—the pulses and durations that give shape and direction to music, allowing its linear progress. But this is a simplification. Any pattern of alternating sound and silence always happens against other patterns of alternating sound and silence; pulse is always pitted against pulse. As Henri Lefebvre argued, rhythm is always a *relational* phenomenon, a function of an "interaction between a place, a time and an expenditure of energy." Lefebvre divided it into various categories—the "circular" rhythms of nature and the cosmos, including regular patterns of the sun, the seasons, the heavens, the earth; the "linear" rhythms of human activity, like the workday, patterns of traffic, sounds of manufacturing; the biological rhythms of the heartbeat, breathing, and other bodily processes; the rational rhythm of the clock's second hand, or, in music, the parceling out of time through bar lines and time signatures. The point is that these categories continuously and ineluctably inform each other—they "measure themselves against one another." And it is only in that measurement that individual patterns gain definition.

Thus we cannot understand even something as simple as a recurring bar of four quarter notes, in 4/4 meter, played at a moderate tempo, without also referencing the background rhythms it is immersed in, which can never simply be "turned off." Those quarter notes sound different in the middle of rush hour than they do at midday; different to a child than to a grandparent; different in summer, or when the listener is falling into a nap, or before an anticipated meal. How can such interwoven relationships of time be described notationally, when they are ultimately idiosyncratic for each listener? How can we even speak of musical rhythm as anything other than an incomplete concept? Whatever we can get down on the page will only ever tell part of the story of the interrelated pulses and silences that all music is enmeshed in.

Looked at decompositionally, even the part of the story we can tell—the part of "rhythm" we can transcribe—is greatly compromised in the telling. Digital recording software has opened up new ways of seeing how rhythm occurs in practice, as anyone who has ever tried to edit a recording session will have noticed. The waveforms of a program like Pro Tools provide compelling visual evidence of just how inexact tempos, attacks, and cutoffs can be—even when they sound consistent or are performed by experienced musicians. In a duet recording, for instance, you can see where players misalign an entrance that is supposed to be together—where one waveform begins a little more to the right or left than the other. The phenomenon is often visible even when that discrepancy can't be heard. Forced by a limited notational system, and a flawed human ear, to regularize these small discrepancies—these moments of quantum aesthetic difference—transcribers typically round up or down, making a rhythm easier for the reader to understand. A quarter note in a tempo of 120 beats per minute may cut off a few microseconds early, but there is no way to accurately represent this, assuming the transcriber even hears it. It will be written as a quarter note.

A variation of this rounding problem occurred recently in a transcription of a three-bar excerpt from the Duke Ellington work "Mood Indigo." Critiquing Gunther Schuller's mistranscription of that piece, composer Darcy James Argue corrected the pitches performed by three horn players: Arthur Whetsel on trumpet, Joe "Tricky Sam" Nanton on trombone, and Barney Bigard on clarinet. But with respect to the *rhythm* of the excerpt, Argue follows Schuller, indicating that each musician played a whole note (held for four beats in bar one of the excerpt), followed by two half notes (each held for two beats in bar two), and then another whole note (held for another four beats in bar three). To my ear, Whetsel and Bigard come much closer to this exact rhythmic sequence than does Nanton, who cuts off noticeably early in bars one and three, thus performing something less than a whole note each time. (The pitches Nanton was performing were rather high for his instrument, and he presumably needed more air to sustain them.) It is an extreme example of the ear's willingness to adjust rhythms so as to impose a kind of aesthetic rationality—in this case, having the horn players execute the same rhythm in all three bars makes better compositional sense, and is probably what the musicians intended. And yet if we allow ourselves such editorializations, in what sense is this a "transcription"?

Swing—not the genre we discussed a few chapters ago, but the time feel—has long suggested other ways a rhythmic concept can elude

those trying to write it. Early-twentieth-century bandleader James
Reese Europe, whose ensemble played an inchoate form of what is
usually called "symphonic jazz," was one of the first to confound listeners with the indescribability of the swing concept. When Europe
toured France during World War I, local musicians were so taken with
the new style that they asked to peruse several of his scores, and were
quickly frustrated when their study did not automatically lead to the
same effect in their own playing. There is some irony in this anecdote,
incidentally, given that modern swing had a much older forerunner in
the Baroque practice of *notes inégales*—a swinglike feel in which notes
with a technically consistent rhythmic value were in practice emphasized inconsistently. ("We always made the first of each pair a little
longer than the second," French composer François Couperin wrote
of the style.)

By the end of the twentieth century, musicians who had grown up
knowing swing fared no better notating it than had Europe. It's another
problem Dapogny calls attention to in his Morton transcriptions. Even
Schuller, who offers a detailed examination of swing in his *Early Jazz,*
writes that "like the description of a primary color or the taste of
an orange," the word "swing" becomes meaningful "only when the
thing defined is also experienced"—seemingly a direct admission of
the futility of trying to describe it with notation (and an exception to
the textualism Schuller adopts elsewhere). Complicating matters further is the fact that, as Richard Lawn and Jeffrey Hellmer point out,
"there can be many subtle variations of swing, as many variations as
there are players." Thus it is common to speak of jazz drummers, for
instance, by referring to their idiosyncratic expressions of the concept,
as in "Billy Higgins's swing," "Elvin Jones's swing," or "Dannie Rich-
mond's swing." But for even a single player the range of swing feel can
vary from nearly straight eighths to a quarter-note eighth-note triplet,
depending on the ensemble, piece, or mood.

Notwithstanding Schuller's caveat, there have been textualist attempts to notate the swing feel using conventional symbols. Lawn and
Hellmer indicate that in the 1930s and '40s, for instance, swung eighth
notes were often written as a dotted eighth note followed by a sixteenth note—until jazz musicians decided this "was much too stiff and

machine-like to accurately express the smoother flow of swing eighth notes." Some have argued that triplet rhythms (implying a 12/8 meter) come closer, but are ultimately too awkward for extensive passages. In the end, Lawn and Hellmer inform us, swing was understood as an orally (and aurally) transmitted convention, rather than something that could be denoted on the page.

What is one to do in the face of all of this perceptual confusion? Do the vagaries of pitch and rhythm mean that transcription is a pointless exercise?

I think not—but there are better ways to respect the confusion. Berliner, like Tirro, raises questions about the ultimate faithfulness of any transcription, even as he too includes several transcriptions in his book. But Berliner goes farther than Tirro in building uncertainty directly into these texts, adapting traditional notation to that purpose. He uses parentheses, for instance, to signify "incomplete or implied chords at structural points in the music in which, for example, the piano is absent." He uses braces "around the analysis of harmonic structures open to multiple interpretations that defied consensus among transcribers." He draws up a chart of new symbols that paradoxically hint at the shortcomings of notation while simultaneously trying to give an idea of the sounds notation fails to represent. These symbols signify, for instance, a "split attack" that might include an "extraneous pitch or unpitched sound," symbols for a "pitch with a raspy or buzzy sound," or symbols for a "ghosted pitch" that included "barely audible or implied sound." (In *Early Jazz*, Schuller does something similar, employing a "square note head," for instance, to represent "a blue note, whose pitch may vary by more than a half tone.")

These alterations of traditional notation are useful because they point to the questions that transcription is hard-pressed to answer. How, for instance, would it be possible to agree on the exact auditory content of an "unpitched sound," or a "barely audible or implied sound," or a sound that "may vary by more than a half tone," or a set of parentheses indicating an implied chord? How could someone reading those instructions ever know they had reproduced the original note faithfully? At best, the symbols act as placeholders for a content that escapes representation. They make ambiguity—*qua* ambiguity—explicit, accounting for the things that cannot be represented while acknowledging the fact that transcription can never completely do the job we expect it to.

Part III

ART AND COMMERCE

7.

DIGITAL WITNESS

We are in the business of art.

—Lars Ulrich

Being the owner of a power boat, and speaking a little conversational French, I think it's safe to say I know something about the music industry.
—Scott Thompson, in a *Kids in the Hall* sketch

When I started thinking about this book in the late 1990s, I assumed it would end up being primarily about the past: Duke Ellington, player pianos, Ludwig van Beethoven, and so on. Digital technology, already everywhere, was exciting and new, but Internet or no Internet, workstation or no workstation, Pro Tools or no Pro Tools, I didn't yet appreciate the impact these developments would eventually have, or their potential relevance to questions of authorship and authenticity.

In 2000 all that changed. That year, a number of powerful labels, and one powerful rock band, sued the company behind a file-sharing program called Napster. That suit followed another, from earlier in the year, against MP3.com—one of the first social networking sites for music, with which I was familiar because I had used it to share some of my own recordings. In part these cases came to seem emblematic because of how they synced with other dramatic events at the time. The rumors of a technological doomsday (2000), the spectacle of a contested presidential election (2000), and the horror of a dramatic terrorist attack on the United States (2001)—events that followed in relatively rapid succession—all provided a weird 60-cycle hum of anxiety that informed the debate Napster and MP3.com generated, giving it shape and definition. In some details, the connections were more explicit: like 9/11, the digital music fight provoked new state and corporate surveillance measures, establishing a common ground between counterinfringement and counterterrorism that continues to this day. And like Y2K, the digital music fight drew some of its power from a narrative of technology run amok.

More important, the lawsuits helped establish a template for how music would be discussed in the new century. Surely the issues they raised factored into music's death cult, described at the beginning of this book, helping to produce its sharp divisions. On one side, optimists celebrated the emergence of a "leveled playing field" for artists, focused on an apparent effusion of creative activity, and generally anticipated benign impacts from technology. At one point, the Computer and Communications Industry Association sponsored a report, *The Sky Is Rising!,* which detailed some of these developments. "By any measure, it appears we are living in a true Renaissance era for content," wrote Michael Masnick and Michael Ho, the report's authors. "More money is being spent overall. Households are spending more on entertainment. And a lot more works are being created."

That's a perhaps selectively cheerful take on things. Yet I might as well admit up front that when it comes to digital culture, I have generally sided with the optimists, however cautiously. My personal history is undoubtedly a factor here. I came of age in the late 1980s, when the "official" music industry seemed overwhelmingly trite, oppressive, and irrelevant. The years since have done little to convince me that the system was not badly broken; my few brushes with its centers of power inevitably left a bad taste. I have always wanted something better for the art form, and today I remain excited by the possibilities of digital culture: by the fact that it is technically easier for audiences to find music than it was twenty years ago, for instance; by the fact that recordings are more plentiful and more varied; by the fact that artists have greater direct access to listeners and thus potentially more control over their own careers. (Frankly, given the odd music I enjoy making, I doubt I would have much of a "career" at all if these possibilities did not exist.)

At the same time, as a professional musician with close friends and associates who are, to say the least, uneasy about the new landscape, I don't want to dismiss out of hand the argument that Napster and its ilk opened the door to a dystopia, in which artists faced unprecedented penury, or worse. (Indeed, I have experienced a little of what feels like unprecedented penury myself.) To the aesthetic and economic pessimism of Glenn Branca, Andrew Keen, Andrew Shapter, and *Frontline,* cited at the beginning of this book, we could add the writer Cal Stamp, who began a recent article about the music-sharing service Spotify—the latest in a series of post-Napster technologies—with the tendentious assertion that "to the average music consumer, a song is worth less than a candy bar." Or David Byrne, who expanded on Stamp's argument when he wrote that in its current form, digital culture is "unsustainable as a means of supporting creative work of any kind. Not just music. The inevitable result would seem to be that the internet will suck the creative content out of the whole world until nothing is left." Or David Lowery, of the 1990s indie band Camper van Beethoven, who in 2012 staked out a critique that included an angry and widely shared essay, "Meet the New Boss, Worse Than the Old Boss?" Or journalist Robert Levine, whose 2011 book *Free Ride* was partially subtitled, "How Digital Parasites Are Destroying the Culture Business." (Frustratingly, the subject of the second half of that subtitle—"And How the Culture Business Can Fight Back"—occupied a rather small section of Levine's book.)

I disagree with the pessimists, but they are not crazy, and I share their concern for economic justice. The digital revolution has been at times ruthless in its idealism. Working musicians, just as beholden to the demands of capitalism as anyone else, are in a particularly difficult position for the time being, continuing to feel the brunt of the system as it is, instead of as it might be. The words of Metallica drummer Lars Ulrich—"We are in the business of art"—perfectly, though perhaps unintentionally, capture the paradox. And they reveal a complex ambivalence about decomposition. We—musicians—may have a deep and experiential understanding of the collaborative and mediated nature of musical creativity (only the least self-aware of us could ignore it), yet the fight over digital music reveals just how much we have learned to expect fans to believe in authorship and authenticity, and to routinely express that belief in the marketplace.

Why should it be otherwise? Musicians today have little material incentive, for instance, to openly acknowledge that their own work is derived from a complex welter of influences and collaborators. It's hard enough to get yourself paid; how much harder it would be to fairly remunerate the collaborative forces I have been championing in this book (or to even determine what that fair remuneration was). Musicians also have little material incentive to openly acknowledge the ways their work lacks authenticity; in fact, we have learned to understand lack of authenticity (especially expressive authenticity) as an aesthetic and even moral weakness. Consequently, many of us have become territorial in the face of change. Successful artists "quietly believe that they have to keep many more people 'out' in order to hold onto what remains," claims Tadhg Kelly. "We live in a curious age when the freest of thinkers (artists of various stripes) are the ones that want to curtail freedom the most."

THE CLASS SYSTEM OF MUSIC

> Like it or not, we have this system of money in place, and that has to be dealt with one way or another.
> —Chris Ruen

But there is more to the digital music fight, and the music death cult it stokes, than a simple struggle between optimism and pessimism. We can think of the music industry as a microcosm of the class conflicts that characterize the broader economy (itself undergoing great trauma in this period). Certainly, music, like all industries, has its elites—those who control and benefit most from the system, and who can be found, typically, in major record labels, high-profile presenting venues, powerful trade groups, superstar bands, and, increasingly, gigantic technology companies. For clarity's sake, I divide these into the "traditional elite" (those who dominated the pre-Internet era), and, for want of a better term, the "Web 2.0 elite" (what Jaron Lanier calls the "siren

servers"—entities like Google and Amazon and Facebook and Spotify); originally at odds, in some ways the interests of these groups have
been converging. In turn, music also has its "masses," its middle and
lower classes—independent or developing artists, technology start-
ups, small labels, freelance engineers, underground venues, and others
who lack the economic muscle of the elites, and who have borne the
brunt of the digital era's stresses. Finally, both the masses and the elites
depend on an audience, which of course has its own class affiliations.

Considered from a distance, all three groups describe merely the
general outlines of the system. An "independent" artist whose work is
distributed by a major label, for instance, may be said to have a foothold in both the musical middle class and the musical elite. Moreover,
"audience" and "music industry" are not mutually exclusive entities.
Professionals in the industry can be audience members too, while even
so-called nonmusician fans collaborate contextually with the music
they love, exhibiting their own artistry. In other words, there is overlap
and contradiction in this class model.

Yet even with that caveat the model is broadly useful for understanding some of the tensions that have defined the music industry
over the last hundred years. The key issue, I think, is whether that
industry privileges *listening,* or *consumption.* As I use the term here,
listening—or as Daniel Cavicchi calls it, "audiencing"—connotes an
active, autonomous, participatory experience of music. It is the audience's part in contextual collaboration, whether one is an "intimate"
listening to Beethoven play the piano, or a blond in a black dress listening to "Diminuendo and Crescendo in Blue" at Newport, or a record
collector enjoying your favorite 78s. From the rationalizing standpoint
of the early publishing industry—the foundation of what would later
become the record industry—the unpredictable behavior of contemporary audiences was potentially dangerous. After all, nineteenth-century
concertgoers enjoyed "a degree of sovereignty" and "regularly engaged
in socializing which was oblivious to the stage action, or made inter-
ruptive demands that paused and startled productions with applause,
stomping, and catcalls." How could a publisher capitalize on listeners'
pleasure when that pleasure seemed so chaotic and fickle? If we under-

stand business as a form of gambling, and consider the huge sums of money that can today be tied up in the manufacture, marketing, and selling of music, the incentives to reduce unpredictability become clear. From the beginning, the elites of the music industry preferred to think of audiences—and tried to get audiences to think of themselves—as *consumers,* passively receiving music as it was apportioned in controlled doses. In this context, the quibbling critics of chapter 4 signified not merely a psychological quirk but a business liability.

In practice, of course, consumption is a more complex phenomenon. Rebecca Tushnet and others have pointed out that even the most commercially contrived product can be used as an effective tool of self-actualization and identity formation. We all buy, display, discuss, and manipulate things—including musical things—in part to establish an existential claim, and to express our values. Fans proudly display passion for a band or artist, whether on a T-shirt or a Facebook page, using their cultural affinities to establish (or avoid) relationships with other listeners. Contextual collaboration takes this idea a little further—listeners help *produce* the music from which identity is constructed, decomposing what is heard into a new work with a personal relevance.

Yet the question here is not how consumption functions in practice. The fact of contextual collaboration, and of our potentially redemptive interaction with things, doesn't necessarily alter the elite's *expectation* that we be consumers, in the most unflattering, flat sense of that word. And to some extent the argument generated by MP3.com and Napster at the turn of the twenty-first century had to do with whether that expectation would continue to be viable. Arguably, fans had turned to these digital tools in the first place as a way of resisting the worst offenses of an industry that seemed to view them purely as consumers. Many listeners felt abused by the typical album's imbalance of "good songs" and "filler," by the aggressive pricing of CDs, by the sense that each new format (from LP to cassette to CD) was merely a pretext for remarketing old material, and eventually by a concern about new legal prohibitions against music sharing and community building. They looked at digital culture and imagined for the first time what it might be like to turn the system on its head.

A HISTORY OF TENSION

That imagined possibility was new, but the history of the music indus-try has always been shot through with moments of audience pushback against being proactively defined as cogs in a commercial machine. In the early days of recording, for instance, rural phonograph aficionados were so enamored of the myth of Edison that when a salesman from Columbia (Edison's chief competitor at the time) approached in an attempt to win their allegiance, "he was fortunate to escape without bodily injury," as Walter Welch and Leah Burt wryly put it. On the one hand, it is tempting to see this anecdote merely as an instance of inchoate brand loyalty. But we should not overlook the personal revolt against commercial power it also reveals. That hapless salesman was an emissary from the world of increasingly ubiquitous hard-sell advertising—itself disseminated through an increasingly immersive media environment. (Note that radio, for instance, would soon make the transition from content free-for-all to orderly format with paid sponsors.) Seen in light of the effort to force a narrow idea of con-sumption, the cranky resistance of the anonymous Edison aficionados was remarkable.

The example suggests a simple schism between industry and audi-ence, but in fact each subculture of what became the global music ecosystem—audiences, A&R reps, DJs, engineers, musicians, and so on—has had its own economic and aesthetic interests. And they have not always been in sync. Consider, for instance, how James Petrillo, head of the American Federation of Musicians, temporarily prohibited musicians from making new records in the middle of the twentieth century. Petrillo's intentions were good—he believed recording was a threat to musicians, and sought compensation through increased roy-alties. But in practice the recording bans produced unintended fissures, which would ultimately lead to new conflicts within the larger class system of music. And their actual effect on the commercial fortunes of musicians was uneven. Historians have suggested that the bans con-tributed to the demise of the big band, after its heyday in the 1930s, and inadvertently prompted the popularity of vocal stars like Frank Sinatra (singers belonged to a different union at the time, and so were not required to go on strike). And some have also lamented how the first ban in particular now obscures our understanding of the contemporaneous emergence of bebop.

Seen one way, the bans articulated a tension between competing elites—the streetwise AFM leadership and the profit-minded labels. But many rank-and-file musicians were ambivalent about these developments, even as they were caught up in them. Dinah Washington hinted at the dilemma on her "Record Ban Blues," singing, "Don't ask me when I'll record again, because only Petrillo knows." More problematically, the bans seemed to introduce a rift between artists and fans. Why, for instance, did the big bands not become popular again after the strikes? That genre's commercial fortunes need not have shifted unidirectionally. Whatever other factors may have been involved, it appeared in this case that audiences were all too willing to be led by the elites of the industry—to be consumers rather than listeners. And so whatever material gains the strikes produced, they also left behind lingering contentiousness.

Over time, musicians developed a keener awareness of the awkward situation in which they found themselves—their potential exploitation by both industry and fans. Pop stars of the late 1960s and early 1970s even developed a genre of reflexive critique, an early example of which is the Byrds' single "So You Wanna Be a Rock 'n' Roll Star," released in 1967. "Sell your soul to the company," the group sings, "Who are waiting there to sell plastic ware / And in a week or two / If you make the charts / The girls'll tear you apart." The double entendre—"tear you apart"—is telling here, but the double affront of being mishandled by both "the company" and "the girls" is the real key to understanding this song. Billy Joel's "The Entertainer," released in 1974, before the songwriter had achieved the sort of fame his lyrics bemoan, is a similarly bitter litany of the threats presented by music's commodification—threats that mirrored the commodification of the artist himself: "But if I go cold / I won't get sold / I'll get put in the back / In the discount rack / Like another can of beans."

Other artists complained even more directly. Consider the aggressiveness of the Sex Pistols' "EMI" (1977) (with its scathing pronouncement, "I can't stand these useless fools"), or Prince's much-publicized struggle with Warner Brothers, which in 1993 led to his appearing in public with the word "slave" written on his cheek. Indeed, if it is hard to find a critically reflexive song about the industry before the late 1960s, the decades since have been chock-full of them—from the Kinks' "The Moneygoround" (1970), to Pink Floyd's "Have a Cigar" (1975), to Frank Zappa's "Packard Goose" (1979), to Graham Parker's "Mercury Poisoning" (1979), to Dire Straits' "Money for Nothing" (1985), to Ice-T's "Rap Game's Hijacked" (1996), to Matthew Sweet's "Write Your Own Song" (1999), to Tom Petty's "The Last DJ" (2002), to Sara Bareilles's "Love Song" (2007). Most expressed resentment at the exploitative mechanisms of the mature industry—its capacity for confusing art and commerce, and for generating complex antagonisms between elites, masses, and audience.

By the time of the MP3.com and Napster lawsuits, then, the class conflicts of music were already well established. That foundation made it easier for modern stakeholders to take the tension to new extremes. As the public face of the plaintiffs, the Recording Industry Association of America (RIAA) came to symbolize the power of the elites. The digital technologies, on the other hand—whatever wealth they later produced, or however venal their board members and venture capitalists later turned out to be—seemed to naturally align with the masses and the audience. Napster seemed a cool invention created by a humble college dropout. MP3.com seemed a useful tool, created by hardworking, risk-taking entrepreneurs. In retrospect, these conclusions may have been naïve, but it was at least true that the new technologies allowed for audiencing, radically exploiting the web's capacity for sharing, and blurring the distinctions between artists and listeners. Indeed, listening was emphasized as a source of power, rather than merely a data point to be collected in a shareholder presentation.

Although the RIAA eventually prevailed over Napster and MP3 .com, its legal victories proved Pyrrhic. Flustered, but convinced of its own rectitude, the organization was goaded into a desperate step: suing listeners directly. And it was here that the lopsidedness of the situation became most apparent. Though promising to avoid "small violators," the RIAA quickly developed a reputation for choosing defendants reck-lessly: completely innocent and, in at least one case, even dead people did not escape the dragnet. (The strategy was reminiscent of some of the errors contemporaneously committed by the U.S. Department of Homeland Security, as the wrong people were placed on no-fly lists or worse.) But it almost didn't matter, because the true purpose of these lawsuits was intimidation. Given that intellectual property is a "strict liability" system—meaning, as James Boyle puts it, that "it is generally not a legal excuse to say that you did not believe you were violating copyright, or that you did so by accident, or in the belief that no one would care, and that your actions benefited the public"—the complex details of the law were far less pertinent than the more immediate real-ity of impending legal fees. Under the glare of the subpoena, listeners became atomized, interchangeable units of potential economic value, rather than distinct individuals with separately subjective experiences of music.

The new legal strategy posed serious risks for the plaintiffs too. According to testimony given by Sony BMG's head of litigation, the "entire campaign" to sue customers was "a money pit"—one reason the RIAA called it off in the latter part of the decade. Yet by then it was too late. Today, the RIAA may no longer be the visible bogeyman it once was, but its strategy has left a mark, institutionalizing a confron-tational momentum that now seems self-perpetuating. Like American politics, the discourse around digital music has become locked in a vicious cycle, an endless game of one-upmanship. When major labels flooded file-sharing networks with "spoofs" (dummy files) in 2003, for instance, listeners could only respond in kind. One spoof featured Madonna asking, "What the fuck do you think you're doing?" Angry fans answered by hacking the singer's website, uploading spoofs of their own that proclaimed, "This is what the fuck I think I'm doing." Today, the discussion has not improved much. An incisive critique of file sharing, published in 2012 by bassist and blogger Ronan Guil-foyle, bore a title seething with rage: "F**k The Filesharing Websites (and their apologists . . .)." Those apologists could be just as brutal; Chris Ruen's "The Myth of DIY: Towards a Common Ethic on Piracy" prompted a flurry of hate mail, including one message recommending suicide. And the legal music services have hardly relieved the tension. In 2011, U.K. distributor STHoldings pulled 238 labels from Spotify (and similar companies), posting a statement encouraging listeners to "keep the music special, fuck Spotify." When electronica musician and producer Jon Hopkins echoed that sentiment on Twitter, blogger Tom Clements ridiculed him with a sarcastic post entitled " 'Fuck Spotify'—a Rant in D minor."

"Irrespective of what any court says, a debate has crystallized: it's legitimate versus illegitimate," RIAA head Mitch Bainwol wrote in 2004. A "debate" that has "crystallized" is no longer really a debate, of course—it's more of a hardened, Manichean standoff. Yet for all the discursive back-and-forth over consumption and audiencing, the real battle over what was or wasn't "legitimate" would happen in the legal arena. For the traditional elites, even suing customers turned out to be a palliative; what they really wanted was a kind of legal preventive medicine. What they really wanted, that is, was to change copyright. In a moment we will see how successful they were in that goal.

DIGITAL CULTURE: A NEW CONTEXT FOR DECOMPOSITION

Technology reveals the active relation of man to nature, the direct process of the production of his life, and thereby it also lays bare the process of the production of the social relations of his life, and of the mental conceptions that flow from those relations.

—Karl Marx

One thing about which all sides in the digital culture debate agree is that the technological developments of the last few decades have the potential to change the way we think about music. As we saw with the player piano, technology is not only a tool, but also a barometer of our time, a sounding board for our aspirations and beliefs. But a sounding board can also feed back into cultural change. And as the peculiar affordances of digital technologies uncover, in music more than anywhere else, some of our underlying assumptions about copyright, capitalism, and aesthetic value, they bring long-festering disagreements over authorship and authenticity suddenly and sharply into focus.

Napster and MP3.com, for instance, demonstrated the new technology's capacity for the decompositional processes of collaboration and mediation, multiplying the listeners and contexts for each work. Through these tools, each composition could be—instead of reified—dissolved into the ether, and then brought back again; literally remade by the contextual collaboration of a computer. You could see it happen on the screen, as a song requested from the search box suddenly appeared on your desktop.

One of my favorite examples of how digital culture is decompositional, however, dates from late 2011, when composer and trombonist Alex Heitlinger created "The Lick," a short video inspired by a Facebook group of the same name. "The Lick" was compiled of sharply juxtaposed musical excerpts, copied from nearly fifty different source videos and spanning many different periods and genres, but with one thing in common: each featured the same seven-note "lick"—musicians' slang for a phrase, motif, or fragment of melody—deployed by a different artist in a different improvisation or composition.

Conceptually, there was some precedent for this piece in the political videos that became popular during the 2004 presidential campaign—see for example Sim Sadler's "Hard Working George," in which President George W. Bush's compulsive utterances of the words "hard work" during a single debate were spliced together into a seamless viewing experience. And like "Hard Working George," Heitlinger's video was a hit. By the end of its first week it had accrued nearly sixty thousand views—no small feat given the narrow focus of its subject matter.

"The Lick" would not have been impossible to create in the years before consumer-grade digital technology. But it would have been much more difficult. For one thing, the process of finding the raw material from which it is made was facilitated by the so-called hive mind of social networking. For nearly two years, volunteers posted instances of the phrase—sound clips, video clips, textual descriptions, and so on—to the aforementioned Facebook group. Many of these were already available in video form on the web, via sites like YouTube, and as such were easily "rippable" by anyone with a laptop and a modicum of technological know-how. In the predigital era, assembling these clips into a composite video would have required access to (or ownership of) not only a broad library of source material—which would most likely have been subject to stricter copyright policing—but also costly editing tools. Nowadays, inexpensive, widely available software (Apple's iMovie, for instance) has the same capabilities. And once created, "The Lick" was disseminated via the same social networks that had spawned it in the first place. In the predigital era, comparable dissemination would have required access to old-fashioned broadcast technology and distribution channels.

More important, hilarious as it is, "The Lick" makes a serious point about creativity. For one thing, it is dramatic evidence of one kind of musical collaboration: the borrowing of preexisting musical material. The musicians who wove "the lick" into their performances were, in a rudimentary way, channeling an Ellingtonian method, in which, as we saw in chapter 1, a composer makes creative use of phrases generated by musicians around her. In terms of the Lick's seven notes, at least, none of the cited musical performances could be considered purely original. In addition, the video has been broadly embedded on blogs, Facebook pages, and other sites, and so, like the *Mona Lisa* and its constantly changing Louvre audience, is not experienced in a vacuum, but rather in the context of the extended comment streams and browser frames that are the web's most obvious evidence of mediation. Given this context, the video discourages an authentic reading before we even view it.

Some viewers ignored that warning. "People cop licks all the time," wrote one, "but this is ridiculous." But was it? Most musicians intuitively understand that music in general relies on an abundance of shared licks, rhythms, lyrical phrases, and chord progressions; a version of "The Lick" could have been made about any one of them. Though the process occurs with what an individual listener would consider greater or lesser degrees of creativity, the point is that borrowing happens so frequently as to be a fundamental dynamic rather than a curious exception. What was so memorable (and, from one perspective, threatening) about "The Lick" was not the exposure of this or that borrowed item, but how extensively the act of borrowing was documented.

The digital revolution has produced other memorable artifacts, with similarly forceful displays of the collaboration and mediation that have been under our cultural radar for so long. Mashups, for instance, make the point as a genre, creatively juxtaposing preexisting recordings, building on a practice engaged in by underground radio DJs in the 1960s and 1970s, who, as Jesse Walker notes, sometimes amused themselves on air by playing two records simultaneously. Instead of borrowing a lick, mashups borrow entire sections of songs, playing them alongside other entire sections of songs. *The Gray Album* (created by Brian Burton, also known as Danger Mouse) is often cited as the exemplar—in this case, a creative melding of vocal tracks from Jay-Z's *The Black Album* with excerpts from the Beatles' *The White Album*.

W. David Marx and Nick Sylvester argue that cheaply available digital technology makes mashups easier to produce, but simultaneously "obscures" the fact that " 'mashing up' is the fundamental process for music making," one that involves "combining and recombining different sounds into pleasing and/or hopefully-not-boring configurations." But "obscures" is precisely the wrong word here: the technology makes that "fundamental process" more obvious than ever. That is what is so compelling about mashups: most of them deliberately let their seams show, rather than attempting to hide their source material. The word "mashup" itself suggests the use of brute force to join disparate elements in fascinating if not always elegant ways.

But though Marx and Sylvester draw the wrong conclusions from mashups' shameless delight in their component parts, they are right that the genre beautifully illustrates a basic directive of all composition: put together two already existing things in order to create a new thing. Mashing up the guitar part from one song with the drum part from another is, as a fundamental creative gesture, no different from mashing up two pitches, or a pitch and a chord, or a rhythm and a series of pitches—or any other constructive procedure of conventional composition. In this sense anyone who makes music is like a curious child playing with blocks, persistently and sometimes compulsively assembling them in different configurations until something finally works.

SAMPLING: A CASE STUDY

Get a license or do not sample.
—Sixth Circuit Court of Appeals in the *Bridgeport* case

The mashup has roots in other recombinant creative practices of the mid- to late twentieth century, most obviously musique concrète and then the sampling techniques that became so popular in the 1980s, both in hip-hop and in the work of composers like John Oswald. But the underlying method has *always* been important to musical creativity, and is basic to the aesthetics of decomposition. Sampling, for instance, is really just another way of describing quotation, the centuries-old practice of classical music, in which a fragment from one composition is inserted into another. Think of the modern example of Charles Ives, who frequently imported popular hymns, ragtime songs, and marches into his work. Quotation is also used in both popular music and jazz. The band Men at Work played a fragment of the song "Kookaburra" in their hit "Down Under," underlining the latter's geographical themes. Miles Davis played a fragment of the song "Maria" (from *West Side Story*) during an improvisation on "Bye Bye Blackbird," making a comment on race by juxtaposing music from a Broadway show about miscegenation with a tune that had minstrelsy associations.

Some—most notably the courts—insist that sampling is fundamentally different from quotation, that the former is a specific technological process that exactly reproduces the timbre, acoustics, and other performative details of an original recording. But aside from the fact that even in sampling, truly exact reproduction is not possible—at the very least, at the level of the bit, there can be tiny discrepancies in voltage between an "original" and a sample—the alleged material differences between sampling and quotation pale in comparison with their common purpose and effect. And insisting that quotation and sampling are qualitatively unlike practices starts us down a slippery slope of using subjective notions of "good" and "bad" aesthetic appropriation to drive copyright infringement claims—even though copyright law says nothing about good or bad art.

Let's consider this point for a moment. "Immature poets imitate; mature poets steal; bad poets deface what they take; and good poets make it into something better, or at least something different," T. S. Eliot once wrote, in a comment that is frequently misquoted. "The good poet welds his theft into a whole of feeling which is unique, utterly different from that from which it was torn; the bad poet throws it into something which has no cohesion." The "good taking" Eliot refers to here is usually understood as "authorship," in which the "taking" becomes unremarkable in itself and seems to disappear. And that is the crux of the problem—no one is going to sue an author whose appropriations, they believe, are used to create a new work that has "a whole of feeling that is unique." Thus sampling lawsuits too often participate in arbitrary distinctions between "bad art," which (it is assumed) relies on appropriation, and authorship, which (it is assumed) does not. To put that another way, a judge who dislikes a particular appropriation on aesthetic grounds is less likely to find in favor of it on legal grounds.

This helps explain why sampling, unlike quotation, incited a furious burst of litigation starting in the late 1980s. (It is not that there were no quotation infringement cases in the same period—Men at Work were sued for their use of "Kookaburra," for instance—but they were less visible.) The music that provided the fodder for these lawsuits—primarily hip-hop and rap—had a largely undetermined cultural status at the time, despite its popularity. It was not broadly considered "art," and, even more problematically for conservative judges, it originated in an African-American street culture about which they had little understanding. Not surprisingly, most of the first sampling cases were driven by standard assumptions regarding authorship and authenticity, and utterly failed to account for the contextual collaboration that occurs when a sample is situated in a new piece of music. They ignored, for instance, that singer-songwriter Gilbert O'Sullivan's piano part for his 1972 number one hit "Alone Again (Naturally)"—a song that prompted a landmark copyright lawsuit in 1991—simply has a different valence, or "feel," when chopped up and juxtaposed with the rapping of Biz Markie. It is no longer the same sound in this new environment, but rather participates in the striking uncanniness that is one of the unsung features of hip-hop: we simultaneously recognize the sample and are taken back with how different, how odd it sounds.

Yet a sample can be transformed even more dramatically and literally than that—contextual collaboration can easily become direct collaboration. In the 1980s, samples were routinely doctored, processed with effects or filters, slowed down, pitch-shifted, and so on. As Chris Cutler points out, there are "manipulations which take the sounds plundered and stretch and treat them so radically that it is impossible to divine their source at all." Even radical manipulations have not been safe from copyright infringement claims, however. The usual example is *Bridgeport Music, Inc. v. Dimension Films* (2005), another landmark copyright case that concerned a mere two seconds taken from a Funkadelic song—music that goes by in less time than it took you to read this sentence. The outcome of *Bridgeport*—the defendants lost on appeal—ensured that when it comes to sampling, charges of infringement are not contingent upon what is actually perceived by the listener. Sounds that have been altered past the point of recognition are still considered the property of the original rights holder. It is as if the proponents of this view believe there is a genetic code for music, something *in* the sound, *regardless of what it sounds like*. (Yet how can a sound—by definition, something heard—ever be anything other than what it sounds like?)

This "genetic" understanding of music gives us absurd situations like the aforementioned lawsuit between Gilbert O'Sullivan and Biz Markie, technically known as *Grand Upright Records v. Warner Brothers Music*. Decompositionally speaking, the collaborative work in Biz Markie's song ("Alone Again," from the album *I Need a Haircut*) made any claim of copyright infringement moot. Yes, the four-bar introduction of O'Sullivan's hit had been sampled without permission. But as the chords looped, the progression (roughly, I / iii / ii–V7b9 / I) also articulated an overall harmonic sequence unique to the Biz Markie song—one that sounded like stasis rather than the ongoing change that had characterized the pop song. And while the rapper did borrow the words and rhythm of the phrase "Alone again, naturally"— admittedly the original song's "hook"—even here, he was unfaithful to

O'Sullivan's melodic content, and to the phrase's original placement at the end of a sixteen-bar melody. In the rapper's version, "Alone again, naturally" becomes its own four-bar chorus.

In other words, very little of the musical information that went into the O'Sullivan recording was actually used by Biz Markie, and the musical information that *was* used was put to a different aesthetic purpose. That this argumentative weakness in the plaintiffs' case did not prevent the court from finding for them suggests that the suit was weighed down by subtext. Aside from O'Sullivan's status as a seasoned pop star, who had been mistreated by a manager and so was understandably suspicious about the intersection of art and commerce, he also seems to have been "exercised," as one analyst put it, "not by how much copyrightable expression defendant appropriated but rather by the potentially demeaning association inherent in defendant's use of key music and words closely identified in the ears of the public with the plaintiff's song." Yet however much O'Sullivan may have disliked "Alone Again" (and the question arises: in what way was Biz Markie's song "potentially demeaning" to the singer?), copyright law—in the United States and the UK, anyway—is not designed to punish the makers of a piece of music simply because it is unpleasant or even offensive to some listeners.

In his decision, which granted an injunction and recommended criminal prosecution, Judge Kevin Duffy wrote scornfully of the defendants' argument that "they should be excused because others in the 'rap music' business are also engaged in illegal activity." (Note the scare quotes.) In doing so, he missed the bigger point. The "illegal activity" that Biz Markie engaged in was not merely endemic to rap music—it was not a bug plaguing a single genre, but a feature of all musical creativity. For what it's worth, O'Sullivan too surely "stole" (if we must put it that way) from his environment to make new art. His very persona was the product of artistic appropriation. Born Raymond Edward O'Sullivan, he had riffed on the nostalgia of British art rock (the same nostalgia that drove the Beatles in their *Sgt. Pepper* phase) and had, through the encouragement of his manager—who also handled another pop star with an antiquated pseudonym, Englebert Humperdinck—fused the famous last names of the nineteenth-century operetta team of W. S. Gilbert and Arthur Sullivan to create his own brand. As pretty as "Alone Again (Naturally)" is, and as clearly as it shows signs of individual craft, it did not spring fully formed from the godhead of this brand. Rather, it was the outcome of one songwriter's complex personal history, and of the various trajectories of influence that intersected with that—each of which could in turn claim some authorship role, if they could somehow be discovered.

SPEAKING DECOMPOSITIONALLY

"The universality of appropriation is an open secret," Marcus Boon insightfully writes, "known to everyone but almost impossible to speak of." Which is not to say that this knowledge has not been exploited, in a trivialized form, by the Web 2.0 elite. But most of the time, we marginalize a more nuanced discussion of appropriation—whether we term it "remixing" or "sampling" or "quotation" or "borrowing" or "theft" or "collaboration"—in a way that signals a kind of hypocrisy. "It is striking how often musicians condemn a younger generation's practice of musical appropriation as theft, while viewing their own musical development and indebtedness as benign and organic," writes James Boyle, citing the example of soul icon James Brown, whose music has been sampled copiously—according to Kevin Nottingham, Brown's "Funky Drummer" is the most sampled record ever. Brown disliked when hip-hop musicians used guitar riffs or drum grooves from his songs. But he "celebrated" his own "process of borrowing from gospel standards and from rhythm and blues"—or, in the case of "Funky Drummer," from Clyde Stubblefield, the drummer in his band. Brown was not the only artist ever to straddle this contradiction, of course. But his example demonstrates that no one who polices appropriative practices has figured out a way to make art that does not rely on appropriative practices. Kirby Ferguson distills that idea nicely, quipping a parodic mantra (itself adapted from the Eliot quote we looked at earlier) for the artist who advocates creative theft only when she is not the one being stolen from: "Great artists steal, but not from me."

Admittedly, although this insight comes too late for Biz Markie and other first-wave digital copyright defendants, today the "open secret" sometimes seems more open and less secret. In his 2012 SXSW keynote address, for instance, Bruce Springsteen emphatically described the musical debt he owed classic rock pioneers the Animals. "We Gotta Get Out of This Place," one of that band's hits, featured a riff that Springsteen joked was also in "every song I've ever written." Indeed, Springsteen's album *Darkness on the Edge of Town* "was filled with Animals," as he explained to the audience. After playing some of that band's song, "Don't Let Me Be Misunderstood," he compared it to his own "Badlands." His analysis? "It's the same fucking riff, man. Listen up, youngsters: this is how successful theft is accomplished."

Other articulations of the "open secret" come from Ferguson, who points to obscure sources for famous Bob Dylan songs; Boyle, with a much more detailed treatment of one of Ray Charles's earliest hits; John Tehranian, who finds in Thomas Pynchon's *Gravity's Rainbow* a lyrical prototype of Nirvana's "Smells Like Teen Spirit"; and Lawrence Lessig, tracing the origins of the character of Mickey Mouse. (Robert Levine's critique of Lessig, after Stephen Manes, misses the point: the question is not how much of Mickey Mouse was borrowed from Buster Keaton's film *Steamboat Bill Jr.*, but whether Mickey Mouse would have been invented at all without the earlier film.) A decade earlier, Judge Alex Kozinski had summarized the point while litigating a copyright case involving Vanna White. "Nothing today, likely nothing since we tamed fire, is genuinely new," Kozinski wrote. "Culture, like science and technology, grows by accretion, each new creator building on the works of those who came before."

Yet in the end the critique amplified by these figures—Springsteen, Lessig, Ferguson, Boyle, Kozinski, among others—remains frustratingly outside our cultural mainstream, even as it is subject to pat advertising slogans like Apple's "Rip. Mix. Burn." Indeed, it can be downright controversial when voiced by someone other than a beloved rock star surrounded by an audience of fans, or when broadcast to a larger audience than any law professor or judge can hope to reach. "If you were successful, somebody along the line gave you some help," Barack

Obama said at one point during the 2012 presidential campaign, in a statement that may have been inspired by the earlier remarks of Elizabeth Warren, who was running for Senate that year. "There was a great teacher somewhere in your life. Somebody helped to create this unbelievable American system that we have that allowed you to thrive. Somebody invested in roads and bridges." And then came the line that drew the most attention: "If you've got a business—you didn't build that." Obama, of course, was describing the interdependence of individual citizens, the economy, and a federally supported infrastructure. He was, in fact, describing a version of the collaborative theory as it applied not only to the arts, but also to society: roads, bridges, and education are all forms of contextual collaboration. The idea was simply that our actions are connected, and that society, as Kozinski put it, grows by accretion. The president could just as easily have said, "No man is an island," as John Donne did several centuries before, with much less controversy.

Yet the simple truth of Obama's remarks drew scorn from his critics. His campaign rival, Mitt Romney, responded with the rhetoric of genius, emphasizing the iconic personalities lauded by a culture in love with its own branding. "To say that Steve Jobs didn't build Apple, that Henry Ford didn't build Ford Motors, that Papa John didn't build Papa John Pizza," Romney said at an event in Pennsylvania, "to say something like that, it's not just foolishness. It's insulting to every entrepreneur, every innovator in America"—as if entrepreneurs and innovators do their work in a vacuum. A photoshopped image, one of many attempts to capitalize on what became the "You didn't build that" meme, also revealed the nerve that had been touched, drawing a link between politics and art. In it, Obama is made to point accusingly at Walt Disney, implying that the latter didn't "build" Mickey Mouse—another a superficial reading of Lessig's work.

The contrived outrage showed that in twenty-first-century culture, whatever the philosophical awareness prompted by digital technology, the concepts of decomposition continue, for the time being, to be overwhelmed by old ways of thinking about art—by authorship and authenticity.

THE ELITE RESPONSE

This is true partly because authorship and authenticity continue to be asserted, forcefully, by the industry elite. Consider the view of musical creativity expressed in a PR text originally published on the RIAA website in 2002. In a revealing example of how the organization sought to publicly define and represent itself at an early moment in the post-Napster landscape, the text insisted that "the artist creates the music that jolts you back in your chair, whisks you across the dance floor, or freezes you in reverie"—an unambiguous statement of the "telegraphic model" of "mere transmission" critiqued by Vijay Iyer in chapter 1 of this book. Channeling the religious imagery that pervades the rhetoric of genius, the PR text also stressed the godlike qualities of those who make music, noting that they are globally "embraced, honored, banned and sometimes feared." Audiences, on the other hand, were posited as mere consumers, in the worst sense of that word. Perpetually on the receiving end of creativity, they existed to be acted upon, whether that meant being jolted, whisked, or frozen.

This specific wording has since been removed, but the underlying concepts continue to inform RIAA aesthetic ideology. In an online obituary for Michael Jackson, for instance, Joel Flatow (the RIAA's "Senior VP, Artist and Industry Relations") referred to Jackson's "absolutely unique" artistry, adding that

> there's something profound here occurring with Michael but is beyond Michael which is . . . how all of us relate to music. How it defines our lives. That song at that moment, that album when we needed it, that love forever associated. That other person or group of friends who get that artist that you worship that makes you smile inside and determines that you are, well . . . friends!

Whatever the specific meaning of this passage, its general thrust is clear: Jackson is one of those "artists you worship," and whose "music defines our lives." Flatow later subjected Whitney Houston to a similarly insipid eulogy, describing her talent—which was undoubtedly impressive—in terms almost reminiscent of a teenage fan letter. "With THAT VOICE," Flatow gushed, "Whitney made YOU feel what she felt, what she sang." Her hits, "like 'You Give Good Love,' 'Where Do Broken Hearts Go,' 'Saving All My Love' or 'Didn't We Almost Have It All' could be studied, imitated, emulated—but never, ever matched." The capitalizations here underscore the hierarchy between the (active) "VOICE" and the (passive) "YOU." It's a hierarchy also evident in the stylized cover art of the standard Top 40 release. One could choose, almost at random, albums and singles featured on the homepage of the RIAA website—in 2012 it featured Chris Young's "Tomorrow," Justin Bieber's "As Long as You Love Me," Lee Brice's "A Woman Like You," Luke Bryan's "Don't Want This Night to End," Rascal Flatts' *Changed,* Blake Shelton's "Honeybee," the Black Eyed Peas' "I Gotta Feeling"—noting that they all visually evoke the rhetoric of genius, primarily through solo portraiture, whose subjects exude faux sincerity, piercing gazes, and nearly comical self-importance, all in contrast to an implied passive audience.

Ultimately the very notion of music has been reduced in this discourse. "Music moves us," the RIAA had said in the PR text. "Music unites us. Not many art forms are as expansive, evocative, or powerful." Such platitudes mask an underlying incongruity. It is contradictory to say that music "unites" even as it is "expansive," for instance, since expansiveness suggests the divergence of musical perception we looked at in detail in chapter 4. Yet the bigger point is that the elite is not really interested in "music," but *songs*. Songs, after all, are a specific, monetizable form, hardly representative of "the music" as a whole. When the PR text informs us that "no one drops from the sky a rock star" or starts at the top "on the Billboard chart," or when it suggests that our "memories of first loves, bitter battles, and sweet triumphs are all brought back by that favorite song," it is counting on us to make the same assumptions about what music is—assumptions that eMusic also made when it tried to lure me with the promise of "13+ million tracks," or that Spotify makes when it touts "access to millions of songs."

Of course, similar substitutions happen frequently in the wider culture too. Though *Best Music Writing 2009*, for instance, includes interesting articles on a variety of genres, it advertises itself with a blurb from the *Boston Phoenix* that makes the same conflation, calling the *Best* series a "compendium that's become, next to free Radiohead tickets, the rock critic's highest professional honor." Here, the song-based genre of "rock" is privileged over the broad category of "music" referenced by the book's title. A similar problem characterizes Chris Ruen's *Freeloading*, which speaks generally of "music" even though it mostly concerns the indie rock scene based in Brooklyn, NY. "Copyright laws," writes promoter Jeff Cameron, in yet another example of this discursive sleight of hand, "are the only things that protect what musicians do for a living: write songs."

Not to belabor the obvious, but not all musicians (and probably not even a majority of them) "write songs," or play rock, or live in Brooklyn, or care about Radiohead or *Billboard*. In this context, Theodor Adorno—who when it came to pop music was wrong about many things—was right when he pointed out the inadequacy of the elite assumption that music depends on "eight-beat symmetrical treble melody," which is "catalogued as the composer's 'idea' which one thinks he can put in his pocket and take home, just as it is ascribed to the composer as his basic property." In modern culture, Adorno acerbically pointed out, all music is "examined in terms of the category of ideas, with musical larceny being hunted down with all the zeal of the belief in property, so that finally one music commentator could pin his success to the title of tune detective" (a reference to Adorno's contemporary Sigmund Spaeth, a broadcaster and educator who went by that moniker). Adorno's nicely satirical reference to an "eight-beat symmetrical treble melody" that one can "put in his pocket and take home" is of course another way of describing music's reification. "Song" is shorthand for "music," just as "composer-genius" is shorthand for the collaborative creative process, and just as "authentic work" is shorthand for the many works generated by mediation and perception.

All of which, in turn, are shorthand for decomposition.

A BRIEF INTRODUCTION TO COPYRIGHT

How would the great musical traditions of the twentieth century—jazz, soul, blues, rock—have developed under today's copyright regime? Would they have developed at all?

—James Boyle

As I have suggested, the tensions we have been looking at so far come to a head in the discourse over copyright. But what exactly is copyright?

For one thing, it is easy to forget that its claims are just that—claims, not facts of nature. Copyright is a Western social construction, a kind of imperfect bargain or necessary evil, with which we have historically made peace. Yes, there have always been antimonopolist and "tax on literacy" arguments against it—arguments that it forced unfair competition around information and culture—even going back to its eighteenth-century origins. But for most of the era of electronic mass media, and even as recently as the 1970s, we have assumed that copyright was just and uncontroversial. Partly this was because infringement was harder to commit. And partly it was because the laws seemed fairer. While there was litigation (presumably there will always be litigation), there was no large-scale movement to challenge the scope of the law.

Some of the contentiousness we see today has to do with how criticism of copyright is often painted with a broad brush, as if all copyright's critics want it eliminated rather than curbed. And some of it has to do with how copyright's different traditions are invoked, haphazardly, and for political reasons, by the music industry's many stakeholders. One set of copyright traditions, for instance, draws heavily on the rhetoric of genius and authenticity. Consider the French idea of *droit d'auteur,* or the moral right of authors—what Robert Levine calls "copyright as a human right"—which emphasizes an author's inherent rights, including the right of paternity (in the collaborative theory I distinguished this as the "initiating act") and the right of integrity (the right to control how a work is used). *Droit d'auteur* has been very influential on the European continent, and also in the Berne Convention's articulation of international copyright law. In Great Britain, John Locke's "labor-desert" theory of property similarly avowed the natural rights of authors. The labor of a person, Locke wrote, "and the *Work* of his Hands, we may say, are properly his. Whatsoever then he removes out of the State that Nature hath provided, and left it in, he hath mixed his *Labour* with, and joyned it to something that is his own, and thereby makes it his *Property*."

Early in the eighteenth century, the English parliament devised the Statute of Anne, which for the first time posited copyright as a utilitarian arrangement entered into by authors, publishers, and audiences. The Statute of Anne redirected the emphasis of authorship—not toward the natural rights of authors, held in perpetuity, but toward a broader idea of the public good, as measured by the advancement of culture, which in turn depended on an audience's ability to interact with works through use, commentary, or appropriation. Under this statute, authors and publishers shared, for a limited time, a monopoly benefit from their mutual labor. During that limited monopoly, audience access to a work would largely (but not exclusively) be determined by how authors and publishers chose to make it available. The monopoly incentivized the production of works in the first place, but because the law did not privilege a natural rights conception of authorship, transformative uses—translation, parody, abridgement, quotation, and so on—were also permitted, understood as "accretive to progress in the arts." More important, after the limited monopoly period of twenty-eight years (at most), the copyright expired and the work entered the public domain, where it could be put to a wide range of uses by other authors, thereby potentially advancing culture even more.

Crucially, the Statute of Anne, and not labor-desert or *droit d'auteur,* became the model for copyright law in the United States. The first American expression of copyright, the Copyright Clause of the Constitution, gave Congress power to "promote the progress of Science and useful Arts, by securing for limited Times to Authors and Inventors the exclusive Right to their respective Writings and Discoveries." Note how the sentence structure here foregrounds the societal benefit that superseded, even as it was produced by, the short-term personal privileges of "Authors and Inventors." Thus this foundational statement of American copyright established it as a way of nurturing a culture into viability—a goal of particular concern for the new country—and only secondarily as a way of ensuring the livelihood of professional creative people.

PROPRIETARY TOTALISM: THE LOGIC OF COMMERCIAL MUSIC

I think the entire government should be privatized. Chuck E. Cheese could run the parks. Everything operated by tokens. Drop in a token, go on the swing set. Drop in another token, take a walk. Drop in a token, look at a duck.

—Ron Swanson, *Parks and Recreation*

Over the last few decades, we have moved away from this foundational notion of copyright. In music, traditional elites like the RIAA, sometimes called "maximalists" because of how they seek to strengthen and expand copyright law, have responded to the chaos of profusion by imagining a listening environment of what I call "proprietary totalism"—Lessig calls it a "permission culture," though that seems too benign to me—in which musical experience is pervasively subject to financial frameworks. Under such a system, the average listener could not hear music without paying for it first, or without being exposed to an atmosphere of compulsive consumerism. Of course, not all intimations of proprietary totalism are explicitly connected to traditional elites. Consider the mania with which listener taste is subjected to analytical algorithms by entities like Amazon. Consider commercials routinely appended to the front of YouTube music videos—even though most viewers are likely to opt out of them once presented with the opportunity to do so (usually after a few seconds). Consider younger audiences' reputed comfort with what used to be called "selling out"—an ironic outcome of the "leveled playing field" promised by digital advocates.

It sounds like a bad science-fiction premise, but the dream of proprietary totalism is also the logical end point of the mass commercialization of music that began in the late nineteenth century, a predictable outcome of the desire to get every last bit of economic value out of what is ultimately a finite resource: listening. It's an example of how the music business has been a type of "progress trap"—to borrow Ronald Wright's term for cultural "improvements" that then obliquely generate new problems. Progress traps complicate the usual evolutionary narrative of how societies develop. Looking back to early human history, for instance, we find that as hunting techniques were refined, certain animals were killed off entirely. The advancements made possible by hunters' ingenuity (figuring out that you could kill many mammoths at once by driving them off a cliff) also led to unintended, undesirable effects (no more mammoths). And where art intersects with commerce, progress traps occur too. In a capitalist system, artists, labels, technology companies, and other music professionals naturally seek to grow their profits. ("If you sell fifty million records one year and seventy the next year," notes Jeff Gold, describing the expansion of Warner Music in the 1990s, then soon someone is going to ask "how are you going to sell eighty?") As elites become more efficient at producing, marketing, and selling music, that increased efficiency stresses the system. Music becomes, as William Patry puts it, "a zero sum game, where the more people vie for the top, the fewer make it, but the rewards are disproportionately greater." In the process, the thoughtful listener is left with a nagging feeling that just as we cannot understand music outside of recording, or our own thoughts about it outside of writing, it is now difficult to even conceive of it outside of money—outside of our transactional roles as producers, consumers, or both. TV On The Radio's Kyp Malone makes the point when he poignantly notes that almost greater than the musician's annoyance at having to deal with piracy is her "frustration with having to sell anything" at all—a frustration at least some audiences surely share.

One could argue that a formal framework of proprietary totalism was laid out in an influential white paper created in the U.S. Patent Office in the mid-1990s. Produced by the Clinton administration's Information Infrastructure Task Force, and coauthored by Bruce Lehman and Ronald Brown, this white paper, according to Boyle, responded to the challenges of the then-emerging digital era by proposing a "pervasively monitored digital environment." Lehman and Brown wanted to make copyright stronger, to lengthen its term, to increase its penalties, and to criminalize infringement even in noncommercial situations. They also wanted to regulate the technology used to enjoy copyrighted works. It should be illegal, they proposed, to disable (or to produce tools that could disable) the digital "fences" that protect such devices, "even if you do so to make a 'fair use' of the material on the other side." Anticipating the shift from ownership to licensing, Lehman and Brown further argued that works should be subject to control even after purchase. Boyle summarizes the document as a call to "make this technology of the Internet, which was hailed as the great 'technology of freedom,' into a technology of control and surveillance."

Which is not to say that everything in the document came to pass. Even Boyle admits that the legal and technological changes of the twenty-first century have "not brought about the worst of the dystopian consequences that some people, including me, feared might result." It may be that for every new legal restriction the white paper anticipated—and in a moment we will look at a few of those that were actually implemented—listeners found corresponding work-arounds. Some repeatedly turned to new file sharing platforms—trading Napster for Kazaa, for instance, or trading Kazaa for BitTorrent. Many eventually took advantage of putatively "free" legal streaming services, like Pandora or Spotify (which of course were not free at all, given their dependence on advertising, and given that they required regular investments in technology). Others chose to boycott the products covered by the most egregious protections—such as the CDs outfitted with harmful digital rights management. Some turned from the music offered for sale in the official marketplace to the music they made themselves—one explanation for the seeming growth of amateur and semiprofessional music making in this period. Even professional artists explored ways around the potential restrictiveness, taking advantage of new licenses, such as those innovated by the nonprofit group Creative Commons, which explicitly allowed for remixing and other forms of appropriation, or trying "pay what you want" pricing schemes that let audiences decide what a recording was worth.

But all of this does not mean that there is no longer any cause for concern about proprietary totalism in music. The worldview of the white paper has been hard to back away from, given the intensity and economic force with which the PR people and lobbyists of the content industries embraced it. In other words, the imagination of proprietary totalism has in some ways been bad enough. We may be in a lull at the moment—the last big battle in the copyright wars, the Stop Online Piracy Act fight, happened a few years ago—but the push for greater control is insistent. As this book goes to press, Congress is conducting a series of copyright hearings that may result in what Register of Copyrights Maria Pallante calls "The Next Great Copyright Act." Some, like NYU Law professor Christopher Sprigman, are less than sanguine about the process. "The public interest doesn't appear," Sprigman notes. "There is no real principle that drives this, it's basically just a bunch of people fighting over money."

Meanwhile, the excesses of a superstar-oriented culture have been not only pardoned but admired, even as similar excesses in other fields are widely criticized. "Musicians and labels at the top of their game have been making too much money for a long time—I don't think that's fair in the same way I don't think hedge fund salaries are fair," says bassist Ira Wolf Tuton, making the connection. The fact that our obsession with authorship and authenticity continues to impact the discussion suggests that there is no reason to blithely assume that new legislation will point in a direction that is healthy for culture. And there are numerous reasons to fear it won't.

LEGAL EFFORTS

Somewhere along the line copyright became a law everyone breaks.
—Tim Wu

Even before Lehman and Brown's white paper, for instance, the 1976 Copyright Act, as Tehranian points out, had "dramatically altered our default regime from one of nonprotection to one of protection." Before 1976, copyright required paperwork; artists were supposed to register their creations with the U.S. Copyright Office. Today, every expression—from e-mail to demo recordings to personal videos posted on YouTube to love notes to grocery lists—is assumed to be copyrighted the instant it is created, whether or not it is registered, and providing it is fixed in a "tangible medium." This, Tehranian notes, means "virtually the entire universe of creative works created after 1978 is now subject to copyright protection"—though registration is still a factor in determining remedies for infringement.

To understand the potential harm here, we should review the wording of the Copyright Clause. One can only speak of "securing for limited times" in the context of an environment that is normatively *insecure*—in this sense, copyright ought to be a way of carving out a limited space of protection against an implicitly larger background of nonprotection. The 1976 law reversed that relationship by protecting *everything* as a default and making nonprotection the exception. That reversal was further complicated by the fact that the "entire universe of creative works" continues to expand, thanks to population growth, the increasing availability of powerful creative tools, and the cumulative effect of history. Suddenly, copyright has become a demographic problem. Everyone has a claim to make, and convenient means for making it. After all, there's now an easy way to find out if your own music is being downloaded against your will: just google it.

Of course, musicians had impressive surveillance tools at their disposal even before Google. Performing rights organizations (PROs), even from their inception in the nineteenth and twentieth centuries, have always monitored listening as if audiences already lived in a world of proprietary totalism. And while such monitoring can provide an important revenue stream for artists, the compulsive visibility of the Internet may have inspired PROs to police new contexts for performance, even without new legal mandates. In 1996, for instance, the American Society of Composers, Authors and Publishers demanded an unprecedented fee—$561—of a Girl Scout day camp, so that scouts could continue to sing ASCAP-affiliated songs. That demand was fairly sweeping—the number of protected songs ran into the millions, and included such summer camp warhorses as "God Bless America," "Puff the Magic Dragon," and "This Land Is Your Land." Similar fees were soon foisted on venues that hosted open-mic nights—those informal public gatherings of aspiring singer-songwriters—even when the performers themselves had written the featured music. In a confrontation with a restaurant in North Carolina, Broadcast Music Incorporated, another PRO, demanded payment before checking to see whether the establishment even played music publicly. (More recently, BMI sued an Ohio bar for $1.5 million for failing to obtain the license required to feature a cover band.) And perhaps most ludicrously of all, the United Kingdom's Performing Rights Society sued a car mechanic company, charging that its employees "routinely use personal radios while working at service centers across the UK and that music, protected by copyright, could be heard by colleagues and customers."

These are just a few examples of a new PRO aggressiveness. The point, as Steve Jansen puts it, is that PROs started "using over-the-top, heavy-handed policing tactics," demanding fines even "when no copyrights have been violated." Yet while PROs are not blameless in their zeal, they have acted in the context of a legal zeitgeist that can be traced to the 1976 law. Again, the goal has been to effect dramatic change to notions of intellectual property. Even concepts as fundamental to culture as the public domain—the shared repository that has historically served as a prompt for creativity and learning, and without which new music would not be possible (as the examples of sampling, quotation, mashups, and "The Lick" demonstrate obviously, but not exclusively)—are now in danger of being critically compromised. Sonny Bono's Copyright Term Extension Act (1998), for instance, drew on the recommendations of the white paper by adding twenty years to the copyright term, weakening the constitutional stipulation that copyright should last for "limited times" only. But CTEA was merely the latest effort in a longer project. For a single author, the period of "limited monopoly" has slowly but steadily grown, because of occasional changes in the law, from twenty-eight years (in 1790) to now roughly *105 years* (assuming a work produced when the author is thirty-five, and that she lives to be seventy-five). The CTEA may not even be the final word on the matter; a few of its advocates actually wanted copyright to be perpetual. Indeed, it is some measure of where our culture is going that we have started taking works *out* of the public domain (a precedent recently established by *Golan v. Holder*).

FAIR USE: FAIRLY USELESS

We have generally assumed that proprietary totalism is prevented by what Nancy Kranich calls the "traditional safety valves" of copyright—mechanisms that ensure a balance between the interest of audiences and the interest of producers, stressing the utilitarian bargain expressed in the Copyright Clause. One of these safety valves is the public domain, which, as we have just seen, is in crisis. Another is fair use.

Variations on fair use have played a role throughout the history of copyright, but the concept would not be codified until the 1976 law, which provided courts with four tests to which infringement claims could be subjected: the nature of the use, the nature of the work being used, how much of the work had been used, and the effect of the use. Yet even in the wake of this legal "clarification," the concept remained elusive. "Use," after all, is extremely difficult to describe or quantify, philosophically, let alone legally. It is what happens in the idiosyncratic trajectory from sound generation, to vector, to subjective perception. How do we determine that trajectory in ourselves, let alone in others? Indeed, if, as I have been arguing, we create works *as* we listen, and through the act of listening, then listening itself is fair use, regardless of whether a work is protected. No wonder then that disinterested attempts to explain this exemption, well-intentioned though they may be, are frustratingly uninformative. Patricia Aufderheide and Peter Jaszi, for example, suggest that fair use is the right to incorporate copyrighted material without a license "when the value to society is greater than the value to the copyright owner"—even though it is difficult to know how "value" in either case could be definitively measured. They add that fair use should be understood "within the specific cultural practice in which the use occurs." Yet cultural practices are as wide-ranging as can be; do they *all* potentially provide exemption? The Copyright Office is even less helpful. "The distinction between what is fair use and what is infringement in a particular case," it writes, "will not always be clear or easily defined." It is hard to imagine a more opaque statement.

As William Patry points out, the vagueness of fair use is supposed to be its strength. But in practice that vagueness has led to a scenario that is full of risk for the very people who are supposed to benefit. Fair use is now treated as both an anomaly and a joke (RIAA president Cary Sherman once mocked it as "the old standby"; other critics have derided an imagined notion of "fair use creep"). We live in a world in which an aspiring singer-songwriter, working on a new piece, may unexpectedly generate a melody that sounds vaguely familiar—and at that moment, if she has an even passing familiarity with prevailing attitudes to fair use (exemplified recently by a problematic lawsuit alleging that Led Zeppelin stole the introduction to "Stairway to Heaven"), she may be tempted to put her pen down. The threat of litigation and its baggage of cultural shame can cause the most confident artist to forget that an inchoate melody is subject to transformation; that "all art," as Glenn Gould put it, "is really variation on some other art." It can cause her to ignore the initiating act's potential—its capacity for being edited, or sounding different in the context of a certain harmony, when wedded to certain lyrics, or when played by certain instruments. Like the modern hip-hop artist, frustrated at the outset of the creative process by a post-*Bridgeport* zeitgeist (most labels now demand a list of potential samples before a record is even made), this hypothetical singer-songwriter will write from a position of caution rather than abandon. Such inhibitions do not serve creativity well.

It doesn't help that the other major legislative development of the digital era, the Digital Millenium Copyright Act (like the CTEA, passed in 1998), encourages content producers to assume fair use is a rarity rather than a basic gesture of musical experience. Among other things, the DMCA has been the legal justification for the takedown notices now sent to allegedly infringing websites. While the DMCA also provides "safe harbor" for those sites—complying with a notice limits liability—it also abets the compulsive generation of infringement claims, leading content producers to obsessively monitor the web for instances of alleged wrongdoing. Such notices are exhausting for most everyone involved. And though the DMCA may curtail infringement some of the time, it also places serious limitations on our ability to realize the cultural purpose of copyright. In intellectual property parlance, the term

is "chilling effect": instead of influencing subsequent expression, protected works are "frozen" like fossils embedded in a cultural glacier.
Decompositional collaborations and mediations are too often subject
to a set of absurd, unnatural, creativity-killing legal formalities.

Mutual musical interest between listeners is "chilled," for instance,
when music bloggers must pause to weigh the pros and cons of sharing
a favorite band's song online. Writers in this fan-based genre, which
emerged in the middle of the last decade, have established a niche in
which they obsessively discuss and promote their favorite music, often
offering samples or entire albums for download or streaming. Blog
aggregator Hype Machine—a favorite resource for the music blogging
community—reveals the passion of its mission ("to help this vibrant
culture spread") when it proclaims, simply, "This is why we wake up."
Yet although many artists now submit their own material expressly
for sharing in this context, some music bloggers still feel compelled to
proactively defend themselves against potential infringement claims,
alerting surfers accordingly—perhaps an oblique recognition of the
fact that many of the first music blogs were killed by such claims a few
years after the phenomenon began. Even a blog as blatantly named as
"WE FUCKING LOVE MUSIC" leads with the disclaimer, "we fucking love music is a blog about awesome music"—as if with a name
like that it could be about anything else. Readers, the WFLM bloggers remind us, should support the promoted artists "by buying their
albums and merchandise, and going to their shows"—as if readers
who "fucking love music" too are unlikely to do either of those things
without being prodded.

Maybe it's silly to carp about such obviously ass-covering boilerplate,
now appended to the headers of many music blogs and tumblrs. Yet I
don't think it's an exaggeration to say that there is something patho-
logical going on here. In the digital world, love for music is no longer
assumed as a given—even in the case of websites whose *entire purpose
is to express love for music*. And so, for instance, we are now apparently capable of shrugging it off when the federal government seizes
and disables a popular hip-hop blog, without making charges, and at
the behest of the very industry that the blog was helping to promote,
only to imply its own mistake later by letting the blog go back online

without comment—all of which happened recently to the blog Dajaz1 .com. We are, that is, already starting to perceive musical passion from within the mind-set of proprietary totalism, in which that passion is neither believable—too easy to mistake for crass materialism—nor sufficient in itself. To those with an interest in prosecution, the complex variations of musical love seemingly matter less and less.

It may even be that fair use has been weakened in one of the areas it should be strongest: education. The problem is that the 1976 articulation of fair use encourages us to think of education as a narrow category of experience clearly separable from entertainment—as if "education" is an activity that can only happen in a room with a blackboard and desks, and only when studying certain kinds of music. But surely works of "entertainment" can be educational; surely they can be studied and learned from, even in informal settings, and regardless of their musical merits. Similarly, education can be entertaining—or, to put that another way, the sort of pleasure given by entertainment is not *only* given by the music we label "entertainment," but can be found in intellectual accomplishment as well. Beyond the shallow rhetoric of contemporary marketing terms like "edutainment," actual, honest-to-goodness learning can produce enjoyment, delight, and fun. In practice, then, the distinctions between education and entertainment are blurred. And that is precisely the problem once the issue enters a court of law. Music that happens to be popular and lucrative—like the Beatles' "Yellow Submarine," of which more in a moment—is assumed to have a purely commercial purpose, so that its sharing or appropriation is automatically indefensible on fair use grounds.

Today, professional educators know that digitally sharing music with students—depending on what that music is—can be a good way to invite trouble. John Covach recently wrote of his experience teaching a MOOC (Massive Open Online Course) on the history of rock, noting that "we could not play or post any music in the course because of copyright restrictions"; in response, "students began posting playlists in the discussion forum, employing various servers to get all the music posted (including a server in Russia)." Cynthia Cyrus, associate provost for undergraduate education at Vanderbilt University, notes of music-based MOOCs that "there is no case law to determine whether there is fair use in this area, and nobody wants to be the one to provide the case law!" I hesitate to admit it in print, but I like to think my own students have benefited from my distribution of MP3s and YouTube videos (just as twenty years ago they would have benefited from my mixtapes). Yet I know from experience that if I were to force students to purchase official recordings, often I would be adding yet another expense to their already debt-ridden lives, and thus providing an additional disincentive for them to learn about music in the first place.

Ted Gioia made a similar point in a recent Facebook discussion about the release of the audiobook version of his *The History of Jazz*—when a friend asked whether musical examples had been integrated into that release, Gioia noted that "to secure rights to include musical examples in the audiobook would add substantially to the cost and [make] it prohibitively expensive." But the other option—removing recorded musical examples from a curriculum altogether—is equally problematic. Collectively listening to music—discovering it, experiencing it, discussing it—is a vital part of learning the art form. "Nobody has ever learned to play jazz from a book only," as Mark Levine puts it, in a comment that could apply to any kind of music. In the end, neither way of being legal (forcing a purchase that may not be in the student's budget, or removing musical examples from a curriculum) is likely to produce the "progress" of "useful arts" that the Copyright Clause mandates; both inhibit formative listening experiences, contributing to the very disengagement with music that the elites attribute to file sharing and the curmudgeons attribute to a decline in taste.

Of course, there is now a third way: many instructors use streaming services for musical examples. Spotify, for instance, is often touted as a library of all music—it's "the 'celestial jukebox' we dreamed of a decade and a half ago," writes Taylor Hatmaker. Why not just have students listen to playlists on that? The pedagogical issue is that Spotify only works for this purpose until you get to a song that isn't on Spotify. Such was the case, for instance, when the elementary school choir I help lead learned the Beatles' "Yellow Submarine" a few years ago (the Beatles are one of the many artists not on Spotify). Ironically, at around the same time, a group of older kids were tweeting, in response to the 2012 Grammy Awards, "Who the fuck is Paul McCartney?" I was struck by that meme, and by its juxtaposition with the experience of my own students, many of whom, at a much younger age, already knew how to answer the question—partly because of YouTube videos I had shared.

THIEVING KIDS

It wasn't a rip off, it was a love in.

—John Lennon

The deeper problem here is a disconnect over where we think music comes from. Theft has been the shibboleth. In terms of digital music, the term was originally used to decry file sharing, and it is now understood as a metaphor for much of what happens online. Indeed, it is increasingly used to describe streaming too, given that technology's growing popularity and the current controversy over Spotify royalties. As Chris Ruen recently put it, "You can't separate streaming from illegal downloading. It's a part of an ecosystem." But whether or not file sharing turns out to be a brief unhappy phase in the history of digital music, the argument against it has revealed certain deeply held assumptions about musical creativity.

"If someone in a low-income community—who has no Internet or computer access—goes to a record store and steals a CD or DVD, he is fined and/or put in jail," New York representative Edolphus Towns once wrote, in a pro-RIAA article that could stand, like the PR text we looked at earlier, as a template for the elite worldview. "If an affluent child with broadband access downloads (i.e., steals) 10 CDs from online sharing services," he continued, by way of comparison, "there are no visible repercussions and parents often praise that child for being tech savvy." In part, Towns's comments drew on what used to be called the "digital divide," or the gap between those who own a computer and have the means to get online and those who don't. Yet that was a distraction from his main point, which was a comparison between lawful purchase and theft. It's an understandable rhetorical technique, of course: framing downloading as theft makes it that much less defensible. Yet downloading—whether from a music blog, or an online storage site, or a file-sharing program, or an e-mail from a friend—has never been theft. Even in cases where the act is illegal, nothing is literally being taken, only copied. And some of the time, downloading is not even infringement. The child in Towns's example might be accessing music for a school research assignment, for instance, at least raising the possibility of fair use. That music might not even be protected. (Copyright, as we saw earlier, is now assumed by default—but Towns leaves aside the possibility that the recordings in question could have been published under a Creative Commons license.)

On the other hand, only the most benighted observer would dismiss outright the idea that sometimes downloading copyrighted material is a lot *like* conventional stealing. Towns's comparison, in other words, is not entirely unwarranted—it *doesn't* seem fair that someone could be prosecuted for illegally removing music from a brick-and-mortar store, while their cyber-counterpart escapes prosecution for illegally accessing music with digital tools. The real weakness in Towns's argument is that it ignores the question of why anyone—from any community, but perhaps most especially a low-income community, where cultural capital is often hard to come by—would be motivated to steal music in the first place, regardless of whether they did it online, in a store, or at a neighbor's house. If we grant, for a moment and with some hesitancy, that "theft" is an adequate metaphor for illegal downloading, and maybe for the pursuit of free or inexpensive music in general, then we must ask ourselves: *why* do people steal music?

The answer is complex, but it has to do with the kind of commodity music is. Unlike other products that get stolen on a regular basis— Honda Accords, for instance—music's appeal as an item of potential resale is negligible. Rare recordings, of course, can be very valuable— you would suddenly be quite wealthy if you could get your hands on a 45 of Buddy Holly's "That'll Be the Day," as performed by the Quarrymen (a skiffle group that featured the young John Lennon, Paul McCartney, and George Harrison). Even MP3s can be valuable, if they are the right MP3s—as a recent theft of unreleased tracks from Lady Gaga suggests. But more often than not, shops that specialize in used recordings pay at most half the original value of an item brought in for resale. In fact, the main reason people sell preowned physical record-ings at all is not to make money, but to make room for new physical recordings. And as digital files become more popular, the idea of there being *any* street value to "used" music becomes increasingly absurd. Once you have purchased an album from iTunes, chances are you are not ever going to sell it to anyone, even if the music eventually bores you. You are more likely to delete it.

Thus for most people the value of recorded music is in its being heard. It follows that to the extent that illegal downloading can be called "theft," it is not the sort of theft that has the goal of increas-ing the thief's material wealth. Except in cases of raw vandalism, it has the very different goal of actually experiencing the music that has been stolen. Of course, some critics have assumed *all* downloaders are vandals, problematically generalizing the self-righteous anarchists of the world as stand-ins for the curious student, say, or the musically engaged adult. But we can criticize the unfairness of music theft with-out also overlooking that there is a cultural need that it sometimes seeks to satisfy: music must be heard.

Could we survive as a culture if we ignored this need? Thomas Jeffer-son, who helped devise early American copyright law, thought not. A talented violinist with a large personal library of scores, Jefferson once referred to music as the "passion of my soul." But he had more than platitudes for the subject. His subsequent remarks are often left out when the "passion" quote is cited, but according to Douglas Wilson, Jefferson spoke from what he saw as a perspective of "extreme depri-vation," because "fortune has cast my lot in a country" in which music "is in a state of deplorable barbarism." The urgency he expressed— and this was a problem that American composers and listeners would wrestle with throughout the nineteenth century as they tried to estab-lish a national musical identity independent of European influence— suggested that he wanted more from music than the private pleasures that came from his personal library of scores or his violin. Music, he knew, was *socially* important.

Most of us have this same sense of music's social value, whether we personally understand it as an escape from the stresses of daily existence, or a means of establishing identity, or a backdrop for recreation, or a marker of private memory, or an outlet for emotion, or an intellectual exercise, or any of the other subjective listening positions suggested in chapter 4. Yet what we sometimes lose in the copyright debate is that, like Jefferson, Towns's "affluent child"—or at least a portion of the anonymous crowd she is supposed to represent—loves music too. She might not be able to articulate that love, or to delineate its role in her life. Unlike Jefferson, she might not ever learn to play the violin or to read a musical score. In some cases, the music she downloads (or streams) may seem trite to outsiders. But there is nevertheless a social benefit to her love, just as there is to yours or mine. Even in its brazen disrespect for authority, or its compromised relationship to the advertising that now sometimes makes it possible, her action remains a marker of art's irrational power. It is a mute indictment of music's commercialism, its supporting narrative of heroic individuals producing great works out of thin air, its habit of reified fetishism, and the limitations thereby placed on musical experience. It is an attempt to replace consumption with listening.

A culture won't make music if it can't love music. And that's the uncomfortable question inadvertently raised by the cliché of this imaginary child's careless theft. We know we love music enough to have created an industry around it in the first place. But in an increasingly fenced-in, branded, proprietary society, can we recognize when someone else loves music enough to steal it?

THIEVING ARTISTS

All my jazz records were stolen, pretty much.

—John Zorn

The point might be clearer if we shift the discussion from affluent children stealing music to those who identify as artists. Artists, after all, are thieves too. The record shows that they have always accused each other of aesthetic larceny, have always considered the direct and contextual collaboration of their peers as potential affronts to authorial private property. Yet their example also shows that even cruder forms of theft can sometimes be expressions of creative curiosity. The history of art suggests that the impulse to unlawfully "download" predates the first Napster user by centuries.

Whether or not there is something we could consistently call an "artistic personality," artists are generally ego-driven, and at times almost self-destructively unconcerned with social convention. Consider the following anecdote about the young J. S. Bach. It appears in an obituary published in 1754, four years after his death:

> The love of our little Johann Sebastian for music was uncommonly great even at this tender age. In a short time he had fully mastered all the pieces his brother had voluntarily given him to learn. But his brother possessed a book of clavier pieces by the most famous masters of the day—Froberger, Kerl, Pachelbel—and this, despite all his pleading and for who knows what reason, was denied him. His zeal to improve himself thereupon gave him the idea of practicing the following innocent deceit. This book was kept in a cabinet whose doors consisted only of grillwork. Now, with his little hands he could reach through the grillwork and roll the book up (for it had only a paper cover); accordingly, he would fetch the book out at night, when everyone had gone to bed and, since he was not even possessed of a light, copy it by moonlight. In six months' time he had these musical spoils in his own hands. Secretly and with extraordinary eagerness he was trying to put it to use, when his brother, to his great dismay, found out about it, and without mercy took away from him the copy he had made with such pains. We may gain a good idea of our little Sebastian's sorrow over this loss by imagining a miser whose ship, sailing for Peru, has foundered with its cargo of a hundred thousand thaler. He did not recover the book until after the death of his brother.

Or this one, from an autobiographical article of Frank Zappa's, in which the composer describes his high school listening habits:

> My real social life revolved around records and the band I played with. There wasn't much work for us then. We'd get a job maybe, every two months at a teen hop, but most of the time, I was back in my room listening to records. It was the records, not TV, which I didn't watch, that brainwashed me. I'd listen to them over and over again. The ones I couldn't buy, I'd steal, and the ones I couldn't steal I'd borrow, but I'd get them somehow. I had about six hundred records—45s—at one

time, and I swear I knew the title, group and label of every one. We all used to quiz each other.

Like a Baroque version of Towns's affluent child, Bach surreptitiously, and against the explicit wishes of his brother, steals the coveted book of scores. ("A teenager in a small town," Paul Elie calls him, "up late, alone in the dark, sitting rapt next to a piece of cabinetry with music coming out of it.") And Zappa, who always jealously guarded the copyrights on his own work, admits to stealing records as a kid, or else to getting them "somehow." That Bach and Zappa were very different kinds of musicians suggests that theft is a broader modus operandi here. Indeed, these stories are not exceptional, but point to a deeper truth: at least some of the time, creativity is about breaking laws, even if only those of routine, convention, or propriety.

It is not that we need to assume a moral equivalence between trying out a forbidden chord progression, say, and shoplifting a guitar. Some forms of theft are clearly antisocial for the sake of being antisocial, and may not correlate with creative potential at all. As adults, most artists sublimate whatever baser desires they harbor in a way that is not harmful to others—indeed, some psychologists say that art *is* that sublimation. Yet this does not take away from the fact that there is something fundamentally transgressive about creativity too. Composition and illegal downloading (or stealing scores, or stealing records) are positions on a continuum, rather than mutually exclusive categories of "creativity" and "theft."

In youth, this continuum is more fluid and more obvious—so the age similarity between Towns's "affluent child," the "little Johann Sebastian," and the teenaged Frank Zappa is no coincidence. Indeed, there is a resonance between thieving artists and thieving kids. While Tehranian is right when he says that, today, "copyright enforcement is not just a problem for teenagers downloading music and movies on the latest file-sharing networks," nevertheless, it *is* a problem for those teenagers. And why wouldn't it be? Over the last century, young people—with increasing access to discretionary cash and to new means for organizing themselves—repeatedly aligned with outcast musicians, generating a powerful market force. Post–Tin Pan Alley, popular music owed at least part of its economic success to its capacity for evoking narratives of defiance and deviance, whether those narratives had to do with actual crime, generalized social aggressiveness, or other kinds of nonconformity. This is the flip side of the comfort and redundancy attributed to the genre by Suisman and Schafer—the anodyne to social upheaval described in chapter 3. When musicians transgressed in their art, young people who longed to transgress in their lives had another reason to purchase and listen to it. It became a tool of identity establishment, a way for the listener to distinguish herself from propriety.

Such was one source of jazz's initial popularity, certainly—to take just one example. We can resist the stereotype here while pointing out that in the 1920s, the music provided a sonic context for Prohibition, the flaunting of social mores, the development of urban organized crime, and the "Lost Generation." The Ellington Orchestra epitomized these connections quite literally during its tenure at the Cotton Club, a venue both owned and frequented by gangsters. Jazz musicians eventually used the term "legit" to describe playing "not jazz music," with the implication that jazz was (admirably, desirably) *not* "legit." Indeed, much of the vernacular used by popular musicians even today strongly hints at danger and deviance. Many refer to quality performances as "killer," "bad," "badass," "sick," "dope," or "ridiculous." Gigs are "hits." The word "hit" also describes a top-selling recording. Albums or singles that become popular quickly are said to move up the charts "with a bullet." Skilled performers engage in "cutting contests" and play "axes." "Boogie woogie," "rock and roll," "swing," and other related words ("gig," "juke," "jelly roll") all have pejorative etymologies, mostly having to do with sex. Even the recently discovered earliest use of the word "jazz" in print—a 1912 *Los Angeles Times* article about the baseball team the Portland Beavers—refers to pitcher Ben Henderson's "jazz curve," so named because the ball "wobbles and you simply can't do anything with it." That definition may refer to physical deviation in the air, but it has connotations of both aesthetic and social unconventionality.

The linking of popular music with impropriety—part marketing, part expressive authenticity quest, and part lived experience—is now so common as to be almost a cliché. The juvenile delinquency of rock and roll, the aggressive demeanor of punk, the "gangsta" imagery of rap, the jailhouse motifs of country or folk music all make the connection. Nor is it limited to popular culture, as the Bach anecdote demonstrates, or as is revealed by the modern fascination with Mozart's scatological propensities, or as Christopher Marsh suggests when he writes of the early modern period in England that "the very term 'minstrel' came, in some minds, to signify debauchery and disorder." Its roots go much deeper than American culture, in fact. Christopher Small notes, for example, that in many African societies musicians' status is characterized by the "high level of tolerance for the deviant behavior that seems almost to be expected of them."

The point takes on a kind of hypocrisy in the context of the debate over digital music, however, because of how traditional elites in the industry have decried the thievery of downloading kids—as if the same record labels that issued subpoenas hadn't romanticized deviance for young listeners in the first place. Indeed, calling kids "thieves" may have been the best way to *promote* infringement, particularly when musical profusion meant that available choices would overwhelm the typical young person's entertainment budget. Philo T. Farnsworth, owner of the Illegal Art label, which has released Girl Talk's most critically acclaimed mashups, notes with pride how Illegal Art has avoided major label involvement. Simply put, Farnsworth does not *want* sample-based music to become culturally acceptable. Maintaining at least the soupçon of illegality (in this case, helpfully woven into Illegal Art's name) means "there is a subversive edge to sampling that gives it more essence, more meaning." Compromising with the "larger music industry" would cause the music to "lose that edginess." It is fair to say the same dynamic exists for any of the appropriative practices of digital culture.

Critics often miss these nuances almost completely. But for many young listeners, in both past and present, theft *is* love. And while that dynamic frustratingly glosses over certain economic realities, the rub is that theft-as-love—a key facet of decomposition—is also essential to creativity. No wonder then that many of the music business professionals who openly criticize file sharing—now that such critiques have become more common—nevertheless cannot deny having engaged in some form of the practice themselves. ("I feel that jadedness when I see the blogs where all they do is post the album art thumbnail and a link to a free Mediafire download," says Chris Swanson, of the record label Secretly Canadian. "That said, I still download from their sites.") On the other hand, given how little we actually know, sociologically, about the human face of what is usually called "piracy"—and how much we are starting to know about how fans are willing to support alternate music economies like Bandcamp.com—it may be that, for the vast number of listeners, online infringement is a fleeting practice, informed in part by temporarily unstable material resources. And given that those artists who came of age in the post-Napster era are presumably just now reaching some kind of creative maturity, it may also be that we have yet to hear the full musical impact of the abundance file sharing helped unleash.

COPYRIGHT, COPY IT

> We all have access to a pool of sounds, clusters of sounds, your personal tool kit. They're based on what you remember from a lifetime of listening . . . what it is that you loved and collected in your mind as sounds that you like and then you go for those sounds all the time. Sometimes you don't even *like* the sounds, but you're stuck with them.
>
> —Paul Simon

If theft is the shibboleth in this debate, work is its loudly celebrated foil. "No one drops from the sky a rock star," the RIAA told us, drawing a stark contrast to thieving kids. "It's hard work. Breaking through is a struggle." Robert Levine makes a similar point, accusing audiences of laziness by saying, in the very title of his book, that digital culture is populated with "parasites" out for nothing more than a "free ride." Andrew Keen too argues that "music file sharing" (and a range of other behaviors that he groups under the heading of "co-opting other people's creative work") may undermine "a society that has been built upon hard work." John Beeler, of Asthmatic Kitty Records, argues that "if piracy is a rebellion, it's the laziest rebellion anyone could ever imagine." Similar critiques are leveled at other decompositional practices of the digital era. Entertainment lawyer Anthony Berman notes of sampling that "the view on the traditional side was that this is a very lazy way of songwriting and making records"; producer Steve Albini similarly calls sampling "an extraordinarily lazy artistic choice." In 2000, *Gig* magazine featured an aesthetic defense of "turntablism" by Oakland DJ Mike Salamida, which provoked a backlash of criticism; one complainant asserted that "any kid with a hundred bucks can buy a turntable and call himself a DJ. But not just anybody can pick up an instrument and make music, real music." (The suggestion was that Salamida's art was not worth discussing, because it was easy.)

There is a technological determinism to this view, in how it focuses on the speed, minimal copying costs, and other material advantages of digital tools. In that sense, the outrage is perhaps understandable. It is true, for instance, that copying a recording is functionally much easier now than it has ever been. In the cassette or LP era, home copying required that the original media play in real time; in contrast, the first commercially available high-speed CD burners seemed almost magical—one merely dropped the recording and a blank disc in the machine, clicked the relevant buttons, and waited a few minutes. Alas, eventually even a few minutes came to seem like an eternity— especially when compared with how long it would take to download (that is, copy) an MP3, once faster Internet access became common. In the hands of the "vandals" I referred to earlier, one can see how this would be a problem.

But what about in the ears of the curious students or musically engaged adults who are also part of the ecosystem? For such listeners, perhaps *especially* at this moment in history—in this digital environment, with its capacity for fostering profusion—copying also requires effort. A recent article criticizing the frequency of skipped songs among Spotify users, for instance, overlooks how skipping is also a symptom of search, which of course is work. Whether copying takes the form of file sharing, streaming, ripping, sampling, uploading, or downloading, the tools are easy to implement and use, assuming a basic level of tech savvy. But the tools are only part of the experience. What do you copy? And when do you find the time to love it all? For the listener, as opposed to the consumer, technologically enhanced copying does not destroy work; it actually creates new kinds of work. And like "theft," it is a part of creativity, not its antithesis.

Copying, in fact, has a long history as a pedagogical tool. Bach's score thievery may seem less offensive if we consider that he was schooled in the tradition of *exempla classica,* which Christoph Wolff describes as the process of "memorizing and emulating" favorite "models by eminent masters" (like transcription, which, as we have seen, is still used as a learning technique in jazz). "By copying down exemplary works of different kinds," Wolff explains, "Handel, Bach, and their contemporaries learned the principles of harmony and counterpoint, melody and voice leading, meter and rhythm." By the time of his death, Bach had a sizable library of scores by other composers, many of which were transcriptions or works he had copied out by hand. In a review of Kirsten Beisswenger's book on the subject, George B. Stauffer notes how "the major shifts in Bach's collecting interests closely parallel the major shifts in his compositional interests." Clearly this model of copying, collecting, and creating informed Zappa too; the records referenced in the above anecdote ultimately gave rise to a running pattern of doo-wop and R&B references in his work, most blatantly on the album *Cruising with Ruben and the Jets.*

Of course, copying a score by hand, as Bach did, is not illegal under modern copyright law, and is not a practice that currently concerns the elites of the music industry. But despite the Latin name, *exempla classica* still seems vaguely illicit in the context of the push toward proprietary totalism, the weakening of fair use, and the constriction of the public domain. The point is that, to rephrase the decompositional argument, learning to make music *always* involves *exempla,* whether they are scores or MP3s or audio streams or live performances. Recall Dave Restivo's exhortation, cited in chapter 1, to "use pieces you like as templates for creating your own works." Without examples, you have no influence, and without influence, you have stasis. Creativity thus requires access. Just as you won't make music if you can't love music, you won't love music if you can't first hear it. ("People desire or decide to become musicologists, composers, or ethnomusicologists because they have heard music that excited them," as Joseph Kerman once put it.) Copying a work, then—whether reproducing a score by hand, lovingly saving a recording to your hard drive, or painstakingly constructing a Spotify playlist—can be a way of marking, and trying to understand, the music that has excited you. It allows a kind of reverse engineering, a way of getting inside someone else's musical creativity—to the extent that such a thing is possible—more directly than merely reading about it.

To put that neurologically, the human brain possesses a "perception-production link," as Daniel Levitin points out—a mechanism by which "every song you know how to sing, every word you speak" is reproduced "with your own voice based on something you originally heard." And that thing "originally heard" was itself based upon a similar perception-production link experienced by someone else in the past, and so on back through history. Paul Simon's reference to a "pool of sounds" that is "based on what you remember from a lifetime of listening" is thus a key point. All musical production is in this sense part of a great chain of influence, through which we decompose what we hear, turning it into new compositions.

And so the RIAA is right: no one drops from the sky a rock star. For that matter, no one drops from the sky a composer, or a session musician, or an audience member. Composing, performing, and listening are work, regardless of the technological contexts in which they occur. Indeed, even with the new helpmeets of digital technology derided by Levine, Keen, Beeler, Berman, Albini, and others, there may be more work involved in being a musician or listener today than there has ever been. This is especially true if we consider that modern educators encourage students to *embrace* musical profusion—in other words, to know their history. The problem is simple and inevitable: today there is much more history to know. A century ago, a conservatory student had to absorb a two-hundred-year art music tradition; her modern descendant is faced with the same task, but must also figure in an extra hundred years' worth of art music, produced at an ever-quickening pace, by a larger group of people—plus a wide range of popular genres, world music traditions disseminated by ethnomusicology and decolonization, and historical rediscoveries.

That's a lot of listening, and one can diligently work at the task without doing much more than scratching the surface. In his book on twentieth-century classical composition, Stefan Kostka insists that students obtain recordings of the more than one hundred works discussed in his text. Mark Levine similarly exhorts readers of his jazz piano book to listen broadly, selecting generously from a lengthy recommended discography. "Many of the albums listed are currently out of print," Levine advises. "To put together a good record collection, you need to haunt used record stores *regularly*." In a blog post called "Sixty Postwar Pieces to Study," composer Christian Carey lists works he thinks every composer should know—and then qualifies his selections, because "on a different day, we could come up with sixty different pieces." A young composer, Carey argues, must "be prepared for a lifetime of listening, score study, and learning," while simultaneously being "humbled by the fact" that it is only possible to "get to a fraction of all the good stuff out there!" (How Carey knows for certain that there is a bigger corpus of "good stuff" out there, if any one listener can only ever get to a "fraction" of it, is another question.)

Embracing musical profusion, as anyone with a decent record collection knows, can be expensive. Digital albums are considerably cheaper than CDs, but still typically cost around $10; at that rate a modest fifty-album-a-year habit can set you back $500 annually. Perhaps that's not much, for the gainfully employed adult with a dedicated entertainment budget. On the other hand, it's much more than the $64 a year cited by David Pakman as what the "typical music buyer" spent in 1999. More to the point, fifty albums a year are fewer than Carey, Levine, or Kostka (who don't account for any listening not related to their educational goals) imply are necessary for a typical music student—or, for that matter, for an educated listening public. And the recommendations of these educators, and the corresponding budgets, seem downright inadequate when compared with the listening habits reported by devoted fans like Jimi Yamagishi (an album a day), or David Adler (seven hundred albums a year).*

I for one think the world would be a better place with more devoted fans like Yamagishi and Adler. And I believe the growing artist and the

* See page 11.

curious, musically passionate citizen each has to find a way to hear the music she needs to hear, even though, whatever her tastes, that music is sure to exist in abundance. How else can she can love and learn from it? But if she is to do so legally, she has to find a way to pay for it too, beyond her other financial commitments, and despite a season of ongoing economic struggle. If she can't, and if she is serious about her love, is it surprising that she would choose file sharing or streaming as the next best thing? For this ideal listener, the current state of digital music is merely a predictable consequence of profusion.

ACCESS NETWORKS: THE RIGHT PLACE, THE RIGHT TIME

> I don't want to sell my music. I'd like to give it away because where I got it, you didn't have to pay for it.
> —Don Van Vliet, a.k.a. Captain Beefheart

All of this leads us to the fact that creativity relies on "access networks": environments that nurture a relationship with music simply by making it available. It is thus not enough to say, as Astra Taylor does, that "production is a precondition of access"; access is also a precondition of production. That, indeed, is the essence of the dilemma we find ourselves in: how do we fairly fund production without restricting the kind of access that makes subsequent production just as vibrant and interesting?

Access networks are the safe creative spaces—artistic sandboxes, if you will—that allow for and even encourage transgressive appropriation, not to mention a wandering of the imagination, openness to failure, and freedom from consequences. Hank Shocklee describes how his band Public Enemy initially thought nothing of packing its compositions with layer upon layer of illegally appropriated samples, because "we always felt like, you know, when you're creating, you create." From that perspective, we can appreciate how hard it is for a dedicated artist to respect the point at which an access network ends and the fenced-in "real world" begins. Indeed, in some ways it's a shame when she does. "The child we were and are," writes Stephen Nachma-novitch, "learns by exploring and experimenting, insistently snooping into every little corner that is open to us," even when those corners are "forbidden." And it can be frustrating when social proprieties kick in. "The real world created by grown-ups comes to bear down upon growing children, molding them into progressively more predictable members of society"—and progressively less engaged artists. And that may be the final indignity of proprietary totalism.

We know access networks are important because of how they factor into musician biographies. Bach, for instance, was born into the fourth generation of a family of musicians, and surrounded by profession-als as a boy. The theft anecdote we just looked at is perhaps easier to understand when we consider that he was simply accustomed to having music around. When it came to the book of famous clavier pieces, why would there be any reason to respect his brother's prohibitions? Music was there to be heard; that's where its power came from. Mozart's case was similar. Meticulously groomed for a career as a composer and per-former, he too was always surrounded by music. As a boy not yet fully versed in the ways of the outside, propertied world, why should he ever have expected that immersion to stop? Transcribing the *Miserere*—an act that from the Vatican's point of view was theft—may to young Mozart have seemed just an inevitable expression of music's natural tendency toward self-propagation. Again, music was there to be heard.

But we need not go so far back for examples of the music made possible by access networks. Saxophonist Jackie McLean grew up in the Sugar Hill district of Harlem, at the time a community full of jazz musicians. McLean worked in his stepfather's record store, describing it as an "amazing musical environment" in which he could not only hear a lot of great music, but also benefit from interactions with icons like Bud Powell, who "was always dropping by the house and playing with him, encouraging him to develop, and inviting him along on gigs." Historically, shops like this—as well as "cooperative record-sharing 'extended families' who circulated records from house to house"— encouraged informal musical education. Guitarist and writer Lenny Kaye similarly reminisces about visits from his friend Patti Smith while he was working as a clerk in an independent record shop. "When it was quiet I'd take out records from the stacks and put 'em on, and we'd play and we'd dance in the store and had a good time," Kaye recalls. "And it was almost like a place where we got to know each other." Importantly, it was also a place where they got to know music.

Access networks have been larger, of course. Some spill out of private contexts, into towns and cities. In his autobiography, Louis Armstrong talks about the music he could regularly hear in the streets of New Orleans as a boy. "That neighborhood certainly had a lot to offer," Armstrong wrote, describing the Liberty, Perdido, Franklin, and Poydras intersections where he spent much of his youth. "Of course, we kids were not allowed to go into the Funky Butt"—a local club— "but we could hear the orchestra from the sidewalk." By following the bands that accompanied local parades—a practice known as second lining—Armstrong "started to listen carefully to the different instruments, noticing the things they played and how they played them." Before long he could recognize the individual styles of some of the more prominent players—Buddy Bolden, King Oliver, Bunk Johnson. Later he would use those experiences—his personal "pool of sounds"—to develop his own style.

Later still, Armstrong would *become* an influence, moving in similarly informal communities when he wasn't performing in expensive halls or on film. Steve Isoardi describes the fertility of Los Angeles' Central Avenue, where even a child could learn about music just by hanging out. "Not only were most members of the bands—such as Duke's, Basie's, and Lunceford's—accessible," Isoardi writes, "but many would also take the time to talk with these kids, who were hanging around stage entrances and the Dunbar hotel waiting for their heroes." One regular was Armstrong himself—by that time a bona fide star—who was apparently so approachable that he "could be hailed as he crossed the intersection at 17th and Central on his way to the musicians union." The point is that Armstrong and his peers, as Isoardi notes, were a "visible, everyday presence."

This is a precise inversion of the megaconcert dynamic described in chapter 5, and an upending of the dream of proprietary totalism.

Those things emphasize the physical and economic distance between artist and fan. At the megaconcert, for instance, even listeners who get close—who sit in the front row, or who have a backstage pass—are only able to do so because they possess the right material resources or social connections. But the rope lines, limousines, bodyguards, and other barricades that can today inhibit access to music were less conspicuous in the historical Central Avenue, or New Orleans, or indie record shop. In those contexts, one did not need a front-row ticket or a backstage pass to approach even a figure as revered as Armstrong. Learning about his music did not require the considerable financial resources necessary to be enrolled in a university, or to possess a record collection, or to own audiophile equipment. These things were not the price of entry into the world of music. With informal access networks, compelling new trajectories of creativity freely took root, unnoticed though they may have been at the time.

Today, these older forms of access are increasingly rare. "What people don't realize," says social media scholar danah boyd, in seeking to understand the online activity of those who are growing up digital, "is that over the last thirty years, we have made it much harder for young people to get together in face-to-face settings." In music, the impact of this shift has been significant. There are fewer "mom-and-pop" record stores like those McLean, Kaye, and Smith benefited from—thanks in part to downloading, but also thanks to the consolidation of major record labels in the 1990s, and the price wars instigated by big box chains. And thanks in turn to gentrification and the privatization of public space, there are fewer "open" city neighborhoods, where kids can feel comfortable approaching well-known musicians—who today are mostly not interested in being found in such spaces anyway. There seems to be less publicly performed music in general, in parades or other types of community gatherings—and where it occurs, it tends to be remarkable precisely because it is exceptional. (Most of the public music we do hear is recorded, and is found in commercial contexts.) No wonder, then, that the sorts of relationships and interactions that make for a healthy musical culture now seem to occur mostly online. Even with their faults, music blogs, Spotify, YouTube, Facebook—and whatever versions of these technologies may be in store for us in the decades ahead—allow for new kinds of networking around music. Like their antecedents, they remind us that love depends on interaction with the thing loved.

The wrong response to the digital dilemma would be to push back against decomposition, and to inhibit online access networks with proprietary totalism, shoring up old ways of thinking about art. Of course that also means thinking carefully about how those access networks can be made sustainable for both audiences and artists; how artists can continue to engage in the "business of art." Some critics are already doing important work along these lines. Jaron Lanier, for instance, has pointed out the ways that the system as currently configured is depleting the cultural middle classes. Yet I'm skeptical of his "solution," that users be compensated for digital interactions through the issuance of nanopayments—as if the world is not commodified enough already. Astra Taylor offers a number of more persuasive, progressive ideas: from the ethos of sustainability itself; to a revivified national arts policy that builds on the history of the National Endowment for the Arts, or public broadcasting, or even the Works Progress Administration; to regulating service providers and popular Internet platforms as public utilities; to increased subsidies and taxes to be paid by advertisers and technology companies; to inchoate microeconomies built around practices like crowdfunding or sites like Bandcamp.com (Taylor doesn't mention this last example by name, but it certainly qualifies). It goes without saying that in the United States at least, all of these ideas will require significant consciousness-raising.*

Keeping a watchful eye on Congress's "comprehensive review" of copyright law—a phrase that experience indicates could ultimately mean anything—we need to look for a way beyond both the old system of the major labels and the new system accruing around unprecedentedly large corporations like Apple, Amazon, or Google. We need to be sure we have learned the right lessons from past legislation like the

---

*For my review of Taylor's (recommended) book, *The People's Platform: Taking Back Power and Culture in the Digital Age*, please see my own "These Are Not the Droids We Were Looking For," http://uglyrug.blogspot.com/2014/06/these-are-not-droids-we-were-looking-for.html.

CTEA and the DMCA—to remind ourselves that creativity stands to suffer from overprotection at least as much as it ever has at the hands of infringers. We need to find a way to fight back against the din of advertising and consumerism that surrounds us whenever we go online. But most of all, we need to work toward a concept of music that relies less on hero-worship and the accumulation of musical objects, and more on a vibrant, dispersed experience of connection making and participation. In other words, we need to stay vigilant about the value of listening over consumption. Economic justice, I believe, will flow naturally from such a shift.

AFTERWORD
The Benefits of Aesthetic Confusion

Online activists present the choice about our online future as one between control and creativity, but it's really about commerce or chaos.
— Robert Levine

The most precious thing in life is its uncertainty.
— Yoshida Kenkō

There's a passage in Joseph Conrad's novel *Lord Jim* in which the character Stein expresses a philosophy that has intrigued readers ever since the book's publication. "A man who is born," Stein says, "falls into a dream like a man who falls into the sea. If he tries to climb out into the air as inexperienced people endeavor to do, he drowns." But there is a better way, Stein suggests. That is to "submit yourself" to the "destructive element," using "the exertions of your hands and feet in the water" to "make the deep, deep sea keep you up."

I have returned to this passage many times since I first read it in an undergraduate survey course back in the early 1990s, always understanding it as a philosophy that counterintuitively embraced life's ambiguity—its "destructive element," which could be both terrifying and beautiful. But Stein's metaphor is also a fitting description of the decompositional complexity of musical experience. One must be willing to be immersed in music without grasping for the easy way out of the paradoxes it presents. That comparison is not as untoward as it might first seem: like the roiling sea (or Heraclitus's river) music resists our attempts to make it stand still—to analyze, rationalize, catalog, record, or write it. In truth, it cannot be reified, no matter how emphatically we assume its reification. To quibble with Levine's point, quoted in the epigraph above, creativity *is* chaos. If you try to escape it, into the safety of clarity, you drown. Or at least you discover, as historian Edward Tenner once put it, that "clarity is overrated."

Whatever clarity's benefit in the hard sciences, its overrating in music is, I think, the root of our current dilemma. It is what drives music's death cult. It is why we make the mistake of asserting that genius is an objective fact of nature. It is why we overlook the artistic role of technology—whether in a player piano or a phonograph or a drum machine or a saxophone mouthpiece—and the creativity of so many other contexts. It is why we put undue faith in the pat idea of a composer's original score—as if any writing is ever transparent or fixed. It is why we override our misgivings about saying what "listening" and "music" even are. And it is why the music elite push for new laws to expand a business model that has, in comparison with the whole history of music, been around for but an inkling, during which it has sometimes served us well—but sometimes not well at all.

I won't end by advocating complexity for complexity's sake, but rather complexity for honesty's sake. What I am most interested in is the generosity, empathy, and compassion of listeners. Listening, I can hear those qualities in a remarkable letter Ferruccio Busoni wrote to his wife in 1907. Through twenty years of study, Busoni noted, Mozart's score for *The Marriage of Figaro* had "remained unchanged in my estimation, like a lighthouse in surging seas." Even so, he admitted, "when I looked at it again, a week ago, I discovered human weaknesses in it for the first time; and my soul flew for joy when I realized that I am not so far behind it as I thought, in spite of this discovery being a real loss, and pointing to the lack of durability in all human activities." The idea that one could respond with bittersweet euphoria to the discovery of weakness in an idolized composer, to realize that the lighthouse wasn't really there, and that you were both still at sea, is I think an instance of what Thelonious Monk called "ugly beauty"—an exquisite idea of beauty, which does not pull any one "genius" down, but lifts everyone up. It is the new growth on the other side of the death cult—decomposition leading into new composition. And it demonstrates the possibility of demythologizing music without demeaning it.

As a culture, we are at a crossroads, but the crisis we face is not limited to the question of whether file sharing is killing music, or whether a single listener will ever have time to hear every song she has the potential to enjoy, or whether composers have become lazy in a postmodern cut-and-paste free-for-all. Those are all interesting questions, but more important is whether we can learn—or perhaps relearn—to hear music, make music, and think about music in a way that shows we are truly comfortable with complexity. Can we understand Ellington properly when he says music is "beyond category"? It is hip to quote that phrase, but how many of us are truly willing to set aside the complacency of our enduring aesthetic presumptions?

ACKNOWLEDGMENTS

No book is ever written without the assistance of collaborators—much less a book like this one, which takes collaboration as a fundamental theme. That's not to say there weren't times I *felt* alone writing it—not just physically, but existentially. Yet we are all products of our interactions. If *Decomposition* is worth reading, that has to do with the help of an awful lot of people. (At the same time, any mistakes or oversights it contains are mine alone.)

My colleagues at the University of Southern California were of course crucial to my thinking over the last two decades. Conversations at the Institute for Multimedia Literacy—with Chris Gilman, Sharon Sekhon, Veronica Paredes, Steve Anderson, Bob Stein, Frank Kearl, and many others—were very helpful in getting a handle on digital culture. Seminars with Alice Gambrell, Carol Muske-Dukes, Jim Kincaid, and Ron Gottesman were great opportunities to get feedback on (very) early versions of some of these chapters and ideas—and I thank fellow participants in some of those seminars, including Christian Hite, Rosalee Shim Hite, Jinny Huh, Annemarie Perez, Michael Blackie, Jennifer Morrow, and Sarah Shute. Others, with whom I was never lucky enough to share classes, nevertheless were generous in sharing feedback, ideas, and friendship: Michael Frisoli, John Bruns, Joan Jastrebski, Litz Brown, and Kuba Zielinski. And I am still grateful to some of the people who influenced me most as an undergraduate, especially Ann Saltzman, Jaqueline Berke, Shannon Olin, and Wendy Kolmar. Also, I would be remiss if I neglected to mention the wonderful librarians at the Brand Library in Glendale, California; USC's Music Library; and the Multnomah County Library system.

Of course, I have also been influenced by the musicians I have known, starting from my first bands back in high school, on to the various song-oriented groups I led in my early twenties, and through my descent into jazz. I learned more from these experiences—and from rehearsals, gigs, and tour van dialogues with Jill Knapp, Evan Francis, Ian Carroll, Mike Richardson, Kris Tiner, Dan Schnelle, Damon Zick, Cory Wright, Phil Rodriguez, Damian Erskine, Joe Tepperman, Jason Polland, Josh Sinton, Tany Ling, Josh Rutner, Marcus Milius, Sam Bevan, Gabriel Sundy, Mary-Sue Tobin, Dan Rosenboom, Andre Canniere, and many others—than anything I ever read in a book about music. And then there were the musicians who never played in any of my groups, but whose intelligence and experience was generously shared—either in person, or in the "blogosphere," or in other forms of social media: David Ocker, Dan Krimm, Jim Scully, Dan Clucas, Jim Romeo, Steve Lawson, Jason Parker, Phillip Greenlief, Darcy James Argue, Steve Morgan, Ethan Iverson, Lewis Porter, Jeff Albert, Susan Wenger, Ted Gioia, Jason Crane, Dennis Bathory-Kitsz, and others whose names I do not know, because they went by online avatars like "the improvising guitarist" and "godoggo."

As a grad student, I wrote the initial version of *Decomposition* as a dissertation thesis, and for that experience I am particularly grateful to the people who were on my committee: Peggy Kamuf, Ron Gottesmann, Peter Manning, Jim Kincaid, and especially my chair, Joseph A. Dane. It is quite possible that without JAD in particular there never would have been a dissertation, let alone a book. By the time I presented the player piano paper that would become the basis for *Decomposition*'s chapter 2, I was almost ready to quit grad school. Instead, JAD heard it, helped get it published as an article, and gave me the courage to follow through on what I had started. He has since become a consistent advocate, an engaging and critical reader, and a valued friend.

Various people gave the gift of their time and readership as *Decomposition* traveled the long road to becoming the book it is now. I am forever in their debt, both for wading through my ideas in their inchoate form and for speaking honestly about the manuscript's shortcomings. Many thanks to Frank Mabee, Sean Utt, Gary Lawrence Murphy, Jeff Kaiser, Alex Tarr, and especially Alex Rodriguez and Mike Reynolds (Alex went so far as to read some sections *twice*, and Mike went so far as to print out and mark up the chapters I asked him to read). Thanks also to Henry Andrew Caporoso, for reading the dissertation version of *Decomposition* many years ago, and for sharing his thoughts as a smart "lay reader."

I have special gratitude for one of my oldest and closest friends, Paul Badalamenti, who has the distinction (indicative of unbelievable stamina) of having read and commented on every single chapter of the book as I revised it, in the year before it was finally completed. I have known Paul for about thirty years now, and throughout that time he has been a consistent touchstone for playing or thinking about music, discussing philosophy, and trying to make sense of what Prince called "this thing called life." He possesses one of the sharpest minds I know, and I am honored that he lent it to the sometimes trying and always time-consuming process of fashioning *Decomposition* into the work it is now.

I still cannot believe my good fortune in connecting with the person who formally introduced me to the world of publishing: Barbara Clark, my amazing and dedicated agent. Barbara took the risk of contacting me about *Decomposition,* back when I was recklessly posting it, in dissertation form, on my blog. Anyone who has read that initial version and compared it with the book as it exists today will understand what a leap of faith that must have involved. Barbara has also been very supportive and patient at every step of the revision process, even after I started sending her chapters that I thought were finished—until I later decided they were not. I will always be deeply grateful.

At Pantheon, a whole range of people have been similarly supportive and helpful. Thanks to my editor, the brilliant Erroll McDonald, for being willing to take a chance on an unknown author, and for pushing me to make the book both more engaging and more accessible. Caroline Bleeke was an always thorough and conscientious editorial assistant. Josefine Kals was an extremely dedicated publicist.

Finally, I thank my family. Ruth Ann Durkin, Ron and Elaine Durkin, and my brother Glenn and his family all consistently expressed faith in the book—even if they had no proof that it would ever be finished. Of course, my biggest thanks go to the love of my life—my wife, Daphne—and our darling and brilliant daughter, Thandie. For three years these remarkable, beautiful ladies calmly endured my writerly moods. I have tried to be the best father and husband I could in this time. To the extent that I have failed, they are to be thanked the most—for their saintly patience, and for continuing to provide the energizing love that eventually helped me muddle through.

NOTES

INTRODUCTION

3 "There are so many approaches": Jourdain, *Music, the Brain, and Ecstasy,* 239.

3 "The eighteenth century musician": Dart, *The Interpretation of Music,* 164.

4 "it's quite conceivable that we will see the end of a cultural economy": Andrew Keen quoted in Dworsky and Köhler, *PressPausePlay.*

4 "For more than half a century": Branca, "The Score: The End of Music."

5 "Absolutely, read the poetry of John Donne": Cornel West quoted in Astra Taylor's documentary *Examined Life* (Zeitgeist Films, 2008).

7 "interesting property": Iverson, "All Our Reasons?"

7 In certain Pacific Northwest Native American tribes: Jourdain, *Music, the Brain, and Ecstasy,* 59. A Smithsonian recording of the Nootka, a tribe from British Columbia, indicates that "the fieldwork experience gathering songs in this region was very challenging due to the fact that each individual song was traditionally personally owned, and permission from the owner was needed in order to sing it." (The musicologist doing the research was Dr. Ida Halpern.) *Nootka Indian Music of the Pacific North West Coast* (Folkways Records, 1974), http://www.folkways.si.edu/nootka-indian-music-of-the-pacific-north -west-coast/american-indian/album/smithsonian.

7 And in the tradition of Somali sung poetry: Finnegan, *Oral Poetry,* 74.

8 "the reduction in capitalist society": Rosen, "Theodor Adorno: Criticism as Cultural Nostalgia," in *Freedom and the Arts,* 249.

8 "one of the things taken away": Abbate, "Music—Drastic or Gnostic?," 506.

8 Lydia Goehr and Richard Taruskin: See, for instance, Goehr's *The Imaginary Museum of Musical Works* or Taruskin's *The Danger of Music and Other Anti-Utopian Essays.*

8 "music primarily in terms of entities": Small, *Music of the Common Tongue,* 45.

8 "seeing music as an open 'process' and not a closed 'object'": Cavicchi, "From the Bottom Up," 6.

8 as trumpeter and composer Kris Tiner has pointed out: Comment on Durkin blog post, "The world we have lost."

9 "pleasure gardens": Small, *Music of the Common Tongue,* 250.

9 Evan Eisenberg: See *The Recording Angel,* 11–33.

10 "If there was anything the human race had a sufficiency of": Joseph Mitchell, quoted by Fleagle, "His Own Sweet Time.

10   "Papa, how do you ever think of so many tunes?": Nachmanovitch, *Free Play*, 4.

10   Several decades ago: Storr, *Music and the Mind*, 50.

10   "for every sensible line": Borges, *The Total Library*, 216.

11   "I have EXACTLY one hour a day": Yamagishi, *MusicThoughts*.

11   "overchoice": See Toffler, *Future Shock*, chapter 12.

11   "I listen to some 700 CDs a year": Adler, "Of big bands, critics' priorities, etc." Ted Gioia recently surpassed this figure when he wrote that "in 2013 I listened to around 900 new releases (the exact number was 886)." Gioia, "The 100 Best Albums of 2013."

13   "are myriad": Certeau, *The Practice of Everyday Life*, 97.

14   "some of his comments": Ratliff, *Coltrane*, 76.

14   "Some people have said": Ibid.

15   "For reasons that I think are relatively obvious": Argue, "Irony, Man."

15   "are an embarrassment": Cavicchi, "From the Bottom Up," 4.

15   "I have spent a lot of time": Ben Ratliff, "The Art of Writing About Listening," *New York Times*, May 30, 2013.

15   "the myth of musical autonomy": Taruskin, *The Danger of Music*, 3–4.

15   "the discipline's institutional commitment": Cavicchi, "From the Bottom Up," 4.

16   "There's a song as it exists in my mind": Conor Oberst quoted in Kot, *Ripped*, 100.

16   "If one says 'Red' ": Albers, *The Interaction of Color*, 3.

16   "transduction": Colin Symes (*Setting the Record Straight*) and Jonathan Sterne (*The Audible Past*) have both previously looked at the role of transduction in music, though not precisely in the same way.

17   "quite independent of the phenomenal world": Eisenberg, *The Recording Angel*, 242.

17   "wiggling air molecules": Zappa, *The Real Frank Zappa Book*, 161.

17   "is basically a specialized form of touch": Glennie, "Hearing Essay."

17   "audio-tactile": See, for instance, McLuhan's *The Gutenberg Galaxy* (1962).

17   "played outside a situation": Lucy Green quoted in Frith, *Performing Rites*, 250.

17   "One can even assume": Stockfelt, "Adequate Modes of Listening," 133.

18   "bears no relationship to how ordinary people hear": Nicholas Cook quoted in Frith, *Performing Rites*, 63.

18   "two quite different pieces": Kathryn Bailey quoted in ibid., 63.

18   "infrathin": Marcus Boon's excellent discussion of this concept (including the quote "composed of unique physical matter, occupies a unique point in the space-time continuum, and has a unique passage through that continuum") can be found in his *In Praise of Copying*, 193–94.

19   "distinguishes the same from the same": Russell, "Marcel Duchamp's Readymades," 3.

I. A THOUSAND WROUGHT LIKE ONE

23   "It takes a thousand men": Mark Twain quoted in Vaidhyanathan, *Copyrights and Copywrongs*, 65.

23 "If we would stop and attribute too much to genius": Ives, "Essays Before a Sonata," 113.

23 "preoccupation, even obsession": Youngren, "Duke Ellington, by James Lincoln Collier," 86.

23 "rotting mint julep": Baraka, "Jazz Criticism and Its Effect on the Music," 81.

23 "insipid, sloppy and irresponsible": Crouch, "Stanley Crouch on *Such Sweet Thunder, Suite Thursday,* and *Anatomy of a Murder,*" 442.

24 Instead, he implied: Collier, *Duke Ellington,* 303.

25 "As an artist, as a musician": Einstein, *Mozart,* 3.

25 "the most stupendous miracle" and "is a colossus": Richard Wagner and Charles Gounod quoted in *Gramophone,* "Is Bach Best?"

25 "his emotions at their greatest level": H. L. Mencken quoted in Powell, "Ludwig van Beethoven's Joyous Affirmation of Human Freedom."

25 "the hero of Western music": Burnham, *Beethoven Hero,* xvi.

26 "the greatest, the most exalted of composers": Hans von Bülow quoted in Alan Walker, *Hans von Bülow,* 289.

26 "in tune with the infinite": Johannes Brahms quoted in Jourdain, *Music, the Brain, and Ecstasy,* 170.

26 "the greatest musical interpreter who ever lived": Lawrence Gilman quoted in Horowitz, *Classical Music in America,* 279.

26 "Louis Armstrong is quite simply": Burns, "Ken Burns on the Making of *Jazz.*"

26 "the celestial realm": Small, "The Perception of Music."

26 "I thought I saw all of heaven before me"; "was dictated to me by God": George Frideric Handel and Giacomo Puccini quoted in Jourdain, *Music, the Brain, and Ecstasy,* 170.

26 "To realize that we are one with the Creator": Johannes Brahms quoted in Nyquist, *Visions of Reality,* 260.

27 "a benevolent god": Claude Debussy quoted in Day, *A Century of Recorded Music,* 66.

27 "Alas! how could I declare the weakness": Beethoven, *Beethoven's Letters,* 38.

27 "partially concealing your meaning": Orwell, "Politics and the English Language," 28.

28 "high-intensity, often frantic bravura manner": Gooley, *The Virtuoso Liszt,* 206.

29 "The mass cultural notion of stardom": Frith, *Performing Rites,* 31.

29 "In one sonnet": Grigely, *Textualterity,* 34.

29 "canonical Keats"; "embarrassing Keats": Ibid.

29 "played such fantastic tricks": Ibid.

30 "the 'ban Comic Sans' movement": Lacher, "I'm Comic Sans, Asshole."

30 "We are traditionally inclined": Grigely, *Textualterity,* 140.

31 "The people scurry by": Weingarten, "Pearls Before Breakfast."

31 "right of paternity": See, for instance, Lillick, *International Copyright,* 283.

32 "When I get interviewed": Babbitt quoted in Duckworth, *Talking Music,* 80.

34 "Whether we like it or not": Zorn, *Spillane,* liner notes.

34 resisted the word "jazz": Ellington, *Music Is My Mistress,* 309.

34 Jørgen Mathiasen: See Teachout, *Duke,* 348.

35 "countless"; "consistently high quality": Yanow, "Duke Ellington," 1213.

35 Harvey Cohen: See Cohen, *Duke Ellington's America.*
35 "During the past year or more": Tucker, ed., *The Duke Ellington Reader,* 54.
35 "one of the most extraordinary moments": George Avakian, in ibid., 290.
35 "written against the glass partitions": Richard O. Boyer, in ibid., 216.
36 "the view from the mountaintop": Stanley Crouch, in ibid., 442.
36 "Duke Ellington holds a privileged position"; "single-handed": André Hodeir, in ibid., 297–98.
36 "all the musicians in jazz": Miles Davis, in ibid., 364.
36 "always considered his orchestra to be his main instrument": Yanow, "Duke Ellington," 1213.
36 "In order to do what his creative appetite": Stanley Crouch, in Tucker, ed., *The Duke Ellington Reader,* 443.
36 "Unlike the European concerto": André Hodeir, in ibid., 285.
37 "snippet of melody": Teachout, *Duke,* 211.
37 "a bright luster": Ibid., 92.
37 "Hodges's sliding, passionate way with ballads": Hasse, *Beyond Category,* 298.
38 "none of Ellington's recordings can be considered": John Edward Hasse, *Beyond Category,* 322.
38 that were then incorporated by Ellington: It should be pointed out that Ellington too was a victim of this sort of appropriation, at the hand of Irving Mills, the band's manager. See Cohen, *Duke Ellington's America.*
38 "the central melodic ideas": Collier, *Duke Ellington,* 302–3.
38 "I don't consider you a composer": Lawrence Brown quoted in ibid., 130.
39 "Ellington and his men"; "a rougher sound": Gunther Schuller quoted in Rattenbury, *Duke Ellington,* 16.
39 Schuller contends: Ibid., 16–18.
39 "Camp Meeting Blues": See Teachout, *Duke,* 67.
39 "no more than Beethoven or Stravinsky": Ibid., 112.
39 In retelling that story: For a particularly deft handling of Teachout's strengths and weaknesses, and a response to the controversies attending his book, see Iverson, "Interview with Terry Teachout" and "Reverential Gesture."
39 "is a central part of": Payton, "Duking It Out with Teachout and Other Racist Assailants."
40 gratingly superior tone: "It was well within [Ellington's] power to familiarize himself with the structural techniques of the great classical composers, to learn how to write for string sections instead of hiring orchestrators, even to figure out how to write songs that drove the plot of a musical comedy rather than sounding as though they'd been written without prior knowledge of the script," Teachout argues at the beginning of *Duke* (pp. 14–15), in an attempt to illuminate Ellington's extended works. But then comes the sucker punch: "But accomplishing any of these goals would have taken more time than he cared to spare . . . so he chose to keep on being Duke Ellington." Note how Teachout packs three problematic assumptions into one claim: the assumption that the works in question were no good, the assumption that Ellington lacked discipline, and, strangest of all, the assumption that Ellington could have been anyone other than Ellington.
40 "attitude of hortatory, contentious reverence": Horowitz, "Mozart as Midcult," 16.

40 "In considering Ellington's rich and productive life": Tucker, *The Blanton-Webster Band*, liner notes, 1.

40 "*Cotton Tail* emerges as a simple, straightforward romp": Ibid., 8.

41 "is solely credited to Ellington": Teachout, *Duke*, 215.

41 "to produce one of the greatest periods": Cohen, *Duke Ellington's America*, 176.

42 sequences of notes not found: Cutler, "Plunderphonia," 142.

43 "Donna Lee": Berliner, *Thinking in Jazz*, 78. See also http://www.jazzstandards .com/compositions-1/donnalee.htm.

43 "Ko Ko": Vitale, "The Story of Charlie Parker's Ko Ko."

43 "an eight bar interlude": Kelley, *Thelonious Monk*, 101, 111. See also Berliner, *Thinking in Jazz*, 88.

44 "use pieces you like": Dave Restivo quoted in Hum, "Jazz composers' roundtable."

44 *Moonlight Sonata*: See Miles, *Beatles in Their Own Words*, 102.

45 A remarkable composer in his own right: Walter van de Leur is an essential resource on this point, which has too long been overlooked in jazz history. See his *Something to Live For: The Music of Billy Strayhorn* (New York: Oxford University Press, 2002).

45 he met Ellington in 1938: David Hajdu's *Lush Life: A Biography of Billy Strayhorn* (New York: Farrar, Straus & Giroux, 1996) is still the best biography of Strayhorn.

45 "the exact nature of their collaboration is difficult to elucidate": See also my own blog post "A meandering post on collaboration."

45 "my right arm, my left arm": Ellington, *Music Is My Mistress*, 156.

46 "So many people suggest a question": Tucker, ed., *Duke Ellington Reader*, 502–3.

47 "to be a facile melodist": Teachout, *Duke*, 112.

47 "closed feedback loop": Gene Santoro quoted in Davis, *Outcats*, 21.

47 "At one point, I went down to the Jersey shore": Emily Remler quoted in Berliner, *Thinking in Jazz*, 115.

48 It took him three years of hermetic study: Sonny Rollins, "Bio," http://www .sonnyrollins.com/biography.

48 "It took me twenty years": Miles Davis quoted in Ellington, *Music Is My Mistress*, 244.

49 "he marched up and down the street": Art Pepper quoted in Dawson, "Deacon's Hop," 83.

50 "created some sort of resonance": Bob Willoughby quoted in Myers, "Photo-Story4: Big Jay McNeely."

51 "a notion of communication as process": Iyer, "Exploding the Narrative in Jazz Improvisation," 394.

51 "you have to watch people close when you do this": Big Jay McNeely quoted in Myers, "Interview: Big Jay McNeely (Part 2)."

51 "dance engagements": Hasse, *Beyond Category*, 159.

52 "provoked pandemonium": Stanley Dance, *Ellington at Newport*, liner notes, 4–5.

52 "A moment later somebody else": George Avakian quoted in Teachout, 290.

52 "vernacular dance": See Stearns, *Jazz Dance*.

52 early jazz in general: For more on this history, see Hill, *Tap Dancing America*.

52   "and the rest of the musicians listened to the drummer": Charles "Honi" Coles quoted in Hill, *Tap Dancing America*, 217. Paul F. Berliner (in *Thinking in Jazz*, 788) has written too that "the association of rhythm and dance expresses itself most dramatically in the context of African-American tap dancing, which made strong impressions on learners from Bud Freeman . . . to Miles Davis."

53   "The relationship between music and dance": Theberge, *Any Sound You Can Imagine*, 171.

53   "one of the principal claims to supremacy": McClary, *Feminine Endings*, 57.

53   "Many, if not all, of music's essential processes": Blacking, *How Musical Is Man?*, x–xi.

54   codified and presented as a contract: See, for instance, pianofortephilia .blogspot.com/2013/02/a-short-guide-to-concert-etiquette.html.

54   "ascent of inwardness": Peter Gay quoted in Cavicchi, *Listening and Longing*, 148.

55   "My case illustrates how success is always rationalized": Lewis, "Don't Eat Fortune's Cookie."

56   "explore 'music's social meaning' with no reference to the music": Rosen, "Did Beethoven Have All the Luck?," 9.

56   Self-appointed critics from the lay audience: Amazon.com, Customer Reviews: *Beethoven and the Construction of Genius: Musical Politics in Vienna, 1792–1803*, http://www.amazon.com/Beethoven-Construction-Genius-Politics -1792-1803/product-reviews/0520211588/ref=cm_cr_dp_see_all_btm?ie=UT F8&showViewpoints=1&sortBy=bySubmissionDateDescending.

57   "If one were to come to believe": Kivy, *The Possessor and the Possessed*, 250.

57   "Beethoven's talent": "Beethoven's Genius: An Exchange," *New York Review of Books*, April 10, 1997.

58   "Not all Viennese-based composers": DeNora, *Beethoven and the Construction of Genius*, 118.

58   "a passage in the finale of the third trio": Ibid.

58   Beethoven also responded to advice: Knight, *Beethoven and the Age of Revolution*, 90.

58   "separate gospels": Comini, *The Changing Image of Beethoven*, 121.

58   "Opera was always composed for a special occasion": Einstein, *Mozart*, 109.

59   "musical architecture": Palmer, *Beethoven—Eleven Bagatelles, Op. 119 for the Piano*, 2.

59   "Beethoven reworked existing music in more than a third of his compositions": Olufunmilayo Arewa quoted in Tucker, "Musical Borrowings from Bach to Hip Hop."

59   "it would be hard to think of a composer": Mencken, *A Mencken Chrestomathy*, 525.

59   "One of the most intriguing moments": Yoshihara, *Musicians from a Different Shore*, 11–12.

59   "The Romantics heard": Guerrieri, *The First Four Notes*, 89.

60   "apparent temporal priority of discovery": Michael Mulkay quoted in DeNora, *Beethoven and the Construction of Genius*, 5.

60   "discoveries become virtually inevitable": Merton, *The Sociology of Science*, 371.

60   "resemblance": Guerrieri, *The First Four Notes*, 41.

61 "constantly renewed through the reflexive interplay": DeNora, *Beethoven and the Construction of Genius*, 7.

62 "in Vienna it was virtually impossible for a local musician": Ibid., 55.

62 "exceptionally well-placed": Ibid., 61.

62 Prince Karl Lichnowsky, his wife, Princess Christiane, and especially Baron Gottfried van Swieten: Van Swieten, in fact, was important to the careers of all three composers of the First Viennese School (Beethoven, Haydn, and Mozart), in part because of his generosity in sharing scores by the best-known composers of previous generations, particularly Bach and Handel. As an indication of the breadth of Van Swieten's influence, Albert Einstein claims that without him "Haydn would never have written *The Creation* or *The Seasons*"—presumably referring to the fact that Van Swieten served as a librettist-translator of those works (Einstein, *Mozart*, 148.) As for *The Creation* itself, Van Swieten acted as a musical consultant of sorts. On the Lichnowskys, see DeNora, *Beethoven and the Construction of Genius*, 115–18. On Van Swieten, see ibid., 20–27.

62 "being in exactly the right place": Guerrieri, *First Four Notes*, 89.

62 DeNora develops the point: DeNora, *Beethoven and the Construction of Genius*, chapter 4 ("Beethoven's Social Resources").

63 "the exposure to visitors and teachers": Ibid., 66.

63 "positioned from the start"; "to get practical experience"; "Unlike Dussek": Ibid.

64 Consider, for instance, the famous: As Matthew Guerrieri has pointed out, Beethoven himself may have been somewhat ambivalent about the "Haydn's hands" trope. Although he had briefly been a student of Haydn, Beethoven, according to Ferdinand Ries, resisted being known as a "Pupil of Haydn," because "he never had learned anything from him." Guerrieri, *The First Four Notes*, 96.

64 "You are going to Vienna": Ibid., 84.

64 "Haydn's hands": Ibid., chapter 5 ("'From Haydn's Hands': Narrative Constructions of Beethoven's Talent and Future Success").

64 Merton is again useful: Merton: "The Matthew Effect in Science," *Science*, 1968.

65 "to exaggerate his relationship": Guerrieri, *The First Four Notes*, 49

2. METAL MACHINE MUSIC

66 "Ever since I'd been writing music": Conlon Nancarrow quoted in Carlsen, *The Player-Piano Music of Conlon Nancarrow*, 2.

66 "appear to be in different tempos": James Tenney, *Conlon Nancarrow: Studies for Player Piano*, liner notes, 3–4.

66 "extreme musical isolation": Carlsen, *The Player-Piano Music of Conlon Nancarrow*, 2.

66 while preparing for a 1941 performance: Ibid., 3.

67 Bach was capable: Jourdain, *Music, the Brain, and Ecstasy*, 188.

67 "once lobbed a whole kettledrum"; Mahler was regularly challenged: Ibid., 192.

67 "a martinet": Anita O'Day quoted in Chusid, *The Music of Raymond Scott / Reckless Nights and Turkish Twilights*, liner notes, 11.

67 "actually reduced a promising young saxophonist": Berliner, *Thinking in Jazz*, 271.

67 punched trombonist Jimmy Knepper in the mouth: As related in Don McGlynn's documentary *Charles Mingus: Triumph of the Underdog* (1998).

67 Igor Stravinsky, Paul Hindemith, Nicolai Lopatnikoff: See, for instance, the Musikproduktion Dabringhaus und Grimm CD compilation *Player Piano 4: Piano Music Without Limits: Original Compositions of the 1920s*, released in 2007 (MGD 645-1404-2).

67 "All percussive": George Antheil quoted in Oja, *Making Music Modern*, 80–81.

67 "Anything you can dream up can be typed or played": Zappa, *The Real Frank Zappa Book*, 172–73.

68 With poetic symmetry: See Artis Wodehouse's description of converting piano rolls to MIDI files in the brief introduction to her *Jelly Roll Morton: The Piano Rolls* (Milwaukee: Hal Leonard, 1999).

68 the first "digital" keyboard: See John H. Lienhard ("My scratchy records were analog devices. Player pianos use pure on-off digital logic to store sound"). Via the *Engines of Our Ingenuity* website, episode 692, http://www.uh.edu /engines/epi692.htm.

68 the Great Depression virtually destroyed: See Suisman, "Nancarrow in Context."

69 "not be played by any living performer": Henry Cowell quoted in Carlsen, *The Player-Piano Music of Conlon Nancarrow*, 3.

69 "some of the advantages gained": Henry Cowell, "Music of and for the Records," 254.

69 "fascinated": Carlsen, *The Player-Piano Music of Conlon Nancarrow*, 3.

69 "what the computer now": Amirkhanian, *Conlon Nancarrow: Studies for Player Piano*, liner notes.

69 "the most significant composer": Gyorgy Ligeti quoted in Hocker, http:// www.nancarrow.de/buch.htm.

69 "Igor Stravinsky referred to himself": Oswald, interview with Norman Igma, *Plunderphonics*, 17.

70 "musically gifted": Chanan, *Musica Practica*, 167.

70 "clever craftsmen": Haynes, *The End of Early Music*, 6.

70 "the open mind of the self-taught man": Schweitzer, *J. S. Bach*, 1:198–99.

70 although its currency: See Yo Tomita, "Title and Its Historical Background," *The Inventions and Sinfonias*, http://www.music.qub.ac.uk/~tomita/essay /inventions.html#1.

70 "architectonic": See, for instance, Wilfred Blunt quoted in Sartorius, "Baroque Music Performance"; Wolff, *Bach*, 102, 306, 313; and Duckett, "Bach Choir presents lovely pair of works for Christmas concert."

70 "mere mechanicus": Einstein, *Mozart*, 237.

71 "splendid advantage": Ibid., 238.

71 "pleasure in playing with figures": Ibid., 25.

71 "musical dice games": See Cope, *Virtual Music*, 4–5.

71 "obscured to the point of meaninglessness": Holland, "What Did Beethoven Hear in His Dreams?"

71 Battle Symphony; "Maelzel": Knight, *Beethoven and the Age of Revolution*, 84–85.

71 an invention he actually stole: Guerrieri, *The First Four Notes*, 25

72 most middle-class: See Roell, *The Piano in America;* or Loesser, *Men, Women, and Pianos.*

72 "music, like clothing": Roell, *The Piano in America,* 53.

72 "REQUIRES NO MUSICIAN": Ibid., 51.

73 "a marked deterioration": Ibid., 54.

73 "canned music": Thompson, "Machines, Music, and the Quest for Fidelity," 139.

73 Interestingly, Sousa's reputation: See, for instance, Suisman, *Selling Sounds,* 164–65.

73 "Your Victor Talking Machines are all right": Roland Gelatt, *The Fabulous Phonograph,* 136.

73 "The piano exempts a pupil from learning music": Louis Pagnerre quoted in Loesser, *Men, Women, and Pianos,* 414.

74 "foster that wholesale ignorance": Vernon Lee quoted in *Musical Times,* "Chats on Current Topics."

74 "the appalling number of miserable platitudes": Hector Berlioz quoted in Jourdain, *Music, the Brain, and Ecstasy,* 176.

74 "The trumpet can blare": Quoted in *Three Classics in the Aesthetic of Music,* 101.

74 "Anything that didn't come out of wood": Robert Moog quoted in Hans Fjell-estad's documentary *Moog* (Plexifilm, 2004).

75 "the greatest composer you've never heard of": Roddy, "London music fest gambles on little-known Nancarrow."

75 "I dream of instruments": Varèse, "The Liberation of Sound," quoted in Holmes, *Electronic and Experimental Music,* 17.

75 "only for the instruments available to him": Rosen, *Critical Entertainments,* 209.

76 the composer originally punched all of his rolls: Carlsen, *The Player-Piano Music of Conlon Nancarrow,* 4. This story is also recounted by Nancarrow in Gann, *The Music of Conlon Nancarrow,* 43–44; neither the machinist (Nancarrow calls him an "absolutely accurate metal worker") nor the technician ("this fantastic mechanic") are named. "As agreed beforehand," Gann notes, "Nancarrow paid the New York machinist $300 for his work, though the man said, 'I told you $300, but if I had to do it again, I'd charge you I don't know what!' Years later Nancarrow sent the machinist another $500." This is probably the same person Nancarrow discussed with Duckworth, *Talking Music,* 45.

76 Jürgen Hocker frames the issue much the same way: Hocker, "Encounters with Conlon Nancarrow."

77 Horst Mohr and Walter Tenten: "Conlon Nancarrow: Studies for Player Piano vol. 3," http://www.sonoloco.com/rev/mdg/1405/player3.html.

77 "People think that if I can write for player piano": Conlon Nancarrow quoted in Duckworth, *Talking Music,* 45.

77 "invaluable": Amirkhanian, *Nancarrow: Studies for Player Piano,* liner notes, 13.

78 "Until records and radio shut them up": Eisenberg, *The Recording Angel,* 229.

78 rolls manufactured by one company: Edwards, "The Piano as Phantom," 36.

78-79 spark chronograph: A good overview of this technology can be found in the

Pianola Institute's article "The Reproducing Piano—Ampico," http://www
.pianola.org/reproducing/reproducing_ampico.cfm.

80 "Easy to Play": Roell, *The Piano in America,* 117.

80 "The amount of practice necessarily": Ibid., 111.

81 "Playing the player piano properly takes years": Durkin, "What passes," comment available as a screen capture.

81 "remains unfettered": Roell, *The Piano in America,* 111.

81 "You *do not* operate the Manualo": Ibid., 115.

81 "player pianists," "playerists," or "pianolists": See Henderson, "Definition of a 'Reproducing' Piano"; or Anatole Leikin, *The Performing Style of Alexander Scriabin* (Burlington, VT: Ashgate, 2011), 7.

81 "It is no good anybody sitting at the instrument": Townley, "Ragtime, Blues, and Jazz," 20.

82 "the pianolist can play with expression": Wodehouse, *Gershwin Plays Gershwin,* liner notes, 6.

82 "sit quietly in the middle of the bench": Gordon Nevin, *First Lessons on the Organ,* 18.

82 "Let the feet caress the pedals": Ord-Hume, *Pianola,* 259.

83 "When you sit down at a strange player": Ibid., 255.

83 "played the rolls over": Artis Wodehouse quoted in Walsh, "Gershwin, by George," 113.

83 were often produced [. . .] with the help of a real piano player: Montgomery, Trebnor, and Hasse, "Ragtime on Piano Rolls," 94.

84 "I do not play these passages evenly": Paderewski quoted in Husarik, "Musical Expression in Piano Roll Performance of Joseph Hoffman," 48.

84 "The original perforated rolls": Nordin, *Conlon Nancarrow.*

84 The dynamics and accents to be performed: One good resource on the complicated world of reproducing pianos is the Pianola Institute. The organization's essay on the Welte reproducing piano, considered by many to be one of the most realistic brands, is fascinating, though it seems to raise as many questions as it answers. Pianola Institute, "The Reproducing Piano—Welte-Mignon," http://www.pianola.org/reproducing/reproducing_welte.cfm.

84 "put on the note roll": Hamer, "Don't shoot the Pianola," 51.

85 "The Blue Danube": Edwards, "The Piano as Phantom," 36.

85 technicians' interpretation of that interpretation: An essay at the Pianola Institute website explains that "a not inconsiderable army of musical technicians was employed by Ampico, measuring and transcribing the information on the spark chronograph rolls, and converting it by means of tables and charts into pre-ordained crescendo, decrescendo and intensity coding." Pianola Institute, "The Reproducing Piano—Ampico," http://www.pianola.org/reproducing/reproducing_ampico.cfm.

85 "merely a starting point": Montgomery, Trebnor, and Hasse, "Ragtime on Piano Rolls," 94.

85 "color and variety": Berkman, "Tribute to J. Lawrence Cook."

85 Frank Milne; "Milne and Leith": Wodehouse, *Gershwin Plays Gershwin,* liner notes, 4–5.

86 "Automated player pianos were in vogue": David A. Jasen quoted in Confrey, *Ragtime, Novelty & Jazz Piano Solos,* 2.

86 "Living Soul of the Artist": Henderson, "The Pianola News."

87 In November 1917, pianist Harold Bauer: Roell, *The Piano in America,* 44.

87 Grieg, Debussy, Respighi: Ibid., 42–43.

87 "I am sorry, but I am capable of seventeen": Artur Schnabel quoted in Lichtman, "Hit Gershwin Disc Sparks New Interest in Piano Rolls."

87 "an instrument which reproduces so faultlessly": Quoted in Gaida, "Ampico Salesman's Manual."

88 "played Gershwin's rolls": Wodehouse, *Gershwin Plays Gershwin,* liner notes, 7.

89 Hal Boulware: Montgomery, *Scott Joplin,* liner notes, 2.

90 "All of these movements": Montgomery, *Greatest Ragtime of the Century,* liner notes, 2.

91 "Phonograph": Pekka Gronow, "Phonograph," in *Continuum Encyclopedia of Popular Music of the World,* 2:517. See also Symes, *Setting the Record Straight,* 19–22. (Also note that overseas, "gramophone" became the generic term.)

91 "always provided a glass window": Thompson, "Machines, Music, and the Quest for Fidelity," 144–46.

91 "Victorian camouflage for the industrial machine"; "Victor's viola": Kenney, *Recorded Music in American Life,* 51. For an interesting discussion of the etymology of "Victrola," see Bilton, "Who put the ola in Victrola?"

92 flower-shaped playback horn; emotions onto a recording; "Golden Throat"; "Magic Brain": Millard, *America on Record,* 127, 146, 202. See also Hoenack and Hoenack, "Behold the MAGIC BRAIN."

92 compared to the sizzle of a heated frying pan: See "Science and Invention," *Literary Digest* 42 (May 20, 1911): 997. ("These harsh notes that rend the rendition of a soprano just when she is soaring to the topmost peaks are called 'frying-pan noises.'")

92 "unable to reproduce all the frequencies": Day, *A Century of Recorded Music,* 9.

92 the *Firebird Suite* and *Till Eulenspiegel; Tristan un Isolde:* Gelatt, *The Fabulous Phonograph,* 198, 240–41.

93 Fats Waller: Lipskin, *Turn on the Heat,* liner notes (no page numbers).

93 As Eric Hobsbawm has written: Hobsbawm, *The Jazz Scene,* 157.

93 Puccini, for instance: Symes, *Setting the Record Straight,* 52.

94 "In popular movies": Nachmanovitch, *Free Play,* 86.

94 "For years in the minds of nearly everybody": Compton Mackenzie quoted in Eisenberg, *The Recording Angel,* 147.

95 Tim Gracyk and Frank Hoffmann: See their *Popular American Recording Pioneers, 1895–1925,* 11–12.

96 "If Caruso can be made to sing": Kozinn, "Have You Heard the New Caruso? (No Kidding)."

96 "provide any computer-based recording": *Musician,* May 1998, 65.

97 "Devotees of acoustic recording": Millard, *America on Record,* 8.

97 phonograph societies: See, for instance, antiquephono.org, capsnews.org, hoosierantiquephonographsociety.com, antiquephonograph.org, otaps.org, and 78records.wordpress.com.

97 "Listeners should be aware": Lipskin, *Turn on the Heat,* liner notes (no page numbers).

97 "the recording apparatus was defective": Marston, *Enrico Caruso: The Complete Recordings,* liner notes, 5.

98 "very, very fussy about recording": Hasse, *Beyond Category*, 242.

98 "recording engineers at Victor": Ibid.

99 "regarded as a device": Eno, "The Studio as Compositional Tool."

99 "sound photographs": Day, *A Century of Recorded Music*, 40.

99 "over the relative levels of sounds that went onto the machine": Eno, "The Studio as Compositional Tool."

99 Walter Legge: Ibid.

100 "to pay him by far the largest fee": Suisman, *Selling Sounds*, 106.

100 "Volga Boat Song"; Violin Concerto in B Minor: Eisenberg, *The Recording Angel*, 95.

100 peculiar demands of the recording process: Symes, *Setting the Record Straight*, 39–40.

100 "in a single afternoon": Griffith, *Enrico Caruso: The Complete Recordings*, vol. 1, liner notes, 2.

101 "musical text which endures after the composer's death": Michael Chanan, *Musica Practica*, 72–73.

101 "In the more extreme forms of this discursive polarity": Theberge, *Any Sound You Can Imagine*, 189.

102 "The music itself is a jangle of shattered nerves": Compton Mackenzie quoted in Gelatt, *The Fabulous Phonograph*, 231–32.

102 "symphonic debut"; "we must at once dethrone": Compton Mackenzie in *Gramophone*, January 1926.

102 "Mellowness and reality have given place to screaming": Quoted in Gelatt, *The Fabulous Phonograph*, 232.

102 "so antagonistic at times": Burns, *The Life and Times of A D Blumlein*, 96.

103 "superior listening experience": Frith, *Performing Rites*, 25.

103 Alfred Brendel expressed a similar bias: Symes, *Setting the Record Straight*, 42.

103 "the collector of 78 recordings had to be an 'active' listener": Frith, *Performing Rites*, 25.

103 "The sound of the record": Paul Elie, *Reinventing Bach*, 339.

104 "the work of technology can never quite become invisible": Belton, "Technology and Aesthetics of Film Sound," 63.

104 "it is art to conceal art": Eugene Ehrlich, *Amo, Amas, Amat and More: How to Use Latin to Your Own Advantage and to the Astonishment of Others* (New York: Harper & Row, 1993), 56.

3. AN INTRODUCTION TO AUTHENTICITY

107 "It's so obsessed with the real": Prickett, "Speaking in Tongues."

107 "Frank never did intend": Art Jarvinen interviewed by Trubee.

107 "Any sound the audience hears": Zappa, *The Real Frank Zappa Book*, 175.

108 "a wall of hiss"; "I slunk down in my seat": David Ocker quoted in Lantz, "The David Ocker Internet Interview."

108 "Much to my surprise": Ibid.

108 "The man who ran the concert series": Zappa, *The Real Frank Zappa Book*, 175.

108 "produced quite a scandal": Ibid.

108 "were made to feel very ashamed": Art Jarvinen quoted in Trubee.

109 "Several members of the ensemble": Zappa, *The Real Frank Zappa Book,* 175–76.

109 What about the listener who, as Ocker notes: David Ocker quoted in Lantz, "The David Ocker Internet Interview."

110 "embodied knowledge": Smith, "Listening to the Wild Blue Yonder," 39.

110 pseudo-porn audiotape: Zappa, *The Real Frank Zappa Book,* 59.

111 "You put together two notes": David Lang quoted in Da Fonseca-Wollheim, "Keeping the Magic Without the Thunder."

111 "With things that go together": Conlon Nancarrow quoted in Gann, *The Music of Conlon Nancarrow,* 39.

111 Bach reperformed Palestrina: Brown, "Pedantry or Liberation?," 34.

112 Stravinsky's [. . .] rewrite of commedia dell'arte: See Maureen A. Carr, ed., *Stravinsky's Pulcinella: A Facsimile of the Sources and Sketches,* Issue 6 (Middleton, WI: A-R Editions, 2010).

112 later revealed: Haskell, *The Early Music Revival,* 75.

112 "dark, sly, distancing maneuver": Wallmark, "Turning Back the Clock."

112 "immutable laws of music": On Schenker, see Guerrieri, *The First Four Notes,* 199–211.

113 "experienced an inner emptiness": Kenney, *Recorded Music in American Life,* 56.

113 "resettled": Hyde, "Stravinsky's Neoclassicism," 98.

113 Miles Orvell observes: Orvell, *The Real Thing,* xviii.

113 "providing redundancy and therefore stability": Schafer, *The Soundscape,* 114.

113 comforting lyrics about domestic and moral order: Suisman, *Selling Sounds,* 53.

114 "a spiritual transcendence of the sterility of modern life": Kenney, *Recorded Music in American Life,* 56.

114 In contemporary France: See, for instance, Rowley, "Defining neoclassicism."

114 *collegia musica;* "a simpler past": Brown, "Pedantry or Liberation?," 34–36.

114 "The period from the mid-thirties onward": Ross, *The Rest Is Noise,* 237.

114 "the countries most invested": Elie, *Reinventing Bach,* 157.

114 As Mike Dash has shown: Dash, "Hitler's Very Own Hot Jazz Band."

114 "pieces in foxtrot rhythm": Joseph Škvorecký quoted in Gould, "Josef Skvorecky on the Nazis' Control-Freak Hatred of Jazz." Some have maintained that Škvorecký's piece was intended as satire. He insisted otherwise.

115 "end very badly": Quoted in Ross, *The Rest Is Noise,* 216.

115 "culture of the factitious": Orvell, *The Real Thing,* xxiii.

116 "the foremost spiritual quest of our time": Potter, *The Authenticity Hoax,* 3.

116 "A rockist": Sanneh, "The Rap Against Rockism," *New York Times,* October 31, 2004.

116 the laws and mores historically segregating black and white: See, for instance, Monson, *Freedom Sounds,* 61–62 and passim.

116 the viciousness of the "Disco Sucks" campaign: Myers, "Why 'Disco Sucks!' sucked."

116 Max Roach allegedly punching Ornette Coleman: Litweiler, *Ornette Coleman,* 83.

116 Keith Jarrett's infamous proclivity: See, for instance, Swanson, "Keith Jarrett and the Audience."

116   long history of booing: Huynh, "Boo . . . Who? A New Freakonomics Radio
      Podcast."
116   Amateur Night at the Apollo: Ibid.
116   the murders of Brian Deneke and Sophie Lancaster: See Lyons, "Anarchy in
      Amarillo"; and Taylor, "Sophie Lancaster: The murder that caused a subcul-
      ture to fight back."
117   the death threats received by Los Angeles DJ Fei-Fei Wang: Haithcoat, "DJ
      Gets Death Threats for Playing Dubstep."
117   "to suspend our aesthetic judgments and acquiesce to its claims": Mehldau,
      "Ideology, Burgers, and Beer."
117   "politics of style": Ross, *The Rest Is Noise,* 118.
117   "meaningful life"; "also good for society": Potter, *The Authenticity Hoax,*
      126.
118   *Swingjugend:* See Fackler, "Swing Kids Behind Barbed Wire."
118   "East Coast Swing is more of a purer": Behrens, *Big Bands and Great Ball-
      rooms,* 50.
119   "the American century, the Jazz century"; "the rise and fall of America"; "I
      think the messages of Rap": Lydon, "Ellington, Newport and the American
      Century."
119   "That's perhaps the word of the current era": Grella, "The Anxiety of Au-
      thenticity."
120   "true dat": Ibid.
121   "musical fascism": Rudhyar, "Musical Fascism."
121   "The Big Question": *The Atlantic,* June 2014.
122   "Music critics love to make lists": Moon, *1,000 Recordings to Hear Before
      You Die,* x.
122   "Lists are ridiculous": Ebert, "The Greatest Films of All Time."
122   "How the shit Danny Carey didn't end up on this list"; "Ringo?"; "Go
      to YouTube": Greene, "Rolling Stone Readers Pick Best Drummers of All
      Time."
124   "Why are you bent on destroying": Patrick Jarenwattananon, "The Year-
      End List of Lists 2010," December 23, 2010, www.npr.org/blogs/ablog
      supreme/2010/12/24/132274520/the-year-end-list-of-lists-2010.
124   Ellington himself complicated the issue: Note that the phrase "beyond cat-
      egory" is used as the title of Hasse's biography of Ellington.
124   "the other kind": Duke Ellington, in Tucker, ed., *The Duke Ellington Reader,*
      326.
125   "moldy figs": See Gabbard, *Jazz Among the Discourses,* 19.
125   "One side—the traditionalist faction": Argue, "Dispatches from the End of
      the Jazz Wars."
126   "Black American Music": Payton, "An Open Letter to My Dissenters on Why
      Jazz Isn't Cool Anymore."
126   "For the second year running": Piazza, *Blues Up and Down,* 162.
126   It is true that by 1956 Gonsalves: Teachout, *Duke,* 288.
127   "it was painful to watch": Davis, *Outcats,* 206.
127   "the Middle Mind mediocrity of NPR fern bar jazz": Chris Rich quoted in
      Adler, "Fern bar."
127   "This sort of self-righteous, us-versus-them": Ibid.
127   Rich later softened his stance: The blog post Adler references has since been

deleted, though Rich has continued to use the term "fern bar" in the same way in later postings.

128 "Jazz Nerds International": Chris Barton, "Jazz War, Anyone?"

128 "Here's some real swing for your ass": Kenny Drew Jr. quoted in Hum, "On Vijay Iyer, Kurt Rosenwinkel, HuffPo, greatness, prizes and hype."

128 "I wish we lived in a time": Mike Doughty, interview, *Village Voice,* October 29, 2009.

128–129 "a true expression of the artist's *self*": Potter, *The Authenticity Hoax,* 78.

129 the honest signal theory of biology: See, for instance, "The Honest Signalling Theory: A Basic Introduction," http://octavia.zoology.washington.edu/handicap/.

129 the facial action encoding system of psychology: See for instance Ekman and Rosenberg, *What the Face Reveals.*

129 Roger Watt's idea that listeners personify their music: Mithen, *The Singing Neanderthals,* 24.

129 "nine inviolable rules": Irving Berlin quoted in Suisman, *Selling Sounds,* 45–46.

129 noted K-pop impresario Lee Soo-man: Seabrook, "Factory Girls."

129 Emily Howell: Cope, "Emily Howell."

129 recent *Wall Street Journal* article: Doucleff, "Anatomy of a Tear-Jerker."

129 Mike Daisey's interview with *This American Life:* Isherwood, "Speaking Less Than Truth to Power."

129 James Frey's book *A Million Little Pieces:* Wyatt, "Best-Selling Memoir Draws Scrutiny."

129 the *lonelygirl15* videos: Keen, *The Cult of the Amateur,* 78–79.

129 "true self": Potter, *The Authenticity Hoax,* 79.

130 "nominal authenticity": Dutton, "Authenticity in Art," 259.

130 "virtually every artist of note": Potter, *The Authenticity Hoax,* 82.

130 Joyce Hatto comes to mind: See, for instance, Dutton, "The Joyce Hatto Scandal."

130 the "Milli Vanilli of American politics": Dunn, "Palin No Longer Writing Her Own Script."

130 "Milli Vanilli of Sports Coverage": Filler, "ESPN: The Milli Vanilli of Sports Coverage."

130 "Milli Vanilli of book publishing": Schmidt, "Don't Be the Milli Vanilli of Book Publishing"

131 "deceived record buyers": Cocks, "Music: Fans, You Know It's True."

131 Angry fans were prompted to send in for a rebate: Friedman, "Milli Vanilli and the Scapegoating of the Inauthentic."

131 a New Jersey congressman tried to prohibit unacknowledged lip-synching: Ibid.

131 a chewing gum commercial: Ibid.

131 The real Milli Vanilli singers: See, for instance, "The Real Voices Behind Milli Vanilli Share Their Side of the Lip Syncing Scandal," *Huffington Post,* February 27, 2014, http://www.huffingtonpost.com/2014/02/27/milli-vanilli_n_4860222.html; and UFAlien, "Milli Vanilli and the Dark Side of Music," *Earthsong* forum post, September 6, 2010.

131 Martha Wash: See, for instance, Bernstein, "Martha Wash Gets Her Form Back."

131   "a pact with the devil": Antczak, " 'Pact with the Devil.' "

131   Pilatus eventually died of a drug overdose: Pilikington, "Hollywood pays lip service to Milli Vanilli."

131   "the new Elvis": Worrell, "Rebutting Milli Vanilli."

132   Long before Milli Vanilli: "He's a Rebel," a number one hit in 1962, was credited to the Crystals, but was actually sung by the Blossoms when producer Phil Spector decided to record the song while the first group was on tour. The Blossoms were right to be upset by this; no one else seemed to be. See *20 Feet from Stardom*, directed by Morgan Neville, Gil Friesen Productions and Tremolo Productions, 2013, DVD.

132   "shift from live performance to the re-enactment": Kooijman, "Michael Jackson," 127.

132   Milli Vanilli too was initially given a pass: See Goodman, "Milli Vanilli: Behind the Music."

133   infamously booed: For possible alternate interpretations of the booing, see *Mojo*'s 2007 interview with Murray Lerner, "Exclusive: Dylan at Newport: Who Booed?"

133   "scapegoating": Friedman, "Milli Vanilli and the Scapegoating of the Inauthentic."

133   Elisabeth Schwarzkopf had sung a high C: Gould, "The Prospects of Recording," 340.

134   "a particularly sinister invention": McCormick, "The Truth About Lip-Synching."

134   "Fifty Worst Inventions": *Time*, "Fifty Worst Inventions," http://www.time.com/time/specials/packages/completelist/0,29569,1991915,00.html.

134   "I truly feel like the Guitar Hero games": Franich, " 'Guitar' Hero Is Dead, but We'll Always Have 'Strutter.' "

135   "it's still possible for a band to get heard": Quoted in Kot, *Ripped*, 128.

136   "If we dare attempt this tribute to Rush": Rodman, "Tribute bands are music to fans' ears, wallets."

136   "truly authentic"; "the very essence"; "Seeing the Return": See the Return's website, http://www.thereturnonline.com/meet-the-return.html.

136   "groupies with": Newell, "Tribute Band Groupies."

136   "but if they liked a song enough": Suisman, *Selling Sounds*, 60.

137   "the recording industry's sacrifice": Friedman, "Milli Vanilli and the Scapegoating of the Inauthentic."

4. DO YOU HEAR WHAT I HEAR?

138   "Every act of perception": Gerald Edelman quoted in Sacks, *Musicophilia*, 157.

138   "An old friend of mine once defined tragedy": Feldman, *Speaking of Music at the Exploratorium*.

138   "fine, resonant, splendidly balanced"; "the conductor waved his hand": Wilson, *Tone Deaf and All Thumbs?*, 62.

139   "full of contradictory explanations of the same music": Blacking, *How Musical Is Man?*, 93.

139   fundamental incompatibility: Gracyk, "The Aesthetics of Popular Music."

139 "either one of the two": Wilson, *Tone Deaf and All Thumbs?*, 62–63.
139 "Collective music making may encourage social cohesions": Levitin, *This Is Your Brain on Music*, 252.
140 "not only do we dislike physical isolation": Meyer, *Emotion and Meaning in Music*, 21.
140 Tin Pan Alley–era publishers and songwriters: Suisman, *Selling Sounds*, 44.
140 "the music-buying public": Harry Von Tilzer quoted in ibid., 22.
140 "alone in company": Blacking, *How Musical Is Man?*, 62.
141 "powerless to express anything": Ross, *The Rest Is Noise*, 117.
141 "cannot distinguish musical tones a semitone apart": Levitin, "Tone Deafness," 2.
142 "can only be determined on a case-by-case basis": Gracyk, "The Aesthetics of Popular Music."
143 "very clearly; they sound like different instruments": Levitin, *This Is Your Brain on Music*, 45.
143 "Decades of research on music cognition": Levitin, *The World in Six Songs*, 17.
143 "perceptual constancy": Epstein, "The Metahistorical Context."
145 "Recording introduced the idea": Levitin, *The World in Six Songs*, 282.
145 "Records are dynamic artifacts": Symes, *Setting the Record Straight*, 149.
146 "Every single one of us": Glennie, "How to truly listen."
147 "Do persons five miles from the explosion"; "The sound": Perkins, *Sensing the World*, 171–72.
148 "life cycle": Wang, "Amplitude of Sound."
148 Thurston Dart distinguishes: Dart, *The Interpretation of Music*, 57–58.
148 "the offstage trumpet in Beethoven's": See Wilson, *Tone Deaf and All Thumbs?*, 101.
149 Producer Bob Margouleff calls this feature: *Musician*, September 1998, 70.
149 the ability to localize sound: Levitin, *The World in Six Songs*, 246; see also Grothe, Pecka, and McAlpine, "Mechanisms of Sound Localization in Mammals."
149 the 1962 opening of the original Philharmonic Hall: Pierce, *The Science of Musical Sound*, 154–59; see also Sekuler, "Architectural Acoustics: The $20,000,000 Mistake."
149 "caused a single note to sound like two notes": Sekuler, "Architectural Acoustics: The $20,000,000 Mistake."
151 "A delicate, sensitive ear": Mainzer, *Music and Education*, 9.
151 "modular model of music processing": Mithen, *The Singing Neanderthals*, 62.
151 "the raw sensation of toothaches and redness": Pinker, *How the Mind Works*, 60.
152 "an unfamiliar term for something": Dennett, "Quining Qualia," 619.
152 pitch, volume, and key, for instance: See Levitin, *This Is Your Brain on Music*, 15.
152 "the physical facts of time and space": Smith, *The Acoustic World of Early Modern England*, 8.
153 "very, very differently": Kay Shelemay quoted in *The Music Instinct* (PBS documentary, 2009).
153 "When we watch TV": Pinker, *How the Mind Works*, 29.
154 "sonic barber pole": Rudd, "The Sonic Barber Pole: Shepard's Scale."

154   "Men of the most confined knowledge": Hume, "Of the Standard of Taste," 115.

155   it is common to point out: See, for instance, Schafer, "Open Ears," 25.

155   "we change, correct, or reverse our opinions": Albers, *The Interaction of Color*, 17.

155   "Doth not the appetite alter?": Shakespeare, *Much Ado About Nothing*, act 2, scene 3.

155   "how I could have not liked it": Lucy Lowell quoted in Cavicchi, *Listening and Longing*, 116.

155   "Don't you wonder sometimes": David Bowie, "Sound and Vision," *Low* (RCA, 1977).

156   "use visual and tactile cues": Sacks, *Musicophilia*, 159.

156   "the entire sensory apparatus as an operational complex": Ong, *The Presence of the Word*, 6.

156   Ultimately, our senses collaborate: Soukup, "Looking Is Not Enough," 4.

157   as Jonathan Winawer and others have recently shown: see Winawer et al., "Russian blues reveal effects of language on color discrimination."

157   "We all sometimes block out the visual world": Sacks, *Musicophilia*, 173.

157   "The listening system is used primarily as an alert and support system": Hertsens, "How We Hear."

158   "It did me good": Walt Whitman quoted in Cavicchi, *Listening and Longing*, 127.

158   "positioned Janus-wise": Eisenberg, *The Recording Angel*, 122.

159   "are exquisitely sensitive to the physical gestures": Levitin, *This Is Your Brain on Music*, 206.

159   "prominent holes and stains in/on their jeans": Osby, "Jazz Bums."

159   as saxophonist Chris Kelsey suggested in a response to Osby: Kelsey, "Dressin' for Success: A Clusterf*** in Three Movements," currently unpublished, referenced by permission of the author.

160   "Is the distinction between 'thoughtful' and 'thoughtless' music": Levinson, "Musical Thinking," section 2.6.

160   "objectivity" is itself a construction of the Enlightenment: Cavicchi, *Listening and Longing*, 46.

161   "oblate spheroid": Asimov, "The Relativity of Wrong."

161   a tension Meyer reminds us: Meyer, *Emotion and Meaning in Music*, 39–40.

161   "rock 'n' roll music gets right through to you": John Lennon quoted in Miller, *Boxed In*, 175.

161   Glenn Gould once claimed: Kivy, *Music Alone*, 86. (Gould's words: "What's there to think about?")

162   "loving music dearly as I do": Caroline Healey Dall quoted in Cavicchi, *Listening and Longing*, 146.

162   "chord progressions that have never been used before": Gann, "Naïve Pictorialism."

163   though often misattributed: See Johnston, "OT: We Hear from Martin Mull."

163   "much more subtle and varied": Meyer, *Emotion and Meaning in Music*, 8.

163   Consider the range of statements: I am grateful to Peter Kivy for this example; see Kivy, *Music Alone*, 85.

165   "many people are essentially deaf to complex harmony": Jourdain, *Music, the Brain, and Ecstasy*, 112.

166 "approaching epidemic proportions": Cited by Prochnik, *In Pursuit of Silence,* 15.

166 World Health Organization: Bouton, *Shouting Won't Help,* 247.

166 *loudness recruitment:* on loudness recruitment and paracusis, see Jourdain, *Music, the Brain, and Ecstasy,* 19, 116–17; on hyperacusis, see www.hyperacusis.org; on diplacusis, see http://www.healthyhearing.com/content/articles/Hearing-loss/Causes/51055-Understanding-diplacusis; on presbycusis, see Hain, "Presbycusis."

166 "between 30 and 50 million Americans": Bouton, *Shouting Won't Help,* 197.

166 consider research suggesting that boys have less acute hearing than girls: Sax, "Sex Differences in Hearing," 15.

167 "blessed with much 'better' ears than other people": Terhardt, "Absolute Pitch."

167 "Sometimes when a piano is a whole tone flat": Lhévinne, *Basic Principles in Pianoforte Playing,* 12.

167 "may end up feeling cranky": Wilson, *Tone Deaf and All Thumbs?,* 74.

168 More than one observer has speculated: Bouton, *Shouting Won't Help,* 201.

168 Evelyn Glennie's concept: As evoked, for instance, in the title of the film *Touch the Sound.*

168 "noise is the most erotic form of sound": Masami Akita (Merzbow) quoted in Cox and Warner, "The Beauty of Noise," 60.

168 "literally touches the audience"; "what they play": Grella, "First, the Sound."

168 "the materiality of music": Reynolds, "Noise," 57.

169 George Prochnik argues that Cage himself had tinnitus: Prochnik, *In Pursuit of Silence,* 182.

169 "I heard two sounds, one high and one low": John Cage quoted in Vitale, "Music Is Everywhere."

169 "for a comfortable length of time": Carroll, "A Simulation of the Tuning Meditation."

170 "Isn't it wonderful?": Kazunori, "The Day I Saw Van Gogh's Genius in a New Light."

170 "say exactly the notes, chords, intervals": Alicia de Larrocha quoted in Jourdain, *Music, the Brain, and Ecstasy,* 117.

170 "I may truly say that my life is a wretched one": Beethoven, *Beethoven's Letters,* 20.

170 Michael Chorost's quest to find a scientific solution: See Chorost's *Rebuilt.*

171 "amateur" once meant, literally, "lover": Cavicchi, *Listening and Longing,* 141–42.

171 "almost tone deaf yet passionately sensitive to music": Sacks, *Musicophilia,* 313.

171 hearing loss in musicians may be more widespread: Ibid., 148.

172 "I don't have an ear for music": John Cage interviewed in Duckworth, *Talking Music,* 7.

172 Evelyn Glennie, Brian Wilson: I am grateful to Katherine Bouton for many of these examples.

172 "Everyone Deserves Music": The video can be viewed at https://www.youtube.com/watch?v=_oNUNs2nWHY.

172 "a distinct cultural group": Prochnik, *In Pursuit of Silence,* 246.

172 "the stigma of deafness": Bouton, *Shouting Won't Help,* 75.

172   "adapted to another sensory mode": Sacks, *Seeing Voices*, 121.

173   "We can feel this": Glennie, *Touch the Sound*.

173   "often listened to recordings": Thompson, "Machines, Music, and the Quest for Fidelity," 169. Edison, it should be noted, was only one contributor to the development of early recording technology.

5. LIVE TO TAPE, AND BACK AGAIN

174   "Within the cultural field of music": Suisman, *Selling Sounds*, 109.

174   "megaconcert": It can be tricky to get exact numbers for megaconcert attendance, especially in unticketed or open-seating scenarios. For Woodstock, see *FOH Online*, "Parnelli Innovator Honoree, Father of Festival Sound." For the New York Philharmonic's 1986 performance in Central Park, see *Noise Addicts*, "Concerts with Record Attendance." Some concerts have been even bigger than these, but one is tempted to call Rod Stewart's 1994 performance at Copacabana Beach, which the *Guinness Book of World Records* claims drew 3.5 million people, not a megaconcert but a temporary metropolis.

174   similarly large political rallies: Bendersky, *A History of Nazi Germany*, 152.

174   "Peace Jubilees": See, for instance, Cavicchi, *Listening and Longing*, 119–20; or Horowitz, *Classical Music in America*, 15–28.

174   the term was not originally meant pejoratively: Cavicchi, *Listening and Longing*, 119.

175   The record-breaking audience of fifty-five thousand: Capo and Borzellieri, *It Happened in New York*, 116.

175   "It was a very strange location": Paul McCartney quoted in *The Beatles Anthology*, 321.

176   "Listening to records is generally less gripping": Rosen, *Critical Entertainments*, 316.

176   The mashup artist Girl Talk: See, for instance, performance footage of Girl Talk in Gaylor, *Rip!: A Remix Manifesto*.

176   "Listening now to the Pablo Casals recordings": Nachmanovitch, *Free Play*, 33.

177   "Recording introduced the idea": Levitin, *The World in Six Songs*, 282.

177   "it seems hugely preferable for me": Smith, "Repeatability: The Biggest Benefit of a Recording."

178   "We have been taught to mistakenly view online": Jurgenson, "The IRL Fetish."

179   "No matter what may be your mood": This recording is available on the Internet Archive under the artist/composer name "Len Spencer." http://archive .org/details/iamed1906.

180   commerce, medicine, forensics: See, for instance, handheld recording devices (useful for memos), answering machines, voice mail technology, ultrasound recordings, wiretaps, recording authentication (e.g., Rebecca Morelle, "The Hum That Helps to Fight Crime"), Muzak, advertising.

180   *Voyager*'s Golden Record: For more on this recording, see "The Golden Record," http://voyager.jpl.nasa.gov/spacecraft/goldenrec.html.

181   "intimate unity with the time and place of performance": Chanan, *Repeated Takes*, 18.

181 "schizophonia": Schafer, *The Soundscape*, 88.

181 Carolyn Abbate claims: Abbate, "Music—Drastic or Gnostic?," 505–6.

181 "appears to lead inevitably"; "Just as the photograph has led to the trivialization of the visual image": Gioia, *The Imperfect Art*, 8–9.

182 Chanan concurs that the ubiquity of recordings: Chanan, *Repeated Takes*, 18.

182 "In a time like ours": Debussy quoted in Eisenberg, *The Recording Angel*, 55.

182 "a 'boundless surfeit' which would wear music out": Arnold Schoenberg quoted and paraphrased in Day, *A Century of Recorded Music*, 213.

182 "was now being used to provide a discreet accompaniment": Day, *A Century of Recorded* Music, 213.

183 "What infuriated me": Roger Sessions quoted in Chanan, *Repeated Takes*, 119.

183 "The very great drawback of recorded sound": Aaron Copland quoted in Sanden (after Glenn Gould), *Liveness in Modern Music*, 37.

183 the Music Defense League: Novak, "Musicians Wage War Against Evil Robots."

184 the AFM: For a good, if dated, history of Petrillo and American musicians' unions, see Leiter, *The Musicians and Petrillo*. For a concise history of the tensions leading to the strikes, see Knapp, Morris, and Wolf, eds., *The Oxford Handbook of the American Musical*, 181.

184 Local 802: For more on this protest, see "Protect Live Music at Lincoln Center," http://www.local802afm.org/2012/11/protect-live-music-at-lincoln-center-3/.

184 "the thrill of seeing and hearing a live orchestra": For more on the Council for Living Music, see the "Save Live Music on Broadway" website, http://savelivemusiconbroadway.com/about.

184 "Live Music Is Better": Neil Young, "Union Man," *Hawks & Doves* (Reprise, 1980).

184 "Whoever has approved": T. S. Eliot quoted in Dart, *The Interpretation of Music*, 163.

185 "A present-day musician's idea of harpsichord tone-color": Dart, *The Interpretation of Music*, 164–65.

185 "The aura of listening": Leon Botstein quoted in Kun, "How We Listen."

186 and indeed many working-class homes: Thompson, *The Rise of Respectable Society*, 194.

186 piano reductions of ensemble works: Lockhart, "Listening to the Domestic Music Machine."

186 when Boston's Handel and Haydn Society: Cavicchi, *Listening and Longing*, 68.

186 they had been fortified with cast iron frames: Barron, *Piano: The Making of a Steinway Concert Grand*, 102; see also Schafer, *The Soundscape*, 109.

186 "painful outcry"; "offensive power and offensive character": Eduard Hanslick quoted in Schafer, *The Soundscape*, 109.

187 "a continual subject of controversy": Ibid., 65.

187 "instrument of torture"; "assassinate him": Prochnik, *In Pursuit of Silence*, 178–79.

187 "daily interrupted": Schafer, *The Soundscape*, 66.

187 " 'One afternoon, when I was watering flowers' ": Quoted in Suisman, *Selling Sounds*, 56.

187 the name comes from the idea: Suisman, *Selling Sounds,* 59.

188 "We'd sing a song to them thirty or forty times a night": Quoted in ibid., 72.

188 "Romantic theatergoers": Judith Pascoe quoted in Cavicchi, "Romanticism, the Voice, and the History of Listening."

189 "repeated encounters with the same performer": Cavicchi, *Listening and Longing,* 105.

189 "I should like to hear just the same thing over again": Ibid., 107.

189 "I never can satisfy myself about music": Ibid., 131.

189 "recalled a listener": Day, *A Century of Recorded Music,* 203.

189 It was understood as a request for the reperformance: See, for instance, Horo- witz, *Classical Music in America,* 127.

189 "There is music that I have listened to": Pat Metheny quoted in Small, "The Perception of Music."

189 "cold repetition"; "constructive repetition": Goehr, "The Dangers of Satisfac- tion," 58.

190 "has become literally disembodied": Chanan, *Repeated Takes,* 18.

190 "a familiar record in fresh company": Quoted in Day, *A Century of Recorded Music,* 216.

190 "these are works so rich": Davis, *Outcats,* 199.

190 "increasing profundity and value for me"; "For instance": Nisenson, *Blue,* 7.

191 "a recording might not change": Leonard Bernstein paraphrased in Day, *A Century of Recorded Music,* 216.

191 "unchanging sounds": Day, *A Century of Recorded Music,* 216.

192 "recording tends to dilute and disperse": Rosen, *Critical Entertainments,* 317.

192 "the increased 'efficiency' of modern musical language": Eisenberg, *The Recording Angel,* 136.

193 "hand down a verdict": Ibid, 137.

193 "The obvious lack of any form of contact": Rabl, *Caruso 2000,* liner notes, 16.

194 There have been complaints about this feature: See, for instance, Braue, "iTunes: Just how random is random?"

194 "miraculous button": Corbett, *Extended Play,* 1.

195 "tactic"; "the cracks that particular conjunctions open": Certeau, *The Prac- tice of Everyday Life,* 37.

195 "records give you more of what you want": For variations on the same sleeve, see http://www.flickr.com/photos/lwr/8451947329/ or http://blog.vinylrecord architect.com/2009/05/04/heres-how-records-give-you-more-of-what-you -want.aspx.

195 "has these advantages": The image is archived at http://mtr.arcade-museum .com/MTR-1915-60-21/MTR-1915-60-21-38.pdf.

195 "Often I don't like the sequence of musical numbers": Fantel, *Durable Plea- sures,* 105–6.

196 that industry helped pioneer modern marketing: See, for instance, chapter 1 of Suisman, *Selling Sounds,* "When Songs Became a Business."

196 "The phonograph": Chanan, *Repeated Takes,* 40.

197 "I fancy him listening to those 'talks' ": National Phonograph Company, *The Phonograph and How to Use It,* 138.

197 "Indestructible Cylinder Record": Gelatt, *The Fabulous Phonograph,* 165.

197 "withstand any amount of rough handling": The image is archived at http:// www.cedmagic.com/history/gramophone-1900-ad.html.

197 "indefinitely": The image is archived at http://78records.wordpress.com /2011/08/02/berliner-advertisments-1896-1897/.

197 "made the opera": The image is archived at http://www.tjsrecords.com/vic trola.htm.

198 "Jenny Lind is only a memory": Quoted in Millard, *America on Record*, 9.

198 "fleeting documents": Russell Sanjek paraphrased in Cohen, *Duke Ellington's America*, 66.

198 "For all the grandiloquence about messages": Sterne, "The Preservation Paradox in Digital Audio," 59.

199 "awaken their music at will": Claude Debussy quoted in Eisenberg, *The Recording Angel*, 55.

199 "phonophobia"; "commit more errors": Symes, *Setting the Record Straight*, 45.

199 "conscious the whole time": Ferruccio Busoni quoted in Day, *A Century of Recorded Music*, 46.

200 "The sound recording": McWilliams, *The Preservation and Restoration of Sound Recordings*, 23.

200 "machine ensemble": Suisman, *Selling Sounds*, 95.

200 "When we wake up and cruise into our studios": Stephen St. Croix, *Mix*, February 1999, 249.

200 electromigration; parameter drift; transient electrical stresses: See, for instance, Phil Koopman, "Why Things Break."

200 new media is even shorter-lived than its predecessors: Bollacker, "Avoiding a Digital Dark Age," 1.

201 the frying pan noise of the 78: Millard, *America on Record*, 203.

201 digital error correction can actually make: Stephen St. Croix, *Mix*, January 1999, 20.

201 the National Academy of Recording Arts and Sciences: See National Academy of Recording Arts and Sciences, "Recommendation for Delivery of Recorded Music Projects."

201 "no medium has proved stable enough": See Brylawski, "Preservation of Digitally Recorded Sound."

201 "entire digital life was destroyed": Honan, "How Apple and Amazon Security Flaws Led to My Epic Hacking."

203 disc drives have become optional on some brands: Zibreg, "Apple killed the disc drive, but it's for your own good."

203 Bollacker tells about the NASA archivist: Bollacker, "Avoiding a Digital Dark Age," 4.

204 "The political economy of the recording industry": Symes, *Setting the Record Straight*, 9.

205 "intelligibility"; "quality of tone": Thompson, "Machines, Music, and the Quest for Fidelity," 135 and passim.

205 "The manufacturers of talking machines": Millard, *America on Record*, 202.

205 "As we fumbled with wraps and gloves": National Phonograph Company, *The Phonograph and How to Use It*, 135–36.

206 "A Man's Voice, Anyhow"; "the phonograph's power": Kenney, *Recorded Music in American Life*, 55.

207 "tone tests": Thompson, "Machines, Music, and the Quest for Fidelity," 132.

207 "The purpose of this hearing": Ibid., 151.

207 "admirers of Edison's tinfoil phonograph": Copeland, *Sound Recordings,* 71.
207 "the common ear of the day really was gulled": Eisenberg, *The Recording Angel,* 111.
208 "a strip of paper travels": Quoted in Welch and Burt, *From Tinfoil to Stereo,* 9.
208 "The sound was lifted clear of the machine": Quoted in Thompson, "Machines, Music, and the Quest for Fidelity," 144.
208 "fascination": Chanan, *Repeated Takes,* 41.
208 Thompson points to the similarity: Thompson, "Machines, Music, and the Quest for Fidelity," 162.
208 some of the ads played with this paradox quite openly: See for instance "Memorex VHS Tapes Ad from 1982—Is It Live or Is It Memorex?," YouTube, http://www.youtube.com/watch?v=EZyFcJcZiaU.

6. DOTS ON A PAGE

210 "Unless sounds are held": Isidore of Seville quoted in Weiss and Taruskin, *Music in the Western World,* 34.
210 "Though the distance between": François Couperin quoted in Dart, *The Interpretation of Music,* 79.
210 "The text of music is a performance": Carolyn Abbate quoted in Taruskin, *The Danger of Music and Other Anti-Utopian Essays,* 32–33.
211 "Gutenberg Galaxy"; "spectrum of effects"; "just a convulsive": McKenna, "Riding Range with Marshall MacLuhan" and "Marshal MacLuhan: Shamans Among the Machines."
211–212 "drastic"; "ephemeral"; "phenomenal"; "ineffable": Abbate, "Music—Drastic or Gnostic?," 510.
212 "The authority of the score": Chanan, *Musica Practica,* 72.
212 *Texttreue:* Edberg, referencing Bruce Ellis Benson, in "Why Classical Musicians Don't Improvise, Part III: Textualism."
212 "sacralization": Horowitz, *Classical Music in America,* 251.
212 "textualism": Edberg, "Why Classical Musicians Don't Improvise, Part III: Textualism."
213 "the despair of every organist": Schweitzer, *J. S. Bach,* 1:308.
213 "ideal of self-effacing textual fidelity": Horowitz, *Classical Music in America,* 277.
213 "must produce what the printed score directs that he produce": Ibid., 408.
213 composer-conductor Felix Weingartner and pianist Artur Schnabel: Botstein, *Tanner Lectures.*
213 "the musical score, and not the performance": Nelson Goodman paraphrased in Gioia, *The Imperfect Art,* 103.
213 "You've got how it has to be in front of you": Sviatoslav Richter quoted in Auerbach, "Sviatoslav Richter: Musical Strict Constructionist."
213 "the composer and his score *have* to be respected": Gunther Schuller quoted in Taruskin, *The Danger of Music and Other Anti-Utopian Essays,* 462.
214 "post-literate"; "the extinction of a musical medium": Halle, "Meditations on a Post-Literate Musical Future."
214 "piously": Levin, "Performing Mozart's Keyboard Music," 5.

214 "beer and hugs": Wakin, "Rockers Playing for Beer: Fair Play?"

214 Palmer's peer Beck Hansen: Beck's sheet music can be found at http://www
.songreader.net/.

215 "In the last analysis": Russell, *ABC of Relativity*, 143.

216 "there is no such thing": Walter Emery quoted in Brett, "Text, Context, and
the Early Music Editor," 90.

217 Nineteenth-century domestic pianists: Cavicchi, *Listening and Longing*,
89–90.

217 "ideal beauty": Schweitzer, *J. S. Bach*, 1:308.

218 "One should not": Ludwig van Beethoven quoted in Guerrieri, *The First Four
Notes*, 9.

218 Cees Nieuwenhuizen's 2012 "reconstruction": Nieuwenhuizen called the
piece "Fantasia Sonata for piano in D (1791/92)"; see http://ceesnieuwenhui
zen.com/ for more details and for other reconstructions.

218 the type of writing implement or paper: Tyson, *Mozart: Studies of the Autograph Scores*, 22.

218 "asked only to rate the probability": Beyerstein, "How Graphology Fools
People."

219 "I have a gub": *Take the Money and Run*, directed by Woody Allen (ABC
Films, 1969).

220 "scribal errors, 'Freudian slips,' and shorthand elisions": Peter Schillingsburg
quoted in Brett, "Text, Context, and the Early Music Editor," 110.

220 "patent errors": Ibid., 102–3.

220 "rests, accidentals, ties, meter markings, clefs": Nemire, "Errata to scores of
the player piano studies," 294–302.

220 composer's mistaken metronome markings: Somfai, *Béla Bartók*, 254–58.

220 "was quite capable of making mistakes in manuscript": Rosen, *The Frontiers
of Meaning*, 14.

220 "impulsive scrawls and hen scratches": Nachmanovitch, *Free Play*, 27.

220 losing the original score for his opera *Fidelio*: Knight, *Beethoven and the Age
of Revolution*, 90.

220 forced placement of everything from accidentals to articulation marks: For
more on this critique of standard notation software, see http://www.lilypond
.org/essay.html.

221 "One of the tricks is that if you play something": Kenny Barron quoted in
Berliner, *Thinking in Jazz*, 212.

221 "I can adopt the traditional attitude": Nachmanovitch, *Free Play*, 90.

222 "The more he looked at the misprint": Rosen, *The Frontiers of Meaning*, 21.

222 "was mistrustful of a mechanical approach to his method": Brett, "Text, Context, and the Early Music Editor," 103.

222 "famous and controversial A-sharp": Rosen, *The Frontiers of Meaning*, 13.

222 "the note we would expect"; "modernism and the hope of establishing a difficult reading": Ibid., 16.

222 "gross error": Ibid., 22.

223 defended by other musicologists, notably Anatole Leikin: See, for instance,
Leikin's "Repeat with Caution." He also addresses this issue with respect
to Beethoven's *Pathétique* Sonata (Op. 13 in C Minor) in "A Refined Precision."

223 "taste is, after all, a matter of will": Rosen, *Critical Entertainments*, 309.

224 "almost incredible," "the authentic ones": Schweitzer, *J. S. Bach,* 1:336–37.

224 "it is possible that this or that 'original' work of Bach": Ibid., 1:194.

224 "come closest to the modern pianoforte style": Ibid., 1:324.

225 "like shorthand": Haynes, *The End of Early Music,* 4.

226 "preluding": Botstein, *Tanner Lectures.*

226 "living conventions of performance": Chanan, *Musica Practica,* 70.

226 "In repeating the Air": Pier Francesco Tosi quoted in Donington, *Baroque Music,* 95.

226 Such practices: Haynes, *The End of Early Music,* 4.

226 "full of detailed and descriptive instructions": Kostka, *Materials and Techniques of Twentieth-Century Music,* 280.

227 "In the award-giving and commission-granting sectors": Gann, "The Case Against Over-Notation."

227 "seem not infrequently to strike sounds": Quoted in Schuller, *Early Jazz,* 50.

227 "fully subject to the performer's conscious control": Chanan, *Musica Practica,* 77.

228 "To play this motif 840 times in succession": See Whittington, "Serious Immobilities."

228 "notation has been so overburdened with meaning": Samples, "Notation's Last Hurrah?"

228 "in the spirit of Zen Buddhism"; "musical koan": John Cage quoted and paraphrased in Whittington, "Serious Immobilities."

229 *Octet '61 for Jasper Johns:* For more on this piece, see Morrison, "Cornelius Cardew's move from notes to performance notes"; and Kostka, *Materials and Techniques of Twentieth-Century Music,* 284.

229 Martin Bartlett's *Lines from Chuang-Tzu:* Kostka, *Materials and Techniques of Twentieth-Century Music,* 290.

229 "Overtake the others": Ibid., 291.

230 "I can't tell you what a joy": Customer quote taken from John Zechiel's music transcription site, http://www.zechiel.com/transcribe/index.html.

230 *The Real Book* was created: For more extensive discussions of *The Real Book,* see O'Donnell, "The Real Book: A History and Commentary"; and Kernfeld, *The Story of Fake Books.*

231 "Any music, no matter": Bill Dobbins quoted in Argue, "Arranging Ellington: Interview with Bill Dobbins."

231 he is reputed to have transcribed Gregorio Allegri's *Miserere: Classical Net,* "Miserere."

232 "sheets of sound": Gitler, "Trane on the Track."

232 "nobody could transcribe even one Coltrane solo": Lewis Porter, e-mail to author (unpublished).

233 "relative sensitivity to different features of music": Berliner, *Thinking in Jazz,* 508.

233 "the tremendous difficulty in obtaining": Frank Tirro, *Jazz: A History,* 271.

233 Gunther Schuller: Darcy James Argue has recently uncovered other examples of errors in Schuller transcriptions; see, for instance, "Arranging Ellington: The Ellington Effect" and "Misunderstanding in Blue."

233 Tirro's own transcription of Louis Armstrong's solo: Tirro, *Jazz: A History.* Tirro's transcription is found on page 63 in the appendices section.

234   "many sounds"; "every note": Jourdain, *Music, the Brain, and Ecstasy,* 33–35.

234   James Dapogny is revealingly frank: See the introduction to Dapogny's *Ferdinand "Jelly Roll" Morton: The Collected Piano Music.*

235   "relatively weak upper octave doublings": Dapogny, *Ferdinand "Jelly Roll" Morton,* 33.

235   "what I know Morton played": Ibid.

236   "In final (third-less) chords": Storr, *Music and the Mind,* 59.

236   "the final big chord": Rachel, *Infused Knowledge,* "The Barbershop Overtone, and Other Music Stuff," Oiboyz.blogspot.com/2009/04/barbershop -overtone-and-other-music.html.

236   combining alto and tenor saxophone in octaves; "especially if the figure is heavy": Russo, *Composing for the Jazz Orchestra,* 74.

237   "A mystery surrounds the solo that begins": Kernfeld, *What to Listen For in Jazz,* 178–79.

237   "In terms of the human organisim": Lewis Mumford, *Technics and Civilization,* 15.

237   what psychologists call "flow": For more on this concept see Csíkszentmihályi, *Flow.*

238   "interaction between a place": Lefebvre, *Rhythmanalysis,* 15.

238   "measure themselves against one another": Ibid., 8.

239   A variation of this problem: Argue, "Misunderstanding in Blue."

240   When Europe toured France during World War I: Lawn and Hellmer, *Jazz Theory and Practice,* 150.

240   "We always made the first of each pair a little longer": François Couperin quoted in Dart, *The Interpretation of Music,* 80.

240   "like the description of a primary color": Schuller, *Early Jazz,* 6.

240   "there can be many subtle variations of swing": Lawn and Hellmer, *Jazz Theory and Practice,* 154.

240–241   "was much too stiff and machine-like": Ibid.

241   "incomplete or implied chords": Berliner, *Thinking in Jazz,* 510.

241   "square note head": Schuller, *Early Jazz,* 45.

7. DIGITAL WITNESS

245   "We are in the business": Lars Ulrich quoted on RIAA website circa 2001, archived at http://web.archive.org/web/20030409055214/http://www.riaa .org/Artists-Issues-1.cfm.

245   "Being the owner": Scott Thompson, *Kids in the Hall,* episode 318, http:// www.kithfan.org/work/318.html. Skit archived at https://www.youtube.com /watch?v=UXCwgHyAgAw.

246   like 9/11, the digital music: In his documentary *I Need That Record,* for instance, Brendan Toller notes that "After September 11, the Recording Industry Association of America . . . tried to piggyback anti-file-sharing proposals on the Patriot Act, to make it legal to search computers and sabotage systems."

246   "By any measure, it appears": Masnick and Ho, *The Sky Is Rising!,* 5.

247   "to the average music consumer": Stamp, "Kids These Days: Spotify, Radiohead, and the Devaluation of Music."

247   "unsustainable as a means of supporting creative work": Byrne, "The internet will suck all creative content out of the world."

247   "Meet the New Boss, Worse Than the Old Boss?": Available at http://the trichordist.com/2012/04/15/meet-the-new-boss-worse-than-the-old-boss-full-post/.

247   "How Digital Parasites Are Destroying the Culture Business": Levine, *Free Ride.*

248   "quietly believe that they have to keep": Kelly, "Why Pro-Amateurs Are the Future."

248   "Like it or not": Ruen interviewed by Bambury, "Is our addiction to free content killing creativity?"

249   "audiencing": Cavicchi, *Listening and Longing,* 4 (see also the note on this page).

249   "a degree of sovereignty"; "regularly engaged": Ibid., 123.

250   Rebecca Tushnet and others have pointed out: Tehranian, *Infringement Nation,* 52.

251   "he was fortunate to escape": Welch and Burt, *From Tinfoil to Stereo,* 60.

251   the transition from content free-for-all: Walker, *Rebels on the Air,* 35.

251   Petrillo's intentions were good: For more on Petrillo, see Leiter, *The Musicians and Petrillo.*

251   the bans contributed to the demise of the big band: McClellan, *The Later Swing Era,* 41.

252   "Record Ban Blues": *The Complete Dinah Washington on Mercury,* Vol. 1 *(1946–1949).* Also available at https://www.youtube.com/watch?v=qJXvecksZtg.

252   "So You Wanna Be a Rock 'n' Roll Star": Jim McGuinn and Chris Hillman, "So You Wanna Be a Rock 'n' Roll Star," *Younger Than Yesterday* (Columbia, 1967).

252   "The Entertainer": Billy Joel, "The Entertainer," *Streetlife Serenade* (Columbia, 1974).

253   "EMI": Sex Pistols, *Never Mind the Bollocks, Here's the Sex Pistols* (Virgin, 1977).

253   Prince's much-publicized struggle: Heatley, *Where Were You . . . When the Music Played?,* 191.

253   whatever wealth they later produced: See Kotkin, "America's New Oligarchs," for an unflattering look at the point to which big technology companies—the descendants of Napster and MP3.com—have evolved today.

253   however venal their: See Knopper, for instance, on John Fanning, 124–26 passim.

254   completely innocent and, in at least one case: Bylund, "RIAA sues computerless family, 234 others, for file sharing."

254   "it is generally not a legal excuse": Boyle, *The Public Domain,* 12.

254   "the 'entire campaign' to sue customers": Bangeman, "RIAA anti-P2P campaign a real money pit, according to testimony."

254   " 'spoofs' ": Mason, *The Pirate's Dilemma,* 68–69.

254   "F**k The Filesharing Websites": *Mostly music,* January 28, 2012, http://ronanguil.blogspot.com/2012/01/fk-filesharing-websites-and-their.html.

254 "The Myth of DIY": Ruen, *Freeloading*, 24–35.
255 "keep the music special": *The Wire*, "STHoldings Labels to Leave Spotify"
255 blogger Tom Clements: Clements, Tom: " 'Fuck Spotify'—a rant in D Minor."
255 "Irrespective of what any court says": Borland, "Judges rule file-sharing software legal."
255 "Technology reveals the active relation of man to nature": Karl Marx quoted in Røyrvik, *The Allure of Capitalism*, 94.
256 One of my favorite examples: Heitlinger, "The Lick."
256 Sim Sadler's "Hard Working George": Archived at https://archive.org/details /hardwork.
257 "People cop licks all the time": Heitlinger, "The Lick."
258 a practice engaged in by underground radio DJs: Walker, *Rebels on the Air*, 8.
258 "obscures": Marx and Sylvester. "Theoretically Unpublished Piece About Girl Talk," 147.
259 "Get a license or do not sample": Sixth Circuit Court of Appeals, *Bridgeport Music, Inc. v. Dimension Films*, 410 F.3d 792 (6th Cir. 2005), http://www .ca6.uscourts.gov/opinions.pdf/05a0243a-06.pdf.
259 The band Men at Work: Tehranian, *Infringement Nation*, 75.
259 Miles Davis played: I am grateful to John von der Heide for suggesting this example. The recording can be found on the Miles Davis album *The Legendary Prestige Quintet Sessions* (Concord, 2006).
259 at the very least, at the level of the bit: Boon, *In Praise of Copying*, 199.
260 "Immature poets imitate": Eliot, "From Philip Massinger," 153.
260 Men at Work were sued for their use of "Kookaburra": Tehranian, *Infringement Nation*, 75.
261 "manipulations which take the sounds": Cutler, "Plunderphonia," 155.
262 "not by how much copyrightable expression": Columbia Law School and USC Gould School of Law, "Grand Upright v. Warner 780 F. Supp. 182 (S.D.N.Y. 1991)."
262 "they should be excused because others": Ibid.
262 through the encouragement of his manager: See "Gilbert O'Sullivan," http:// www.classicbands.com/osullivan.html, and also Harrison, *Music: The Business*, 25.
263 "The universality of appropriation": Boon, *In Praise of Copying*, 209.
263 "It is striking how often musicians condemn": Boyle, *The Public Domain*, 130.
263 "Brown's 'Funky Drummer' ": Nottingham, "The Ten Most Sampled Songs in Hip Hop."
263 "process of borrowing from gospel standards": Boyle, *The Public Domain*, 130.
263 "Great artists steal, but not from me": Ferguson, "Embrace the remix."
264 "every song I've ever written": Springsteen, "SXSW Keynote Address, 2012."
264 "Smells Like Teen Spirit": Tehranian, *Infringement Nation*, 45–46. It should be noted that though Tehranian claims Kurt Cobain got the title of this song from Pynchon, it actually came from Kathleen Hanna, who once spray-painted the phrase "Kurt smells like Teen Spirit" on Cobain's wall. (Of course, it is possible that Hanna was also inspired by Pynchon.) See Tom Breihan, "Kathleen Hanna Covers, Explains Nirvana's 'Smells Like Teen Spirit,' " *Pitchfork*,

December 17, 2010, http://pitchfork.com/news/41059-video-kathleen-hanna -covers-explains-nirvanas-smells-like-teen-spirit/.

264   Levine's critique of Lessig: Levine, *Free Ride*, 89–91.

264   "Nothing today, likely nothing since we tamed fire": Alex Kozinski, *Vanna White v. Samsung Electronics America, Inc.*, 989 F.2d 1512 (9th Cir., 1993), archived at https://www2.bc.edu/~yen/Torts/Vanna%20White%20 Koz%20ed.pdf.

264   "If you were successful": C-SPAN, "President Obama Campaign Rally in Roanoke," July 13, 2012, http://www.c-spanvideo.org/program/307056-2.

265   "No man is an island": John Donne, "Meditation 17" (1624).

265   "To say that Steve Jobs": Blake, "Obama's 'You didn't build that' problem."

265   A photoshopped image: Viewable at http://didntbuildthat.tumblr.com/post /30895935136.

266   "the artist creates the music"; "embraced, honored, banned": This RIAA PR text is archived at http://web.archive.org/web/20020205125701/http://riaa .org/Artists-Voices-1.cfm.

266   "there's something profound here": Flatow, "Michael and the Power of Music."

267   "With THAT VOICE": Flatow, "Whitney Soars in Our Hearts."

267   One could choose, almost at random: See Vicki Anderson's "Yawn, Another Brick Wall" for an extended complaint against this aesthetic as manifested in the stereotypical band-against-a-brick-wall publicity shot, at www.stuff .co.nz/the-press/opinion/blogs/rock-and-roll-mother/7490552/Yawn-another -brick-wall.

267   "Music moves us": RIAA PR text.

267   "no one drops": RIAA PR text.

267   "access to millions of songs": www.spotify.com/us/.

268   "compendium that's become": Greil Marcus, ed., *Best Music Writing 2009* (New York: Da Capo, 2009).

268   "Copyright laws": Jeff Cameron quoted in RIAA, "Recording Industry Sues Napster for Copyright Infringement."

268   "eight-beat symmetrical treble melody": Adorno, *Essays on Music*, 294.

269   "How would the great musical traditions": Boyle, *The Public Domain*, 124.

269   "tax on literacy" arguments: Ibid., 36.

269   "copyright as a human right": "Presentation: Robert Levine."

270   "labor-desert" theory: See Tehranian, *Infringement Nation*, 54.

270   "and the *Work*": John Locke quoted in ibid., 18.

270   the Statute of Anne: See Tehranian, *Infringement Nation*, 17–19.

270   "accretive to progress in the arts": Ibid., 16.

270   "promote the progress of Science and useful Arts": Quoted in ibid., 19.

271   "permission culture": Lessig, *Free Culture*, xiv.

271   what used to be called "selling out": Chris Robley, "Stop Trashing Millenials; They Like Music More Than You Ever Did," May 21, 2014; diymusician /cdbaby.com/2014/05/stop-trashing-millenials-like-music-ever-2/.

272   "progress trap": Wright, *A Short History of Progress*, 30.

272   "If you sell fifty": Knopper, *Appetite for Self-Destruction*, 57.

272   "a zero sum": Patry, *How to Fix Copyright*, 88.

272   "frustration with having to sell": quoted in Ruen, *Freeloading*, 141.

272   an influential white paper: Boyle, *The Public Domain*, 55–56.

273 "not brought about the worst": Ibid., 119.

274 "The Next Great Copyright Act": "Fixing Copyright? The 2013–2014 Copyright Review Process," Electronic Frontier Foundation, www.eff.org /issues/2013-copyright-review-process.

274 "The public interest doesn't appear": quoted in Holpuch, Amanda: "US music copyright: 'It's basically just a bunch of people fighting over money.' "

274 "Musicians and labels at the top of their game": quoted in Ruen, *Freeloading*, 103.

274 "Somewhere along the line": Tim Wu quoted at *Infringement Nation* (website), http://infringementnation.com/reviews/.

274 "dramatically altered our default regime": Tehranian, *Infringement Nation*, xix–xx.

275 "virtually the entire universe of creative works": Ibid., xx.

275 In 1996, for instance, the American Society of Composers: Bannon, "The Birds May Sing, but Campers Can't Unless They Pay Up."

275 Similar fees were soon foisted: Holt, "Play it again . . . and we'll sue."

276 In a confrontation with a restaurant in North Carolina: Jansen, "License to Kill the Music: ASCAP and BMI Bullying Local Music Venues."

276 More recently, BMI: *Northwest Music Scene*, "BMI Sues Bar Owner for 1.5 Million for Allowing Cover Tunes."

276 the United Kingdom's Performing Rights Society sued a car mechanic company: Tehranian, *Infringement Nation*, xxi.

276 "routinely use": BBC News, "Kwik-fit sued over staff radios." (Note that "Performing Rights Society" is the name of the PRO.)

276 "using over-the-top, heavy-handed policing tactics": Jansen, "License to Kill the Music."

276 The CTEA may not: Patry, *How to Fix Copyright*, 57.William Patry puts the copyright term problem succinctly when he asks:

> Was there a single author in the entire world who said, "A term of copyright that only lasts for my life plus fifty years after I die is too short. I will not create a new work unless copyright is extended to last for my life plus seventy years"?

The answer, if we are being honest, is no.

276 a few of its advocates: Rimmer, *Digital Copyright and the Consumer Revolution*, 24. Mary Bono, Sonny Bono's widow, noted that "Sonny wanted the term of copyright protection to last forever. I am informed by staff that such a change would violate the Constitution. . . . There is also Jack Valenti's proposal for term to last forever less one day. Perhaps the Committee may look at that next Congress."

276 taking works *out* of the public domain: Liptak, "Public Domain Works Can Be Copyrighted Anew, Supreme Court Rules."

277 "traditional safety valves" of copyright: Kranich, *The Information Commons*.

277 "when the value to society": Aufderheide and Jaszi, "Recut, Reframe, Recycle," 20.

277 "within the specific cultural practice": Ibid.

277 "The distinction between what is fair use": U.S. Copyright Office, "Copyright: Fair Use," http://www.copyright.gov/fls/fl102.html.

278 As William Patry points out: Patry, *How to Fix Copyright,* see chapter 10.

278 "the old standby": Sherman, "Perspective: Honest Talk About Downloads."

278 "fair use creep": Parker Higgins, "'Fair Use Creep,' and Other Copyright Bogeymen, Appear in Congress," July 25, 2013, www.eff.org/deep links/2013/07/fair-use-creep-and-other-copyright-bogeymen-appear-congress.

278 exemplified recently by a problematic: Eriq Gardner, "See the Lawsuit Claiming Led Zeppelin Stole 'Stairway to Heaven,'" June 2, 2014, www.billboard .com/biz/articles/news/legal-and-management/6106423/see-the-lawsuit -claiming-led-zeppelin-stole-stairway.

278 "all art," as Glenn Gould put it: Quoted in Elie, *Reinventing Bach,* 269.

279 "to help this vibrant culture spread": Hype Machine, http://hypem.com /about.

279 perhaps an oblique recognition: Allen, "The Rise and Fall of the Obscure Music Download Blog."

279 "we fucking love music is a blog about awesome music": See http://wefucking lovemusic.blogspot.com.

280 all of which happened recently to the blog Dajaz1.com: Lee, "Waiting on the RIAA, feds held seized Dajaz1 domain for months."

280 Today, professional educators know: See McSweeney, "Music, MOOCs, and Copyright."

280 "we could not play or post": John Covach: "To MOOC or Not To MOOC?" www.mtosmt.org/issues/mto.13.19.3/mto.13.19.3.covach.php#FN12.

280 "there is no case law": Quoted in McSweeney, "Music, MOOCs, and Copyright."

281 Ted Gioia made a similar point: www.facebook.com/tedgioia/posts/10152125 413256546.

281 "Nobody has ever learned to play jazz from a book only": Levine, *The Jazz Piano Book,* vi.

281 "celestial jukebox": Taylor Hatmaker: "Get Ready for the Streaming-Music Die-Off." December 6, 2013, Readwrite.com.

281 a song that isn't on Spotify: See, for instance, the helpful tumblr: Greatmusic notonspotify.tumblr.com.

281 "Who the fuck is Paul McCartney?": Stopera, "Who Is Paul McCartney?!"

282 "It wasn't a rip off": Lennon quoted in Patry, *How to Fix Copyright,* 96.

282 "You can't separate streaming": Ruen interviewed by Bambury, "Is our addiction to free content killing creativity?"

282 a brief unhappy phase: We should at least cite a recent study that indicates "300 Million Users Swap Files Via BitTorrent Every Month," compared with Spotify's "over 10 million" paid subscribers and "over 40 million" active users. Janko Roettgers, "File Sharing Is Alive and Well, to the Tune of 300 Million Users a Month," May 28, 2014, Gigaom.com/2014/05/28/file-sharing -is-alive-and-well-to-the-tune-of-300-million-users-a-month/.

282 "If someone in a low-income community": Towns, "Piracy hurts everyone both online and offline."

283 "That'll Be the Day": SWNS.com, "First ever Beatles record that original bandmate sold for £12k now the most valuable in the world at almost £1/4m."

283 a recent theft of unreleased tracks from Lady Gaga: Dahlkamp, "Star Wars: Lady Gaga, Ke$ha and the German Hacker Heist."

284 And as digital files: And yet apparently such sales do happen. See for instance, Ernesto, on *TorrentFreak*, "Record Labels: Used MP3s Too Good and Convenient to Resell." April 22, 2014, www.torrentfreak.com/record-labels-used-mp3s-too-good-and-convenient-to-resell-140422/.

284 "passion of my soul"; "extreme deprivation": Wilson, *Thomas Jefferson*, xiii.

285 "All my jazz records were stolen": John Zorn quoted in Duckworth, *Talking Music*, 456.

286 "The love of our little Johann Sebastian": Wolff, *Johann Sebastian Bach*, 45.

286 "My real social life": Zappa, " '50s Teenagers and '50s Rock," 45.

287 "A teenager in a small town": Elie, *Reinventing Bach*, 23.

287 "copyright enforcement is not just a problem": Tehranian, *Infringement Nation*, xxv.

288 Even the recently discovered earliest use of the word "jazz": Zimmer, "How baseball gave us 'jazz.' " But see also the entry for "jazz" in Paul Dickson's *Dickson Baseball Dictionary* (New York: Norton, 2011), 466–67, which suggests (unpersuasively, I think) that the usage should be considered as dating from 1913, not 1912; Dickson notes that in 1913 the word referred more to "pep, energy, fighting spirit, vim, vigor."

289 "the very term 'minstrel' ": Marsh, *Music and Society in Early Modern England*, 23.

289 "high level of tolerance": Small, *Music of the Common Tongue*, 25.

289 "there is a subversive edge to sampling": Philo T. Farnsworth quoted in Kot, *Ripped*, 171.

289 No wonder then that: Ruen's interviews (which are to be found in the section of *Freeloading* called "Ground Clearing") are full of such admissions. Note also his description of his own experience, page 19: "I pirated hundreds of songs during my college years, but I sensed disposability and devaluation affecting my relationship with music. . . . Piracy turned my genuine love for music into just another fidgety online addiction." This, of course, is one person's experience (and it conveniently overlooks other possible explanations for "fidgety online addiction"). In my own case, I never used Napster or its imitators, but came to downloading via music blogs, as a grad student surviving on a meager teaching salary in an expensive city, trying to write a dissertation, and leading an original big band. I found the abundance of free online offerings crucial to my own voracious creativity at the time. My tastes were different than Ruen's: I was a fan of exotica, early roots styles, bootlegs, rare soundtracks, and mashups—music often unavailable through record labels anyway. Most of the blogs I frequented in this period (the early-to-mid-aughts) have since gone defunct.

290 given how little: Which begs a question not often raised in these debates: the extent to which musicians' economic struggles in the twenty-first century have to do with factors beyond piracy—such as the 2008 recession and its aftereffects, or increasing competition from a hyperabundance of entertainment choices.

290 alternate music economies: see for instance Stuart Dredge, "Bandcamp's Ethan Diamond: 'Fans want to support the artists they love,' " http://musically.com/2014/06/12/bandcamp-fans-artists-music-interview/.

290 "We all have access to a pool of sounds": Paul Simon quoted in Levitin, *The World in Six Songs*, 255.

290   "No one drops from the sky a rock star": RIAA PR text.

290   "music file sharing"; "a society that has been built upon hard work": Keen, *The Cult of the Amateur,* 145.

290   "if piracy is a rebellion": Beeler, quoted in Ruen, *Freeloading,* 90.

291   "the view on the traditional side": Anthony Berman quoted in Franzen, *Copyright Criminals.*

291   "an extraordinarily lazy artistic choice": Steve Albini quoted in ibid.

291   "any kid with a hundred bucks": *Gig,* January 2001, 6 (Letters to the Editor).

291   A recent article: Chris Martins, "A Quarter of Spotify Songs Are Skipped in First Five Seconds," *SPIN,* May 6, 2014.

292   Copying, in fact: For more on this idea, see Patry, *How to Fix Copyright,* 90–99.

292   "memorizing and emulating"; "Handel, Bach, and their contemporaries": Wolff, *Johann Sebastian Bach,* 48.

292   "the major shifts in Bach's collecting interests": See George B. Stauffer's review of Kirsten Beisswenger's "Johann Sebastian Bachs Notenbibliothek," *The Free Library,* http://www.thefreelibrary.com/Johann+Sebastian+Bachs+Notenbibliothek.-a016087890.

292   "People desire or decide to become musicologists": Kerman, *Contemplating Music,* 29.

293   "perception-production link": Levitin, *The World in Six Songs,* 266–67.

294   Stefan Kostka: Kostka, *Materials and Techniques of Twentieth-Century Music,* xv.

294   "Many of the albums listed": Levine, *The Jazz Piano Book,* 275.

294   "on a different day": Carey, "Sixty Postwar Pieces to Study."

294   Embracing musical profusion [. . .] can be expensive: For a discussion of the historical relationship between copyright and financial barriers to the creation of a reading public, see Patry, *How to Fix Copyright,* 84–85.

294   On the other hand, it's much more than the $64: Jordan Weissmann, "Spotify Is Growing Like Gangbusters. Is It Doomed Anyway?" *Slate,* May 21, 2014.

295   "I don't want to sell my music": Captain Beefheart (Don Van Vliet) quoted in Fong-Torres, ed., *The Rolling Stone Rock 'n' Roll Reader,* 110.

295   "production is a precondition of access": Taylor, *The People's Platform,* 177.

295   "we always felt like, you know, when you're creating": Hank Shocklee quoted in Franzen, *Copyright Criminals.*

296   "The child we were and are": Nachmanovitch, *Free Play,* 116–17.

296   "amazing musical environment": Sidran, *Talking Jazz,* 127.

296   "was always dropping by the house": Don Sickler quoted in Berliner, *Thinking in Jazz,* 38.

296   "cooperative record-sharing 'extended families' ": William Howland Kennedy, *Recorded Music in American Life,* 21.

297   "When it was quiet": Lenny Kaye in Toller, *I Need That Record!*

297   "That neighborhood certainly had a lot to offer": Armstrong, *Satchmo,* 23.

297   "started to listen carefully": Ibid., 24.

297   "Not only were most members of the bands": Isoardi, liner notes, *Central Avenue Sounds,* 17.

297   "could be hailed as he crossed": Isoardi, *Central Avenue Sounds,* 17.

298   "What people don't realize": danah boyd (the lowercase spelling is correct),

interview on *Science Friday,* February 28, 2014, http://www.sciencefriday
.com/guests/danah-boyd.html#.

299 Of course that also means thinking: For organizations thinking productively
about how to move forward in the new landscape, see the Content Creators
Coalition, http://contentcreatorscoalition.org, or the Future of Music Coalition, http://futureofmusic.org.

299 Jaron Lanier, for instance: See Lanier's *Who Owns the Future?*

299 Astra Taylor offers a number of more persuasive: See Taylor's *The People's
Platform,* especially her concluding chapter.

299 "comprehensive review": For more on this, see "Chairman Goodlattee
Announces Comprehensive Review of Copyright Law," U.S. House of Rep-
resentatives Judiciary Committee, April 24, 2013, http://judiciary.house.gov
/index.cfm/2013/4/chairmangoodlatteannouncescomprehensivereviewofcopy
rightlaw.

AFTERWORD: THE BENEFITS OF AESTHETIC CONFUSION

301 "Online activists present the choice": Levine, *Free Ride,* 240.

301 "The most precious thing in life is its uncertainty": Kenkō quoted in Varley,
Japanese Culture, 110.

301 "A man who is born": Joseph Conrad, *Lord Jim* (New York: McClure, Phil-
lips & Company, 1905), 199.

302 "clarity is overrated": Tenner, "Clarity Is Overrated: Could Opacity Be the
New Transparency?"

302 It is why we make: Leung, "Prodigy, 12, Compared to Mozart."

302 "remained unchanged in my estimation": Ferruccio Busoni, letter to his wife,
quoted in Horowitz, "Mozart as Midcult," 3.

302 "ugly beauty": Thelonious Monk, "Ugly Beauty," *Underground* (Columbia
Records, 1968).

WORKS CITED

Abbate, Carolyn. "Music—Drastic or Gnostic?" *Critical Inquiry* 30 (Spring 2004).

Aczel, Peter. "The Ten Biggest Lies in Audio." *The Audio Critic*, no. 26 (2000).

Adler, David R. "Fern bar." *Lerterland*, June 10, 2009. http://blog.adlermusic.com/2009/06/fern-bar.html.

———. "Of big bands, critics' priorities, etc." *Lerterland*, January 19, 2010. http://blog.adlermusic.com/2010/01/of-big-bands-critics-priorities-etc.html.

Adorno, Theodor. *Essays on Music*. Selected, with introduction, commentary, and notes by Richard Leppert; new translations by Susan H. Gillespie. Berkeley: University of California Press, 2002.

Albers, Josef. *The Interaction of Color*. New Haven, CT: Yale University Press, 2006.

Allen, Mark. "The Rise and Fall of the Obscure Music Download Blog: A Roundtable." *The Awl*, November 27, 2012. http://www.theawl.com/2012/11/the-rise-and-fall-of-obscure-music-blogs-a-roundtable.

Amirkhanian, Charles. Liner notes, *Conlon Nancarrow: Studies for Player Piano*. Wergo, 2000.

Ankeny, Jason. "Gilbert O'Sullivan." *AllMusic*. http://www.allmusic.com/artist/gilbert-osullivan-mn0000546735.

Antczak, John. "'Pact with the Devil': Milli Vanilli Duo Say They Were Seduced by Money." *Los Angeles Times*, November 20, 1990. http://articles.latimes.com/1990-11-20/entertainment/ca-5210_1_milli-vanilli.

Argue, Darcy James. "Arranging Ellington: The Ellington Effect." *Musical Exchange*, October 25, 2013. http://musicalexchange.carnegiehall.org/profiles/blogs/arranging-ellington-the-ellington-effect.

———. "Arranging Ellington: Interview with Bill Dobbins." *Musical Exchange*, December 14, 2013. http://musicalexchange.carnegiehall.org/profiles/blogs/arranging-ellington-interview-with-bill-dobbins.

———. "Dispatches from the End of the Jazz Wars." *NewMusicBox*, July 16, 2008. http://www.newmusicbox.org/articles/Dispatches-From-the-End-of-the-Jazz-Wars/.

———. "Irony, Man." *Darcy James Argue's Secret Society*, September 20, 2007. http://www.secretsocietymusic.org/darcy_james_argues_secret/2007/09/irony-man.html.

———. "Misunderstanding in Blue." *Do the Math*, March 21, 2014. http://dothemath.typepad.com/dtm/misunderstanding-in-blue-by-darcy-james-argue.html.

Armstrong, Louis. *Satchmo: My Life in New Orleans*. New York: Da Capo, 1986.

Asimov, Isaac. "The Relativity of Wrong." *Skeptical Inquirer* 14, no. 1 (Fall 1989): 35–44. Archived at http://chem.tufts.edu/answersinscience/relativityofwrong.htm.

Auerbach, David. "Sviatoslav Richter: Musical Strict Constructionist." *Waggish,* March 30, 2007. http://www.waggish.org/2007/sviatoslav-richter-musical-strict -constructionist/.

Aufderheide, Patricia, and Peter Jaszi. "Recut, Reframe, Recycle: The Shaping of Fair Use Best Practices for Online Video." *I/S: A Journal of Law and Policy for the Information Society* 6, no. 1 (Winter 2010). Archived at http://moritzlaw .osu.edu/students/groups/is/files/2012/02/Aufderheide.pdf.

Bangeman, Eric. "RIAA anti-P2P campaign a real money pit, according to testimony." *Ars Technica,* October 2, 2007. http://arstechnica.com/tech-policy/2007 /10/music-industry-exec-p2p-litigation-is-a-money-pit/.

Bannon, Lisa. "The Birds May Sing, but Campers Can't Unless They Pay Up." *Wall Street Journal,* August 23, 1996. Available at http://www.southcoasttoday.com /apps/pbcs.dll/article?AID=/19960823/LIFE/308239949.

Baraka, Amiri: "Jazz Criticism and Its Effect on the Music." In *Digging: The Afro-American Soul of American Classical Music.* Berkeley: University of California Press, 2009.

Barron, James. *Piano: The Making of a Steinway Concert Grand.* New York: Times Books, 2006.

Barton, Chris. "Jazz War, Anyone?" *Pop & Hiss: The LA Times Music Blog,* March 21, 2010. http://latimesblogs.latimes.com/music_blog/2010/05/jazz-wars-jason -marsalis-v-jazz-nerds-international.html.

BBC. "Kwik-fit sued over staff radios." October 5, 2007. http://news.bbc.co.uk/2 /hi/uk_news/scotland/edinburgh_and_east/7029892.stm.

Beadon, Leigh. "Bruce Springsteen, Another Pirate Remixer!" *Techdirt,* March 16, 2012. http://www.techdirt.com/articles/20120316/08413818131/bruce-spring steen-another-pirate-remixer.shtml.

Beatles, the. *The Beatles Anthology* [book]. San Francisco: Chronicle Books, 2000.

Beethoven, Ludwig van. *Beethoven's Letters.* Translated by J. S. Shedlock. New York: Dover, 1972.

Behrens, Jack. *Big Bands and Great Ballrooms: America Is Dancing . . . Again.* Bloomington, IN: AuthorHouse, 2006.

Belton, John. "Technology and Aesthetics of Film Sound." In *Film Sound: Theory and Practice,* edited by Elisabeth Weiss and John Belton. New York: Columbia University Press, 1985.

Bendersky, Joseph W. *A History of Nazi Germany.* 2nd ed. Chicago: Burnham, 2000.

Berkman, Bob. "Tribute to J. Lawrence Cook." *Ragtime—Blues—Hot Piano— J. Lawrence Cook,* 2002. http://www.doctorjazz.co.uk/page11.html.

Berliner, Paul F. *Thinking in Jazz.* Chicago: University of Chicago Press, 1994.

Bernstein, Sharon. "Martha Wash Gets Her Form Back." *Los Angeles Times,* December 14, 1990. http://articles.latimes.com/1990-12-14/entertainment/ca -6706_1_black-box-videos.

Beyerstein, Barry. "How Graphology Fools People." *Quackwatch.* http://www .quackwatch.org/01QuackeryRelatedTopics/Tests/grapho.html.

Bilton, Lynn. "Who put the ola in Victrola?" September 2005. http://www.inter tique.com/WhoPutTheOla.htm.

Blacking, John. *How Musical Is Man?* Seattle: University of Washington Press, 1973.

Blake, Aaron. "Obama's 'You didn't build that' problem." *Washington Post,* July 18, 2012. http://www.washingtonpost.com/blogs/the-fix/post/obamas-you-didnt -build-that-problem/2012/07/18/gJQAJxyotW_blog.html.

Bollacker, Kurt. "Avoiding a Digital Dark Age." *American Scientist,* March– April 2010. http://www.americanscientist.org/issues/pub/2010/2/avoiding-a-dig ital-dark-age.

Boon, Marcus. *In Praise of Copying.* Cambridge, MA: Harvard University Press, 2010.

Border, Terry. "I'm just writing this to get it out of my system." *Bent Objects,* January 27, 2012. http://bentobjects.blogspot.com/2012/01/im-just-writing-this-to -get-it-out-of.html?utm_source=feedburner&utm_medium=feed&utm_cam paign=Feed%3A+BentObjects+%28Bent+Objects%29.

Borges, Jorge Luis. *The Total Library.* New York: Penguin, 2007.

Borland, John. "Judges Rule File-Sharing Software Legal." *CNET,* August 19, 2004. http://news.cnet.com/2100-1032_3-5316570.html.

Botstein, Leon. *Tanner Lectures.* http://grad.berkeley.edu/tanner/1011.shtml.

Bouton, Katherine. *Shouting Won't Help: Why I—and 50 Million Other Americans—Can't Hear You.* New York: Farrar, Straus & Giroux, 2013.

Boyle, James. *The Public Domain: Enclosing the Commons of the Mind.* New Haven, CT: Yale University Press, 2008.

Branca, Glenn. "The Score: The End of Music." *New York Times,* November 24, 2009. http://opinionator.blogs.nytimes.com/2009/11/24/the-end-of-music/.

Braue, David. "iTunes: Just how random is random?" *CNET,* March 8, 2007. http://www.cnet.com.au/itunes-just-how-random-is-random-339274094.htm.

Brett, Philip. "Text, Context, and the Early Music Editor." In *Authenticity and Early Music,* edited by Nicholas Kenyon. New York: Oxford University Press, 1988.

Brown, Howard Mayer. "Pedantry or Liberation? A Sketch of the Historical Performance Movement." In *Authenticity and Early Music,* edited by Nicholas Kenyon. New York: Oxford University Press, 1988.

Brylawski, Samuel. "Preservation of Digitally Recorded Sound." In *Building a National Strategy for Digital Preservation: Issues in Digital Media Archiving.* Washington, DC: Council on Library and Information Resources and Library of Congress, April 2002. http://www.clir.org/pubs/reports/pub106/pub106.pdf.

Bullough, Miles. "Ornette Coleman and the Battle of the Five Spot." *In 1959,* November 21, 2009. http://in1959.blogspot.com/2009/11/ornette-coleman-and -battle-of-five-spot.html.

Burnham, Scott. *Beethoven Hero.* Princeton, NJ: Princeton University Press, 2000.

Burns, Ken. "Ken Burns on the Making of *Jazz.*" PBS. http://www.pbs.org/jazz /about/about_behind_the_scenes.htm.

Burns, R. W. *The Life and Times of A D Blumlein.* Stevenage, UK: IET, 2000.

Bylund, Anders. "RIAA sues computer-less family, 234 others, for file sharing." *Ars Technica,* April 24, 2006. http://arstechnica.com/uncategorized/2006/04 /6662-2/.

Byrne, David. "The internet will suck all creative content out of the world." *Guardian,* October 11, 2013. http://www.theguardian.com/music/2013/oct/11/david -byrne-internet-content-world.

Cage, John. *Silence: Lectures and Writings.* Middletown, CT: Wesleyan University Press, 1961.

Cannon, Bob. "The Who's Nightmare Concert." *Entertainment Weekly,* December 4, 1992. http://www.ew.com/ew/article/0,312557,00.html.

Capo, Fran, and Frank Borzellieri. *It Happened in New York.* Guilford, CT: Globe Pequot Press, 2006.

Carey, Christian. "Sixty Postwar Pieces to Study." *File Under?,* March 20, 2012. http://www.sequenza21.com/carey/2012/03/sixty-postwar-pieces-to-study/.

Carlsen, Philip. *The Player-Piano Music of Conlon Nancarrow: An Analysis of Selected Studies.* Institute for Studies in American Music, Conservatory of Music, Brooklyn College of the City University of New York, 1988.

Carr, Nicholas. "Digital Decay and the Archival Cloud." *Rough Type,* April 5, 2010. http://www.roughtype.com/?p=1355.

Carroll, Michael. "A Simulation of the Tuning Meditation." http://actlab.us/actlab /mcarroll/tuning.html.

Castoro, Rocco. "Downloading Some Bullshit: An Interview with the President of the RIAA." *Vice,* July 31, 2010. http://www.vice.com/read/downloading-some -bullshit-484-v17n8.

Cavicchi, Daniel. "From the Bottom Up: Thinking About Tia DeNora's *Music in Everyday Life.*" *Action, Criticism, and Theory for Music Education* 1, no. 2 (December 2002). http://act.maydaygroup.org/articles/Cavicchi1_2.pdf.

———. *Listening and Longing: Music Lovers in the Age of Barnum.* Middletown, CT: Wesleyan University Press, 2011.

———. "The Musicality of Listening." http://www.academia.edu/215116/The _Musicality_of_Listening.

———. "Romanticism, the Voice, and the History of Listening." *The Ardent Audience,* December 3, 2011. http://theardentaudience.blogspot.com/2011/12 /romanticism-voice-and-history-of.html.

Center for Media and Social Impact. "Documentary Filmmakers' Statement of Best Practices in Fair Use." November 2005. http://www.cmsimpact.org/fair-use/ best-practices/documentary/documentary-filmmakers-statement-best-practices -fair-use.

Certeau, Michel de. *The Practice of Everyday Life.* Berkeley and Los Angeles: University of California Press, 2011.

Chanan, Michael. *Musica Practica: The Social Practice of Western Music from Gregorian Chant to Postmodernism.* London: Verso, 1994.

———. *Repeated Takes: A Short History of Recording and Its Effect on Music.* London: Verso, 1995.

Chorost, Michael. *Rebuilt: How Becoming Part Computer Made Me More Human.* New York: Houghton Mifflin, 2005.

Chusid, Irwin. Liner notes, *The Music of Raymond Scott / Reckless Nights and Turkish Twilights.* Sony, 1992.

Classical Net. "Miserere." http://www.classical.net/music/comp.lst/works/allegri /miserere.php.

Clements, Tom. " 'Fuck Spotify'—a rant in D Minor." Blog post. November 24, 2011. http://tom-clements.com/blog/2011/11/24/fuck-spotify-a-rant-in-d-minor/.

Cohen, Ben. "Life Sans Music." *Vice,* July 31, 2010. http://www.vice.com/read /life-sans-music-495-v17n8.

Cohen, Harvey G. *Duke Ellington's America.* Chicago: University of Chicago Press, 2010.

Coldwell, Maria V. "What is early music?" *Early Music America.* http://www.early music.org/what-early-music.

Collier, James Lincoln. *Duke Ellington.* New York: Oxford University Press, 1987.

Columbia Law School and USC Gould School of Law. "Grand Upright v. Warner 780 F. Supp. 182 (S.D.N.Y. 1991)." *Music Copyright Infringement Resource.* http://mcir.usc.edu/cases/1990-1999/Pages/granduprightwarner.html.

Comini, Alessandra. *The Changing Image of Beethoven: A Study in Mythmaking.* New York: Rizzoli International, 1987.

Confrey, Zez. *Ragtime, Novelty & Jazz Piano Solos.* Edited by Ronny S. Schiff, with an introduction by David A. Jasen. New York: Alfred Publishing, 1985.

Connor, Steven. *Dumbstruck: A Cultural History of Ventriloquism.* New York: Oxford University Press, 2000.

Cope, David. "Emily Howell." http://artsites.ucsc.edu/faculty/cope/Emily-howell .htm.

———. *Virtual Music: Computer Synthesis of Musical Style.* Cambridge, MA: MIT Press, 2004.

Copeland, Peter. *Sound Recordings.* London: British Library, 1991.

Corbett, John. *Extended Play: Sounding Off from John Cage to Dr. Funkenstein.* Durham, NC: Duke University Press, 1994.

———. Liner notes, Sun Ra, *When Angels Speak of Love.* Evidence, 1963/2000.

Council for Living Music. http://savelivemusiconbroadway.com.

Covach, John. "To MOOC or Not to MOOC?" *Music Theory Online* 19, no. 3 (September 2013). www.mtosmt.org/issues/mto.13.19.3/mto.13.19.3.covach .php.

Cowell, Henry. "Music of and for the Records." In *Essential Cowell: Selected Writings on Music by Henry Cowell, 1921–1964,* edited by Dick Higgins. New York: McPherson, 2002.

Cox, Christoph, and Daniel Warner. "The Beauty of Noise: An Interview with Masami Akita of Merzbow." In *Audio Culture: Readings in Modern Music.* London: Continuum, 2004.

Csíkszentmihályi, Mihály. *Flow: The Psychology of Optimal Experience.* New York: Harper, 2008.

Cushing, Tim. "Restaurant Owner Ordered to Pay BMI $30,450 for 'Illegally Playing' Four Unlicensed Songs." *Techdirt,* August 17, 2011. http://www.techdirt .com/articles/20110815/11503015533/restaurant-owner-ordered-to-pay-bmi -30450-illegally-playing-four-unlicensed-songs.shtml.

Cutler, Chris. "Plunderphonia." In *Audio Culture: Readings in Modern Music,* edited by Christoph Cox and Daniel Warner. London: Continuum, 2004.

Da Fonseca-Wollheim, Corinna. "Keeping the Magic Without the Thunder." *New York Times,* November 30, 2012. http://www.nytimes.com/2012/12/02/arts /music/love-fail-by-david-lang-with-anonymous-4-at-bam.html?_r=0.

Dahlkamp, Jürgen, "Star Wars: Lady Gaga, Ke$ha and the German Hacker Heist." *Spiegel Online,* January 27, 2011. http://www.spiegel.de/international/world /star-wars-lady-gaga-ke-ha-and-the-german-hacker-heist-a-741667.html.

Dance, Stanley. Liner notes, *Ellington at Newport* (reissue). CBS, 1987.

Dapogny, James. *Ferdinand "Jelly Roll" Morton: The Collected Piano Music.* New York: Schirmer, 1986.

Dart, Thurston. *The Interpretation of Music.* New York: Harper & Row, 1963.

Dash, Mike. "Hitler's Very Own Hot Jazz Band." Smithsonian.com, May 17, 2012. http://blogs.smithsonianmag.com/history/hitlers-very-own-hot-jazz-band -98745129/.

Davis, Francis. *Outcats: Jazz Composers, Instrumentalists, and Singers.* New York: Oxford University Press, 1992.

Dawson, Jim. "Deacon's Hop" (liner note blurb). *Central Avenue Sounds.* Rhino, 1999.

Day, Timothy. *A Century of Recorded Music: Listening to Musical History.* New Haven, CT: Yale University Press, 2000.

Debussy, Claude, Charles Ives, and Ferruccio Busoni, *Three Classics in the Aesthetic of Music.* New York: Dover, 1952.

DeCurtis, Anthony, James Henke, and Holly George-Warren, eds. *The Rolling Stone Album Guide.* New York: Random House, 1992.

Dennett, Daniel. "Quining Qualia." In *The Nature of Consciousness: Philosophical Debates,* edited by Ned Block, Owen Flanagan, and Güven Güzeldere. Cambridge, MA: MIT Press, 1997.

DeNora, Tia. *Beethoven and the Construction of Genius: Music and Politics in Vienna, 1792–1803.* Berkeley and Los Angeles: University of California Press, 1997.

Donington, Robert. *Baroque Music: Style and Performance: A Handbook.* New York: Norton, 1982.

Doucleff, Michaeleen. "Anatomy of a Tear-Jerker." *Wall Street Journal,* February 11, 2012. http://online.wsj.com/news/articles/SB100014240529702036460045 77213010291701378.

Duckett, Jodi. "Bach Choir presents lovely pair of works for Christmas concert." *Lehigh Valley Music Blog,* December 9, 2012. http://blogs.mcall.com/lehigh valleymusic/2012/12/bach-choir-presents-lovely-pair-of-works-for-christmas -concert.html.

Duckworth, William. *Talking Music.* New York: Schirmer, 1995.

Dunn, Geoffrey. "Palin No Longer Writing Her Own Script." *Huffington Post,* September 9, 2009. http://www.huffingtonpost.com/geoffrey-dunn/palin-no-longer -writing-h_b_280161.html.

Durkin, Andrew. "A meandering post on collaboration." *Jazz: The Music of Unemployment,* January 30, 2014. http://uglyrug.blogspot.com/2014/01/a -meandering-post-on-collaboration.html.

———. "What passes for scholarship these days: Chapter two, part two." *Jazz: The Music of Unemployment,* December 30, 2009. http://uglyrug.blogspot .com/2009/12/what-passes-for-scholarship-these-days_30.html.

———. "The world we have lost." *Jazz: The Music of Unemployment,* September 15, 2009. http://uglyrug.blogspot.com/2009/09/world-we-have-lost.html.

Dutton, Denis. "Authenticity in Art." In *The Oxford Handbook of Aesthetics,* edited by Jerrold Levinson. New York: Oxford University Press, 2003.

———. "The Joyce Hatto Scandal." *New York Times,* February 25, 2007. Originally published in *International Herald Tribune.* http://www.nytimes .com/2007/02/25/opinion/25iht-edutton.4712389.html?pagewanted=all&_r=0.

Dworsky, David, and Victor Köhler. *PressPausePlay.* http://www.presspauseplay .com/about/.

Ebert, Roger. "The Greatest Films of All Time." *Roger Ebert's Journal,* April 26, 2012. http://www.rogerebert.com/rogers-journal/the-greatest-films-of-all-time.

Edberg, Eric. "Why Classical Musicians Don't Improvise, Part III: Textualism." *Improvisation and the Classical Musician,* April 23, 2006. http://classicalimprov .blogspot.com/2006/04/why-classical-musicians-dont-improvise.html.

Edelman, Edward. "Building a Picture of the Brain." In *The Brain,* edited by Gerald M. Edelman and Jean-Pierre Changeux. New Brunswick, NJ: Transaction, 2001.

Edison, Thomas A. "The Phonograph and Its Future." *North American Review,* May 1, 1878. Archived at https://archive.org/details/jstor-25110210.

Edwards, James M., Jr. "The Piano as Phantom." *Clavier* 23 (July–August 1984): 36–38.

Einstein, Alfred. *Mozart: His Character, His Work.* New York: Oxford University Press, 1962.

Eisenberg, Evan. *The Recording Angel.* New York: McGraw-Hill, 1987.

Ekman, Paul, and Erika L. Rosenberg: *What the Face Reveals: Basic and Applied Studies of Spontaneous Expression Using the Facial Action Coding System (FACS).* New York: Oxford University Press, 2005.

Electronic Frontier Foundation. "Unintended Consequences: Twelve Years Under the DMCA," March 2010. https://www.eff.org/wp/unintended-consequences -under-dmca.

Elie, Paul. *Reinventing Bach.* New York: Farrar, Strauss & Giroux, 2012.

Eliot, T. S. "From Philip Massinger." In *Selected Prose of T. S. Eliot,* edited by Frank Kermode. New York: Houghton Mifflin Harcourt, 1975.

Ellington, Duke. *Music Is My Mistress.* New York: Da Capo, 1976.

Eno, Brian. "The Studio as Compositional Tool." *Down Beat,* 1979[?]. Archived at http://music.hyperreal.org/artists/brian_eno/interviews/downbeat79.htm.

Epstein, William. "The Metahistorical Context, IV: Perceptual Constancy." In *Perception of Space and Motion,* edited by William Epstein and Sheena Rogers. San Diego: Academic Press, 1995.

Erlich, Eugene. *Amo, Amas, Amat and More.* New York: HarperCollins, 1993.

Fackler, Guido. "Swing Kids Behind Barbed Wire." *Music and the Holocaust.* http://holocaustmusic.ort.org/politics-and-propaganda/third-reich/swing-kids -behind-barbed-wire/.

Fantel, Hans. *Durable Pleasures: A Practical Guide to Better Tape Recording.* New York: Dutton, 1976.

Feldman, Morton. *Speaking of Music at the Exploratorium.* Interviewed by Charles Amirkhanian. San Francisco, January 30, 1986. http://www.ubu.com/sound /feldman.html.

Felsenfeld, Daniel. "Rebel Music." *New York Times,* March 26, 2010. http://opin ionator.blogs.nytimes.com/2010/03/26/rebel-music/.

Ferguson, Kirby. "Embrace the remix." TED Talk, June 2012. http://www.ted.com /talks/kirby_ferguson_embrace_the_remix.html.

Filler, Graham. "ESPN: The Milli Vanilli of Sports Coverage." *Off Tackle Empire,* May 6, 2009. http://www.offtackleempire.com/2009/5/6/867484/espn-the-milli -vanilli-of-sports.

Finnegan, Ruth. *Oral Poetry: Its Nature, Significance and Social Context.* Cambridge, UK: Cambridge University Press, 1980.

Flatow, Joel. "Michael and the Power of Music." RIAA, *Music Notes Blog,* July 23,

2009. http://www.riaa.com/blog.php?content_selector=riaa-news-blog&blog_se
lector=MichaelandthePowerofMusic&news_month_filter=7&news_year
_filter=2009.

———. "Whitney Soars in Our Hearts." RIAA, *Music Notes Blog,* February 13,
2012. http://www.riaa.com/blog.php?content_selector=riaa-news-blog&blog_se
lector=Whitney-Soars-&news_month_filter=2&news_year_filter=2012.

Fleagle, Matthew. "His Own Sweet Time: Joseph Mitchell's Omnibus 20 Years On,
Part II." *January Magazine,* August 16, 2012. http://januarymagazine.blogspot
.com/2006/12/his-own-sweet-time-joseph-mitchells.html.

FOH Online. "Parnelli Innovator Honoree, Father of Festival Sound." http://www
.fohonline.com/index.php?option=com_content&task=view&id=579&Itemid=1.

Fong-Torres, Ben, ed. *The Rolling Stone Rock 'n' Roll Reader.* New York: Bantam,
1974.

Franich, Darren. " 'Guitar' Hero Is Dead, but We'll Always Have 'Strutter.' " *Entertainment Weekly,* February 10, 2011.

Franzen, Benjamin, and Kembrew McLeod. *Copyright Criminals* (documentary).
2009. http://www.pbs.org/independentlens/copyright-criminals/credits.html.

Friedman, Ted. "Milli Vanilli and the Scapegoating of the Inauthentic." *Bad Subjects,* issue 9 (November 1993). http://bad.eserver.org/issues/1993/09/friedman
.html.

Frith, Simon. *Performing Rites: On the Value of Popular Music.* Cambridge, MA:
Harvard University Press, 1998.

Gabbard, Krin, ed. *Jazz Among the Discourses.* Durham, NC: Duke University
Press, 1995.

Gaida, Ed. "Ampico Salesman's Manual." In *Mechanical Music Digest* (archives),
March 24, 1998. http://www.mmdigest.com/Archives/Digests/199803/1998.03
.24.19.html.

Gann, Kyle. "The Case Against Over-notation: A Defense and a Diatribe." June
2000. http://www.kylegann.com/notation.html.

———. *The Music of Conlon Nancarrow.* Cambridge, MA: Cambridge University
Press, 2006.

———. "Naïve Pictorialism: Toward a Gannian Aesthetic." December 2001. http://
www.kylegann.com/naivete.html.

Gatens, William J. "Beside Themselves—Two Harpsichords" (review). *American
Record Guide* 57 (November–December 1994): 225.

Gaylor, Brett. *Rip!: A Remix Manifesto.* http://ripremix.com/.

Gelatt, Roland. *The Fabulous Phonograph, 1877–1977.* New York: Collier, 1977.

Gillam, Barbara. "Perceptual Constancy." In *Encyclopedia of Psychology,* edited by
A. E. Kazdin, vol. 6:89–93. New York: American Psychological Association and
Oxford University Press, 2000.

Gioia, Ted. "The 100 Best Albums of 2013." http://tedgioia.com/bestalbumsof
2013.html.

———. *The Imperfect Art: Reflections on Jazz and Modern Culture.* New York:
Oxford University Press, 1988.

Gitler, Ira. "Trane on the Track." *Down Beat,* October 16, 1958.

Glennie, Evelyn. "How to truly listen." TED Talk, February 2003. http://www.ted
.com/talks/evelyn_glennie_shows_how_to_listen.html.

———. "Hearing Essay." http://tribalvillages.org/deaf/essays/Evelyn-Glennie.html.

————. *Touch the Sound: A Sound Journey with Evelyn Glennie* (film). New Video Group, 2004.

Goehr, Lydia. "The Dangers of Satisfaction: On Songs, Rehearsals, and Repetition in *Die Meistersinger.*" In *Wagner's "Meistersinger": Performance, History, Representation,* edited by Nicholas Vazsonyi. Rochester, NY: University of Rochester Press, 2004.

————. *Elective Affinities: Musical Essays on the History of Aesthetic Theory.* New York: Columbia University Press, 2011.

————. *The Imaginary Museum of Musical Works.* New York: Oxford University Press, 2007.

Goodman, Jason. "Milli Vanilli: Behind the Music." VH1, 1997. http://vimeo .com/6659561.

Goodman, Nelson. *Languages of Art.* Indianapolis: Hackett, 1976.

Gooley, Dana Andrew. *The Virtuoso Liszt.* Cambridge, UK: Cambridge University Press, 2009.

Gould, Glenn. "The Propects of Recording." *High Fidelity* 16, no. 4 (April 1966): 46–63. Reprinted in *The Glenn Gould Reader.* New York: Alfred A. Knopf, 1984, 331–53. Available at https://www.collectionscanada.gc.ca/glenngould/028010 -4020.01-e.html.

Gould, J. J. "Josef Skvorecky on the Nazis' Control-Freak Hatred of Jazz." *Atlantic,* January 3, 2012. http://www.theatlantic.com/entertainment/archive/2012/01 /josef-skvorecky-on-the-nazis-control-freak-hatred-of-jazz/250837/.

Gracyk, Theodore. "The Aesthetics of Popular Music." *Internet Encyclopedia of Philosophy.* http://www.iep.utm.edu/music-po/.

Gracyk, Tim, and Frank W. Hoffmann. *Popular American Recording Pioneers, 1895–1925.* New York: Routledge, 2000.

Gramophone. "Is Bach Best?" http://www.gramophone.co.uk/editorial/is-bach-best.

Greene, Andy. "Rolling Stone Readers Pick Best Drummers of All Time." *Rolling Stone.* http://www.rollingstone.com/music/pictures/rolling-stone-readers-pick -best-drummers-of-all-time-20110208.

Grella, George. "The Anxiety of Authenticity." *The Big City,* November 10, 2010. http://thebigcityblog.com/the-anxiety-of-authenticity/.

————. "First, the Sound." *The Big City,* September 25, 2009. http://thebigcityblog .com/first-the-sound/.

Griffith, Hugh. Liner notes, *Enrico Caruso: The Complete Recordings,* vol. 1. Naxos, 2000.

Grigely, Joseph. *Textualterity: Art, Theory, and Textual Criticism.* Ann Arbor: University of Michigan Press, 1995.

Gronow, Pekka. "Phonograph." In *Continuum Encyclopedia of Popular Music of the World,* vol. 2, *Performance and Production,* edited by John Shepherd et al. London: Bloomsbury Academic, 2003.

Grothe, Benedikt, Michael Pecka, and David McAlpine. "Mechanisms of Sound Localization in Mammals." *Physiological Reviews* 90 (2010): 983–1012. http:// physrev.physiology.org/content/90/3/983.full.

Guerrieri, Matthew. *The First Four Notes.* New York: Vintage, 2014.

Hain, Timothy. "Presbycusis." http://www.tchain.com/otoneurology/disorders /hearing/presby.html.

Haithcoat, Rebecca. "DJ Gets Death Threats for Playing Dubstep." *LA Weekly,*

March 20, 2012. http://blogs.laweekly.com/westcoastsound/2012/03/dj_death_threats_fei_fei_beyond_wonderland_dubstep.php.

Halle, John. "Meditations on a Post-Literate Musical Future." *NewMusicBox,* August 1, 2004. http://www.newmusicbox.org/articles/Meditations-on-a-Post Literate-Musical-Future/.

Hamer, Mick. "Don't shoot the Pianola." *New Scientist* 104 (December 20–27, 1984): 1435–36.

Handel, Jonathan. "Broadway Musicians' Union Sounds Off About Recorded Music." *Hollywood Reporter,* May 16, 2011. http://www.hollywoodreporter.com/news/broadway-musicians-union-sounds-recorded-188567.

Hansen, Beck. *Song Reader.* http://www.songreader.net/.

Harrison, Ann. *Music: The Business; The Essential Guide to the Law and the Deals.* New York: Random House, 2011.

Haskell, Harry. *The Early Music Revival: A History.* Mineola, NY: Dover, 1996.

Hasse, John Edward. *Beyond Category: The Life and Genius of Duke Ellington.* New York: Da Capo, 1995.

Haynes, Bruce. *The End of Early Music: A Period Performer's History of Music for the Twenty-First Century.* New York: Oxford University Press, 2007.

Heatley, Michael. *Where Were You . . . When the Music Played? 120 Unforgettable Moments in Music History.* New York: Readers Digest, 2008.

Heitlinger, Alex. "The Lick." November 12, 2011. http://www.youtube.com/watch?v=krDxhnaKD7Q.

Henderson, L. Douglas. "Definition of a 'Reproducing' Piano." *Artcraft Music Rolls.* http://www.wiscasset.net/artcraft/electric.htm.

———. "The Pianola News." *Artcraft Music Rolls.* http://www.wiscasset.net/artcraft/rollnews.htm.

Hertsens, Tyll. "How We Hear." *HeadRoom.* http://www.headphone.com/learning-center/how-we-hear.php.

Hill, Constance Valis. *Tap Dancing America: A Cultural History.* New York: Oxford University Press, 2010.

Hobsbawm, Eric. *The Jazz Scene.* New York: Pantheon, 1993.

Hocker, Jürgen. Conlon Nancarrow Biography. http://www.nancarrow.de/buch.htm.

———. "Encounters with Conlon Nancarrow." http://www.nancarrow.de/buch.htm#Encounters.

Hoenack, Laura, and Dave Hoenack. "Behold the MAGIC BRAIN." *Hymie's Vintage Records,* April 11, 2010. http://hymiesrecords.com/behold-the-magic-brain/.

Holland, Bernard. "What Did Beethoven Hear in His Dreams?" *New York Times,* August 28, 1994. http://www.nytimes.com/1994/08/28/arts/classical-music-what-piano-did-beethoven-hear-in-his-dreams.html.

Holmes, Thom. *Electronic and Experimental Music: Technology, Music, and Culture.* New York: Routledge, 2012.

Holt, Tim. "Play it again . . . and we'll sue." *Christian Science Monitor,* January 9, 2009. http://www.csmonitor.com/The-Culture/Music/2009/0109/p14s01-almp.html.

Holpuch, Amanda. "US music copyright: 'It's basically just a bunch of people fighting over money.'" *Guardian,* June 24, 2014. http://www.theguardian.com/business/2014/jun/24/spotify-riaa-music-copyright-licenses-house.

Homan, Shane. *Access All Eras: Tribute Bands and Global Pop Culture.* New York: Open University Press, 2006.

Homzy, Andrew. Liner notes, Duke Ellington, *Black, Brown, and Beige.* RCA, 1990 (original recording remastered).

Honan, Mat. "How Apple and Amazon Security Flaws Led to My Epic Hacking." *Wired,* August 6, 2012. http://www.wired.com/gadgetlab/2012/08/apple -amazon-mat-honan-hacking/.

Horowitz, Joseph. *Classical Music in America.* New York: Norton, 2005.

———. "Mozart as Midcult: Mass Snob Appeal." *Musical Quarterly* 76, no. 1 (Spring 1992): 1–16.

Hum, Peter. "Jazz composers' roundtable." *Ottawa Citizen,* May 16, 2011. http:// blogs.ottawacitizen.com/2011/05/16/jazz-composers-roundtable/.

———. "On Vijay Iyer, Kurt Rosenwinkel, HuffPo, greatness, prizes and hype." *Ottawa Citizen,* October 2, 2013. http://blogs.ottawacitizen.com/2013/10/02 /on-vijay-iyer-kurt-rosenwinkel-huffpo-greatness-prizes-and-hype/.

Hume, David. "Of the Standard of Taste." In *Philosophy of Art and Aesthetics,* edited by Frank Tillman and Steven M. Cahn. New York: Harper & Row, 1969.

Husarik, Stephen. "Musical Expression in Piano Roll Performance of Joseph Hoffman." *Piano Quarterly* 32, no. 125 (1984).

Huynh, Diana. "Boo . . . Who? A New Freakonomics Radio Podcast." *Freakonomics,* November 10, 2011. http://www.freakonomics.com/2011/11/10/boo-who-a -new-freakonomics-radio-podcast/.

Hyde, Martha M. "Stravinsky's Neoclassicism." In *The Cambridge Companion to Stravinsky,* edited by Jonathan Cross. Cambridge, UK: Cambridge University Press, 2003.

Isherwood, Charles. "Speaking Less Than Truth to Power." *New York Times,* March 18, 2012. http://theater.nytimes.com/2012/03/19/theater/defending-this -american-life-and-its-mike-daisey-retraction.html?_r=0.

Isidore of Seville. *Etymologiae.* Cambridge, UK: Cambridge University Press, 2006.

Isoardi, Steve. Liner notes, *Central Avenue Sounds.* Rhino, 1999.

Iverson, Ethan. "All Our Reasons?" *Do the Math,* March 14, 2012. http://dothe math.typepad.com/dtm/2012/03/all-our-reasons.html.

———. "Interview with Terry Teachout." *Do the Math,* January 6, 2014. http:// dothemath.typepad.com/dtm/interview-with-terry-teachout.html.

———. "Reverential Gesture." *Do the Math,* January 4, 2014. http://dothemath .typepad.com/dtm/reverential-gesture.html.

Ives, Charles. "Essays Before a Sonata." In *Three Classics in the Aesthetic of Music.* New York: Dover, 1962.

Iyer, Vijay. "Exploding the Narrative in Jazz Improvisation." In *Uptown Conversation: The New Jazz Studies,* edited by Robert O'Meally et al. New York: Columbia University Press, 2013.

Jansen, Steve. "License to Kill the Music: ASCAP & BMI Bullying Local Music Venues." *Phoenix New Times,* August 14, 2008. http://blogs.phoenixnewtimes .com/uponsun/2008/08/license_to_kill_the_music_asca.php.

Johnston, Mike. "OT: We Hear from Martin Mull." *The Online Photographer,* July 17, 2010. http://theonlinephotographer.typepad.com/the_online_photo grapher/2010/07/ot-we-hear-from-martin-mull.html.

Jourdain, Robert. *Music, the Brain, and Ecstasy.* New York: William Morrow, 1997.

Jurgenson, Nathan. "The IRL Fetish." *The New Inquiry,* June 28, 2012. http://thenewinquiry.com/essays/the-irl-fetish/.

Kamlet, Rick. "Listening Evaluation." *Sound and Video Contractor,* November 1, 2005. http://svconline.com/mag/avinstall_listening_evaluation/.

Kazunori, Asada. "The Day I Saw Van Gogh's Genius in a New Light." *Asada's Memorandum.* http://asada0.tumblr.com/post/11517603099/the-day-i-saw-van-goghs-genius-in-a-new-light.

Keen, Andrew. *The Cult of the Amateur: How Blogs, MySpace, YouTube, and the Rest of Today's User-Generated Media Are Destroying Our Economy, Our Culture, and Our Values.* New York: Doubleday, 2008.

Keener, Roberta. "The Elevator Music Company?" *Straight to Plate,* April 12, 2011. http://www.muzakblog.com/index.php/new/the-elevator-music-company/.

Kelley, Robin. *Thelonious Monk: The Life and Times of an American Original.* New York: Free Press, 2009.

Kelly, Tadgh. "Why Pro-Amateurs Are the Future." *Gamesbrief,* January 24, 2012. http://www.gamesbrief.com/2012/01/why-pro-amateurs-are-the-future/.

Kenney, William Howland. *Recorded Music in American Life: The Phonograph and Popular Memory, 1890–1945.* New York: Oxford University Press, 1999.

Kerman, Joseph. *Contemplating Music: Challenges to Musicology.* Cambridge, MA: Harvard University Press, 1985.

Kernfeld, Barry. *The Story of Fake Books: Bootlegging Songs to Musicians.* Lanham, MD: Scarecrow Press, 2006.

———. *What to Listen For in Jazz.* New Haven, CT: Yale University Press, 1995.

King, L. R. E. *Do You Want to Know a Secret: Making Sense of the Beatles' Unreleased Recordings.* Tucson, AZ: Storyteller Productions, 1988.

Kivy, Peter. *Authenticities.* Ithaca, NY: Cornell University Press, 1998.

———. *Music Alone.* Ithaca, NY: Cornell University Press, 1991.

———. *The Possessor and the Possessed: Handel, Mozart, Beethoven, and the Idea of Musical Genius.* New Haven, CT: Yale University Press, 2001.

Knapp, Raymond, Mitchell Morris, and Stacy Wolf, eds. *The Oxford Handbook of the American Musical.* New York: Oxford University Press, 2011.

Knight, Frida. *Beethoven and the Age of Revolution.* London: Lawrence & Wishart, 1973.

Knopper, Steve. *Appetite for Self-Destruction: The Spectacular Crash of the Record Industry in the Digital Age.* New York: Free Press, 2009.

Kooijman, Jaap. "Michael Jackson: *Motown 25,* Pasadena Civic Auditorium, March 25, 1983." In *Performance and Popular Music: History, Place, and Time,* edited by Ian Inglis. Aldershot, UK: Ashgate, 2006.

Koopman, Phil. "Why Things Break," October 1998. http://www.ece.cmu.edu/~koopman/des_s99/why_things_break.pdf.

Kostka, Stefan. *Materials and Techniques of Twentieth-Century Music.* Upper Saddle River, NJ: Prentice Hall, 1989.

Kot, Greg. *Ripped: How the Wired Generation Revolutionized Music.* New York: Scribner, 2010.

Kotkin, Joel. "America's New Oligarchs—Fwd.us and Silicon Valley's Shady 1 Percenters." *The Daily Beast,* May 14, 2013. http://www.thedailybeast.com/articles/2013/05/14/america-s-new-oligarchs-fwd-us-and-silicon-valley-s-shady-1-percenters.html.

Kozinn, Allan. "Have You Heard the New Caruso? (No Kidding)." *New York*

Times, February 20, 2000. http://www.nytimes.com/2000/02/20/arts/have-you-heard-the-new-caruso-no-kidding.html.

Kranich, Nancy. *The Information Commons: A Public Policy Report*. Free Expression Policy Project, Brennan Center for Justice, NYU School of Law, 2004. http://www.fepproject.org/policyreports/InformationCommons.pdf.

Kun, Josh. "How We Listen: A Conversation Between Josh Kun and Leon Botstein." *Guilt & Pleasure*, no. 6 (2007). http://www.guiltandpleasure.com/index.php?site=rebootgp&page=gp_article&id=70.

Lacher, Mike. "I'm Comic Sans, Asshole." *McSweeney's Internet Tendency*, June 15, 2010. http://www.mcsweeneys.net/articles/im-comic-sans-asshole.

Lanier, Jaron. *Who Owns the Future?* New York: Simon and Schuster, 2013.

Lantz, Bill. "The David Ocker Internet Interview" (compiled 1994–95). Via alt.fan.frank-zappa. Archived at http://members.shaw.ca/mitb/ocker/#Lantz.

Lawn, Richard J., and Jeffrey L. Hellmer. *Jazz Theory and Practice*. New York: Alfred Publishing, 1996.

Lee, Timothy B. "Waiting on the RIAA, feds held seized Dajaz1 domain for months." *Ars Technica*, May 4, 2012. http://arstechnica.com/tech-policy/2012/05/waiting-on-the-riaa-feds-held-seized-dajaz1-domain-for-months/.

Lee, Vernon. *Studies of the Eighteenth Century in Italy*. London: T. F. Unwin, 1887.

Lefebvre, Henri. *Rhythmanalysis: Space, Time and Everyday Life*. London: Bloomsbury Academic, 2004.

Leikin, Anatole. "A Refined Precision." *San Francisco Classical Voice*, October 23, 2007. https://www.sfcv.org/reviews/refined-precision.

———. "Repeat with Caution: A Dilemma of the First Movement of Chopin's Sonata op. 35." *Musical Quarterly* 1, no. 3 (Fall 2001).

Leiter, Robert. *The Musicians and Petrillo*. New York: Bookman Associates, 1953.

Leonard, Anne. "Picturing Listening in the Late Nineteenth Century." *The Art Bulletin* 89, no 2 (June 2007): 266–86.

Lessig, Lawrence. *Free Culture: How Big Media Uses Technology and the Law to Lock Down Culture and Control Creativity*. New York: Penguin, 2004.

Leung, Rebecca. "Prodigy, 12, Compared to Mozart." CBS News/*60 Minutes*, November 24, 2004. http://www.cbsnews.com/news/prodigy-12-compared-to-mozart/.

Levin, Robert. "Performing Mozart's Keyboard Music." *Mozart Society of America Newsletter* 6, no. 2 (August 27, 2002): 1, 4–6. Archived at http://mozartsocietyofamerica.org/publications/newsletter/archive/MSA-AUG-02.pdf.

Levine, Mark. *The Jazz Piano Book*. Milwaukee: Hal Leonard, 2005.

Levine, Robert: *Free Ride: How Digital Parasites Are Destroying the Culture Business, and How the Culture Business Can Fight Back*. New York: Doubleday, 2011.

———. "Presentation: Robert Levine." *You Are in Control*. http://youareincontrol.is/presentation-robert-levine-usa.

Levinson, Jerrold. "Musical Thinking." *Journal of Music and Meaning* 1 (2003). http://www.musicandmeaning.net/issues/showArticle.php?artID=1.2.

Levitin, Daniel. "Tone Deafness: Failures of Musical Anticipation and Self-Reference." *International Journal of Computing and Anticipatory Systems* 4 (1999): 243–54. http://daniellevitin.com/levitinlab/articles/1999-Levitin-IJCAS2.pdf.

———. *This Is Your Brain on Music*. New York: Penguin, 2006.

————. *The World in Six Songs: How the Musical Brain Created Human Nature.* New York: Penguin, 2008.

Lewis, Michael. "Don't Eat Fortune's Cookie." Princeton Baccalaureate speech, June 2012. http://www.princeton.edu/main/news/archive/S33/87/54K53/.

Lhévinne, Josef. *Basic Principles in Pianoforte Playing.* New York: Dover, 1972.

Lichtman, Irv. "Hit Gershwin Disc Sparks New Interest in Piano Rolls." *Billboard,* 1994. Archived at http://www.artiswodehouse.com/billboar.html.

Lillick, Paul Goldstein: *International Copyright: Principles, Law, and Practice.* New York: Oxford University Press, 2001.

Lilypond. Essay at http://www.lilypond.org/essay.html.

Lipskin, Mike. Liner notes, Fats Waller, *Turn on the Heat.* RCA CD reissue, 1991.

Liptak, Adam. "Public Domain Works Can Be Copyrighted Anew, Supreme Court Rules." *New York Times,* January 18, 2012. http://www.nytimes.com /2012/01/19/business/public-domain-works-can-be-copyrighted-anew-justices -rule.html?_r=0.

Litterst, George F. "Tackling Technology: Transcribing Piano Roll Performances into Notation with Computers." *Piano Quarterly* 38, no. 148 (1989–90).

Litweiler, John. *Ornette Coleman: A Harmolodic Life.* New York: Da Capo, 1994.

Lockhart, William. "Listening to the Domestic Music Machine: The Keyboard Arrangement in the Nineteenth Century." Max Planck Institute for the History of Science. http://www.mpiwg-berlin.mpg.de/en/research/projects/DeptII_Lock hart_CompositionalListening.

Loesser, Arthur. *Men, Women, and Pianos.* New York: Simon & Schuster, 1954.

Lowery, David. "Meet the New Boss, Worse Than the Old Boss?" *The Trichordist,* April 15, 2012. http://thetrichordist.com/2012/04/15/meet-the-new-boss-worse -than-the-old-boss-full-post/.

Lydon, Christopher. "Ellington, Newport and the American Century." *Radio Open Source,* August 16, 2006. http://www.radioopensource.org/ellington-newport -and-the-american-century/.

Lyons, Julie. "Anarchy in Amarillo." *Dallas Observer,* October 21, 1999. http:// www.dallasobserver.com/1999-10-21/news/anarchy-in-amarillo/.

McClary, Susan. *Feminine Endings.* Minneapolis: University of Minnesota Press, 2002.

McClellan, Lawrence. *The Later Swing Era, 1942 to 1955.* Westport, CT: Green-wood, 2004.

McCormick, Neil. "The Truth About Lip-Synching." *The Age* (Australia), October 13, 2004. http://www.theage.com.au/articles/2004/10/12/1097406567855.html.

McKenna, Terrence. "Riding Range with Marshal McLuhan" and "Shamans Among the Machines" (recorded lectures). UbuWeb. http://www.ubu.com /sound/mcluhan.html.

McSweeney, Ellen. "Music, MOOCs, and Copyright: Digital Dilemmas for Schools of Music." *NewMusicBox,* September 25, 2013. http://www.newmusicbox.org /articles/music-moocs-and-copyright-digital-dilemmas-for-schools-of-music/.

McWilliams, Jerry. *The Preservation and Restoration of Sound Recordings.* Nash-ville: American Association for State and Local History, 1979.

Mainzer, Joseph. *Music and Education.* Cambridge, UK: Cambridge University Press, 2013. Originally published 1848.

Marsh, Christopher. *Music and Society in Early Modern England.* Cambridge, UK: Cambridge University Press, 2013.

Marston, Ward. Liner notes, *Enrico Caruso: The Complete Recordings,* vol. 1. Naxos, 2000.

Marx, W. David, and Nick Sylvester. "Theoretically Unpublished Piece About Girl Talk, for a Theoretical New York Magazine Kind of Audience, Give or Take an Ox on Suicide Watch." In *Best Music Writing 2009,* edited by Greil Marcus. New York: Da Capo, 2009.

Masnick, Mike. "Copyright Finally Getting Around to Destroying Player Piano Music." *Techdirt,* July 26, 2010. http://www.techdirt.com/articles/20100712 /18325210185.shtml.

———. "How ASCAP and BMI Are Harming Up-and-Coming Singers." *Techdirt,* January 12, 2009. http://www.techdirt.com/articles/20090109/1823043352.shtml.

———. "RIAA Totally Out of Touch: Lashes Out at Google, Wikipedia and Everyone Who Protested SOPA/PIPA." *Techdirt,* February 8, 2012. http://www.tech dirt.com/articles/20120208/01453517694/riaa-totally-out-touch-lashes-out -google-wikipedia-everyone-who-protested-sopapipa.shtml.

Masnick, Michael, and Michael Ho. *The Sky Is Rising!* (report). *Techdirt,* January 2012. http://www.techdirt.com/skyisrising/.

Mason, Matt. *The Pirate's Dilemma: How Youth Culture Is Reinventing Capitalism.* New York: Free Press, 2008.

Mehldau, Brad. "Ideology, Burgers, and Beer." *Jazz Times,* December 2003. http:// jazztimes.com/articles/14267-brad-mehldau-ideology-burgers-and-beer.

Mencken, H. L. *A Mencken Chrestomathy: His Own Selection of His Choicest Writings.* New York: Alfred A. Knopf, 1949.

Merton, Robert K. "The Matthew Effect in Science." *Science* 159, no. 3810 (January 5, 1968): 56–63.

———. *The Sociology of Science: Theoretical and Empirical Investigations.* Chicago: University of Chicago Press, 1973.

Meyer, Leonard. *Emotion and Meaning in Music.* Chicago: University of Chicago Press, 1956.

Miles, Barry. *Beatles in Their Own Words.* New York: Putnam, 1979.

Millard, Andre. *America on Record: A History of Recorded Sound.* Cambridge, UK: Cambridge University Press, 2005.

Miller, Mark Crispin. *Boxed In: The Culture of TV.* Chicago: Northwestern University Press, 1988.

Mitchell, Dan. "Amazon's Cloud Nightmare." *Fortune Tech,* April 22, 2011. http:// tech.fortune.cnn.com/2011/04/22/amazons-cloud-nightmare/.

Mithen, Steven. *The Singing Neanderthals.* Cambridge, MA: Harvard University Press, 2006.

Mojo. "Exclusive: Dylan at Newport: Who Booed?" October 25, 2007. Archived at http://archive.is/Fa1f.

Monson, Ingrid. *Freedom Sounds: Civil Rights Call Out to Jazz and Africa.* New York: Oxford University Press, 2010.

Montgomery, Michael. Liner notes, *The Greatest Ragtime of the Century.* Biograph, 1992.

———. Liner notes, *Scott Joplin: "Elite Syncopations": Classic Ragtime from Rare Piano Rolls.* Biograph, 1993.

Montgomery, Michael, Trebor Jay Tichenor, and John Edward Hasse. "Ragtime on Piano Rolls." In *Ragtime: Its History, Composers, and Music,* edited by John Edward Hasse. New York: Schirmer, 1985.

Moon, Tom. *1,000 Recordings to Hear Before You Die.* New York: Workman, 2008.

Morelle, Rebecca. "The Hum That Helps to Fight Crime." BBC News, December 11, 2012. http://www.bbc.com/news/science-environment-20629671.

Morrison, Iain. "Cornelius Cardew's move from notes to performance notes." *Permanent Positions,* March 31, 2013. https://permanentpositions.wordpress.com /tag/octet-61-for-jasper-johns/.

Mumford, Lewis. *Technics and Civilization.* New York: Harcourt, Brace & World, Inc., 1963.

Musical Times. "Chats on Current Topics," February 1, 1890. Available at http:// www.jstor.org/pss/3361981.

Myers, Ben. "Why 'Disco Sucks!' sucked." *Guardian,* June 18, 2009. http://www .guardian.co.uk/music/musicblog/2009/jun/18/disco-sucks.

Myers, Marc. "Interview: Big Jay McNeely (Part 2)." *Jazzwax,* July 31, 2009. http://www.jazzwax.com/2009/07/interview-big-jay-mcneely-part-2.html.

———. "PhotoStory4: Big Jay McNeely." *Jazzwax,* July 10, 2009.

Nachmanovitch, Stephen. *Free Play: The Power of Improvisation in Life and the Arts.* New York: G. P. Putnam's Sons, 1990.

NASA. "The Golden Record." http://voyager.jpl.nasa.gov/spacecraft/goldenrec .html.

National Academy of Recording Arts and Sciences. "Recommendation for Delivery of Recorded Music Projects." Last revised August 1, 2007. http://www2 .grammy.com/PDFs/Recording_Academy/Producers_And_Engineers/Delivery Recs.pdf.

National Phonograph Company. *The Phonograph and How to Use It.* 1900. Archived at http://ia600406.us.archive.org/23/items/phonographhowtou00nati /phonographhowtou00nati.pdf, and at https://archive.org/details/phonograph howtou00nati.

Nemire, Julie Scrivener. "Appendix A: Errata to Scores of the Player Piano Studies." From "Representations of Time and Space in the Player Piano Studies of Conlon Nancarrow." PhD dissertation, Michigan State University, 2002. http://home pages.wmich.edu/~jscriven/Nancarrow%20scores-Errata.pdf.

Nevin, Gordon Balch. *First Lessons on the Organ.* Bryn Mawr, PA: Oliver Ditson Company, 1923.

Newell, Ruth. "Tribute Band Groupies." http://www.sandiegoreader.com/weblogs /roody2shoes/2011/aug/06/tribute-band-groupies/.

Nisenson, Eric. *Blue: The Murder of Jazz.* New York: St. Martin's, 1997.

Noise Addicts. "Concerts with Record Attendance." http://www.noiseaddicts .com/2009/08/concerts-with-record-attendance/.

Nordin, Invar. *Conlon Nancarrow: Studies for Player Piano,* vol. 1 (review, Sonoloco Record Reviews). http://www.sonoloco.com/rev/mdg/1401/nancarrow1 .html.

Northwest Music Scene. "BMI Sues Bar Owner for 1.5 Million for Allowing Cover Tunes." April 4, 2014. http://www.northwestmusicscene.com/2014/04/bmi-sues -bar-owner-for-1-5-million-for-allowing-cover-tunes/.

Nottingham, Kevin. "The Ten Most Sampled Songs in Hip Hop." http://kevinnot tingham.com/2009/03/16/top-10-most-sampled-songs-in-hip-hop/. Archived at http://archive.is/ost0.

Novak, Matt. "Musicians Wage War Against Evil Robots." Smithsonian.com,

February 10, 2012. http://blogs.smithsonianmag.com/paleofuture/2012/02/musi
cians-wage-war-against-evil-robots/.

Nyquist, Greg. *Visions of Reality: New Ways of Conceiving Old Problems*. Bloomington, IN: iUniverse, 2008.

Ochoa, Tyler T. "Is the Copyright Public Domain Irrevocable? An Introduction to
Golan v. Holder." *Vanderbilt Law Review,* October 3, 2011.

O'Donnell, Matt. "The Real Book: A History & Commentary." *Bass Frontiers,*
July 21, 2011. http://www.bassfrontiersmag.com/the-real-book-a-history-com
mentary.

Oja, Carol. *Making Music Modern: New York in the 1920s*. New York: Oxford
University Press, 2000.

Ong, Walter. *The Presence of the Word: Some Prolegomena for Cultural and Religious History*. New Haven, CT: Yale University Press, 1967.

Ord-Hume, Arthur W. J. G. *Pianola: History of the Self-Playing Piano*. Boston:
George Allen & Unwin, 1984.

———. *Restoring Pianolas and Other Self-Playing Pianos*. Boston: George Allen
& Unwin, 1983.

Orvell, Miles. *The Real Thing: Imitation and Authenticity in American Culture,
1880–1940*. Chapel Hill: University of North Carolina Press, 1989.

Orwell, George. "Politics and the English Language." In *The Broadview Reader,*
edited by Jane Flick and Herbert Rosengarten. Peterborough, ON: Broadview
Press, 1998.

Osby, Greg. "Jazz Bums." *Indablog,* October 17, 2009. http://blog.indabamusic
.com/2009/10/6199-jazz-bums/.

Oswald, John. *Plunderphonics*. Seeland Records (reissue), 2001.

Palmer, Willard, ed. *Beethoven—Eleven Bagatelles, Op. 119 for the Piano*. New
York: Alfred Publishing, 1971.

Pascoe, Judith. *The Sarah Siddons Audio Files: Romanticism and the Lost Voice*.
Ann Arbor: University of Michigan Press, 2011.

Patry, William. *How to Fix Copyright*. New York: Oxford University Press, 2011.

Payton, Nicholas. "An Open Letter to My Dissenters on Why Jazz Isn't Cool
Anymore." December 2, 2011. http://nicholaspayton.wordpress.com/2011/12
/02/1319/.

———. "Duking It Out with Teachout and Other Racist Assailants." December 8,
2013. http://nicholaspayton.wordpress.com/2013/12/08/duking-it-out-with
-teachout-and-other-racist-assailants/.

———. "On Why Jazz Isn't Cool Anymore." November 27, 2011. http://nicholas
payton.wordpress.com/2011/11/27/on-why-jazz-isnt-cool-anymore/.

Peretti, Burton. *The Creation of Jazz: Music, Race, and Culture in Urban America*.
Chicago: University of Illinois Press, 1992.

Perkins, Moreland. *Sensing the World*. Indianapolis: Hackett, 1983.

Piazza, Tom. *Blues Up and Down: Jazz in Our Time*. New York: St. Martin's, 1999.

Pierce, John Robinson. *The Science of Musical Sound*. New York: W. H. Freeman
and Co., 1992.

Pilikington, Ed. "Hollywood pays lip service to Milli Vanilli." *Guardian,* February
15, 2007. http://www.guardian.co.uk/world/2007/feb/15/usa.musicnews.

Pinker, Steven. *How the Mind Works*. New York: Norton, 2009.

Potter, Andrew. *The Authenticity Hoax: How We Get Lost Finding Ourselves*. New
York: HarperCollins, 2010.

Powell, Jim. "Ludwig van Beethoven's Joyous Affirmation of Human Freedom." FEE (Foundation for Economic Education), December 1, 1995. http://www.fee.org/the_freeman/detail/ludwig-van-beethovens-joyous-affirmation-of-human-freedom#axzz2tX61lJEc.

Prickett, Sarah Nicole. "Speaking in Tongues." *The New Inquiry,* May 7, 2012. http://thenewinquiry.com/essays/speaking-in-tongues/.

Prochnik, George. *In Pursuit of Silence: Listening for Meaning in a World of Noise.* New York: Doubleday, 2010.

Rabl, Gottfried. Liner notes, *Caruso 2000.* RCA, 1999.

Randel, Don Michael. *The Harvard Dictionary of Music.* Cambridge, MA: Belknap Press of Harvard University Press, 2003.

Ratliff, Ben. *Coltrane: The Story of a Sound.* New York: Picador, 2008.

Rattenbury, Ken. *Duke Ellington, Jazz Composer.* New Haven, CT: Yale University Press, 1990.

"The Real Voices Behind Milli Vanilli Share Their Side of the Lip Syncing Scandal." *Huffington Post,* February 27, 2014. http://www.huffingtonpost.com/2014/02/27/milli-vanilli_n_4860222.html.

Reynolds, Simon. "Noise." In *Audio Culture: Readings in Modern Music,* edited by Christoph Cox and Daniel Warner. London: Continuum, 2004.

RIAA. PR text circa 2002. Archived at http://web.archive.org/web/20020205125701/http://riaa.org/Artists-Voices-1.cfm.

———. "Recording Industry Sues Napster for Copyright Infringement." N.d. http://riaa.com/newsitem.php?id=6446F9E7-95A3-F900-5648-43B6CCEFC6EB&searchterms=Napster&terminclude=&termexact=.

Rimmer, Matthew. *Digital Copyright and the Consumer Revolution.* Cheltenham, UK: Edward Elgar Publishing, 2011.

Roddy, Michael. "London music fest gambles on little-known Nancarrow." Reuters, April 5, 2012. http://www.reuters.com/article/2012/04/05/entertainment-us-music-nancarrow-idUSBRE83409C20120405.

Rodman, Sarah. "Tribute bands are music to fans' ears, wallets." *Boston Globe,* March 6, 2010. http://www.boston.com/ae/music/articles/2010/03/06/tribute_bands_are_music_to_fans_ears_wallets/.

Roell, Craig H. *The Piano in America, 1890–1940.* Chapel Hill: University of North Carolina Press, 1989.

Rose, Jay. "On Golden Ears." *Digital Video Magazine,* July 2000. Archived at http://www.dplay.com/dv/ears/index.html.

Rosen, Charles. *The Classical Style.* New York: Norton, 1998.

———. *Critical Entertainments.* Cambridge, MA: Harvard University Press, 2001.

———. "Did Beethoven Have All the Luck?" *New York Review of Books,* November 14, 1996.

———. *Freedom and the Arts: Essays on Music and Literature.* Cambridge, MA: Harvard University Press, 2012.

———. *The Frontiers of Meaning.* New York: Hill & Wang, 1994.

Ross, Alex. *The Rest Is Noise.* New York: Farrar, Straus & Giroux, 2007.

Rowley, Caitlin. "Defining neoclassicism." http://www.minim-media.com/satie/final1.htm.

Røyrvik, Emil A. *The Allure of Capitalism: An Ethnography of Management and the Global Economy in Crisis.* New York: Berghahn Books, 2013.

Rudd, David. "The Sonic Barber Pole: Shepard's Scale." http://www.cycleback.com/sonicbarber.html.

Rudhyar, Dane. "Musical Fascism." *Rudhyar Archival Project,* 2004. http://www.khaldea.com/rudhyar/musicalfascism.html.

Ruen, Chris. *Freeloading: How Our Insatiable Hunger for Free Content Starves Creativity.* New York: OR Books, 2012.

Ruen, Chris, and David Byrne, interviewed by Brent Bambury. "Is our addiction to free content killing creativity?" *Q with Jian Ghomeshi,* March 5, 2014. http://www.cbc.ca/q/blog/2014/03/05/content-creators-coalition/.

Russell, Bertrand. *ABC of Relativity.* New York: Taylor & Francis, 2009.

Russell, Jay D. "Marcel Duchamp's Readymades: Walking on Infrathin Ice." In *Contrapposto* 12 (1997), Special Issue, "Crossing Boundaries/Beyond the Object." Archived at http://www.dada-companion.com/duchamp/archive/duchamp_walking_on_infrathin_ice.pdf.

Russo, William. *Composing for the Jazz Orchestra.* Chicago: University of Chicago Press, 1961.

Sachs, Joel. Liner notes, *Conlon Nancarrow: Orchestral, Chamber, and Piano Music.* Musical Heritage Society, 1990.

Sacks, Oliver. *Musicophilia.* New York: Vintage, 2008.

———. *Seeing Voices.* New York: Vintage, 1989.

Sadler, Sim. "Hard Working George." 2004. Archived at http://archive.org/details/hardwork.

Samples, Mark. "Notation's Last Hurrah?" *The Taruskin Challenge,* February 6, 2012. http://taruskinchallenge.wordpress.com/2012/02/06/notations-last-hurrah/.

Sanden, Paul. *Liveness in Modern Music: Musicians, Technology, and the Perception of Performance.* New York: Routledge, 2013.

Sanneh, Kelefa. "The Rap Against Rockism." *New York Times,* October 31, 2004.

Sartorius, Michael. "Baroque Music Performance: 'Authentic' or 'Traditional.'" http://www.baroquemusic.org/barperf.html.

Sax, Leonard. "Sex Differences in Hearing: Implications for Best Practice in the Classroom." *Advances in Gender and Education* 2 (2010): 13–21.

Schafer, R. Murray. "Open Ears." Available at http://www4.ncsu.edu/~mseth2/com307/readings/Schafer.pdf.

———. *The Soundscape: Our Sonic Environment and the Tuning of the World.* Rochester, VT: Destiny Books, 1994.

Scherer, Barrymore Laurence. "Thomas Jefferson, Musician." *Wall Street Journal,* July 2, 2009. http://online.wsj.com/article/SB124648983211082927.html.

Schmidt, Kathleen. "Don't Be the Milli Vanilli of Book Publishing." A Bookish Broad, August 27 [year?]. Available at http://web.archive.org/web/20120901023012/http://kathleenschmidt.tumblr.com/post/30339480149/payingforreviews.

Schuller, Gunther. *Early Jazz.* New York: Oxford University Press, 1986.

Schweitzer, Albert. *J. S. Bach.* 2 vols. Translated by Ernest Newman. New York: Dover, 1966. Originally published 1911.

Seabrook, John. "Factory Girls: Cultural Technology and the Making of K-Pop." *New Yorker,* October 8, 2012. http://www.newyorker.com/reporting/2012/10/08/121008fa_fact_seabrook?currentPage=all.

Sekuler, Robert. "Architectural Acoustics: The $20,000,000 Mistake." 2004. http://people.brandeis.edu/~sekuler/SensoryProcessesMaterial/archi_acoustics.html.

Shapter, Andrew. *Before the Music Dies*. BSide entertainment, 2006.

Sherman, Cary. "Perspective: Honest Talk About Downloads." *CNET*, October 16, 2002. http://news.cnet.com/2010-1071-962279.html?tag=fd_nc_1. Cached at http://webcache.googleusercontent.com/search?q=cache:2keWNAVDiOkJ:news .cnet.com/Perspective-Honest-talk-about-downloads/2010-1071_3-962279 .html+&cd=1&hl=en&ct=clnk&gl=us&client=safari.

Sidran, Ben. *Talking Jazz: An Oral History*. New York: Da Capo, 1995.

Small, Christopher. *Music of the Common Tongue: Survival and Celebration in African American Music*. Middletown, CT: Wesleyan University Press, 1999.

Small, Mark. "The Perception of Music." *Berklee Today*, Summer 2010. http:// www.berklee.edu/bt/221/perceptions_of_music.html.

Smith, Ben. "Repeatability: The Biggest Benefit of a Recording." *Classical Convert*, April 14, 2007. http://classicalconvert.com/2007/08/repeatability-the-biggest -benefit-of-a-recording/.

Smith, Bruce R. *The Acoustic World of Early Modern England: Attending to the O-Factor*. Chicago: University of Chicago Press, 1999.

———. "Listening to the Wild Blue Yonder: The Challenges of Acoustic Ecology." In *Hearing Cultures: Essays on Sound, Listening, and Modernity*, edited by Veit Erlmann. New York: Bloomsbury Academic, 2004.

Somfai, László. *Béla Bartók: Composition, Concepts, and Autograph Sources*. Berkeley: University of California Press, 1996.

Soukup, Paul A. "Looking Is Not Enough: Reflections on Walter J. Ong and Media Ecology." *Proceedings of the Media Ecology Association* 6 (2005). http://www .media-ecology.org/publications/MEA_proceedings/v6/Soukup.pdf.

Springsteen, Bruce. "SXSW Keynote Address, 2012." http://www.npr.org/2012/03 /16/148778665/bruce-springsteens-sxsw-2012-keynote-speech.

Stamp, Cal. "Kids These Days: Spotify, Radiohead, and the Devaluation of Music." *New School Free Press*, December 15, 2011. http://www.newschoolfreepress .com/2011/12/15/kids-these-days-spotify-radiohead-and-the-devaluation-of -music/.

Stearns, Marshall. *Jazz Dance: The Story of American Vernacular Dance*. New York: Da Capo, 1994.

Sterne, Jonathan. *The Audible Past*. Durham, NC: Duke University Press, 2003.

———. "The death and life of digital audio." http://sterneworks.org/deathandlife .pdf.

———. "The Preservation Paradox in Digital Audio." In *Sound Souvenirs: Audio Technologies, Memory and Cultural Practices*, edited by Karin Bijsterveld and Jose van Dijck. Amsterdam: Amsterdam University Press, 2009.

Stockfelt, Ola. "Adequate Modes of Listening." Translated by Anahid Kassabian and Leo G. Svendsen. In *Keeping Score: Music, Disciplinarity, Culture*, edited by David Schwarz, Anahid Kassabian, and Lawrence Siegel. Charlottesville: University Press of Virginia, 1997.

Stopera, Matt. "Who Is Paul McCartney?!" *BuzzFeed*, February 13, 2012. http:// www.buzzfeed.com/mjs538/who-is-paul-mccartney.

Storr, Anthony. *Music and the Mind*. New York: Ballantine, 1993.

Stravinsky, Igor. *Stravinsky's Pulcinella: A Facsimile of the Sources and Sketches, Issue 6*. Middleton, WI: A-R Editions, 2010.

Suisman, David. "Nancarrow in Context: A Critical History of Player-Pianos and Mechanical Automation." In *Online Symposium: Conlon Nancarrow, Life and Music,* 2012. http://conlonnancarrow.org/symposium/papers/suisman/suis man.htm.

———. *Selling Sounds: The Commercial Revolution in American Music.* Cambridge, MA: Harvard University Press, 2009.

Swanson, Patrick. "Keith Jarrett and the Audience." *Meadowlark Lemons,* March 14, 2010. http://patrickswanson.tumblr.com/post/449366192/keith-jarrett-and -the-audience.

SWNS.com. "First ever Beatles record that original bandmate sold for £12k now the most valuable in the world at almost £1/4m." November 8, 2012. http:// swns.com/news/beatles-record-original-bandmate-sold-12k-valuable-world -14m-27328/.

Symes, Colin. *Setting the Record Straight.* Middletown, CT: Wesleyan University Press, 2004.

Taruskin, Richard. *The Danger of Music and Other Anti-Utopian Essays.* Berkeley: University of California Press, 2010.

Taylor, Astra. *The People's Platform: Taking Back Power and Culture in the Digital Age.* New York: Metropolitan Books, 2014.

Taylor, Jerome. "Sophie Lancaster: The murder that caused a subculture to fight back." *Independent,* April 4, 2013. http://www.independent.co.uk/news/uk /crime/sophie-lancaster-the-murder-that-caused-a-subculture-to-fight-back -8560733.html.

Teachout, Terry. *Duke: A Life of Duke Ellington.* New York: Gotham Books, 2013.

Tehranian, John. *Infringement Nation.* New York: Oxford University Press, 2011.

Tenner, Edward. "Clarity Is Overrated: Could Opacity Be the New Transparency?" *Atlantic,* January 21, 2011. http://www.theatlantic.com/technology /archive/2011/01/clarity-is-overrated-could-opacity-be-the-new-transparency /69623/.

Tenney, James. Liner notes, *Conlon Nancarrow: Studies for Player Piano.* Wergo, 2000.

Terhardt, Ernst. "Absolute Pitch." February 11, 2000. http://www.mmk.ei.tum.de /persons/ter/top/absolute.html.

Theberge, Paul. *Any Sound You Can Imagine: Making Music/Consuming Technology.* Middletown, CT: Wesleyan University Press, 1997.

Thompson, Emily. "Machines, Music, and the Quest for Fidelity: Marketing the Edison Phonograph in America, 1877–1925." *Musical Quarterly* 79, no. 1 (1995): 131–71.

Thompson, Francis Michael Longstreth. *The Rise of Respectable Society: A Social History of Victorian Britain, 1830–1900.* Cambridge, MA: Harvard University Press, 1988.

Thompson, Terri. "A Virtuoso Ghost at the Keyboard." *U.S. News and World Report* 110, no. 1 (January 14, 1991): 60–62.

Tillman, Frank A., and Steven M. Cahn. *Philosophy of Art and Aesthetics.* New York: Harper & Row, 1969.

Tirro, Frank. *Jazz: A History.* New York: Norton, 1993.

Toffler, Alvin. *Future Shock.* New York: Random House, 1970.

Toller, Brendan. *I Need That Record! The Death (or Possible Survival) of the Independent Record Store.* MVD Visual, 2008.

Torremans, Paul, ed. *Copyright Law: A Handbook of Contemporary Research.* Cheltenham, UK: Edward Elgar Publishing, 2007.

Townley, Eric. "Ragtime, Blues and Jazz: Pianola Recital." *Jazz Journal International* 35, no. 1 (January 1982): 20.

Towns, Ed. "Piracy hurts everyone both online and offline." *The Hill,* May 22, 2002. http://www.thehill.com/052202/ss_towns.shtm. Archived at http://web.archive.org/web/20020606032358/http://www.thehill.com/052202/ss_towns.shtm.

Trubee, John. Interview with Art Jarvinen, October 2007. http://www.united-mutations.com/j/art_jarvinen.htm.

Tucker, Jeffrey. "Musical Borrowings from Bach to Hip Hop." http://archive.mises.org/13476/musical-borrowings-from-bach-to-hip-hop/.

Tucker, Mark. Liner notes, *The Blanton Webster-Band*. Bluebird Records, 1990.

Tucker, Martin, ed. *The Duke Ellington Reader*. New York: Oxford University Press, 1995.

Tuttle, John. "How to Operate a Foot Pumped Player Piano." http://www.playerpianosupplies.com/how_to_operate.html.

Tyson, Alan. *Mozart: Studies of the Autograph Scores*. Cambridge, MA: Harvard University Press, 1990.

Vaidhyanathan, Siva. *Copyrights and Copywrongs*. New York: New York University Press, 2003.

Varèse, Edgard. "The Liberation of Sound." http://music.arts.uci.edu/dobrian/CMC2009/Liberation.pdf.

Varley, H. Paul. *Japanese Culture*. Honolulu: University of Hawaii Press, 2000.

Vitale, Tom. "Music Is Everywhere: John Cage at 100." NPR, September 5, 2012. http://www.npr.org/2012/09/05/160618202/music-is-everywhere-john-cage-at-100.

———. "The Story of Charlie Parker's Ko Ko." NPR, August 27, 2000. http://www.npr.org/2000/08/27/1081208/-i-ko-ko-i.

Wakin, Daniel. "Rockers Playing for Beer: Fair Play?" *New York Times,* September 12, 2012. http://artsbeat.blogs.nytimes.com/2012/09/12/rockers-playing-for-beer-fair-play/?_r=0.

Walker, Alan. *Hans von Bülow: A Life and Times*. New York: Oxford University Press, 2010.

Walker, Jesse: *Rebels on the Air: An Alternative History of Radio in America*. New York: New York University Press, 2001.

Wallmark, Zach. "Turning Back the Clock." *The Taruskin Challenge,* January 27, 2012. http://taruskinchallenge.wordpress.com/2012/01/27/turning-back-the-clock/.

Walsh, Michael. "Gershwin, by George." *Time* 143, no. 5 (January 31, 1994): 113.

Wang, George. "Amplitude of Sound." http://faculty.unlv.edu/gwang/References/Sound/week%202%20amplitude.html.

Washington, Dinah. *The Complete Dinah Washington on Mercury,* Vol. 1 *(1946–1949)*. Mercury/Polygram, 1994 (CD reissue).

Weingarten, Gene. "Pearls Before Breakfast." *Washington Post,* April 8, 2007. http://www.washingtonpost.com/wp-dyn/content/article/2007/04/04/AR2007040401721.html.

Weiss, Piero, and Richard Taruskin. *Music in the Western World: A History in Documents*. Belmont, CA: Cengage Learning, 2007.

Welch, Walter, and Leah Brodbeck Stenzel Burt. *From Tinfoil to Stereo: The Acous-*

tic Years of the Recording Industry, 1877–1929. Gainesville: University Press of Florida, 1994.

Whittington, Stephen: "Serious Immobilities: On the Centenary of Erik Satie's Vexations," 1999. http://www.satie-archives.com/web/article3.html.

Wilson, Douglas. Introduction to *Thomas Jefferson: Musician and Violinist,* by Sandor Salgo. Charlottesville, VA: Thomas Jefferson Foundation, 2000.

Wilson, Frank R. *Tone Deaf and All Thumbs? An Invitation to Music-Making.* New York: Vintage, 1986.

Winawer, Jonathan, et al. "Russian blues reveal effects of language on color discrimination." *Proceedings of the National Academy of Sciences of the United States of America* 104, no. 19 (2007). http://www.pnas.org/content/104/19/7780.short.

The Wire. "STHoldings Labels to Leave Spotify." November 16, 2011. http://www.thewire.co.uk/news/18982/stholdings-labels-to-leave-spotify.

Wodehouse, Artis. Liner notes, *Gershwin Plays Gershwin.* Elektra/Nonesuch, 1995.

Wolff, Christoph. *Bach: Essays on His Life and Music.* Cambridge, MA: Harvard University Press, 1991.

———. "Defining Genius: Early Reflections on JS Bach's Self-Image." *Proceedings of the American Philosophical Society* 145, no. 4 (December 2001): 474–81. http://www.jstor.org/pss/1558186.

———. *Johann Sebastian Bach: The Learned Musician.* New York: Norton, 2001.

Worrell, Denise. "Rebutting Milli Vanilli." *Los Angeles Times,* December 8, 1990. http://articles.latimes.com/1990-12-08/entertainment/ca-5229_1_todd-headlee-rob-and-fab-time-magazine.

Wright, Ronald. *A Short History of Progress.* Toronto: House of Anansi, 2004.

Wyatt, Edward. "Best-Selling Memoir Draws Scrutiny." *New York Times,* January 10, 2006. http://www.nytimes.com/2006/01/10/books/10frey.html.

Yamagishi, Jimi. *Music Thoughts.* October 30, 2003. https://groups.yahoo.com/neo/groups/musicthoughts/conversations/messages/35531.

Yanow, Scott. "Duke Ellington." Entry in *All Music Guide,* 3rd ed. San Francisco: Miller Freeman, 1997.

Yoshihara, Mari. *Musicians from a Different Shore: Asians and Asian-Americans in Classical Music.* Philadelphia: Temple University Press, 2008.

Youngren, William. "Duke Ellington, by James Lincoln Collier." *Commentary,* February 1988.

Zappa, Frank, as told to Richard Blackburn. "'50s Teenagers and '50s Rock." *Evergreen Review* 14, no. 81 (August 1970). Archived at http://www.afka.net/Articles/1970-08_Evergreen.htm.

———. *The Real Frank Zappa Book.* New York: Touchstone, 1990.

Zibreg, Christian. "Apple killed the disc drive, but it's for your own good." *iDownloadBlog,* October 28, 2012. http://www.idownloadblog.com/2012/10/28/opinion-imac-optical-media/.

Zimmer, Ben. "How baseball gave us 'jazz': The surprising origins of a 100-year-old word." *Boston Globe,* March 25, 2012. http://www.bostonglobe.com/ideas/2012/03/24/how-baseball-gave-jazz/CMUIs4osAVhg49mvnhLfjK/story.html.

Zorn, John. Liner notes, *Spillane.* Elektra Nonesuch, 1987.

INDEX

ABOUT THE AUTHOR

Andrew Durkin is a Portland, Oregon, composer and writer, best known as the leader of the Industrial Jazz Group. Durkin has a PhD in English from the University of Southern California, where his mentor was Joseph Dane, author of *What Is a Book?* He was a postdoctoral fellow at the Annenberg Center for Communication at USC, where he worked with digital media pioneer Bob Stein. He blogs at uglyrug .blogspot.com.